Not All At Sea!

In memory of my late wife Christine Mary,
who shared almost fifty years of my life,
and supported and encouraged me in all I did.

NOT ALL AT SEA!

Autobiography of

George O'Brien Kennedy

Morrigan

Morrigan
an imprint of
Morigna MediaCo Teo
Killala
County Mayo

ISBN 0 907677 97 5

Cover by Identikit, Dublin
Typeset by uppercase, Cork
Printed by ColourBooks Ltd, Dublin.

A catalogue record for this book is available from the British Library.

Contents

One

I WAS BORN in 1912. Man was beginning to take to the air. The magic of radio waves had recently been harnessed. George V was ruler of all that British Empire splash of red in school atlases. And there was extreme poverty alongside riches in the city of my birth, Dublin. I was born into a class quite high up on that scale of poor to rich.

My father was Frederick Kennedy, the young barrister son of George O'Brien Kennedy, a wealthy Dublin lawyer and business man,(after whom I was named) owner of Bloomfield House off Merrion Road. Since demolished, the site of the house is now part of the St. Vincent's Hospital complex. The huge arched entrance gateway to Bloomfield still remains, opposite the Merrion Inn pub. The gates lead to an empty avenue, and the avenue leads to nowhere. Except to memories, and the past.

My mother was Ruby, elder daughter of a bank official, G.A.Mullaly. At the time of her engagement she had been living with her retired father and her sister Violet in County Leitrim. Their small estate there, Glenade, had been bought for them as a present by G.A's brother John, who had made a fortune cattle ranching in the Argentine.

The Mullaly sisters were not happy in Leitrim, being town girls who had grown up in Dublin and become used to quite a lively social life. In Glenade there was no such fun. Transport was a pony and trap and the nearest shops were eight or so miles away in Manorhamilton. The winters, then as now, were long and wet. And even though Violet was rather a shy retiring person, a great gardener and bird lover, she became very lonely after Ruby's marriage, living alone with her very elderly father.

The Mullalys, full of good intentions towards the local people of the valley, gave employment and built a creamery on their land with the intention of helping the farming community. But this was a time of unrest in Ireland and opposition to all landlords, good and bad, was strong. The creamery was not sufficiently supported and had to be closed down. The Mullalys sold the estate but I did visit Glenade after that and later on in my childhood.

In summertime it was a most beautiful place, the house under the lee of a mountain typical of the area, barren land sweeping up to crevassed rock ramparts below a flat top. There was a spectacular small waterfall cascading down close to the house, and a stream flowing through the nearby glade. There was a splendid view across the wide valley to the mountains opposite, and through the mouth of the valley in clear weather a segment of sea horizon and the blue of Donegal Bay.

Ruby Mullaly and Frederick Kennedy were married in the little Protestant church in Kinlough at the west end of Lough Melvin, a lake later associated with some of the happiest days of my youth.

One recent year I was passing through Kinlough and was surprised to see that the gates to the church were open. I pulled up and went in and found that the church door was also open. And to my joy I was met by a sight I shall always remember.

The church, in excellent repair, was most beautifully decorated with flowers of every sort, wheat sheaves and vegetables. It was an Ecumenical Harvest Festival effort by women of both denominations and they were just putting the finishing touches to their work. I told the lady in charge that my parents had been married in this church. Delighted to hear this she sat down and played the marriage march beautifully for me on the excellent little organ. And I was able to visualise the scene of some 85 years ago, not without a deep sadness for things that are past, past for all of us.

*

My first journey was from a Dublin maternity home on my mother's lap in the sidecar of my father's Scott motorcycle combination. That journey took me to my first home, Cnoc Aluinn in the village of Dalkey, now a suburb of Dublin. The house is still there and, in later years, was occupied by other Kennedy connections, the Browns.

From about Day Five I was placed in the care of a professional nurse of the highest calibre! This was Miss Merry, later always referred to as Nanny Merry. She was a "Princess Christian" nurse, as was her friend my Aunt Violet, who had made this arrangement for her sister. No doubt Violet considered Ruby quite unfit to look after an infant. During this period my father would have been kept well out of the way. He was quite useless domestically and unlike the fathers of to-day he probably never changed a nappy in his life.

I have no real memories of Dalkey and my first certain recollections are of quite another house. From the age of three or four we lived in a small semi-detached two storey house on Novara Road in Bray. We rented this house, (memories of a small garden back and front, two ground floor rooms with big interconnecting sliding doors)when my father went off to the war in France as a private soldier.

Knowing him a little in later life, I doubt if he had answered Kitchener's call of his own accord, I suspect my mother was one of the white feather brigade! Or, at any rate in the early days of that terrible war, she still had romantic ideas of a gallant officer husband fighting for King and Country. In fact my father refused to be commissioned, something for which I know my mother never forgave him.

Novara Road is not a through road to anywhere, there were no private cars on it, and no petrol anyway- it was 1915 - 16 and the only vehicles were those drawn by horses or donkeys. There were cabs, traps, delivery carts and bread vans, the drivers of the latter and their animals being well known to me and my younger sisters. These were Nancy and Doreen, about 18 months younger than myself. Twins, while not identical, they were very much alike.

Bray has been since far back into last century a seaside resort and so it was in my childhood. The sea front esplanade was only a hundred yards along Novara Road, turn right, under the railway arch and the sea was in front of you. Our first visits to the sea were probably in a perambulator! In summer time the rather stony beach and the esplanade were crowded with holidaymakers mostly from Dublin and Lancashire. It was a very popular resort with the lads and lasses from Liverpool and Manchester, their accents were strong on the air, and they knew how to enjoy themselves, but this influx was probably rather thin during the war years, or perhaps non existent due to transport problems.

In fair weather when the tide was out there was a little sand for children to enjoy. At that time Bray had a proper bathing place in the middle of the sea front with dressing shelters for men and women and two long walkway-piers running out to deep water, with diving boards and on the men's one, a scaffolded high dive,which was also used by women divers who swam the twenty yards between them. Bray seafront is very exposed to the east and north east, and these bathing jetties were frequently demolished in the winter, and even the esplanade severely damaged and the seafront houses, hotels and boarding houses heavily doused in spray.

The next door house in Novara Road was a kindergarten run by two unmarried sisters, the Misses Heffernan and a young lady. They must have all been relatively young. My sisters and I attended this day school for a short time, and I apparently fell for the young teacher, because I told my mother that she was very nice! So she was my first love and Mother gave me some flowers to give her, the presentation must have made a touching scene!

Across the road from our house there was a gap in the opposite terrace, a waste ground fenced off from the pavement with a low wooden pailing, and beyond the waste ground but still quite near our house were the sidings and marshalling yard of the Dublin South Eastern Railway's Bray Station. The DSER (which has always meant different things to different people!) ran on to Greystones, Wexford and Rosslare passing out of sight behind a long red brick warehouse.

I have as good a recollection of sound and smell as of sight and in my memory there was always activity night and day - it was wartime - winter and summer in these yards. Goods trains were being sorted and assembled by little steam locos(0-4-0 side tankers), and the noise of these operations is still clearly in my head, and the smell too of hot steam and metal.

On frosty misty mornings, we watching from an upper window as the loco, belching steam and smoke, tried to start and push or pull a line of wagons on the icy track, its wheels sometimes loosing traction in a furious burst of puffing and steam, before the driver could shut his valve, probably releasing sand onto the track before trying again with deliberately slow chuffing.

We always feared for the man who did the coupling as he dived between the rails and under the buffers with perhaps another wagon free wheeling down the track to whack against the one he was coupling.

In those days we travelled quite a lot on the DSER, it was almost the only form of public transport except the horse drawn cabs and "outside cars" where you sat very much outside. As I mentioned, Bray station was only a few hundred yards away and we walked there in fair weather or someone went to the station to summon a cab in bad weather.

Train travel was always exciting. The arrival of the Dublin bound train at Bray station from Greystones was quite dramatic, with the squeal of brakes, clouds of hot wet steam, excess pressure and energy blowing off through the safety valve of the engine and the banging of the buffers as the carriages pulled up. We stood well back from the edge of the platform and then scrambled aboard to wait for the guard's whistle, his green flag and then the engine's whistle, and we were off to Dublin.

All the stations were plastered with advertisements. Oxo and Bovril vied to put beef into you, and Guinness to give you strength, and all the 'spirits' of those times, to help you forget your troubles, but not those of wives and families! Also everywhere was the compelling picture of Kitchener pointing at you with a big finger and demanding that you come forward and give your services to your King and Country. How many Irishmen did and never returned, or returned severely wounded, and miserably compensated, with a pittance for a pension, they ran into many thousands, and we saw them everywhere, legless and armless and facially injured, in their blue hospital uniforms.

Class distinction was pretty evident on the railways. There were three classes, we took the Second, tolerable! And, a consideration for my mother living on a private soldier husband's pay, cheaper than First. Nonetheless I imagine her income was augmented by the rest of the family.

Class was something of which I became aware quite early in life, although never really understanding it. "Ladies" did not seek employment and were not educated to earn a living, and frequently when the family fortunes failed young ladies were obliged to take employment such as that of governess to children of better-off families or as companion to some elderly spinster or widow, anything which ensured a roof over their heads and a little spending money.

"Gentlemen" did not engage in trade, or of course in manual work. It amuses me now to note that in general it was rather different if your trade was on a big scale, or if you had a big enough bank balance and particularly if your business was connected with distilling, brewing or the supply of raw materials in a big way. I would hear the comment that so and so was not quite out of the top drawer etc, and people of Jewish origin unless very rich were not acceptable in the "best" clubs.

At that time and up to the end of the second World War the D.S.E.R. had two stations in Dublin, Harcourt St. and Westland Row. The Harcourt St. line went inland from just north of Bray - it was closed in the '60s in one of the more stupidly shortsighted actions of the Government of that time - was not very exciting but the Westland Row line was exciting and very scenic, it followed the coast - as does The Dart today - through tunnels, along the face of cliffs above the sea, glimpses of Kingstown Harbour and perhaps the Holyhead Mail Boat.

I recently made a sentimental journey from Westland Row to Bray in the DART along this line. It was a beautiful sunny calm day, the tide out and the vast expanse of Merrion Strand peopled by a few walkers,bait diggers, wader birds and gulls.

The stations seemed to match my memory, except for the advertisements, as did the view of Killiney Bay and Bray Head over a smooth shimmering sea ruffled only by the odd cat's paw of breeze.

Quite unchanged are the inland profiles of the big and little Sugar Loaves and Carrigoona, where among the trees - grown up since I was young - Knockranny, another one of the homes of my youth and dreams still stands.

MY FATHER'S mother was a formidable lady living in some state with an unmarried son and daughter in a big house called for some reason The Ark- I never found out why!- it is still there in Foxrock but the name has been changed. The son was my Uncle George and the daughter my Aunt Sissy. Poor Sissy had been blinded in one eye by a stone and had a glass replacement which fascinated us children. However, because of this she was extremely shy and retiring: she died quite young of what I do not know... but it was probably T.B., which also carried off my mother's younger brother at the age of about 18.

Uncle George took the place of my father during the war years, and kept a great interest in me for many years after, in fact up to the time of his rather late marriage to Marguerite - aunt and mother of four of my cousins, little older than my own children- he was my friend and instructor in all things mechanical and electrical, so that by the time I was ten I could use a lathe and all woodworking handtools. Uncle George was also one of Ireland's first radio hams.

Before the First World War he operated a radio Transmitter-Receiver station which in morse was able to cover the world, and I can remember him explaining to me how pictures could be transmitted as they are today in a much advanced form. Private Radio Telegraphy was not permitted by the British Government during the war, and the vital parts of the equipment were confiscated for the duration. In his workshop at the Ark he made all the coils and condensers and other equipment, and built the lattice mast that I still remember in the garden. One of the rooms in the house was the radio station- in some old records there must be recorded his call sign.

At that time all the bewildering jungle of wires, instruments, dials and gauges was dead and my uncle was running a "cottage" industry with his sisters Sissy and Wiggie (as she was known to the family), and my aunt Vi, making large numbers of simple things for hospitals, such as bed tables, back rests and little machines for rewinding washed bandages.

My Grandmother owned and my uncle drove a splendid motor vehicle of the times, a De Dion Bouton, vintage about 1908 I think, in which I vaguely remember travelling on someone's knee under a heavy waterproof rug, but otherwise exposed to the elements. My father also bought a small car just before the war; a little two seater Singer 9- later converted to carry my sisters and me on a bench seat built on top of the "dicky", (named after the female fashion of earlier times the Bustle!) a sort of embryonic "boot" of today; towards the end of the war my mother drove this vehicle on Red Cross duties, but it only came into its own after the war.

We had two Wartime holidays away from Bray. One was to Rush, north of Dublin, where there was a beautiful sandy strand right outside the wheelless railway carriage my mother had rented for a couple of weeks. My memories are of playing in the sand and paddling along the edge of the waves which came with a frothy leading edge, carrying seaweed and perhaps a jelly fish, and left with a dragging sound as it smoothed the wet sand. And I remember the earwigs with their pincer tails which seemed to infest parts of the carriage.

The daily excitement was the little blimp or airship which sallied forth every afternoon, weather permitting, to meet the Mail Boat from Holyhead and escort her into Kingstown. The blimp which was based just inland of where we were, used to putter over us only a hundred or two feet up and at perhaps 30mph. Her pilot, who seemed to be sitting completely exposed, would wave to us and we could see the small bombs with which it was armed hanging beside him. In 1918 the mail boat "Leinster" was torpedoed and sunk with great loss of life not far off the Irish coast. I have never seen it recorded that the blimp was near the scene at the time but the U boat that sank the Leinster never returned to base.

The other holiday remembered was to Pollduff at Cahore Point Co. Wexford, I don't recall how we got there but I expect it was by train to Gorey and then by pony and trap, a distance of ten or twelve miles.

On this holiday there was great excitement when someone in our party spotted a U boat quite close inshore on the surface- I saw it-. There is deep water quite close inshore north of the point although further north and south there are off-lying sandbanks, which make this a dangerous coast and the graveyard of many of the small sailing coasters of that and earlier times.

A call was made to the R.I.C.(The Royal Irish Constabulary) and in due course but long after the U boat had vanished a small posse of soldiers arrived on bicycles armed with rifles... possibly an invasion was feared! Though more likely a Casement type landing of arms for the Republican forces.

This was of course around the time of the Easter Rising, the destruction of much of central Dublin by fire and the shelling by British troops in their clumsy suppression of it. And finally of the execution of men whose names will live for ever in the history of Ireland, for my childhood period was the beginning of the end for British rule.

I think it was somewhere near Cahore that I first saw a thrashing machine in action. We had probably often seen these big red boxes on wheels being towed by steam traction engines, fascinating enough as they rumbled and lumbered along on their unsprung iron wheels, big drivers at the back and small ones steered by chains at the front. All the brasswork gleaming and on top of the coal fired boiler the big flywheel spinning freely driven by the flashing con rod and the steam cylinder.

In those days most of the grain was thrashed locally by these machines, manned by a small team of the owner-engineer, plus a fireman and perhaps two or three helpers. The team with its machinery would move round a wide area by arrangement with the bigger grain growing farmers, staying as long as necessary on a site to deal with all the grain brought in.

I think we went a few miles inland by pony trap to one of these sites in open country where the thrasher and engine had been in action for some hours.

It was a glorious day, probably in September, we could hear the distinctive hum of the thresher and see the smoke from the engine's tall chimney long before we reached it. Like everyone else we had brought food and drink, for this was a communal picnic and gala day for the district and the schools were closed so that the children could enjoy the fun and excitement.

A most animated scene greeted us on arrival, the central figure being the traction engine itself, a symbol of power in those days, standing in the corner of the field, puffing like a railway locomotive, as the exhaust steam made a draft up the tall brass topped chimney, mixing with smoke from the furnace fired by the engineer from the little coal box at the back, and a heap of coal on the ground beside it.

The flywheel of the engine drove the thrasher via a flapping leather belt. The thrasher itself working with a great humming and clattering as it beat the grain which flowed into bags at the back of the machine and disgorged neatly bundled straw at the side. On top of the machine two sturdy, shirtless, bronzed young men with pitch forks, fed in the stooks forked up to them by other men from carts and drays.

The pace seemed furious as indeed it probably was for the owner and his team would have been paid by results, and harvest time was brief and very weather dependant.

Trestle tables were set up stocked with food and drink by the local women and perhaps by the "gentry" of the locality. Although I do not remember them I expect there were "carpet baggers" selling wares and probably one or two stalls.

In the evening there would certainly have been drinking and dancing in the nearest village.

It might be interesting to recall that traction engines were used whilst stationary for ploughing. One method was to use two engines which had cable drums under their boilers, placed one at each end of the field to be ploughed The multi shared plough was pulled across the field by the cable and drum and then the engines were moved on for the next set of furrows, a somewhat cumbersome operation and I don't think it was used for long.

*

Sometime towards the end of the War we moved to a house which had recently been bought by my maternal Grandfather. Mr Mullaly had sold the house in Leitrim and moved with his daughter Vi to Bellevue on the outskirts of Bray. Outskirts, that is, in those days. Bellevue, (still standing and occupied by the Irish Times columnist Dick Walsh) is now with its garden an oasis in the middle of a large housing estate.

It was in this house on Killarney Road Bray that I really grew up. It did in fact have a beautiful view to the west and north from the upstairs windows. To the west the Wicklow mountains were across open fields, and to the north the small but to me memorable hill (my aunt Vi pointed it out to me as 'a mountain' when I must have been about five) named Kattigoliher. This is actually spelt quite differently on the maps.

Kattigoliher was my first mountain!

The lead mine chimney was even then derelict standing on its north west side. As a teenager I explored this chimney which had- and still has- an external stone staircase spiralling round the tapered masonry, but deliberately broken off to prevent climbing. I also wandered the tunnel-like flue which carried the poisonous gases from the smelter in the valley to the chimney.

First mountain, and first aeroplane... it was at Bellevue that I remember first seeing an aeroplane, it must have been 1918 or '19 and the planes we saw were British military machines. They were quite a thrill for us children. The planes seemed to fly quite low and when they disappeared behind the hedge at the top of the garden we were always convinced they must have come down a few fields away and went rushing off after them over a field or two but never found one on the ground!

A moral there somewhere?

Bellevue outbuildings and garden are full of very happy childhood memories. The house was surrounded by a garden and a lawn and at the back there was a stable yard, a stable and coach house and above them a large hay loft. The enclosed yard was paved with thousands of smooth round beach stones set in lime mortar.

Heavily strapped double timber doors gave onto a side avenue where a garage had been built, wide enough to take two vehicles. This drive sloped down and round to the front of the house, and from a turning area the drive continued between hedges of trees and laurel steeply down to the Killarney Road.

On the north side of the drive was the lawn, at first set out for croquet, later for tennis. On the far side of this there was a summerhouse, overshadowed by a splendid oak tree, and also a long rock garden. To the the rear of the stables and the lawn there was a well matured vegetable garden, a small orchard and a large henhouse and run. And beyond were fields to play in.

The house itself was not particularly large, but of somewhat odd design -if it ever was designed- it seemed to have originated from a much older house, which had become the rear part at a lower level and with rather low ceilings. This was the area of the kitchen, scullery, pantry, larder and also of the room we called the 'school room' because it was the room where as small children we did our lessons and started to learn to play the piano under the instruction of various governesses until we were eight or nine. Dad also took a small part in our early education with reading and arithmetic. He also enjoyed reading to us the classic legends of Greece. We always wanted the story of the flying horse Pegasus. The happiest evenings of childhood were spent in that room playing games with the adults of the family, parents and Aunt Vi and Uncle George, all very loving people.

This room was also used by all the family as a living room in the winter as it had a good fireplace and was easy to warm and very cosy. Apart from this room, this area of the house was paved with limestone flags...the kitchen sink was also apparently hewn from a solid block of limestone!

The groundfloor rooms were gas lit, but for lighting upstairs oil lamps or candles were used, and their somewhat feeble and flickering light, the rattling of the old casement windows, and the booming of the wind in the chimneys of the upstairs bedrooms on a stormy night all added up to a not entirely disagreeable thrill when going upstairs to bed, the escorting adult carrying the lamp. Once in bed you were safe with your head under the blankets!

The house was on three levels although it only appeared to be two from the front.There was no true basement, but the front porch was up a flight of stone steps so the front rooms were well above ground level. The staircase started at this level, with two landings above. The rear rooms were down a few steps, into what was probably the original dwelling. The bedrooms above this rear area were at the level of the first landing.

We three kids shared the nursery off the first landing when we were small, our beds in a row with me in the middle, to keep the twins who were apt to fight apart! At that time my Uncle George had the other room on our landing while my parents and Aunt Vi slept in the two top floor bedrooms.

For some reason Aunt Vi's bedroom was believed by us children to be haunted by some spirit and normally we were afraid to go into it at night. I distinctly remember my sister Doreen telling me in later life that as an older child she had for some reason slept in the room for a period and always felt uneasy; but then I always thought Doreen was a little fae herself!

The other spooky place was the totally unlit stair off our landing which led up to Brigid's room which was on a level all its own, a sort of afterthought room on the back of the house.

Brigid was mistress of the kitchen premises, a woman for whom I have the tenderest of memories. I think she adored us kids being herself childless and unmarried- typical of the servants of her day- and no doubt she spoilt us. Her dress was also typical, a black dress to the ground, a white apron and a bonnet. 'Bri' was my nickname and Brigid always called me Master Bri, the twins being Miss Nancy and Miss Doreen even when we were quite small. Such was the custom of "the serving classes" of those days!

The big kitchen was typical of the times, stone flagged floor, huge black range with bright parts polished and the rest blackleaded, the stone sink in one corner, and a large scrubbed-white pine table with a few wheel backed chairs. The walls were all whitewash plastered, as was the back passage leading to the yard past the pantry and larder which were all under a low pitched slate roofed extension at the back of the house.

There was room in the back passage for a large wooden rollered mangle with a powerful handle through which all the household linen, except items which had to be ironed and starched were passed on washing day. There was also a patent knife sharpening and cleaning machine, a round wooden drum about 20" in diameter and 5" deep, with leather lined slots round its periphery into which knives of different sizes were inserted, and a handle on the front given a few turns. It worked well, too well I seem to remember, it was banned because it was found to be wearing down the knives rather rapidly.

One of the big days in the calender at Bellevue was the spring clean. It had to be the first dry warm day in late April when supervised by Aunt Vi all the ground floor furniture which could be carried by the women folk was transferred to the lawn, followed by all the carpets and mats, to be hung up and beaten. Indoors all the immovable furniture was covered with dust sheets, tea leaves which had been saved for the purpose were dampened and scattered on the floors to kept down the dust of the sweeping operation. At the same time the chimneys were swept by a professional sweep who arrived with his donkey and cart. We would watch this operation from the lawn, the big moment being when the brush popped out of the chimney, possibly pushing out a jackdaw's nest!

None of us had any fear of heights and spent a lot of time out doors climbing trees, our favourite was a very large tree of the Yew variety quite easy to climb and with no rotten branches and so dense that one could hardly fall out of it! Doreen was always a bit of a dare devil at tree climbing, she was very agile and a fast runner she could always catch me easily when playing 'tig and later was a good hockey player.

THE STRANGER who was my father finally came home from France in one piece in 1918. He had gone away a 'gentleman volunteer' who refused a commission, and had carried dispatches by motorcycle and driven lorries on the Western Front throughout the War. When he returned he kept up his friendships with the Dublin lads who had been his comrades at the front...I think a little to the discomfort of the family.

The only stories of the war he ever told us were the funny ones, such as the method of cleaning out petrol cans for use as water carriers; empty them out and then drop in a lighted match...the resulting explosion left them perfectly clean! And he told us of cooking with a petrol burning Primus stove on top of a load of cordite in the back of a lorry! But the mud and the horror of that terrible conflict never surfaced in his stories. He did say he disliked the Belgians whom he thought terribly cruel to their horses and other animals.

At about this same time there was talk of a revolution in Russia. Such talk of revolution meant nothing to me, or how it would change the world, but I do remember the refugees. These seemed all to be women, rather pathetic gentlefolk in bedraggled clothes, they had no possessions and no English and were taken in by some of the Bray families we knew.

Apart from a brief spell at Kindergarten, our early education was at home, given principally by several governesses when we were between five and eight or nine, with some help from our parents, and Aunt Vi at the piano.

The music lessons were rather a disaster.

We loved listening to my Uncle, who was a pretty good violinist and Aunt Vi an equally good pianist although going deaf - and became quite deaf later - playing the classics below the nursery at night, but the daily and enforced practices supervised by some rather stupid people put us off the piano. I never got over the tedium of those early days and the same applied to my sisters. Now I wish I could play but cannot even read a note and I have just given that same piano to a granddaughter!

Child discipline in those days was quite strict and not very intelligent, resulting in childish frustration over rules and conduct which made no sense to childish logic. The resulting tantrums were generally treated by the child being locked in a room until they cooled by sheer exhaustion. I think Doreen suffered the most from this, she was always a determined child and woman. I was reckoned to be pretty placid child. Mother who was not very patient sometimes apologised to me for rough treatment I got, which was really intended only for the twins. We never received real corporal punishment at home, mother would spank our bottoms hard at times but I never remember ever receiving any sort of physical punishment from my father.

When we were quite small but yet capable of walking several miles, Aunt Vi loved to take us children for country walks in the spring, which we much enjoyed. Bray Head from the Kilruddery end was a lovely walk through the woods, particularly when the ground was a magical mist of bluebells. Not far away from Bellevue there were several lanes where wild flowers grew in profusion, and we named the lanes to suit the predominant flowers, Violet Lane and several others I have forgotten. But the lanes themselves have vanished so it hardly matters now.

Aunt Vi taught us the names of all the flowers and trees and also of the many birds and their calls which we came across on these walks and around the house. She knew too where the different birds were likely to build their nests and helped us find but not touch them. I remember how the apparent mystery of bird flight intrigued me.

*

I never knew my father intimately or even well, and I greatly regret this. But, from memory, he seemed patient and pretty placid. He left our upbringing to my mother who was undoubtedly the stronger character.

A Greek and Latin scholar, Dad was very well read and inventive, telling us made-up stories as we went for walks about Bray. He was an accomplished sportsman, playing rugby and badminton for Ireland at different times. He was also a good golfer, one time captain of Bray golf club and also for a while the club's secretary.

I feel he was not a happy man in married life. The War had broken up what might have become a career at the Irish Bar, just as the next war broke up my own career. Dad did stay with Law most of his life, but never practiced at the Bar again after the War.

One of his jobs was that of a Sheriff in Dublin Castle... and we children were very impressed when we heard that he had arrested a ship in the docks escorted by a posse of police! He also worked for a time as a solicitor with his brother George but it seems that they spent little time in George's office. Most of the work there was carried out by an elderly clerk and seems to have consisted of disposing of property they had inherited! I imagine a lot of this involved problems of leaking roofs and rent collecting from poor tenants. At this time much of Dublin's once upper class property was turning into tenements and later to the slums of the mid twenties.

I have recollections of this solicitors' office, an establishment which might have come straight out of a Dickens novel. Dusty shelves piled with old files, a bare wood floor, ancient furniture and that elderly clerk sitting at a high desk and stool doing all the work. I don't think there was even a typewriter.

In recent times I met an elderly solicitor, a Mr Kirwin, and I asked him if he remembered George and Freddie Kennedy. "Indeed I do" he said," they were the laziest two men I ever knew in all my life"! End of conversation.

As far as their soliciting this comment was probably true, neither my father nor uncle being being cut out for that kind of life. They were both engineers at heart and in activities that interested them they were far from lazy. There was a third brother, my uncle known as O'B. He was a GP with a practice in Kells in Co. Meath in his later life, having earlier worked in T.B. hospitals. I never knew O'B well, in fact I'm not sure even of his real name!

Dad definitely should have been an engineer, but at the time of his younger days engineering was not for his social class. He also certainly should have owned a sailing yacht of some sort, even quite a small one. I now know he could have well afforded one, and it might have made all the difference to his life. As it was I suspect anything like that was vetoed by his wife. Nonetheless, he did when quite a old man build a Dublin Bay "Wag" -a 14ft dinghy- and joined the Royal Irish Yacht Club. He raced this, crewed for a time by my sister Doreen, but rather sadly for him this was a duty she did not enjoy.

Looking back I think he suffered acute depression in late life, which was not recognised as such by any of his family including me. I was generally far away at this time, but feel I was very insensitive and somewhat cocky about my rather insignificant successes and his apparent overall failure. He gave me every support early in my career, and visited and sailed with me several times when I was in Hamble and later in the New Forest.

After his death I found among his papers a letter written to his wife in Henley - where she had taken us children to stay with an aunt - in which he expressed a deep love for her, and spoke of how acutely he missed her. I don't even know if it was ever sent, and doubt if she would have reciprocated at that stage of their marriage. I think he did not measure up to her expectations in social and public life.

*

Aunty Vi stepped in front of a bus in O'Connell Street in Dublin in 1958 and was killed. This accidental death was caused by her deafness. She had lived with us through all our childhood and later with our parents and had been devoted to us, as I to her in later life. I actually think I loved her more than my own mother. Although I do recall going through a period of excessive secret mother love when a child, probably up to the age of seven or eight, crying myself to sleep over the thought of her dying! Mother actually enjoyed very good health most of her life, so perhaps Freud would have an explanation! I also remember that when I was a very small boy - perhaps four-Mother gave me a little lecture on the elements of how I came to be, how I was born and fed from her breasts. Many years later I suspect she prompted Dad to give me some more explicit advice and instructions, but being rather a shy man on such matters, nothing of substance was transmitted and I just picked it up in the way most boys do. I don't think I did any better when my time came with my own sons!

Vi was a great and a gifted gardener, and Knockranny -our later home, which was actually her property- had a very beautiful rockery and flower garden, as well as an extensive vegetable garden, a big orchard and several plantations of trees,over seven acres in all. The gardens were worked by Aunt Vi herself with the aid of the muscle power of Mr Murtagh, our gardener.

I have strong memories of Aunt Vi and the other women of the household constantly darning socks, stockings, jerseys and other garments by the fire on winter evenings.

While male attire has not changed greatly since my childhood, women's clothes are certainly very different. Most of the ladies at the time of my birth and for several years thereafter wore stays or corsets and I can vaguely remember my mother lacing up hers. (She used to say later that she had a very slim waist and could enclose it in her two hands.) Photographs show her to have been a very good looking if not beautiful woman.

Button boots were also in fashion for children and grown up women, and among my oddments from the past I still have the button hooks and shoe horns necessary for putting them on. Hats were certainly very important too. Visits to Switzers and other hat shops are still in my memory and watching mother and it may have been my great Aunt Evy trying on numerous very elaborate and much adorned hats, and some of the remarks which went with this somewhat mysterious ritual. I could not make out why one hat of dozens suited more than another. Women were then almost invariably wearing their hair long and done up into some sort of bun, secured with numerous hairpins in the daytime.

The problem of securing these millinery creations on top was solved by means of hatpins, long sharp skewers passing thro' both hat and hair. It always worried me to see mother skewering on her hat! She also frequently wore a veil over the lot, thereby adding a bit of mystery to the overall result!

Calary Races was one of the most exciting days of the year. These were point to point races on the high ground of Calary 'Bog', which is actually unfenced (or was unfenced then!) heathland on the high plain to the south of the Big Sugar Loaf.

The races were organised by the Bray hunt, The Bray Harriers. Popular with the ordinary people of Dublin and the surrounding areas, one of the great outings of the year. I will recall this exodus to the hills by many thousands of people, all in festive mood and all passing Bellevue gate. They were fairly sober in the morning and far from sober on the evening's return.

Every conceivable conveyance that could make the trip and ascend and descend what was then known as the Long Hill up to Calary was brought into use. There were Char-a-bancs stuffed to bulging, cars and taxis of every sort, lorries with the rough bench seats, and then every possible description of horse drawn vehicle, old carriages, cabs, outside cars, traps, carts and drays, and of course hundreds of bicycles, tandems and even tricycles! We stood at the gates enthralled, waving and being waved to until the last had passed by. The return started around our bed time and people were still passing long after we were asleep. I think of this day very nostalgically and am reminded of one of the songs we used to sing at school in England, Bladen Races, which seems to epitomise youth, the joy and brevity of it all and shortness of life.

'Lots of lads and lassies there all wie smilin' faces ganning along the Scotsward road to see the Bladen Races.'

As older children we went up to the races ourselves with all the friends we could muster. The racing was great fun, we knew quite a few of the riders, male and female, all amateur. Everyone knew who - barring accidents - would win which race, and so the bookies had a thin time and I remember one or two welshing on their punters! The course which was roughly marked out with flags was quite long and finished with the horsemen charging perilously through the crowd.

Childhood was different then. We had fewer toys than children have today and probably used our imaginations more. My sisters, as seems still to be the way with girls, were a bit horse crazy from quite an early age and either played horses or made the big Airedale or even a nanny goat we had pull a little cart which Uncle George had made for them. True to form I had a little green pedal car of which I am said to have been very selfish, not letting my sisters drive it. I had also already developed an interest in anything to do with boats, no doubt encouraged by my father who although he had no boat took the periodical The Yachting Monthly. These magazines, dated from 1921, are on my shelves as I write!

I was then about nine and very soon understood the basics of boat design. We played boats on the lawn treating it as water, with a serviceable 'ship' made from an old kitchen table covered with a rug - the cabin and upper deck - and the pointed ends made by placing four planks on edge against the table legs at each end... with a few mugs and old plates we could make a voyage!

*

When I was about six or seven Uncle George established his workshop in the old hay loft, based principally on quite a sophisticated Drummond screwcutting metal working lathe, treadle-operated via a heavy flywheel. He taught me to use this for metal and woodwork and he himself made all sorts of other tools and gadgets, from wireless parts to a vacuum cleaner... and many other things of use or just to amuse us kids.

Uncle George and I both suffered acutely from asthma. He went several times to Switzerland for treatment, without much success. I just sat up in bed inhaling smoke from a little burning cone of grey powder to get some relief from this disease...now known of course to be largely a psychological problem. My asthma was left behind when I went to boarding school but George suffered on throughout his life.

Kells Cove is on the south side of Dingle Bay in Kerry and soon after Dad's return from France we went there for a summer holiday, renting the old Coastguard Station overlooking the cove. We children and the women folk travelled down by train to Cahirciveen via Cork City, and thence by horse drawn vehicle to Kells while Dad drove the 230 miles in the little Singer car. This was quite a trip on the roads as they then were, particularly loaded down with luggage. A few days later he drove all the way back with Aunty Vi...a telegram had arrived with news that her father was dying. He did die at that time and is buried at Enniskerry Protestant church, as indeed are my parents and Aunt Vi herself.

In 1919 we had the cove all to ourselves. It was here that I lost all fear of water and learned to swim, as did my sisters, using at first those water wings made of some material that had to be wet to hold the air.

A photo of the times shows two curaghs on the strand. On several occasions during our month's stay we saw these currachs streaking out to the vast shoals of mackerel which we could see from our house above, the shoals in the distance looking like a breeze on the calm water. To my memory they must've been perhaps quarter of a mile across and so the fishermen had no chance of surrounding a shoal...instead they cut off sections and drove them in their nets into the cove. I remember the fry like silver waves on the sand, and then women coming down from the cottages on the hills to gather the mature fish in wicker baskets.

In Kerry as in many country areas transport was largely provided by the donkey or ass. I remember them and their dainty little hooves pulling those overloaded wooden springless carts, and the sound of them clonking along the rough country roads and boreens. That clonking was the knocking of the slack wheel bearings on their axles, and it's a noise which still echoes in my head.

On the roadless hills and across bogs wickerwork panniers were slung across the animals' narrow backs(I have a photo taken in Kerry of me sitting astride a donkey with a sister in each pannier, aged about six and five). The panniers were used to bring in the peat, this "turf" being the only fuel burnt in the open hearth fires of those times. The donkey surely deserves an honourable place in Irish history... and in Animal Heaven!

*

One fine morning at Kells Dad spotted a floating object out in the main bay to the north of us... with the aid of binoculars he saw it was a floating mine from the recent war. A message was sent to the R.I.C. in Cahirciveen...two men with service rifles arrived. They failed to detonate it with rifle fire and a message was sent to the nearest Royal Naval base, probably at Bere Haven.

In the meantime wind and tide combined to set the mine in towards our cove and onto the cliffs below us; so my Father ordered us and the one or two families living near us, to pack up some food and go and have a picnic further inland in case the mine brought the cliff down. Dad went back in the afternoon when he knew the tide would have fallen and possibly grounded the thing.

Sure enough he found it sitting like a giant seaweed covered egg on the sandy bottom of a cleft between rocks, amazingly having floated in without bumping the detonating horns. He got help and ropes and secured it so that it would not bump about when it floated again and he then allowed us to go home.

Soon after dawn the next morning we were awakened by the high pitched high pressure 'shout' of a destroyer's siren, and looking out were thrilled to see the ship tearing up the bay with her high bow wave lit by the rising sun.

She anchored out in the bay and sent in a shore party in a smartly oared 'whaler', which my father met on the strand and escorted the mine disposal party over the rocks, followed by myself and the twins.

I am sure it should not have been permitted, but we watched the whole operation from the rocks above, where we would have been blown highest had it gone off! But the job was done as an obviously routine matter, it didn't explode and later my father was invited on board the ship, a trip which I am sure pleased and interested him.

In retrospect I realise that we kids were afraid of the mine not for what it was but because it was covered with all sorts of creepy and some snake-like marine creatures- probably barnacles which creatures grow quite long and once had the reputation of being embryo barnacle geese!

*

The Tralee to Cahirciveen railway was built principally to bring to markets the herring which was landed at Cahirciveen. The fish were salted and packed in barrels by female labour but for some reason the trade was short lived and the railway was an expensive failure. A very expensive failure indeed as this line was reckoned to have been one of the most costly to build in all Ireland ...and it's not hard to see why! A drive along the south side of Dingle Bay follows the difficult line of the railway just above the road on a steep hillside for a good part of the way.

I have in my possession a Bartholomews county by county atlas of Ireland, dated about 1903, showing the country covered by railway tracks, broad and narrow gauge, they are all gone now with the exception of the few main lines.

It is sad to note that on the current ¼ and ½ inch scale maps no trace of these old tracks are shown. These works,embankments,cuttings, tunnels, bridges and viaducts, represent an immense sum of human sweat and labour, real pick and shovel stuff, and are also examples of great early engineering skills. In my view they should be so recognised and indicated on maps for all time, not only to commemorate the men who built them, but also because they would make wonderful walks for hikers in the wilder parts of Ireland.

There are places on some of these old tracks where on a quiet evening and you are alone it is easy to imagine the presence of those long gone workers, to hear the ring of their tools or even to fancy you can hear a train approaching from around the bend in the cutting.

THE WAR of Independence merged into the Civil War, times of great social and political upheaval in Ireland. To a small boy it meant much excitement. The comings and goings of the Irish Republican Army (I.R.A) irregulars, the R.I.C. and the notorious Black and Tans, as the British Auxiliaries were known to us, and then later the Free State Soldiers in their green uniforms. Little ditties were going the rounds,

"If you see a motor lurry in the devil of a hurry
'tis the Free State comin' by an by.
There'll be lots of money and pots o' honey
from the Free State comin' by an by!"

This period marked the end of the era of the landed Anglo-Irish gentry and saw the destruction of many splendid houses and their contents. To my mind this was rather a sad loss to posterity, but a natural reaction to landlordism, particularly of the absentee variety. In many cases, however, the destruction was quite unjustified.

I had little idea of what was going on. In Bray the troubles meant very noisy nights, and walking to school over pavements strewn with broken glass and brass cartridge cases. Once we found a motor cycle combination inside our gate and somebody had obviously lost a great deal of blood in the sidecar. Our young gym mistress was hit in the neck by a stray bullet and killed.

I remember the 'Tans' in their lorries, wired over to keep out grenades, driving up Killarney road and potting at stray hens just for the hell of it and to terrorise the population.

Through all this my family kept what would now be called a low profile! And as an added survival insurance we flew a large flag from an upstairs window. On an emerald green ground there was depicted a harp, but also a small union jack! This became known as the "sitting on the fence flag"!

On the whole the middle classes did not get much involved in these so called "Troubles". I think my father would have had Republican sympathies but my conservative mother would probably have been a Royalist if anything. In reality the family were a-political, a condition in which I remained until I went to work in an English shipyard at the age of nineteen.

Other recollections of the 'Troubles' were the blown bridges and trenched roads we came across when we went into the hills for picnics in Dad's Singer or down the coast to Brittas, to The Silver Strand or to Jack's Hole. At that time these south Wicklow strands were virtually undiscovered and we would be quite annoyed to find anyone else on our chosen beach. Troubles or not, summertime Sundays were definitely times for picnics. In the early summer it was off to the hills and, later on, when the weather got warmer, and when there were midges in the hills, we went to those empty beaches.

Very often these excursions were with Uncle Berty Plews in a more updated car than ours. Around this time we had begun to see more of Uncle Berty's family, his children Jack and Joan being our only first cousins. The Plews family were living in Blackrock south of Dublin about eight miles away. The connection was through Berty's wife, my father's sister. This was our 'Aunt Wiggie', a family pet name which she never liked but never lost.

This Plews family originally came to Ireland from Yorkshire and had been closely associated with the Great Northern Railways in Ireland. Uncle Berty was, in the twenties, chief accountant to the G.N.R. but during the war he had served as an officer in what was then called Mesopotamia, fighting the Turks and their Arab irregular allies. Judging by his photos and the stories he brought back it must have been a much more interesting and pleasant war than that on the Western Front. Mesopotamia was, of course, the theatre of war in which T.E.Laurence became a legend.

My Dad and uncle Berty had been friends and motor cycling enthusiasts in their bachelor days, and now in the twenties their enthusiasm was cars, which they maintained and tuned themselves.

Dad taught me to be a good motor mechanic. When I was quite a small boy I helped with what were then quite routine jobs, decarbonising, valve grinding, puncture repair, greasing. The cars of those days had many grease points which required lying under the car with a grease gun, and it was while doing this one day that Dad put his knee out, but refused to see a doctor, consequently he was slightly crippled for the rest of his life and walked with a limp. The Singer did not self start and had to be swung with a handle or started down a hill. I always say I learned to drive backwards, I could manage to push the Singer out of the garage, hop in and steer it back down the slope to the front of the house,put the brake on and leave it ready for Dad to start by running forward down the drive and off to Dublin.

In the early twenties Dad sold the Singer and bought a 10/15 Fiat. This was a four seater tourer with a hood but no side curtains. Motoring was still a matter of wrapping up well and being wet and cold at times; but we as a family covered much ground in that car.

On the Singer the petrol tank was just behind the instrument panel, gravity feeding to the engine and the filler projected from the panel! I am always reminded of it when I smell petrol. It surprises me that we never had a fire, Dad who smoked a pipe must have been pretty careful. Filling was done using a tundish from a standard two gallon can, which was carried in a special clip on the running board

The Fiat had a rear mounted tank, I can't remember whether it self-started but it certainly had a crank and seemed quieter than the Singer except at high revolutions. In its extremely low bottom gear the whole car vibrated like mad and had a habit of 'running' big end bearings, letting us down once in the wilds of Achill Island and another time when grossly overloaded in Antrim on the way to Port Ballintrae, where we spent a very wet summer holiday in part of yet another old coastguard station overlooking the harbour. (For me that particular holiday is memorable for the rain, boredom and appalling boils from which I suffered, probably due to bad feeding at prep school in England. The treatment for the boils was bread poultices applied with cotton wool and sticking plaster to my neck and bottom, painful but very effective!)

About the time we got the Fiat, Uncle Berty bought a Sunbeam, a very superior car in its day. This could cope with most of the hills we tackled on picnics in the mountains, but he also had a little Peugeot which Aunt Wiggie usually drove. This was a two seater (but seated tandem!) and was very narrow and somewhat feeble.

If we were going together for a picnic and there were any hills on the way my cousin Jack and I would sit jammed in the back of this car, with Aunt Wiggie driving and then, when the engine began to run out of steam, we bailed out and pushed with all our might. Brakes were not too good and only on the back wheels so that a low gear was always used going down hill, the engine acting as a brake.

Apart from summer picnics, the other great family get-togethers were on Christmas Day. The Kennedys and the Plews alternated, between Blackrock and Bray in early days, and then between Knockranny in Kilmacanogue- our later home-and their new home in Foxrock.

Those were real old fashioned Christmases. Aunty Vi took on the decorating of the house, she and us kids went out and gathered holly (with berries if possible)and ivy, and if we couldn't find mistletoe it was bought. And of course there was a christmas tree. Aunty Vi was also responsible for making the Christmas pudding. In fact she made several, mixed together in an enormous pudding bowl and then dispensed into smaller ones. Manufacture of puddings was done months before Christmas so that they could mature.

I remember sugared ginger fruits, salted almonds and champagne for the adults...and a drop for us so that we could drink the various toasts.

While still at Bellevue we discovered roller skating. There was a rather dingy rink in a big corrugated hall called the Arcadia right opposite Bray railway station. We were given roller skates and soon learned to skate and spent many afternoons after school tearing round and round with all the children of Bray, absorbing dust and germs!

About this time our own parents and those of Jack and Joan, our cousins, were playing a lot of badminton in what is now the library of the Royal Dublin Society at Ballsbridge. This hall adjoins the main exhibition hall. As badminton is a winter game and usually played in the evening, we went along with our parents, plus our cousins and a few other children, to skate in this huge hall, which was unlit and very dark. The hall had a timber floor and had occasionally been used as a rink at the time of my father's boyhood. For us it was the greatest thrill skating in the dark emptiness, torches in our hands, shrieking with excitement.

Picnics and parties, skating and holidays, the high points of our comfortable growing up. It never entered our heads that we were privileged, nor of course did we once query how our lifestyle was financed.

Patchwork was the name of a habitation within one hundred yards of Bellevue's gates. This was a collection of what were little more than hovels by the roadside, with a forecourt dusty or muddy - according to season- and behind a bank sloped down to a little stream.

Patchwork was home to a number of families and innumerable dirty, ragged, barefoot and half-starved children. We passed it indifferently practically every day of our lives. Metaphorically holding our noses.

My father and mother and Aunt Vi were all fairly well endowed with share holdings. Aunt Vi herself actually owned 'our' houses Bellevue and later Knockranny, while Dad I imagine paid all the outgoing expenses. The arrangement seemed to suit everyone, Dad acting as general financial adviser, quite astutely I think. I'm sure none of them ever thought to query how the money actually came to be made but, from conversations I remember overhearing, Aunt Vi and Dad certainly discussed buying this and selling that. This and that had names like Guinness, or other names starting with Imperial!

They mentioned rubber, tea, and chemicals and it all seemed very important to them but a total mystery to me because I saw nothing change hands. With hindsight I now realise that I had been brought up and educated principally on the proceeds of these holdings, in which Guinness predominated.

I think that most people who give the matter of share holdings any thought, other than how much the shares bring in annually or appreciate over time, must be aware that money doesn't simply grow on paper in an office, but ultimately in however roundabout a manner from human labour providing a service or applying skill or physical force to making something, or from rearing or growing animals or crops or from mining.

Many years after my privileged childhood had passed I read a book by Sir Roger Casement. Well known of course for his involvement in Ireland's affairs, he had earlier been employed by the British Government to investigate reports of extreme brutality to the native latex (rubber) gatherers in the Congo and Brazil in the early days of this century. His reports horrified the authorities, which led to some improvements and to his knighthood.

His published book gives a terrible picture of human exploitation in its most extreme form. Nevertheless this was how wealth was actually made, and of course is still being made, particularly in many third world and far eastern countries, from sugar,coffee,cocoa, other cash crops... and from the cheap labour used in all forms of manufacture from electronics to clothing.

I certainly think that had my Aunt and Mother been aware of the sources of their comparative affluence they would have been horrified. Much as the people in today's affluent societies might be horrified...if they thought about the true sources of their wealth and comfort.

NANNY MERRY'S father was the Vicar of St. Feock on Pill Creek, at Falmouth Harbour in England. The whole family were invited there for a holiday and so Dublin to Plymouth passage was booked with The British and Irish Steam Packet Company. This journey then was known as the Long Sea route to London and, in addition to Plymouth, the ships called at Southampton. By present day standards these ships were small; single stack, coal burning three island steamers with single screw and reciprocating engines. They carried cattle and mixed cargoes and ten or twelve passengers.

Our family were practically if not the only passengers, and were virtually given the run of the ship for the first few hours of the trip when it was daylight and fairly calm. We kids took full advantage of the liberty.

The crew were very good to us and no doubt kept an eye out to see that we stayed on board and did not hurt ourselves. My memory of the passage is somewhat dim, I must have been seven going eight and the twins a year younger, but I do distinctly remember playing blind man's buff on the open topped bridge with the mate, who was of course the blind man...I wonder if this game was recorded in the ship's log!

We chased each other round the decks and alleyways of the accommodation. As the ship's motion increased, we began to feel a little queer and then surprisingly to us, were sick every now and then. This was the first night of my life afloat and memorable.

The ship must have run into a considerable head sea as we approached the Scillies and Lands End in the early hours, because I was aware of the ship putting her head down and shuddering alarmingly every now and then, I was quite convinced that her bow was scraping along the bottom of the sea which must be most dangerous? I think my father comforted me in the night, by explaining that it was actually the propeller coming partly out of the water which caused the shudder.

During the voyage I was taken down to the boiler and engine rooms and given a piece of cotton waste for my hands because the hot oily atmosphere made everything greasy. I was very impressed by the fierce heat in the stoke hold, and of the stokers in singlets and trousers, shining with sweat, continuously shovelling coal into the nearly white hot furnaces. In the engine room all seemed to be silent, the quiet massive movement that only a big open and well maintained reciprocating steam engine can produce.

Fifty years later I was to make this passage again. But this time in a little 6ton yacht with my wife Christine and son Simon, we were on the way to race the boat right round Britain and Ireland and the Shetlands. But that journey comes later in this story, many journies lie between.

*

Mr Merry was the Vicar of a small and a poor parish and he had no car or other transport. And Nanny Merry was rather strict, and so we were rather confined on the English holiday, the only way we could get away was by boat!

Pill Creek was typical of the many creeks branching off the main Fall River. It dried into a large muddy ditch at low water, with all the moored boats aground in various attitudes. Several of these were of a type of fishing boat known as Falmouth Quay Punts, shapely little sailing vessels 24 to 26 ft long, cutter rigged, half decked, and engineless. Auxiliary power was provided by the "wooden engine" , this being a long sweep or oar pulling on one side and corrected with the tiller and rudder.

It was arranged for us all to take a number of outings with the elderly and very congenial fisherman owner of one of these little craft - and this was certainly my first experience of sailing. We made trips up the Fall past numerous and to us enormous ships that were laid up light in the river. We also saw one of the "Wooden Walls of England" as the Men-O-War of the early 19th century were called, HMS Implacable. We hauled alongside her and with the permission of the retired Naval Officer caretaker, we went aboard. I have vague memories of huge timbers, low ceilings and lots of old cannons, and darkness.

On another occasion we had a lovely sail out to the open sea and round to the west to the Helford river, where we landed on a beautiful sandy beach, and picnicked before sailing home.

I was allowed to take the tiller on the way back- and that was the first of many many tillers in all sorts of craft in all sorts of weather that I have held over the past 75 years.

One other childhood holiday in England was a spur-of-the-moment decision of my Mother's. She took us to Henley-on-Thames to stay with an aunt. This aunt, a Mrs Rouquette, was widowed shortly afterwards and came to live near us in Ireland. She became almost a part of the family, she was a great golfer and quite a character..

While we were away certain families in the Bray area were hit by a minor epidemic of Sleepy Sickness, a fairly rare disease which attacks the brain. Several children known to us died from it and one of a family of three girls and one boy of about our ages, our closest friends, was struck down by it.

This girl was the eldest and had been a very beautiful and intelligent child. The sickness did not kill her at the time, but left her for several years a mental and physical wreck and with a totally changed nature, so that she seemed possessed of a devil at times. We children never saw her again, but Mother did and learned that she could and did write poetry, possibly indicating that she knew her state.

Mother always said that it was divine inspiration which made her take us three to England when she did.

I WAS nearly nine when I started at Aravon boys school on Novara Road in Bray. Life for small boys really begins with their first school, when they start to fend for themselves. In my case it was also the beginning of some degree of freedom and independence, particularly as I was given my first bicycle and learned to ride and maintain it.

Aravon was a day school with, I think, a few boarders, probably sons of colonials. (It still exists, in a different location, but with much the same ethos!) In the twenties of course there were still a great many Irishmen in various branches of the British colonial service. Aravon was the only Protestant boys school in the area and had its girls equivalent in the French School, situated about half a mile away. They were both privately owned pay schools with a certain snob value in the Bray area. Many of the Aravon boys had sisters in the French school as I had, and although there was not much in the way of joint activities we were pretty closely connected socially.

Physically the school which was on Novara road (Aravon is Novara spelt backwards) and only 100yds from my first remembered home, was based on one or possibly two private houses with timber buildings added, particularly a fine gymnasium and a big class room. It stood in it's own grounds, the playing fields were a short walk away towards Bray Head.

I don't think Aravon did me much good academically. I suppose I picked up a little latin, maths, geometry and algebra, and probably improved my reading and writing, the latter no doubt by writing punishment lines- the same lines or phrase 100 or more times- for some indiscretion or failure, with the horrible pens and nibs of those times. These were very soft, long pointed, in wooden holders, dipped in dirty ink in a small porcelain well fitted into a hole in your desk.

With this implement it was almost impossible to write in other than large copybook style. I think it was I who invented a pen with several knibs, with the object of much reducing the time taken to write lines. This was not a great success, and was never patented!

However a standard paper dart plugged into the metal nib holder made an excellent long range and somewhat dangerous weapon; the timber lined ceiling of the big and very high class room was densely covered with these darts! Later I found a much better nib. 'The Waverley' was obtainable from a Miss Coghlan whose small shop - also a post office - I passed every day on the way to school. Waterman were also producing the first practical Fountain Pens which made ideal birthday and Christmas presents, but they could be rather messy and in school the nib was easily damaged.

My principal memory of Aravon was of learning to play rugby football, and of breaking my collar bone! My father as an ex-international had already taught me how to handle and kick the odd shaped 'ball'. I also remember ragging with other boys in the generally good natured way of small boys, exactly analogous to the play of puppies, who however fierce the play and noise never seem to hurt each other.

Apart from a certain amount of bullying, from which I don't remember suffering or engaging in, I think most us of were fairly civilised. However a new school cap was immediately snatched from your head and kicked around in the dirt to the dismay of the owner.

My main sparring partner was one of the Barrington brothers. We were of about the same size and weight and equal in strength, and I seem to remember rolling about on the dusty and very knotty boarded floor of our class room, struggling for supremacy! We were actually good friends and spent quite a lot time out of school together. I think there was more devilment in the Barringtons than in me... for one thing they were expert in making explosives and delighted in frightening people with loud bangs. I suppose they are staid old gentlemen now and would deny these exploits convincingly. They went into the legal profession.

Another boy I remember well was Lisney, studious and not at all games oriented, founder of the successful estate agency.

The school gymnasium which was very well equipped for its purpose with all sorts of climbing gear and apparatus was also the main assembly hall. Besides the usual P.T. etc to which boys are subjected, we were actually taught to dance the dances of the day, Waltz, Foxtrot, Lancers, Sir Roger de Coverley, Quadrille, Gallop etc, and something of manners and etiquette too!

Once a year this was all put to the test when Aravon hosted a ball around Christmas for The French School. No doubt properly chaperoned! The girls turned up in their best party dresses, and we boys in the juvenile equivalent of evening dress, which consisted of black trousers, short black openfronted jackets- known as bum freezers - and Eton collars, those slightly ridiculous and very uncomfortable lampshade like creations. There was a proper orchestra and an M.C. Most of us boys- particularly myself- were desperately shy, and it was up to the boys to pick partners and get the dances going, I imagine those who had sisters there made a bee line for them. But as the evening wore on we all began to thaw out and anyhow a great many of the dances of those days insured that partners were changing all the time. some of them were quite hectic, and the starch in our Eton collars began to dissolve and the girls dresses to look less pristine! Altogether these rare dances were immense fun, and I have loved dancing in the old style ever since.

My family were not very religious, but we were taught to say our prayers at bedtime, and went to children's service in the little church at the bottom of Bray Main Street just above the Dargle River. (I was sad to see it has now been closed). There we sang childish Hymns such as "There is a green hill far away without a city wall——" and "Onward Christian Soldiers marching as to war——" The words and the melodies played on the organ still come back to me, and even the faint echo of childish voices from down the years. We went to church as a family on Sunday mornings, to Christchurch which was only just up the road, presided over by Canon Scott- we knew his family well-and later to Kilbride church when we moved to near Kilmacanogue about five miles outside Bray.

Mother and I had one problem in common, that of little control over our tear glands! When in Dublin with me alone on some shopping expedition, possibly to outfit me for school, she would take me to the Grafton Cinema, where as likely as not there would be a Chaplin film being shown, or one of some other comedian of the day. One comedienne particularly, a not so young French women Evonne Arnou, who played in many sophisticated comedies and always had mother weeping copiously with laughter, and me too if the humour was within my limited understanding. The funny side of things which make me laugh and sometimes the pathos of a situation still easily and to my embarrassment turn on copious tears!

In a physical sense we were a very loving family, kissing and hugging on all partings and meetings and at bed time. I cannot understand people who do not appreciate human contact. I love the warmth and somehow the comfort it gives me, a poor mortal on life's rather brief, basically sad journey.

And how brief and somehow sad that journey is!

Recently I was staying overnight in Claremorris in County Mayo. To pass the time on the summer evening I was strolling in the overgrown churchyard at the protestant church, vaguely looking for some Lallys, ancestors on my mother's side. I came across the grave of a Mrs Tucker.

Her husband, the Reverend Mr Tucker, was a stout and rather pompous clergyman. Sometime in my eleventh year he had arrived in Ireland, acting as 'recruiting sergeant' for his schools, Trent College in Derby and its nearby prep school, Bramcote Hall in Nottinghamshire.

Mr Tucker was travelling all round what was then the Free State on his recruiting mission, and I think came to us on the recommendation of Nanny Merry. Her brother had gone to Trent. Anyhow, I was conscripted! I think this was rather against my Father's wishes, I am sure he would have preferred me to have gone to his old school and perhaps later to Trinity... and with hindsight I rather wish I had.

But Mother always had other ideas; a great admirer of Captain Scott of the Antarctic, she had all his books and diaries and took me to all the available films on his expeditions. She wanted me to go into the British Navy!

My stars read otherwise, my sight was not good enough and I was saved from what I consider a very narrow life... I have never had any ambition to be a hero in war. And so, in September 1923, my mother escorted me to Bramcote Hall. And thus began my long association with England... a country which pays my pension to-day!

BRAMCOTE HALL was (and it probably still is!) a sandstone edifice built, I would think, at the turn of the century and designed to display the financial success of its owner. It had one quite impressive tower, (ideal as a model glider launch point) a most complicated roof structure with many valleys, (almost designed for illicit roof climbing at night),lots of mullioned sandstone windows, which were already badly weathered, the building all surrounded by terraced gardens and flower beds.

Internally it was quite impressive with a central hall along baronial lines, an overhead balcony all in varnished pitch pine, which incidentally is a timber I delight to work in, next perhaps to well seasoned oak, each having their quite different but lovely smells. The front part of the building provided the living quarters for most of the staff and the bachelor headmaster, the rest of the building being divided into classrooms and dormitories. One of the classrooms on the ground floor was used as the assembly hall, and with its raised platform and a grand piano for concerts and sing-songs.

But of all or any of this I knew nothing when I first arrived. It was late and after brief introductions I was dispatched to bed while Mother was entertained by Mr Johnson the headmaster. The bed I was dispatched to was in a large dormitory shared with about fourteen other new boys. These ranged in age from as young as six years, sons of expatriates, to those about my own age. More than half of the boys were from Ireland.

Parting from Mother in the morning was a bit of a wrench, but soon forgotten when we Irish boys began to gang up and get to know each other and find our where we all came from. In the afternoon the old boys began to arrive, mostly walking up the drive through the chestnut trees, which were conveniently dropping their fruit, giving us "Irishmen" plenty of ammunition with which to pelt the old boys! Quite some cheek for which we paid the next day!

We did of course soon integrate, and made other friends fairly rapidly but for the first week or two there were quite fierce gang fights in the school woods. We were proud of being Irish with a fighting reputation. About half way through the term I was involved in a gang fight and finished up at the bottom of the pile...with a bad compound fracture of my left elbow joint.

My next memory is of finding myself in bed in a huge hospital ward with my extremely painful arm (now bent the right way) with my hand strapped to my chest. All the other inmates were grown men, the one in the next bed having cut his throat, this being stitched up and uncovered.

I don't know how long I was in this the Nottingham general hospital, but I know my arm was x-rayed and examined by the doctors, who apparently decided that the joint was beyond proper repair and had to be fixed in a position which would be most useful to me! The school authorities did not seem to take much interest in the proceedings, and I was somewhat scared when my forearm turned all the colours of the rainbow and by the goings on in the ward, including people dying!

After about a week my father appeared at the bedside with my clothes, got me up, helped me to dress and, obviously very annoyed with everyone, got me down to a waiting taxi. I don't remember the actual journey but next morning I was home. It was the most decisive operation I remember Dad carrying out, and it saved my arm for a normal life, for which I have never ceased to thank him in my heart.

Apparently it was just a hunch he had that all was not well with me, and he decided to go over and bring me home. I was taken to a Mr Pearson at the Adelaide Hospital in Dublin. His indignation when he saw the arm, and heard what had been proposed at the Nottingham hospital, was intense. I was started on a course of exercises and therapy which lasted nearly three months and at the end I had an arm which was almost as good as new. To the late Mr Pearson I owe a great debt of gratitude, I have heard since that he was considered an austere and difficult man but to me he was an angel.

*

I returned to the school in the Spring - Easter term and came in for some very cold weather, to which I was not used on Ireland's east coast. As a preparation for the somewhat tough and austere practices at Trent, we were subjected to twenty minutes of P.T. in front of the building, before a short religious service and then breakfast. I did get used to this after some time, but the first time the cold knocked me out, and I had to be carried from the field!

*

Mr Carr was a Yorkshireman and very proud of that fact. Quite young, he was one of our masters, he had an honours degree from Oxford. Crippled by polio from the waist down, Mr Carr was able to get about on two stout sticks using his legs for balance, thus he had developed an enormously strong upper body. He was a fine pianist, and sometimes played for his own pleasure at night in the big class room, filling the whole building with sound, which I at least much enjoyed. At this time I was a very fair haired little boy, and perhaps a favourite of Mr Carr. He christened me 'twopence' because of my Irish accent- the English pronounced it tuppence. He owned what was in its day quite a hot sports car- a two seater Alvis, in which I several times went to Nottingham...at what seemed a very high speed with an impressive sporty noise.

In retrospect I realise that Mr Carr was a really nice man who loved us boys...he would rag with a whole class of us, starting by sitting in a chair and ending up on the floor with a pile of us struggling on top of him...he never lost his temper and laughed all the time. But, for some reason I cannot remember and don't think I ever knew, we boys turned against Mr Carr towards the end of my time at Bramcote. And from then on we, including myself to my eternal shame, tried to make life hell for him. Little boys and girls too do this and can subject adults to a sort of psychological torture.

*

A rather formidable middle aged lady gave me my piano lessons at Bramcote. She was a pretty mediocre pianist herself, a bit of a martinet, and practices were a real drudgery. Nonetheless I did reach some sort of standard in that I did once play solo at a school concert. I also sang solo, I feel I was much better at singing, in fact I think that had I had more self confidence I could have been quite good when I got my 'proper' voice. But all my best singing has been done when I was alone and couldn't be heard, driving a car or riding a motor cycle. As an adult I once nearly killed myself riding to work soon after my first son was born and I was living in the New Forest. It was a glorious summer day and I got so carried away with my singing that I forgot I was on a bike and 'came round' to realise I was on the grass verge with a telegraph pole rushing at me. I managed to avoid it and finished up in a heap but relatively unhurt!

Our Bramcote piano teacher wore rough tweeds and had set herself up as school disciplinarian, no doubt she considered the male staff much too easy going.

One of her self imposed tasks was to see that we boys 'kept our bowels open!' The boys lavatory, we called it The Bogs, was a corrugated iron shed standing on its own away from the main building. This was incredibly cold and draughty in winter. Seating consisted of a long wide plank with ten holes cut in it, a bucket under each! During the free time before lessons, we were all supposed to visit the bogs and to ensure that we did, this lady would march through it ticking off names!

In addition, to establish our success on the job we were all dosed once a week with what was called the White Mixture, (possibly this also prevented frostbite!) I'm sure this concoction ruined many people's natural function for all time!

The mixture was administered to us by the Matron, a small rather ugly Welsh woman with warts on her chin. It seemed to us boys that she delighted in hurting us- probably not a justified impression- but she did freely apply iodine to open cuts and wounds. She also seemed to delight in lancing and squeezing the dreadful boils which plagued some of us. I think we were short on fresh greens and fruit!

Winters during my time at Bramcote seemed to be very snowy, and I earned the reputation of being the leading toboggan builder, being used to woodworking tools and having a secret source of steel strip for shoeing the runners. Soccer was the sport of winter months, but we started playing rugby in the easter terms, much to the delight of the Irish contingent. We had nearly all played this game at home, and we were able to show the way. But the ground which was practically solid sandstone was very punishing to knees and elbows!

In summer one of the sports was supposed to be swimming. The Bramcote brochures proudly referred to the swimming pool attached to the school. In reality this turned out to be a large sort of tank with a ramp running down into it, which was originally built for bathing horses! Even so, when the school authorities took the trouble to clean it out after the winter and refill it, it was not bad and was deep enough to dive into. I can only remember the 'pool' being in use for one summer, for the rest of the time it was home for innumerable newts!

*

Bramcote village was small and rural but close by was the Stanton Ironworks, at that time possibly the biggest producers of large diameter iron pipes in the world. Stanton had evolved a method of spinning these huge pipes from molten iron, and the process went on night and day all the year round, turning the night sky red.

Except for escorted Sunday walks and occasional outings we were virtually prisoners, but I made one or two lasting friends. One was Bobby Wight, whose father was a director of Cammel Laird's shipyard, and also of a big electrical firm in Sunderland. The family lived in some state outside Birkenhead, and had a chauffeur driven Armstrong Sidley with an early automatic transmission. I was invited to spend part of at least one holiday with the Wights. Bobby was a twin with a girl, and he had a brother a year or two older.

His parents were very kind and friendly, and living with a family where money never seemed to be a consideration was quite a revelation to me after my modest home and way of life. Nearly every day some entertainment or outing was laid on, and the chauffeur-driven car was generally at our disposal.

We went to Liverpool to see the vast and busy docks from the high level dock railway. The railway is gone now, and the shipping a shadow of what it was in those early inter war years.

Many of the great passenger liners docked there then, some of the Cunarders- although they were beginning to move to Southampton for the Transatlantic shuttles-and I think all the White Star ships, the two lines later amalgamated.

Among the many great ships I saw the Barengaria, sister ship of the Lusitania which was torpedoed off the south of Ireland during the 1st World War, also the Aquitania and the Mauritania which held the blue riband of the Atlantic for many years, having crossed at a speed equivalent to nearly 40mph.

I was taken over the Cammel Laird shipyard and was most impressed by the vastness, the dirt and the noise - little did I know then that I was to spend part of my life in that sort of environment.

We climbed onto and into a submarine under construction and also onto a capital ship under construction, the battleship HMS Rodney, which if my memory is correct was sunk by Japanese bombers in the Malacca Straits.

*

My other school friend was Ken Ackerley, who went up to Trent a term before me. His home was in Liverpool, where his father had a managerial job with Fyffes the banana importers and shipowners. Soon after I met Ken his father moved to Dublin and set up his own business, The Tropical Fruit Company. This flourished in a big way up to the outbreak of the 39-45 war, by which time Ken had more or less taken over from his father.

The Ackerleys had a big house just outside Dun Laoghire, which I often visited during holidays. These were another family who seemed to me to be rich by our standards. I was most impressed by a large piece of furniture which was a radio gramophone on which Ken played the latest hit, jazz records, the music coming over with a power I had never heard before.

Ken himself was a jazz fan and played a saxophone in a modest way, and he was one of the few boys at Trent who had a gramophone of his own! That was a wind up H.M.V.,reckoned to be the best of the portables of the times. He also had a good collection of jazz and popular music, I was a bit of a musical snob and affected not to like that kind of stuff, while actually liking at least some of it. Ken also had a little car at home almost as soon as he could have a driving license,(from age 14 at that time!). The car was an M.G.Midget coupé, a pretty little car of which I was very envious.

DURING MY last year at Bramcote School Aunt Vi sold Bellevue and the family moved to a house called 'Knockranny', meaning 'hill of ferns'. The thrill of first seeing and exploring this new home remains with me to this day. I was met off the Holyhead Boat by my parents and driven up the house above Kilmacanogue in Dad's new Chrysler, an open tourer with wooden spoked wheels and detachable rims.

Knockranny had a wonderful situation high on the side of a little hill called Carrigoona (Oona's rock). The house faced the Big Sugar Loaf mountain across the Rocky Valley and the road up to Roundwood Village. To the south Wicklow Head was just visible with a glimpse of the sea through the Glen O' The Downs. Eastward was the Irish sea with the Kish Bank lightship a small speck seven miles out to sea. (On an exceptionally clear day we could see the Welsh Mountains, particularly if there was snow on them.) At night we could see the rather forlorn flash of the lightship, nowadays of course replaced by a fine lighthouse on an artificial island. And further to the north on the part of Howth Head that was visible there was the flash of the Bailey Lighthouse. To the West were the Wicklow mountains which I came to love through my teens, and now look at with a deep nostalgia.

The house stood on about seven acres of land with quite a lot of mature timber of various sorts from eucalyptus with its refreshing smell, to beech and several species of pine and fir. We added to these plantings over the years. There was a large orchard, a vegetable garden, flower beds and a large rock garden. This small 'estate' was worked by Aunt Vi herself, with just the devoted assistance of her gardener Mr Murtagh.

On arrival that summer morning over seventy years ago, I immediately set out to explore this most exciting new domain. In front of the house grass banks dropped down to quite a respectable grass tennis court, later much in use by us and our friends. There were three small fields and from the eastern boundary wall two big fields dropped steeply down to the valley - ideal for our 'winter sports' - towards neighbouring Glencormack House,(since accidentally burnt to the ground). That house was then occupied by Daisy, a member of the Jameson Whiskey family, she was always a good friend to us. We had a right of way through her estate down to the main Dublin/Bray road, but more important to me, she allowed me access to a sizeable pond on the estate.

Knockranny was architect designed and built partly of cut granite blocks with infill of rock and mortar, pebble dashed over, which turned not to be very proof against wind driven rain. The most remarkable feature from the avenue approach was the porch which was inside the north west corner of the house, protected by a massive iron studded, solid teak door, pivoted on the granite corner pillar so that it could be swung to the north or the west side according to wind direction. The house was very exposed to the west, while to the north it was protected by a belt of trees. It was three storeys with six bedrooms and three living rooms. There was only one source of general heat, an anthracite slow combustion stove in the dining room, more-or-less in the middle of the house and an open fire in whichever living room we were using. The top of the house with a big landing and two small bedrooms and one large one was my play area and minor workshop, very cold in winter.

The house had been built and laid out by it's previous owner, Dr Sharf, a German national who had apparently escaped internment in the first war.

It was all very well thought out and executed, from the drains to the water systems -including two wells and an underground tank and filter bed which collected all the water off the roof, to the engine house where what seemed to me a huge engine lived. This was a Ruston Hornsby single cylinder hot bulb engine which ran on paraffin- diesel was not then in general use- and drove from it's big flywheel a dynamo which charged a bank of batteries in a separate compartment and also the water pump which supplied the house. The work of operating this plant was entrusted to Mr Murtagh our faithful gardener. He had been with us at Bellevue and now cycled five or six miles each way summer and winter to work in the garden, and to start and run the engine.

This was no press button task, but Murtagh loved it! First a huge sort of vertical blowlamp had to be lit under the bulb on the cylinder head; this produced much heat flame and smoke - we called it Murtagh's inferno- before the bulb glowed red and it was time to swing the flywheel, (rather in the manner of starting the Bollinder engines familiar to barge owners on the Shannon).The flywheel was spun by gripping one of its spokes and turning the wheel faster and faster until the engine fired and took over, by which time Murtagh would be sweaty and grimy, but happy!

I don't know what Mr Murtagh's wages were, he lived in a cottage on an estate just outside Little Bray with a wife and several children. She must have been a fine woman and he a non-drinker and very careful with what must have been a small wage, because their children were always well dressed, they did very well at school and I also believe in later life.

The grounds of Knockranny had many paths good for cycling, and mother bought some materials for me to build a house in a tree,which I did,- the smell of tar on roofing felt always reminds me of this house-,, However living alone in it was not much fun! and my sisters were away somewhere.

Then I found what we always called Jamesons Pond. It would have been nearly two acres in extent, and with a number of islands. There was a heavy punt on it, more for dredging than for pleasure, however it gave me a lot of pleasure, rigged with a mast and sail of sorts and lots of imagination.

*

I see in my mind's eye a fairhaired boy of about fourteen setting out from Knockranny early one sunny morning in August with a knapsack containing sandwiches, a map, compass and his Dad's field glasses, two dogs, a white Bull terrier and a Cairn as companions. His intention to get to the top of Maulin, a peak of about 1900 feet on the south side of Glencree. And, if making good progress by the time he had shared his sandwiches with the dogs, of also getting to the tops of the two Tonduff peaks, both over 2,000 feet!

This was achieved! The total distance out and back being about sixteen miles, perhaps the longest walk and climb I ever did alone. I loved being alone with only the dogs, I could please myself about the way and the pace to take. I could play imaginary games based on John Buchan's stories...goodies and baddies chasing each other on Scottish moors! I worked out my course to the peaks with the aid of map and field glasses trying to keep below the skyline and out of sight of my imaginary quarry.

But I loved too the the smell of gorse heather and bog plants, and of the bird life, the occasional Kestrel or Sparrow Hawk, and Grouse who burst out of the ground 'crowing' indignantly. There were ravens too in the high rocky areas and all the time the plaintive baa-ing of mountain sheep accompanied me, those sheep almost as wild as the deer in this area, and as sure footed as goats on the steep and very rocky hill sides.

I myself must have been pretty sure footed, I was always very fit and looking back now at some of the places I used to descend full tilt leaping from boulder to boulder, I must have had good balance and nerve, alas I have little of either now. But I can look back and remember then...the moments and the journies...how as a family we used climb Lugnaquilla (over 3000 feet) and, when we were a little older, how we skied and dragged toboggans to the top of Djouce through quite deep snow on top of equally deep heather...that was hard work!

*

The family rented a house in Donegal for holidays. My friend Bobby came over to join us there. The house overlooked Gweebara Bay at its seaward end, a marvellous place for young people. In theory we had with the house about 400 acres of bog, small lakes and nearly half a mile of shoreline, a great crescent of sand in places cut away by the strong tide, so that we could dive off the sand into deep water but we were well aware of the strong current and all were strong swimmers. I had quite a powerful air rifle which I normally used for target shooting but I had it in Donegal and we potted at rabbits without any expectation of hitting one. However Bobby did hit one and we were both very distressed to see it kicking its life away, I think it was the first creature either of us had killed.

The house we rented was owned by an elderly lady whose son was an Air Vice Marshall in the R.A.F. Air Vice Marshall or not he seemed to have totally neglected his mother and she was living in apparent considerable poverty.

It still stands, four square on the skyline to the right of the road between Maas and Portnoo. Stark and bare with not a tree near it, it was bleak inside too but being summer this did not worry us much, although it was rat infested the first year and because we had complained about this it stank of poisoned dead rats on our second visit!

WHEN I was in my fourteenth year I was moved up to Trent, and started in the first form, whose master was a rather dotty old clergyman. I don't think he actually taught us anything academic but he was certainly what we would now call an environmentalist. He had grown a small copse of unusual trees- I probably planted one as we all did- taught us names of birds and plants and made us keep a book of poems which he selected and we wrote out in careful decorative script.

Trent prided itself on being a school where tough empire builders and holders were made. Things were pretty austere and there was little of home comfort. The only heating was from barely luke warm radiators. Sitting on them was a privilege for the more senior boys. We suffered from chilblains and chapped legs in the winter.

The day began, (after a night with all windows partly open, winter and summer), with a cold bath supervised by the prefects, then P.T. outside under the direction of an old sweat army sergeant. Then a twenty minute church service in the chapel, followed by breakfast and the day's work. Twice a week we had games in the afternoon, according to the time of year, cricket or tennis, swimming- there was quite a good swimming pool- rugby, hockey and fives at any time and athletics generally.

Rugger was my favourite game and I worked very hard at it, particularly when I got into the first fifteen as alternative scrum half with another Irish boy Nicholas Ogle. The out half also was an Irishman, Barney Swaine, son of the then Bishop of Limerick and a particular friend of mine, we practiced together in every spare moment. I quite enjoyed cricket but did not excel at it, and gave it up for tennis in my last two summer terms, with ulterior motives (more anon).

Academically I was pretty dud, not least at what was called the classical side of the college, where they tried by every means kind and not so kind to teach me latin. One priest, P.C.Matthews, tried with extra lessons in spare time, but though he tortured me mentally into tears of frustration on many occasions his efforts failed. I know that my recollections of him after leaving College was that he was a sadist but perhaps I drove him mad with my incredible stupidity! I was always hopeless at languages. However P.C. did teach me to learn to some extent because shortly after I went over to the Modern side of the college I immediately found myself near the top of the equivalent class, where I was anyhow much happier doing engineering subjects and science and chemistry.

It seems to be generally accepted that there was always a homosexual tendency in English public schools. I can only say that I as quite a pretty little very fair haired boy might have come in for it but in all my time in prep school and college, I was never aware that anything -even with hind sight- of the sort existed.

Trent was a purpose built college and was well planned and had very extensive playing fields and a good big swimming pool, where in my last term I tested many high speed model boats pulling them across the pool by means of a winch I devised. I was blessed with a very stout heart when it came to long distance swimming and running, at both of which I excelled.

*

At Trent I had been placed in the 'house' called Wright (after some scientist), and shared a cubicle with Ken Ackerley.

An awful lot has been written about English public schools of the period and their unofficial rituals, I think Trent was fairly typical, better in some ways and worse than average in others.

Initiation in Wright consisted of being half drowned in a cold bath and then having to box against one of the older boys. I think because I had several friends up from Bramcote before me, I was let off the first of these and in the second I was pitted against Ken and we had an agreement that we would take it easy. By mistake he punched me on the nose, making it bleed and I rather lost my temper and we had a real set to, to the delight of the thirty or so boys in the dormitory.

Very soon after the start of term Ken and I perpetrated a dastardly outrage in the dormitory, a midnight waterbomb attack on all and sundry. Waterbombs are rather ingenious little boxes made by folding a sheet of square paper in a certain way, they are inflated from flat by blowing into them, and can be filled with water with the aid of a bit of glass lab tube, first drawing the water into your mouth and then blowing it into the little box. We made dozens of these during the day, brought them up to the dorm and then after 'lights out', inflated and filled then from the big water jugs on our bedside tables, waited until everyone seemed to be asleep, stood up on our beds and in the dark showered the whole dormitory with water bombs.

Needless to say there was almost immediate pandemonium. Unfortunately our house master a Mr Tarver was in his room just down the corridor. Tarver was quite an old man with a taste for a dram, but he heard the commotion, and suddenly the door opened and a moment later the lights were switched on and Tarver, a little drunk, surveyed the scene in dead silence. Little pieces of paper in pools of water all over the floor. He then walked the length of the dorm and back again, muttering to himself 'oh oh my glory, oh oh my glory,' and switched off the lights and went out. Everyone in our house knew who had perpetrated the crime and when a notice appeared on the notice board requiring whoever did it to report to Mr Tarvers study, we had no alternative but to report and did.

Ken got a beating, Tarver let me off, he thought I had been led astray, which was most unfair, I was just as much guilty as Ken.

My school reports usually had the standard comment a lot of us know and which must be a disappointment to our parents "could do better if he tried harder". I thought I did try harder when I knew what I wanted to be but I didn't do very much better! (I think he was like one of my sons slightly and one of his daughters quite severely, slightly Dyslectic).

There seemed to be two ways of becoming a Naval Architect. Through pure academic learning at a university, ending in a degree, or through practical work in a shipyard, and part time at a university, backed up with night school, with a diploma and student membership of the Royal Institution of Naval Architects as the objective. To get into university I needed to Matriculate. Well in the end I nearly did, but my Achilles heel- languages- failed me, and I did it the other way.

I have always deeply regretted I never went to University, not because the other did not serve me adequately in the professional sense, but because I longed for the life that went with it. The social life and the life of ideas. Public school life in my time was so totally segregated from life, we were prisoners behind walls. My experience of University was one day a week, I was an outsider only looking in, which was much worse than not seeing it at all, but I will come to that later.

Some time at the beginning of my last year at college, on the way back, I bought a packet of Players from a slot machine on Crewe station, where I had a long wait for the Derby connection, and for the first time lit a cigarette, did not like it and threw it away. It was an expensive cigarette in two ways. First Mother had promised me £100 on my 21st birthday if I had never smoked. I think she was a little hard on me when I later confessed the incident, which was genuinely the only time I had ever touched a cigarette. I never got my £100!

Secondly I took the packet back to school and threw it into some locker of mine and forgot all about it. About six months later in a prefect's raid looking for fags and other banned articles the packet was found.

The first thing I knew about it was a notice on the board requiring me to report to the head prefects study at a specified time. This I did and confronted this boy- little older than myself- across his desk, on which was the packet of Players. ' Yes it was mine but only one was missing, I had not smoked it at college and they were very stale'. He was a big hefty young man - his name was Price, and I shall never forget it- a sadist, he gave me six with a long cane and as hard as he could.

I left his study a different boy and could not sit comfortably for days. It was a gross injustice and turned me into a total rebel so far as school rules were concerned, and I would have happily murdered him.

This beating was on a summer Saturday early in term. I remember because there was a cricket match on against some other school, and we were supposed to watch it, lying on a grassy bank above the cricket pitch. I was extremely uncomfortable, and decided to go for a stroll round the grounds. When I came to the swimming pool enclosure I went in. The enclosure was on the southern boundary of the grounds and when inside I was out of sight of anyone outside it. Over a high stone wall were meadows. These meadows are immortalised in the school song, a rather sentimental and melancholy one of an older man looking back to the days at Trent. I can't remember it all, a bit goes - when the walk on Sawley meadows (an official one on a path!) is but a vanished dream, and only fancy treads the path beside the Derwent stream (the Trent).

The escape was easy, and the first of many. As I was a tennis player there was no check on me on games afternoons. My first outings were down to the canal which passed through the meadows, and I day-dreamed of cruising my little boat, Rusheen, along this reed fringed waterway, intensely happy for miles and miles. I followed the canal in reality, meeting as I went horse drawn gaily painted 'narrow boats' until I came to the wide river Trent. There I was delighted to see some of the beautiful river yachts, the 'Raters' actually racing. These Raters were quite big and very fast 'skimming dishes' with a great spread of sail.

My next discovery was a boat yard where I was able to hire a sliding seat skiff and did so a number of times and then I really was free!

One day sculling up a side water, where there were a number of house boats I found myself looking straight at one of my masters on one of them. He of course saw me but did not acknowledge it because he was with a girl, and I guess he also was supposed to be elsewhere, at any rate we kept each other's secret! I also found my way into Long Eaton - the local town- where I had to be rather more careful and usually went to a cinema for an hour or two. A year or so later I visited the head master when in the area, a Mr Bell and his wife and had lunch with them, and when I was leaving he said to me casually "by the way Kennedy if you want to go for a row on the river you don't have to ask my permission"! Perhaps that master did not keep the secret for ever.

*

I think that the worst feature of the public school system at that time as a preparation for life, was the total segregation from the opposite sex and any preparation for marriage and family life, particularly bearing in mind that most of us were nearly nineteen when we were let out into the real world. I have at the back of my mind some advice given to us from time to time, it may have been part of some school hymn, anyhow it was to the effect that we should look forward to 'wooing and winning some good and gracious *english* girl!! Girls- potential wives- were certainly put on pedestals. I doubt if boys were similarly portrayed to the inhabitants of similar girls institutions.

We did of course get out sometimes in an organised way, sometimes on an O.T.C. route march on roads with full military kit and rifle, usually to somewhere of interest or scenic beauty with the return made by coach. At other times we went by coach to the Peak District for walks through Dove Dale near Matlock, finishing at Donnington Park. These outings were usually in summer time, there were lots of other humans about... and even girls in pretty dresses!

There was one Easter term which I shall never forget, when we had a great freeze which went on for several weeks. Normal games were impossible, we all acquired skates and rules were relaxed somewhat to allow us to make maximum use of them. All spare time was given up to learning to skate on the frozen swimming bath and then on the canals which abounded in that part of Derby.

On half holidays and Sundays we skated for miles, only very loosely escorted by masters. We also found worked-out flooded quarries, where the ice gave off a lovely ring and we could organise ice hockey with ordinary hockey sticks. I got pretty good at skating and later took it up quite seriously when I got to Southampton a year or two later.

In common with most public schools of the times, Trent had an Officers Training Corps and once a week we had to dress up like soldiers of

'The Great War', as we called it. (That war was in fact then less than ten years behind us). We would parade, marching and counter marching in those complicated parade-ground manoeuvres, designed to control in a methodical manner large numbers of men.

It was at the time of I think a Labour Government and there was considerable opposition to things military...and this opposition had infected us boys. The result was that we took rather a delight at times in fouling up the best laid plans of Captain Featherstone our commanding officer and his Sergeant Major. Featherstone was in fact our science master and must have been quite a left winger, he used to lecture us- ex-curriculum- on the worst features of the capitalist system! Particularly as it applied to the pharmaceutical business.

For years after leaving college I had bad dreams of this dressing up as soldiers and putting on all the accoutrements and so forth. For one thing at that time puttees bound your calves and putting these on so that they would not come off at some critical moment in a manoeuvre, when the 'soldier' behind you would take pleasure in treading on the trailing end, was not so easy. Also boys were not too scrupulous about pinching each others equipment if they could not find theirs putting you in a hell of a panic as 'fall in time' approached. Even your rifle was not safe.

We had also to attend at least one military camp during our time at school. I spent mine at Tidworth, somewhere on Salisbury Plain, an established Regular Army Camp, where for a couple of weeks we lived the life of soldiers - quite fun but long enough at that.

From a national point of view no doubt these O.T.C's were a good idea as we partly trained men from all the Public Schools of England no doubt later formed the nucleus of officers in the conscript army of World War Two.

I visited Trent some years ago when driving in the area. Never much of an 'old boy', I was completely out of touch with all but one or two schoolmates, and when I went into the Chapel and scanned the roll of honour, I must say I was very distressed to see how many of my contemporaries had fallen. I had also been very friendly with one of two Ethiopian boys whom I learned had been killed as pilots by the Italians in their brutal war against that country.

One pleasant memory of my last term at college - it was the summer term- was of getting up very early on any fine mornings that came along. There were no rules to discourage this, and I never met anyone else as I walked in the heavy dew on the playing fields. I was in my own private heaven, but then I was in love for the first time. Someone once wrote —- "in all life there is nothing half so sweet as love's young dream".

I wonder does it still apply?

On this second visit Father and I went alone and had a boat each.

For me it was a holiday of a lifetime. The lodge, named Rusheen, after which I named my boat, was -still is- on the north facing shore of a T shaped peninsula on the north shore of the lake, the T making a bay to the east, where Rusheen is, and to the west, shallow sandy and reedy at their heads.

Rusheen had a long narrow plank jetty for boats, and it was just deep enough at the end to allow us to dive off it. When Dad and I were alone we got up early and sprinted naked down this jetty to plunge in for a swim before breakfast. After breakfast it was fishing or sailing all day.

The fishing was good and we lived on trout and bread and butter! In August there were only two kinds of fish which concerned us; two varieties of trout rather special to this lake, the Gilaroo and the Sonahan. The former a fairly docile fish when hooked- we were wet fly fishing from the drifting boat- found generally over sandy bottom, the latter a terrific fighter and found over rocky bottom, and frequently on what we called sunken islands or shallow places in the open lake. When there was any breeze, essential for fishing, the lake got quite rough, and on more than one occasion when alone, rod in one hand and oar in the other I hooked a fish just as I was about to start bumping on the rocks, and had a struggle to avoid damaging the boat and to land the fish with the net.

However the sailing was my great joy, then and for the rest of my active life. With several bays and islands within a couple of miles of the lodge, I had a lovely miniature cruising ground to explore. I am pretty sure Dad kept an eye on me and he was able to give me advice and guidance as well. The improved Rusheen (with rudder which stayed on)sailed and tacked against the wind remarkably well. There is a saying "the smaller the boat the better the fun" and I endorse it. I have owned a few boats in my time and sailed in many others but none gave me quite so much joy as this one.

I HAD two loves in my last two years at college ny little self-built sailing boat...and a girl called Peggy...and they sc f went together.

Up to now my story has been simple and uncompl d, I have not had to name names outside my family or explain perso elationships with other people. But of course I was also growing up wh till at college and although young for my age and knowing little or not ; of the world or sex- although troubled by the reflexes of oncoming m ood, I tended to feel guilt about any thoughts on the matter and tried eep them out of my mind.

At the age of sixteen or seventeen I first became awar f Peggy.

It was at a Christmas time party for young people a Knockmore- the home of the May family, two very sweet middle aged iden ladies and their bachelor brother. The party was given for their t nieces and one nephew. Peggy was the elder of the nieces, about my own e.

Knockmore is a house of unusual style, rather colo l, single storey with big high rooms and windows which in pre-central ting days must have been quite labour intensive to heat. Beyond the ca ge way in front of the house the ground fell away quite steeply, g g the house a beautiful prospect through a wide gap in mature timl the east over Bray, the sea beyond.

The Mays lived in some style, for transport using a ve nart pony and trap, maintained and driven by a liveried groom co an, and their gardener dressed accordingly! Behind the house wa h house and stables, and between the house and the River Dargle w large mature formal garden.

The party was an afternoon one. The Miss Mays c nised games, charades and finally a scene from Shakespeare's "A Midsu mmer Night's Dream" and by chance I was cast as the mortal weaver Bott om. I wore a donkeys head, and Peggy was Titania the Fairy Queen (act 3 scene 1). The spell was cast and I have never quite broken it!

Peggy was physically no fairy, the same age as myself and the same height or taller, slim and to my eyes very beautiful with red-auburn hair in a long single plait down her back. The skin of her arms and face was very freckled. I was to learn later that she was very athletic and courageous.

I was to meet Peggy again, at various times and occasions. Again at Knockmore during a 'paper chase', those long distance cross country runs popular among our class at that period.

Peggy and another girl and two boys were the Hares and the rest including me were the Hounds, we did not catch them, I think we lost the trail. When we got back I saw her there, waiting for us. I have an indelible picture in my mind of Peggy sitting, flushed and happy, with her long legs tucked under her skirt.

Later it was noted that not all the hounds had returned and one of the Miss Mays asked me if I would take Peggy in my car and go and look for them. It wasn't my car but Mother's little "Bull Nosed " Renault (I had had a driving license since I was 14!).

Peggy and I back tracked the roads and lanes of middle Powerscourt and Enniskerry. And on the drive we found out a little more about each other. She had grown up in India, where her father was the District Superintendent of Dehra Dun in the United Provinces of north India. She was at school in England, and because both her parents were in India she spent holidays with her aunts here at Knockmore. She expected to go back to Dehra Dun when she had finished her education.

On other occasions Peggy and I met at Wingfield, at that time the home of the D'Oliers, just off the Bray to Kilmacanogue road. (Mrs D'Olier was the Grandmother of a friend of my sisters', Daphne Wix). Our last meeting for many years was at a formal dance at Wingfield, formal to the extent that it was evening dress for all.

I drove the two miles with my sisters arriving at the house in the dark, all as nervous and keyed up as could be, me secretly praying that Peggy would be there. The house was all lit up and decorated, a small dance band had been engaged, and a buffet supper laid on.

There were a lot of guests, quite a few we knew, but I was only looking for one and I didn't even know if she was in Ireland. I had not let anyone know of my love, then or until much later when I confessed to my sister Nancy. She said she had guessed and later she said one day she was sorry nothing came of it.

Peggy was there with her brother, and I was in heaven and hell at the same time! I danced with other girls I knew and with my sisters, but could not bring myself to ask Peggy. I was mooching around outside when Peggy came looking for me and asked me to come in and dance with her.

I was in heaven!

We had several dances. She used no scent or make up, she wore a simple dress, her freckled arms bare to her shoulders and I was aware that she wore no stays as did a number of other dancing partners, (to pull them into the right shape)!

At those teen age dances then we danced close to our partners, in fact we had been taught to hold our partners close, to dance as one. Maybe we were all young and even innocent for our ages by present day standards but I have no recollection of any sexual stimuli or embarrassment. We danced because- if we had the right partner and could do the steps- we were wonderfully happy just enjoying each others company, the movement and the music.

*

Back at college I plucked up courage and wrote to the Miss Mays asking for Peggy's address. She was at a so-called finishing school at Juvisy on the southern outskirts of Paris. I wrote her, I imagine it was a simple boyish letter about my activities and finished with my love, hardly daring to hope for a reply. But a reply came quickly and so started a long distance correspondence which lasted four or five years. She went for a summer holiday to St Cast in Brittany with some of her family and wrote me from there. Then it was to Dehra Dun and many letters across this great divide all of which I kept most carefully. Over the next six or eight years I was only to meet Peggy twice.

I left Trent in July of 1932.

It was a strange and rather frightening feeling climbing into the station bus on that last morning. I had said goodbye to all the masters and my friends, and walked round the buildings and grounds, through the archways with their latin inscriptions. And I even said a little prayer in the rather beautiful college chapel.

I was quite a believer then.

Two

SOMETIME IN late November 1932 I left home and started my chosen career. Dad had agreed to my wishes and arranged for me to start a premium shipbuilding apprenticeship with John I. Thornycroft of Woolston, Southampton.

It was after dark when I arrived at Southampton Docks with a letter to the shipyard manager in my pocket and a little money, a very green nineteen year old. I went into the first small hotel I came to, where I got a room for the night and almost a woman to go with it, having met a young girl in the corridor of this dockyard hotel who was obviously soliciting, obvious that is to anyone but me! I slept alone my first night, in retrospect a pity perhaps, she looked a nice kid!

The next morning I left my heavy luggage at the station and walked down to the ferry across the River Itchen. These twin car and passenger ferries were known as the floating bridge, shuttling across on wire cables. We passed Vickers Supermarine Seaplane factory just upstream of the ferry, and J.I.Thornycrofts a half mile downstream. I remember seeing on that first journey one of H.M.Destroyers afloat offshore. Downstream and to the right there was the great triangle of Southampton Docks between the estuaries of the rivers Test and Itchen. These docks were then used principally by the transatlantic Cunard liners and by the Union Castle line to South Africa with their buff superstructures and black funnels.

The story had it that in the past when these ships were apparently very much painted up, a rival shipowner told the then chairman of the company that the only reason the line was doing so well was because he painted them pretty colours! The response to this was to paint them the rather dingy black and buff colour, to prove that they did just as well.

Once off the ferry and I walked down through Woolston to the shipyard and nervously asked for the Manager at the gate office inside the closed iron gates. The office I was escorted to was bare walled except for some charts and a few photos of Naval craft. There I presented my letter to a gruff and forbidding Scotsman in a bowler hat.

Gruff yes, but not unfriendly in a rough sort of way. He was, as I came to know over the years, typical of his kind, risen so to speak from the ranks on strength of character and practical knowledge of shipbuilding and of the men who build them. Such men at that time were predominantly Scotsmen.

The bowler hat was also standard for managers and senior foremen. The hard construction workers hat had not been invented at that time. The foreman gave me an address of one or two possible lodgings, and then, after a brief rundown on the layout of the "Yard" and the various workshops and what was done in them, he told me I would be starting in the Mould Loft and gave me a note for the Loft foreman.

I was sent off there in charge of a messenger. The Mould loft turned out to be a huge room, probably about sixty by forty yards in size. It had an all matt black timber floor and there were two glass fronted offices, one for the foreman, one for the masses of drawings. These drawings were the working plans of ships under construction down on the slipways. There was also a large area of template racks.

Jimmy Dalgleish was the foreman, and the original 'very dour Scot'. He seemed to me to be quite an old man with his white goatee beard and moustache. He wore a trilby hat and didn't look particularly pleased to see me! Thinking back I am not very surprised, some of the other premium apprentices tended to be rather truculent. The sons of directors or other 'gentlemen' associated with shipping or shipbuilding , they had no intention of dirtying their hands more than they could help. Their apprenticeship here was just a rather boring interlude on the way to an office job which would lead to the top of some company based in The City.

I think the foreman soon realised I did not come under that category, and he treated me well, even allowing me to get away with making a small model of a somewhat futuristic record breaking speedboat! This of course was the heyday of record attempts by such people as Malcolm Campbell, Kay Don and other Britons. And the designer of most of these boats was Fred Cooper. (He was my hero at the time and a very nice man whom I met later and nearly worked under during the war.)

In the Mould Loft I was appointed to work under Walt, a short, stocky, local man in a boiler suit with knee pads. He permanently wore a cloth cap on his bald head and had a rather ugly square face and the most appalling squint. Whilst one very keen shrewd eye looked at you very straight, the other looked at the ceiling! Over the time I was to work there I think in his own way he came to like and trust me on the job and he treated me well. I probably amused him in some quiet way.

The eye he really used,(and he was the leading hand on the floor),was the one which faired up the hull lines of all the ships passing through the shipyard at that period. The system was that in general the work done in the mould lofts of the time (the early thirties)followed on from design in the drawing office. Our job was to prepare the templates and measurements for every part of the ship's structure in steel, down to the position of every rivet hole in the ship. (I could write another book on this!) Suffice to say here that all the full size drawing was done on the blackboard floor with chalk of the waxy variety which was rubbed on a file to produce a fine line. Straight lines were struck in with a chalk line, a thin cotton string drawn across a lump of soft chalk, then held tight to the floor at each end and plucked and so marking a line, on the principal that a straight line is the shortest distance between two points! The loft floor was thus at all times a cobweb of lines overlapping and criss crossing, quite bewildering to a newcomer but quite clear to the men working it.

*

The first address that I went to in my search for digs was at the upper end of Woolston. It seemed alright. It was on the road out to Bursledon, Fareham and the south coast. I did not have to consider the rate. My wage was only 10/- a week but the firm was paying for my full board and lodging.

I was to have a back bedroom upstairs and the use in the evenings of the front parlour, except on the rare occasions when my landlady might have visitors. This landlady Miss B was a dumpy and rather nondescript little lady in her mid or late thirties. There was a bathroom with a gas geyser, a copper monster of which Miss B was rather scared, and more scared that I would blow up the house with it! The house was at the top of a steep bank in a row of semi detached houses, with only a pedestrian pathway approach in the front; few people in Woolston had cars in those days.

These digs were over a mile from the yard and I decided I must have a bicycle to get to work and back for my dinner in the hour, and also to explore my new environment.

For a very few pounds I bought an old P.O.bike. This was very low geared and heavy, but it served for a year or so...and then Mother agreed to Hire Purchase -goodness knows why- a three speed Raleigh.

*

It was about this time that my Aunt Vi decided to see an ear specialist in Bath in Somerset. She underwent a severe operation -which did no good at all- and because I dearly loved her I decided without telling her to visit her on my old bicycle. It was summertime and the weather was fine but the ride of sixty miles was hard as I had a head wind all the way, largely across the beautiful open country of Salisbury Plain. I had made an early start and got to the hospital in early afternoon, my aunt was most surprised and I think pleased to see me, and although I had planned to ride straight back and had brought nothing with me except sandwiches, she insisted on giving me the money to stay in an hotel for the night. I rode back the next day, and I think the wind was behind me!

*

In the early thirties and I suppose right up to the war most work places which employed a considerable number of men had their own factory hooter. At about 7.25 the air was full of the sound of numerous hooters far and near. I can hear them still.

The Thorneycroft hooter was quite distinct, at least to me! Absolutely on the dot the Iron Gates were shut and you had lost half a day if you weren't in. Many times I cycled furiously with the hooter going, and once or twice I missed it. Apart from loss of pay and a dressing down from your foreman you as like as not had let down your mate on some job.

Needless to say the workmen had ways of taking time off occasionally without loss of part of the rather meagre pay. One of their mates would punch their time card for them, but as there were men watching for this, and the penalties were severe, it could only be done by having a bunch of men round the punch card rack.

A crowd of men on a bet once managed to carry out a blacksmith's anvil when I was there. Certainly a lot of stuff was smuggled out of the yard, but only for personal use. Times were hard and a little paint could make the front of a house look nice!

*

At the time I started in Thorneycroft there were two H.M.Destroyers and one River Gunboat under construction in the yard. This latter was only being bolted together to be shipped out to China and there finally built. (Britain still had a tenuous hold in parts of China, and Gunboat Diplomacy still had a function).

My first job with Walt was accurately putting the draft marks on the bow and stern of the nearly ready-for-launching destroyer, H.M.S. 'Daring'. (The similar ship on the next berth was to become 'Decoy'.) This work involved carrying to the slipway the so-called draft mark box. This was a timber box about one foot square and eighteen feet long. Although no weakling I was quite unused to carrying heavy weights on my perhaps bony shoulders.

Walt carried the front end, apparently with ease. I supported the rear but gritting my teeth in some distress. I have a suspicion he was giving me a little test. I have forgotten just how this piece of rather crude equipment was set up and used, but the marks we made were chiselled into the steel...and went down with her in WW2!

I remember that the weather turned bitterly cold soon after I started work and that one of the jobs of the loft gang was to check the alignment of the keel on both these ships. This would now be done with a theodolite or similar instrument, we did it by rigging up sights at intervals throughout the 300 or so foot length of the keel. It had to be possible to see a light through all the 1/4 inch slots and we had a squad of men available to lift or lower any part of the ship which got out of line. This was done by means of big but very slim ash wedges driven in or knocked back.

The ship's keel was laid on a line of closely spaced built up timber blocks raising it about five feet off the ground, which sloped down to the water. When the ship was ready for launching, the whole weight of the ship was transferred to the launching 'ways' which were built under her in a long and complicated operation, involving a great deal of timber and manual labour, and then the keel blocks were removed. This was the means whereby the biggest ships were prepared for launch, and even the biggest ships could be lifted with wedges when sufficient men with 'mauls' -heavy long hammers- were available to work the length of the ship.

In a similar way we had to align all the propeller shaft bearings, two shafts in each ship. This work gave no chance of keeping circulation going. The slipways were in the open and it was extremely draughty under the ships. I didn't wear gloves but I did wear just about all the clothes I possessed! Since that winter the cold has never worried me unduly!

Our work took us all over the ships where accurate marking off was required, and in those days as far as safety was concerned it was every man for himself and not much hope of compensation in an accident. Moving about on the sometimes icy decks and scaffolding was a bit scary at first.

While on this work I nearly lost my head! I was standing alongside one of the great poles which supported the scaffolding and the partly framed ship, a Corvette in this case. One of the very high shipyard cranes was lifting deckplates off the ground near me aided by workmen, when one being lifted flatwise by the crane jib high above was caught by the wind. I was looking the other way and did not see the plate foul another pole and come spinning round like a great knife at the height of my head or neck. It did not quite reach me and I wasn't even aware of my narrow escape until I turned round and saw my mates quite shaken, they thought I had 'had it' if I moved and so did not shout a warning.

At that time welding was only just coming in for shipbuilding, ships were all rivetted. The noise created by half a dozen pneumatic riveters hammering and perhaps several similar caulkers caulking plate seams was quite deafening and we had a system of sign language...nobody thought of ear mufflers.

The rivetters, some quite deaf, worked in small squads. The actual rivetter worked from the outside of the ship, his mate or 'holder upper' on the inside, and these two were assisted by the rivet boy whose job it was to heat the rivets in a little portable coke forge to the exact redness required. He would then pass them or send them down a pipe into a bucket. They could also throw them very accurately with tongs into a bucket over quite long distances. The mate then fed them into the next empty hole and held them in with a heavy steel "dolly". The rivetter then attacked the 'point' and flattened it expertly into the countersink in the plating, so that when painted over it was almost invisible. These squads and the caulkers worked on a piecework basis, payment by results, they could make what was then good money, but no work no pay, and their work was all the time subject to close inspection, and to some extent to weather.

I found that the coke fumes really bothered me more than anything. I remember once working with Walt in what was known as the steering flat of one of these ships, a small completely closed space, while there was also a rivetting squad working and an arc welder. The fumes and noise was to me impossible to stand for more than a few minutes at a time and I went home that evening deaf and with a very sore chest.

This sort of thing would not be tolerated to-day but at that time of much unemployment the unions were weak and the management was only interested in cutting costs. However, something which I am sure is still tolerated is the four letter adjective applied to just about everything! I have to admit it shocked me for a day or two until I realised it was just part of English as spoken in the shipyard!

As well as work outside I spent a lot of time in the loft making wooden templates from markings on the floor. and after some tuition from Walt, I was allowed to do some marking off on the floor myself. He showed me how to sight a line for fairness, which is best and most easily done by looking along it with your head topside down looking between your legs!

I was in the 'loft' probably about eight months. By that time I knew my way about the yard and visited the boat shop whenever I could, working in timber attracting me much more than in steel. I also made friends with the model maker, who had a little workshop all to himself. Here he was employed full time making most accurate scale models of the ships we built. These are the sort of models you see in the windows of shipping agents, complete in every detail. He was quite a young man and took great pride in his work.

The shipyard was divided into two sections, the hull side and the engineering, I was in the hull side of things but unofficially was able to get around and was interested in all the work that went on. I got a dressing down more than once for not being in my proper place of work, however I did manage to spend time unobserved in the turbine and boiler shops, and in the general machine shops.

The turbines and boilers fitted to H.M.Destroyers probably represented the peak of steam technology. I managed too to get on board 'Daring' after she was launched and the boilers and turbines were being installed. I later even had the cheek to go on board when she was due to go on trials and ask the Engineer Manager if I could go on a trial: he sent me ashore with a flea in my ear, I had no business to be on the ship at all!

In the final fit-out the most dramatic time was when the boilers were tested. There were three oil fired boilers on each ship. These were of extremely high pressure and also with superheaters the working temperature was very high indeed. Steam at these pressures and temperatures is an invisible gas, which can burn like a very hot flame, so that leaks are a hazard for personnel. The actual final testing consisted of pressuring well above maximum working and then 'blowing down' through large valves. The release of all this energy resulted in a roar which could be heard for miles.

*

After leaving the Mould Loft I was for a while in the light plate shop, here all the ventilation trunking and many more items mostly fabricated in aluminium were made. Here I learned how to roll light metal into complex shapes and how to gas weld.

However I wasn't very long in the Light Plate shop before being moved to the Boat Shop, and this was where I really wanted to be.

The Boat Shop foreman was Bill Bartlet and there were six or seven shipwright-boatbuilders, but only two names come back to me. Harry Broadrib who was the 'leading hand' and Bert Belenie whose mate I was to become. The men in the Mould Loft could also in a sense be classified as shipwrights, because they were primarily responsible for seeing that the ships went together according to the plans.

At that time there were several 52ft Naval "Harbour Launches" under construction in the boat shed, big powerful boats, maids of all work for the Navy. (As I shall tell, I was later to be mate on one of these, and just after the end of the war made a bid to buy one fitted with a very nice steam plant-normally they had diesel engines- but missed it by a few pounds). A big ketch rigged sailing yacht was also under construction, and launches and gigs for some of the steam and motor yachts of the period, these were to a very high standard of construction and finish.

For a while I worked with Harry on the harbour launches, holding up a heavy steel 'dolly' against his rivetting of long copper rods driven through the joints in the stem and keel. It was hard physical work and Harry worked me hard. I remember him as a big powerful man who specialised in the bigger craft where the work was not so fussy and where a great deal of the work of fashioning timber -generally oak or teak- was done with the shipwrights adze, a tool with which I became pretty proficient.

My principal memory of those boats was that they were double diagonal teak planked and that in between the skins was a layer of coarse calico plastered with white lead paste. This is now considered a most dangerous substance to handle, but we took little in the way of precautions, and I got a bad attack of dermatitis on my hands. This severe septic blistering took weeks to clear up,and put me out of work for a while. I was lucky not to have been internally poisoned.

Another bad practice which would be more than frowned on to-day was the use of asbestos in the engine rooms of Naval ships. The turbines themselves and all steam piping was encased in asbestos cement and then covered over with heavy asbestos woven matting stitched on in situ. Some men did little else but work in asbestos, and I have since wondered how it affected them; much like the miners in danger of silicosis, nobody in authority worried too much about workers' health in those days.

I spent most of my time in this Shop as mate to Bert. Bert was a small rather hatchet faced man of Italian extraction, and a craftsman of the highest order. He took a great deal of trouble teaching me the skills and tricks of the boatbuilders trade; these I have been able to put into practice through much of my life, and even pass on. It is a skill which has given me great satisfaction. It seems that nowadays the practice of journeymen having their own boy as a helper and trainee is going out. I was lucky in the men I worked with in that they all took trouble to teach me, and in some cases to help me in their spare time when I was building boats in mine.

Bert, with me as his mate, built several all-varnished launches in Honduras mahogany, a beautiful timber to work and quite different from the African which seems to be all that is available to-day.

Bert and I also copper sheathed the bottom of a big yacht, another rather skilled job. In days gone by all timber ships which were trading to the Tropics were copper sheathed in this way to guard them against the Toredo worm, and to reduce marine growths.

Many years years later when I was in India I saw the ravages that can be caused by this horrible creature and on one occasion picked up and broke open a piece of timber that we had found on a beach. It was honeycombed for its entire length with living Toredo worms many feet long, white, soft and about half inch in diameter.

Bill Bartlet paid me a compliment which rather embarrassed me, as I shall relate. While I was serving my apprenticeship I first rebuilt 'Rusheen'- the little sail boat I had built at home- and then over a two year period of spare time, built a 14ft 'International' racing dinghy of the previously mentioned Honduras mahogany. At that time I was living on a small houseboat at Hamble, which was ten or twelve miles by water from Thornycroft's. I occasionally got up early and sailed to work and moored the dinghy to the jetty below the boat shop. One day Bill spotted it there. He apparently had a look at it found out whose it was and called all the men and boys down to see what an apprentice could do! On an earlier occasion Bill found a small rudder I had made for Rusheen on a bench, gave me a blast for wasting firm's time and said he would burn it. A few days later he called me into his office at knock off time and gave it back to me with a warning not to get caught at the gate!

I must have spent nearly a year in the Boat Shop before being allocated to the plate shop, a big drafty area, under a roof but open at the sides. Here I became one of a small squad under a master plater. This was all hard dirty work, handling with mechanical aid the frames and plates that went to make up the ships. Bending and stretching steel plates and angle iron, sometimes cold and sometimes red hot straight out of a huge gas burning furnace. Sometimes hammering them into shape and sometimes rolling them, and finally sheering them in the big guillotine machines, and drilling all the rivet holes.

The forming of the keel plate- aft end- of a destroyer was quite something. To-day it would be done by cutting and welding, but then it was done by heat and muscle power from a half inch thick steel plate about four feet wide and fourteen feet long. By heating and forging we made a trough twelve inches wide at the bottom and eighteen inches deep.

This then had to be bent in the middle to an angle of about fifteen degrees. This was effected by dogging-clamping it to the massive steel honeycomb floor, then bending it up mechanically bit by bit between firings and, as the sides bent outwards, hammering them back while red hot. This caused the steel to thicken in the area of the bend, and so make it stronger.

All the hammering was done with special long handled ten pound hammers known as 'Mondays'. The actual place to apply your hammer was where the master plater indicated with his steel rod. At other times you had to hammer a big steel pad he moved about the plate by means of a long steel handle attached to it. Four of us worked at a time on this and we would each in turn and in rhythm swing our hammers, bang bang bang bang...and as it was a moving target it was not so easy to hit it and if you missed it you marked the plate, and were in the 'dog box'! I think it was the hardest work I have done in all my life, and the hottest!

It was in this 'shop' that I first came across the problem which has bedevilled Northern Ireland, religion and sectarianism. Many of the steel workers of all skills were Catholics from Belfast, who couldn't get work at Harlands, or were the last to be taken on and the first out with little or no chance of promotion. Drawing arbitrary lines on maps to make political divisions has been a disastrous habit of the British when faced with a difficult problem in the past, leaving appalling situations for later generations and administrations to sort out, Ireland and India are just two.

I must record that in the yard I felt completely integrated with the men in every department after the first few days, and I made several very good friends. Bert Bellenie was one and another a driller from Belfast. He was a victim of Polio and could not walk, but he could ride a bicycle using one leg but had to be helped onto it and also onto the plate he happened to be drilling. He helped me build a boat at Hamble at weekends, cycling there and sitting on the ground and 'holding up' for my rivetting.

For a time I was back on the 'building' ways, The two destroyers were fitting out afloat and two 'Corvettes' or 'Sloops' had been started (these were to become H.M.ships 'Harrier' and 'Hussar', and I became one of the erection squad. These were the first naval ships in which a large amount of welding was used instead of rivetting. Little was then known of avoiding distortion and not building in stresses, these ships had lots of both! The methods used to pull and strain bulkheads, frames and plating into position would shock a present day builder. Then, for the last three or four months of my 'time' I was transferred to the Drawing Office, and when my time was up accepted employment as an improver draughtsmen, on about £3 a week.

DURING THESE three years in the yard I was going to classes in Naval Architecture three nights a week during the winter and attending Southampton University one whole day a week during term time. In addition to Naval Architecture, my studies included mathematics, heat engines, and general engineering.

Nonetheless, I did have spare time to myself. I had joined the Southampton Trojans Rugby Football Club soon after arriving in Woolston and attended their practices which included a weekly gym session followed by a visit to the local Turkish baths. I was soon playing scrum half for them and always enjoyed the games, but I'm afraid I was not a proper Rugger-Bugger and didn't enjoy the pub crawls after away matches, nor the bawdy company. I was dependent on others for transport. We did play against pretty rough sides, and as scrum half I was somewhat battered and tired after a match and just wanted to get back to my digs, a hot bath and bed.

I also discovered the Ice Rink and spent many evenings there. I could easily have made friends, as I became aware that I was not unattractive to the opposite sex. I was however still very shy and inhibited by my feelings for Peggy who was writing to me from various distant places.

Early into my first spring, I began to visit Hamble at weekends and there I met Gregory Robinson. A notable marine artist, of the Sailing Ship era (there are pictures by him in the Greenwich Museum), he was secretary of the Hamble River Sailing Club, (H.R.S.C.). He, with his wife and four sons who were of about my own age, became wonderful friends to me. I joined the sailing club and then decided to ask my Dad to try to get my little boat over to me.

Dad arranged for her to be sent to Southampton by B&I as deck cargo, and I duly got word that the ship had docked at the Town Quay, and I went over there with a friend after work. Jim was a well-built redheaded lad of about my own age and he had some small boat sailing experience. (I heard later that he did very well in life and in his career).

We persuaded the mate to put Rusheen over the side with the ship's derrick. Only 10 feet long, she looked tiny beside the ship. Boarding by a rope ladder we got all the gear and the mast on board and rigged her. I had planned to sail her to Hamble that evening but had not given the matter as much thought as it deserved.

In the event, fate was kind.

There was a fresh and favourable wind blowing but I knew it would soon be dark, the trip would take at least four hours, and we had had nothing to eat. Jim must have had doubts about the boat's capability but was game to go and so we did.

It was really a daft decision. We had no lifejackets and the boat had no buoyancy tanks. We would be sailing past very busy docks and down Southampton Water in the dark without even a torch, and this in a boat with freeboard of a bare foot. Furthermore nobody knew what we were doing except possibly the ship's mate and he would be gone by morning.

All went well until we reached the Dock Head, the tide was ebbing strongly from Totton on our side and from the River Itchen on the other and where they met there was- for Rusheen- quite a sea running with the wind blowing across it. With the strength of the tide we had no choice but to go on. We must have had some sort of bailer on board, and I believe there was an angel keeping us afloat because for what must have been about fifteen minutes it was touch and go whether or not we were going to be swamped. Rusheen was partially decked but we were taking in water over it from all sides, not even trying to sail but letting the tide carry us into calmer water. Fortunately it did and the wind held steady and we sailed the rest of the twelve miles in the dark along the west shore of Southampton Water, keeping out of the shipping.

We crossed over to round the flashing Hamble Spit buoy, and then blew up the Hamble River to land at nearly low water at the ferry hard, tieing Rusheen to a stake and hoping that the ferrymen- Mr Bedbrook and Mr Bevis- would look after her in the morning.

These two gentlemen became my friends or, at least, Mr Bevis did! Mr Bedbrook was somewhat surly but not unfriendly. They shared the rights to operate this ferry by some archaic act and spent all their lives rowing people and bicycles across the tide between Warsash and Hamble. they also looked after numerous dinghies belonging to yachts moored in the river during the summer months. (Rusheen was to join these!) They had a small hut for shelter at the top of each 'hard'. The river banks elsewhere were deep grey mud as are all the south coast creeks in that area.

Jim and I walked the ten miles back to Woolston on empty stomachs in the dark small hours and I think we made the gate in the morning!

All through my time at Thornycroft's and beyond I practically lived for the letters from Peggy. When I thought one of these might be due I rode furiously up the hill to my digs at lunchtime. Peggy wrote long and newsy and non-sentimental letters in a neat script about all her activities...riding, shooting, walking in the United Provinces where her father was Chief of Police. Peggy seemed and was awfully far away in time and space. From India in those days the letters between us took a long time by sea and the answers at least seven weeks. All our letters just ended 'with Love'...

My consolation for being unhappy was (as it always has been) just to pitch in and work hard at some project. I remember my mother commenting (possibly when I was home on a short holiday), 'All work and no play made Jack a dull boy'!

And I guess I probably was!

*

Although already a thriving yachting centre, second only to Cowes, Hamble was still for most of the year a sleepy rural village of old cottages and timbered houses. In the summer months the yachting fraternity from all over the south of England moved in, and it literally hummed with the "best people" and their cars. A street wound up from the waterfront and past the Bugle Inn, owned by the brewer Harry Brickwood. Harry was at that time the Commodore of the H.R.S.C. which was built on his land right on the high tide water's edge. The clubhouse was quite small inside and had a flat roof used for starting and watching races from.

The village was centred on Luke Brothers boatyard, the building shed and offices being on the lower road. and the yacht store sheds and mud berths a few hundred yards upstream off Satchell Lane. About a quarter mile out of the village the main road passed through the Air Service Training establishment, the hangers and the airfield being on the side away from Southampton Water. On most week days there were always training flights taking off and landing. (The planes were mostly Avro Cadets. These were nice little fully aerobatic biplanes with radial engines.)

I rebuilt 'Rusheen' extensively before my first sailing season and raced her against miscellaneous dinghies...most successfully! She went to windward quite well and being light and rather flat bottomed skimmed away off the wind. However, it was soon arranged, I expect by Mr Robinson (and possibly with an ulterior motive!) that I should helm the Sea Rangers (Girls) "Hamble Star", taking a girl crew as trainee.

The Hamble Stars were 14ft open undecked sailing dinghies, designed and built to be cheap and simple. They sailed remarkably well as did all the yachts and boats built by Lukes, and as there was quite a fleet of them they gave great racing. The champion sailors were two of the Robinson boys Dick and Nichol. Dick was practically unbeatable, I crewed for him a few times and me taught he a lot particularly in the matter of concentration. His own concentration was absolute and he was furious if you broke it.

Sailing the Rangers boat was great fun, and I did quite well particularly with two particular crews. One of these was Betty Luke, an attractive vivacious girl, (flirtatious too!) but a quite experienced sailor. Her father was the firm's designer and business manager. The other good crew was Nora Bevis, a small quiet girl, very good in a boat and a good swimmer. She was my favourite among the Rangers I think she was fond of me.

We had one capsize together while leading, running up in open water with a strong following wind from the Spit Buoy and against an ebb tide, which produced short steep waves. The boats being completely open -no foredeck- occasionally stuck their noses in and broached. They had buoyancy tanks so did not sink but were impossible to bail out and we had to swim and push her onto a mud bank before we could get going again. We arrived back at the club very wet and cold and muddy, but pleased and happy not to have had to be rescued.

In my first summer I began making friends with some of the yacht owning members of the H.R.S.C. and was invited to go day sailing and racing on bigger yachts. At that time there were a number of classes racing at Hamble or from Hamble to Cowes, particularly the 6 and 8 metre classes, all of which had professional skippers and sometimes a boy as well. Their owners did little except helm them at weekend races and attend regattas in the Solent area, to which they were sailed by their professional crews. I got to know a number of these skippers and sometimes sailed on these delivery trips and learned a lot from them.

In most of the Solent and Southampton Water regattas at that time there was quite a lot of money at stake and great rivalry between working men, fishermen, boatbuilders, aircraft workers and others in the various centres from Lymington to Portsmouth. There were a number of small syndicates building and racing boats particularly in the 18ft restricted class. This gave great scope to local designers and spare time builders. Hamble 'fielded' two very successful boats in this class, the 'Gem' and the 'Triad' whose crews were fierce but friendly rivals. I am not sure who designed the Gem but the Triad was designed by Bill Hobbs who was then by way of becoming Lukes designer. Later he was a very good designer in his own right and became a very good friend and counsellor to me.

That summer also I first met Ernest Nicolay. A young man a few years older than me, he had some sort of share in a small keel yacht with a Miss

Edwards. She was much older than either of us and already an experienced yachtswoman. Nick, as I always called him, and James as Miss Edwards was always called by us, became lifetime friends. James never married and during the war was something high up in the W.R.N.S.

At the time I first knew Nick, who was a Russian emigré as a child with his mother from the Revolution, he was a civil engineering student at Southampton University. He became a very successful civil engineer in later life, building roads and bridges and dams in many parts of the Commonwealth. He was finally responsible for a section of that fairly recently constructed Victoria deep line in London.

As a young man Nick was a bit of an oddity in that he always dressed as a very 'pukka' yachtsman in reefer jacket and yachting cap, white top and flannels at the appropriate time of year. He wore a beard, unusual at that time, and a monocle, I think only for effect! He also spoke with a very cultured la dee da voice. This whole thing which then seemed like an act he has kept up all his life. Nonetheless, I have met men who worked under him and regarded him with the greatest respect professionally.

In the early 1930's there were still quite a few tidal creeks on the West side of Southampton water. The great Fawley refinery is now at the head of what was then Fawley Creek. There was also Badnam Creek and of course that at Calshot which at that time was already a seaplane base, and base for the Schneider Trophy planes, and World speed record holders. I also saw the incredible and useless Dornier DOX fly from there with its twelve engines mounted in pairs along the monoplane wing. These may have been Diesel engines which might account for the fact that it could only just get itself off the water with no load except fuel and a few passengers.

These creeks were my happy cruising ground in Rusheen, which I once very daringly sailed as far as the Beaulieu River in the rather exposed West Solent.

I designed my first International 14 footer on a drawing board on the table of the front parlour of my digs. Somehow somewhere I still have this drawing done some 56 years ago, And even more surprising I had a letter from Wales a few years ago containing a recent photo of the boat, which I had named Evolution. An enthusiast had tracked me down and wanted information on her!

These "Fourteens" were not one design but were designed and built within certain parameters. I partly built Evolution in a dilapidated and junk filled and extremely dirty, drafty shed on the waterfront between the Woolston ferry and the Supermarine seaplane factory. Here I rigged up some lighting but had no power tools.

With some guidance from Bert Bellenie, I worked on this dinghy all my spare time, usually until very late at night in the winter. I remember creeping into my digs at all hours trying not to wake Miss B. On one occasion I found I had no door key and managed to get in by climbing across a very old and rotten greenhouse and in through the bathroom fanlight! I must have left footmarks on the bath because she upbraided me not because I might have wrecked her greenhouse and hurt myself but because she had thought herself safe from intruders! Actually I know she was convinced I had a lady friend somewhere. In fact it was she who had a boy friend, an accountant from one of the Woolston shops. He came to see her from time to time, I was introduced but did not take much notice of him.

I must have been in these digs for about a year when, returning for my dinner, I was violently made aware of the seamier side of real life. On entering my bedroom I was met by what for me was a shocking sight, the real significance of which did not immediately strike me. Poor Miss B had collapsed with a miscarriage there earlier in the morning and had haemorrhaged severely and had unsuccessfully tried to clear up.

I am still filled with remorse that I did not do more for her, call a doctor or something, but I only called to her in her bedroom to ask if she was alright, and as she replied that she was, I fled from the house and did not return until the evening when I was met by a very embarrassed pale woman...she had meantime managed to tidy up my room and put out a cold supper for me in the front room as usual. She seemed to recover from her ordeal in a few days and the matter was never mentioned again.

Sometime after this incident I decided to find digs in Hamble and got a bedroom right in the village belonging to the local baker and his wife. They fed me in their own house across the road where another premium apprentice Peter Thornycroft - third generation of the family well known in shipbuilding and engineering circles - was digging.

My new room in an unoccupied unheated house was far from comfortable-it was wintertime- and the double bed was exceedingly cold and lumpy, the thin mattress had two deep troughs in it and I never decided which was less cold! The only advantage of these digs was that I could go to work in Peter's hotted up Morris Eight, but as Peter always left it to the last moment to leave in the mornings and was often shut out, I went back to using my bicycle for the eight miles to and from work. I decided to try to find a boat to live on and look after myself.

I BOUGHT Betty for £35. Advertised in the local paper as a houseboat, she was lying in a muddy creek a half mile above Bursledon's old timber bridge. I had been living in my first "home", rent free, a first world war M.L. This was around 80ft long, very narrow, (Gregory Robinson who had commanded one said they were dreadful seaboats. Whatever about that, as a residence it was very dark cold and uncomfortable, it was hauled out on dry land, and was deteriorating rapidly.

The decision to find something better (which floated!) led me to Betty. Not that I can say it was love at first sight! Betty was a large box with windows, built on a 30ft ex-Cunard liner's lifeboat. This had been one of those lifeboats of the type which were stowed under the normal boats and had collapsible sides, and thus Betty's hull was very low it the water.

However, there were three rooms in the box and quite a large platform built out over her stern. Or was it meant to be the bow? I forgot to ask the vendor! Anyhow I decided that the platform end was to be the stern. From here a door opened into the galley, which had a minimum of shelving, and little else, and then the 'saloon' which had a table and two chairs, some shelves and a settee berth with a cushion. The fore cabin had two berths with serviceable mattresses and drawers beneath. The boat was just what I wanted, but not where I wanted it!

Betty had no means of propulsion, not even oars or anchor, she was moored to stakes. I might have found someone who would have towed her down to Hamble, but I neither could afford the cost nor had I the nerve to ask some motor boat owner to do it.

I introduced Nick to my 'Yacht' one evening and discussed this problem. The idea of letting the tide do the job occurred to us. We decided that if we could beg borrow or steal a large oar or 'sweep' and lash it to the rail of the stern platform we would have some degree of directional control. And, if we left the berth just after the second high water (of which there are two on each tide due to the Isle of Wight) we should be able to drift to Luke's upper yard on the one tide... provided there was no wind!

A wooden jetty went for about 200 yards along the bank of the Hamble below where the training ship 'Mercury' lay. This jetty connected at it's western end with Luke's upper yard and I arranged a (free) mud berth along here. In winter the bows of numerous yachts would be ranged along it in these mud berths.

It was already early winter and the evenings short, and we decided that night time would be the best time to make the two to three mile voyage. It was unlikely that there would be any water traffic and we would not have an audience for our antics or to report on the moored craft we might bump into!

Nick and I picked on a weekday night when the tide would be right, relying on luck for it to be calm. We got someone to drive us up to Bursledon with the oar lashed on the roof. We brought for a light a paraffin Aladdin-mantel table lamp...very popular at that time for domestic lighting. We stopped off on the way to award our driver, refresh and give ourselves some 'Dutch Courage' for the voyage, plus a little extra for eventualities!

By the time we pushed off it was getting dark. Once into the main stream we were immediately proceeding quite quickly down river, or rather down the course of the river but without any speed through the water and so we had no steerage.

Nick was standing on the little piece of the original bow with his back against the front of the house and could see very well what lay ahead and how to avoid it. I at the stern with the oar could see nothing ahead! And, by rowing sideways, could only change the direction in which we were pointing, not that in which we were travelling!

Our first major hazard was the bridge. As we approached it Nick up forward began shouting back a stream of instructions...I glanced round the port side of the house and saw what he was getting excited about, even in the dark I could see we were going to collide with the bridge! In spite of Nick's now frantic shouts there was nothing I could do except try to make it a glancing blow, and hope that Nick would be all right.

He was and we did, the corner of the boathouse hitting against some of the timber bracing of the old bridge, with a rather horrible crunch, before bouncing through, both now in fits of laughter at our crazy and unseamanlike progress. Below the bridge the current was not so strong and the rest of the voyage was more dignified!

The night was fine and we soon had the lit Aladdin on the roof and were singing lustily and finishing off the beer as we pushed off moored craft and other obstructions. By poling and pushing off boats and things we managed to work Betty in towards the jetty past the 'Mercury', and when we finally grounded it was nearly low water. We forced the oar into the mud and moored to it to await the return of the tide and slept until we could move into our appointed berth at daylight.

Betty spent the winter there, a rather ugly and humble little craft among the elegant yachts, some of which towered over her alongside. This was a very exposed place to get to on a wild winter's night. I had to walk several hundred yards from the shed where I left my bicycle and along a narrow plank walkway in the dark and possibly in a howling gale and carrying my supplies and Betty dark and unheated to greet me. I would be at least a quarter mile from the nearest human being!

And on a wild night at high tide with the wind in the south west the Hamble was really rough, Betty and me bouncing and jolting on our moorings. Nonetheless, with my Aladdin and my Primus stove and my (rather smelly) Valor paraffin heater, I was usually quite warm and happy.

My nearest neighbour was the training ship Mercury moored in the middle of the river. Uninhabited most of the day when the boys were in the shore establishment, they slept aboard her at night in hammocks, Navy style. The nightly business of getting a large number of boys out to her in the dark in oared cutters, big un-handy boats, was quite a business, and I can still hear the shouting and cussing as it came to me against the wind.

When I had got properly settled into my own 'home' I moved the half built dinghy from Woolston to a corner of one of the big yacht store sheds where I left my bicycle. These were open sided and not much better than being in the open, also there was no electricity, and so I could only work at weekends until the evenings lengthened.

It was here that my first real boat was built and launched. She attracted quite a lot of attention from the yard workmen and local dinghy sailors and from my friends the Robinson family who lived within sight of my building area.

It must have been early summer and among the various friends who helped me I remember Nora clad only in a green bathing costume. The yard was a popular bathing place for people who lived on the adjoining Satchell Lane, and I much enjoyed her shy quiet company.

ONE WEEKEND afternoon in the summer of 1934, I was working on the dinghy alone, when a young woman came into the shed and stood beside me, interested in what I was building. Introducing herself as Maud Cooke, she told me she lived with her father and step-mother in the big house just across the road from the boundary fence of the yard. A retired railway engineer, her father had been chief engineer of one of India's principal railway systems for many years. Maud herself had been born in Jaipore and had spent much of her life in India both before and after her education in England. Maud invited me to visit sometime and meet her parents. Her father had a very good workshop over in the big house and she was sure he would be pleased to let me use his lathe and other tools.

This was a fateful moment, possibly the most fateful of my whole life. I do not now and did not then believe in fate, or pre-destiny, but I know that we are not free agents either. I believe that what we do affects others and we have inbred or learned standards by which we live, and that we have varying natures, some hard and strong, some soft and weak.

I do not know whether Maud really fell in love with me or not, but I know that I did not fall in love with her. She was seven years older than me and not at all what I imagined my ideal to be, (my mental picture of Peggy!), but Maud did arouse and attract me physically.

I saw quite a lot of Maud and her family during the winter of 34-35. Mary, Maud's stepmother, was a Scot and extremely kind and hospitable to me in every way, as was her father too. Still at Thornycrofts, I was working on the dinghy at weekends and in the lighter evenings. Through Maud, I came to know several other people in the area, including Maud's cousin Enid (whom I became very fond of), she also had had an Indian upbringing. I also met Jack Hall, son of Admiral Hall who had been commander of submarines in The First World War. I had dinner on more than one occasion with the Hall family in company with Maud. Although only about my own age, Jack was a Pilot Instructor at Airspeed Hamble and it was with him that I had my first flight. This was in an Avro Cadet, one of the basic trainers of that period. These were rugged and fully aerobatic little biplanes with radial aircooled engines and two open cockpits. Jack was completely at home in the plane and gave me a very exciting introduction to flying!

A freckled redhead, Jack was an exceptionally nice and rather quiet and serious young man. He later flew in the early days of the war as a test pilot for Rotol, makers of V.P. airscrews. He lost his life in a Spitfire which disintegrated when the propeller shed a blade in flight.

Maud helped me to complete the dinghy which I named "Evolution" because I thought she incorporated some new ideas. I was short of money to complete her but some of the owners of other boats in this class - nearly all built by the inimitable Uffa Fox- were interested in my efforts and very kindly came up with offers of used spars and sails. Somehow she was completed and rigged in my third summer in England(1935).

I raced Evolution that summer at Hamble and the regattas round Southampton Water with considerable success but usually when the top people in the class were absent. These 'top people' included Peter Scott,(the ornithologist) Stuart Morris, Mrs Richardson, Tom Thornycroft (father of Peter).

Maud often crewed for me, bravely I suppose because I don't think she really enjoyed being wet and cold and these Fourteens were very hard work. They had no decks and a large sail area, and we never thought of wearing life jackets!

Maud had some experience of sex (unlike me!) and she was well versed in the literature of sex and sensuality. The writings of Marie Stopes, Havelock Ellis and D.H. Lawrence were fashionable at the time and Maud seemed to think it was almost her duty to seduce and educate me in these matters. She proceeded to do so and I went along with my education. However this was against my real will and wishes as I was still far too romantically in love with Peggy to love anyone else. Maud seemed to totally disregard this fact, perhaps with some justification. Today the whole situation would be viewed differently.

On one occasion Maud and I sailed over to Cowes and up the Medina river to Newport and it became too late to make the return trip, Maud suggested that we stayed the night on her uncle Dr Dick Cooke's small sailing cruiser 'Fay' which was moored off Uffa Fox's workshop/home at that time. Uffa's establishment had been one of the chain ferries which plied between East and West Cowes,. He had cleverly converted it to a workshop, a design office and a home by roofing in the vehicle carrying area and turning the passenger shelters into a dwelling and an office. One end of this craft was against the bank of the creek and the other out in the stream with its ramp acting as a slipway.

Maud phoned home to say we would not be back that night and were staying on her Uncle's yacht, I don't imagine she said that he was not on board! At this stage my 'education' had hardly begun and I resisted lessons that night with difficulty...but didn't sleep very well! I don't remember what we did for food but we sailed home in the morning.

In the autumn of 1935, about a year after I met her, Maud persuaded her father to pay the rent of a cottage she found at the downstream end of Hamble, which she was supposed to share with her cousin Enid and use as a workshop for a little business she was running making very fancy lingerie and wedding outfits for rather special people. Enid was not often there, I don't think her Father was so indulgent as Maud's and Maud had always had a great capacity for achieving her ends and I became one of them!

The cottage and Betty gave us complete freedom.

While still at Thornycrofts, the calf of my left leg began to swell for no apparent reason, and cycling to work became very painful. I carried on for several weeks thinking it was a strained muscle or tendon until one day something gave and I could hardly walk. I went to a doctor who sent me to the Southampton General, where they operated and removed a dead 'animal' a huge grub about 2 inches long-they showed it to me preserved in alcohol- I did not ask to keep the trophy! These grubs were apparently fairly common among sheep farmers in Australia, and could be fatal if they settled in parts of the body such as the brain, I was lucky that my antibodies had beaten it or it had just died from old age!

The operation left me somewhat incapacitated for a time and I went into very comfortable digs in Hamble, with a Mrs Jurd and her son. While there my Mother and Nancy came over from Ireland and seeing the 'Betty' for the first time they decided to renovate it so that when I moved in again I had mats on the floor and curtains in the windows and the galley was 'properly' equipped and painted. I think now that the real purpose of Mother's visit was to assess the woman I was getting around with and I am afraid they went away not feeling very happy, but I was of age and it was my life.

One little incident I particularly recall from the time I was with Mrs Jurd. Like many young men of the period I rather longed for a sports car, particularly an M.G.Midget. I had no hope of getting one but wrote to Morris Motors for a brochure to drool over! This duly arrived but then one evening (on my return from work in overalls on my bike), there parked outside the gate of my digs was a beautiful new M.G.Midget. And the salesman was waiting inside to give me a trial run! My embarrassment was acute when I had to explain that I was far from being in the market for the car. I think the man who had driven out from Southampton probably thought I would be one of the trainee pilots...but he took it very well and even offered me a drive which in my embarrassment I refused.

*

At around this time I was completing my second International 14 in a floating shed which belonged to another young man. He himself had built two powerful inboard engine speedboats in his spare time; his parents owned a very large yacht permanently moored as a houseboat beside my 'Betty'

This dinghy which I later named 'Dawn' (hoping that she would be the dawn for me of success as a designer) had been partly built on my houseboat Betty, for which purpose I had temporarily to remove the bulkhead between the cabin and the 'saloon', and also one of the bunks in the cabin. This did not leave me with much room to live in once the dinghy was under construction but it did mean that I could work on her at all times day or night, illumination at night being by the Aladdin oil lamp. How I managed not to start a fire I do not know. The place was full of shavings and timber, and as anyone who has ever used one of these lamps will know they hated drafts and the wick had to be carefully tended and watched or they would flare up and fill a room with black smoke and paraffin smuts. When I was offered the alternative building space almost next door I had to cut away the end wall to get the half built dinghy out. After that I put Betty together again.

I completed and launched 'Dawn' and was lucky enough to sell 'Evolution' (she still exists after all these years). I had not been long back aboard Betty after my leg operation in the early autumn of '35, when Hamble and the south coast was struck by one of the worst storms remembered in those parts. After Mother's work I had moved Betty from outside the long timber walkway to inside it, into what was at low water a muddy creek with a firm grass grown bank on either side. She only floated for a few hours on the top of the tide each day and was somewhat more accessible and, I thought, safer. She was moored to two stakes driven into the bank on the west -normally windward- side of the ditch. These banks were usually well above high tide except with abnormal spring tides.

It was still daylight when I got back from work and put my bike away, but already blowing hard. In those days information about weather was not too readily obtainable and we tended to take it as it came. I made my way along the bank carrying my shopping, beginning to worry about Dawn, my beautiful new triple skin dinghy which was on a mooring in the main river off the walkway. After putting my shopping aboard Betty, sitting comfortably on the bottom of the ditch, I walked out along the walkway to see how Dawn was weathering it. She was plunging and bucking into a short steep little sea but did not seem to be taking water aboard, and although the tide was still quite low I could not get to her or do anything about her. Most of the yachts were still on their moorings and the wind was beginning to whistle in their rigging in a shrill chorus and it was getting dusk. On one of the yachts, I could not identify which, I heard a woman shouting for help. In fact it sounded as though she was getting hysterical, but by that time the wind was so strong and the sea out in the river so rough that it would have taken a powerful launch to rescue her (I don't think any lives were lost that night). Anyhow I could do nothing and went back to Betty, and found that the tide was already beginning to fill my creek, and soon Betty was afloat. As soon as she rose out of the ditch the wind began to catch her, and she pulled away from the bank straining on the mooring ropes and the stakes. I had to make a quick decision whether to get ashore while I could or stay with my 'ship'. It was almost dark and I decided to stay.

The wind was pushing the tide up the river and it became evident that there was going to be an abnormally high tide and that the banks were going to disappear and that the low lying land along the river was going to get flooded.

My worry was the stakes to which I was moored were driven into what was comparatively soft mud, and the wind was increasing all the time. I lit the Aladdin and prepared myself a meal. Betty was by now snatching violently on her moorings and healing over in the squalls, and I had to put the lamp on the floor to stop it falling off the table! Having had something to eat I went out on the stern platform and was somewhat shocked at how much the wind had increased to what must have been full storm force.

My home was now entirely surrounded by water and behaving like a wild thing. I was just thinking that if I could tighten the stern warp a little it might reduce the wild behavior, when the stake at the other end pulled out of the bank and Betty swung away down wind now on quite a long rope, began to veer madly from side to side, rolling drunkenly at the end of each swing and putting the low sides of the hull proper under water. I tried to shorten the warp but it was quite impossible as it was just about bar tight. I had to admit to myself that I was quite helpless, scared and soaking wet with the driving rain and spray blowing off the water, on top of which it was pitch dark. I contemplated abandoning ship, somehow swimming and struggling to dry land, but went inside and really had to laugh at the sight that met me. There must have been nearly a foot of water over the floor, the still lit lamp was floating from side to side as Betty rolled, cupboard doors had opened and drawers fallen out and all the contents, food, clothing, books and just about all my possessions were in the water washing about on the floor!

Worse was to come, I sudden felt Betty move in a different direction and knew the other stake had given and we were completely adrift, I dashed out onto the sloping stern platform, it must have been about midnight and I could see nothing except a few lights in the village to orient me. Betty was blowing sideways heavily listed, and obviously taking in water.

She was over the covered saltings but I knew must be heading for the main river and deep water a few hundred yards on, my home a drifting sinking hulk in a raging storm. I decided that she had too much timber in her to completely sink and that if I could hang on she would carry me across to the far bank- which due to the bends in the river would be a long way crossing diagonally- when once again my luck or guardian angel came to the rescue. She 'struck'- as they say in real shipwrecks- when she grounded on the high point of a submerged bank and stuck firm and I knew I was safe because inevitably the tide must be falling. It was and Betty gradually settled safe but at a horrible angle, stern down on the side of a steep bank.

When I got back inside there was no light and I found that most of the water had run down and out at the galley end and that my bunk was on the high side and dry, the lamp had fallen over and fortunately gone out before the paraffin caught fire, I just stripped, off got into my bunk and was asleep in a few minutes.

I got up as soon as I woke at about nine o'clock, dressed and went out on the steeply sloping aft 'deck', the tide was low, the wind had gone down to a stiff breeze and the sun was shining. By the way Betty was lying I knew she would fill when the tide came back and so I went along to the yard and managed to enlist the help of some of the men who were all my friends. We got her to slide down to the bottom of the ditch and I moored her temporarily and then went across the river with some of the men in a rowboat to survey the damage and for me to try to find what I thought would be the remains of my dinghy which had gone from her mooring.

The lee shore on the upstream bend of the river was literally piled with yachts, some of the bigger boats had obviously taken the smaller ones with them and people were already on the scene attempting to assess the damage.

Close along the river bank was a wood of small well spaced oak trees growing from a grassy floor, it was the bottom of somebody's garden, and lying in among the trees I found 'Dawn' with a broken mast but otherwise almost undamaged, and after a search I found her rudder and most of the loose gear. When Betty floated again I got her back to her old berth and accepted temporary accommodation from my very good friends Gregory and Mrs Robinson until I got my home and belongings dried out.

*

From the time I went to England I did not see very much of my sisters. They had always been very keen and very good horsewomen as was our cousin Joan. They did a great deal of riding in their teens mostly on horses hired with their pocket money from a Mr Magee who kept horses further up the valley and probably had a soft spot for the girls. Eventually they managed to scrape up enough money to buy a horse for themselves. This animal they named 'Hilltop', it was the joy of their lives and was very well looked after. They joined the Bray Harriers, a drag hunt, on the same ticket because to most people they were so much alike nobody knew there were two of them! They were fairly small and lightly built girls, but skilled riders with lots of spirit and courage.

Jack Plews and I also rode the same horses from time to time. The twins always scoffed at my abilities as a horseman, I always considered I could ride, but I admit Jack was much better, a completely fearless horseman.

Nancy went out to India a year or so before the War. She went there to help run a school with relatives of some well intended ladies whom we knew... and we didn't see her again until well after the War, at the time of Indian Independence.

In the meantime she had married into the Indian army. Her husband, Mortimore (always known as Morty), was a man who had been brought up very much in the military tradition, to him soldiering was everything and he soon became Colonel of the Rajputana Rifles.

She eventually came home with him and three children, a girl and two boys. They had had a fairly comfortable war, the Rajputs never seeing active service...much to Mortimore's bitter disappointment! The sequel was a sad one.

Morty, as I always knew him, was a soldier through and through and never really settled to civilian life. They tried farming in England but the immediate post war restrictions frustrated him so much that they sold up and moved to Co Wexford in Ireland and tried again. It was not far from our parents, and Nancy and the family were very happy there for a while.

Morty still felt frustrated with civilian life, and rather took out his frustrations on his family to such an extent that when things became impossible for Nancy she ran away. She went to England, had the children made wards of court and eventually got a divorce. When she was in her fifties she married my former wife Maud's brother Reggie Cooke- making him my brother in law for the second time!

Nancy died of Cancer in April of 1984. Very sadly, I just failed to get to see this much loved sister before her death.

Doreen, my other sister remained at home until after the outbreak of War. She felt sufficiently strong about this to break off an engagement because her fiancee had no intention of fighting for the 'King and Country' across the water.

She went to England and joined the WAAF, spending the early part of the War and the Battle of Britain in Dover. She left the WAAF to marry an officer who had been badly wounded at the beginning of the Africa Campaign, Freddie George from Donegal.

He was invalided out of the army and they returned to Ireland, settling in Shankill in County Dublin. As had Nancy, Doreen had two boys and a girl. Freddie George set himself up in an import-export business, not successfully. They emigrated to Canada, and later took Canadian citizenship. I only saw Doreen a very few times during the rest of her life. However I had always felt very close to her and we corresponded a great deal. I think she had a pretty tough time bringing up her family on her husband's rather meagre income in their early days in Canada.

Doreen died of cancer in July of 1986.

IT IS the autumn of 1935 in this part of my story. I had then no interest in politics. At this time England was only beginning to climb out of the great depression, there was still a lot of unemployment and labour unrest in Wales and the North Midlands, but I was too interested in my own affairs to take much notice -it did not affect me and in any case my upbringing was very conservative, and when I read a paper it was probably the Daily Telegraph.

As for Europe, I was hardly aware of what was going on there, except that Mussolini had been 'Il Duce' in Italy since the mid twenties. He was said to have made the Italian trains run to time! This was considered to be quite a compliment from the British upper classes, the only people likely to travel in Italy at that time, and who were little concerned about what else this Fascist was doing in his own country.

*

Maud Cooke and I saw a lot of each other. Ivan, a colleague at Thornycrofts, had a two seater Morris Oxford convertible and I took advantage of his generosity on several occasions to borrow his car. Maud and I and got about quite a bit in this and other borrowed cars. We visited friends as far away as Dartington Hall in Devon. This was then a a co-educational boarding school, considered rather advanced in its philosophy and morality in some circles. Maud's cousin Enid had a staff job there at the time. Dartington Hall was also the home of the Ballet Juss, made up largely of people- particularly Jews- who had seen the writing on the walls in Hitler's Germany, and got out in time. It was at Dartington that I first saw live Ballet, produced and danced in by Juss himself. I remember 'The Three Cornered Hat' and 'The Green Table'. These ballets had political undertones and the dance was very different from the traditional Ballet and the Ballet music of the Russian school, and did not appeal to me.

When Mussolini invaded and brutally conquered Abyssinia (Ethiopia) I did wake up in the political sense. Two of my friends at Trent were nephews of Haile Selassie the Emperor (he probably had dozens of nephews!). Joseph Martin and his brother returned to their country and joined the Air Force, and I found out that they had both been killed.

Maud had been to the Slade Art School. (Indeed many years later at 82 she was still painting in watercolour, rather beautifully, flowers, portraits and landscapes, scenes of Ireland and England and India). I think it was at the Slade that she had made friends with a Miss Errington whose brother George, an aviator, was later test pilot for Airspeed Ltd at Portsmouth. I met George about this time, through Maud and her brother Reggie who owned and flew a D.H.Moth. I was later to meet George again during the War in rather unfortunate circumstances, more of which anon!

*

My apprenticeship at Thorneycroft was up in November 1935 and I was offered employment as an Improver Draughtsman in the Ship Drawing office at £3 per week! This seemed good money, particularly after the 10/- I had been getting. I also was receiving help from my father with materials for my dinghies.

My last job at Thornycroft's was to prepare the 'as fitted' plans of H.M. destroyer 'Daring' to a scale of ¼" to one foot. This made the drawing about six feet long and showed a vertical section and plans of the decks with all details shown correctly and in their correct positions. This was all drawn in Indian ink on tracing linen, so that blue prints could be made from it. This involved a great deal of work and time aboard the ship which was afloat and undergoing final fit out and trials.

I had been on this task for several weeks when disaster struck! Or so it certainly seemed at the time. Another draughtsman was John Hayward, a good friend who had been a great help to me when I first arrived in the drawing office. Wishing to return a book I had lent him, at 'knock off' time he threw it across to me from his board and knocked over the bottle of indian ink which I had not yet corked. The bottle rolled across the great drawing, spilling its contents as it went! Indian ink cannot be removed from tracing linen, the drawing was ruined and weeks of work lost.

John was of course horrified at what had happened, I immediately went to the office of the assistant chief draughtsman to tell him. He accepted that it was a genuine accident and did not hold it against us, (He was my tutor at night school in Naval Architecture) but something had to be done about it quickly and it was agreed between us that John and I would work overtime -unpaid- to trace it off the original, working together until complete. This had to be done quickly because the ship was nearly due to be handed over to the Navy. Well we did it between us on time and I'm sure it was better than the original because for one thing John was a much neater printer than me.

John was quite a character and a never ending source of funny stories, some of which I still remember and no doubt bore people in the retelling. He was a little older than me and married. He wanted a family but they never arrived...he kept poultry in his small suburban back garden and swore that he loved hens whom he reckoned were creatures of intelligence and great character. John had a very different outlook on life to me. I had never really thought of making money, even less of saving it, but he had already started seriously saving for his old age! I lost touch completely, with John for a time when I left Thorny's, which was soon after the incident of the ink but met up with him during and after the War. After that I lost touch completely, but I sincerely hope he had a comfortable old age!

About the same time I was involved in what now seems a rather silly prank with my friend Ivan. It concerned the bicycle rack of all draughtsmen and office staff, male and female. There must have been at least three dozen bicycles (generally known as 'Irons') in it at the time, and there was always an almighty rush to get away after work.

Ivan had got hold of a length of greasy wire rope from somewhere in the yard and we slipped out of the office in the dark of one winter evening. We removed our own bikes from the rack and then passed the wire through the front wheels of all the bikes in the rack, and made the ends fast to the rack by knotting the wire. We made off before we got deservedly lynched but we were under suspicion for some time!

Ivan too was an Irishman!

*

It was towards the end of '35 that I acquired my first motorcycle, a rather elderly 350cc side valve Triumph. This gave me some independence but I don't think Maud was ever a very enthusiastic pillion rider; the unsprung bikes of those days were far from comfortable! I once took Maud's cousin Enid on the pillion to the home of Beatrice and Sidney Webb, where for a time she was their housekeeper. I had a meal with the Webbs who seemed very old to me at the time... although Sidney lived until after the war. Like so many other people of the left in those days the Webbs were deceived about what was going on under Stalin in the Soviet Union in the name of Communism.

In the winter months of 1935 the Hamble River Sailing Club had weekly lectures given by various people on racing tactics, navigation and theory of sail and aerodynamics. This last subject was given by Beverley Shenstone, who was chief aerodynamicist at Vickers Supermarine in Southampton. Beverly was, I believe, of French Canadian stock, and although quite young, not over forty, he was a rather serious man, tall and very thin and gaunt. I was very interested in his lectures and one evening quite out of the blue he asked me if I would like to join Supermarine's design staff.

I had always been, next to yachts, most interested in aircraft and their design and had done a lot of model making in my school days. The offer thrilled me. I said I certainly would! Soon after that I had an interview with the chief draughtsman at Supers who offered me a job at £5 per week on the understanding that, if my work was satisfactory, I would move up in status to the Technician-Design Office.

The Chief Draughtsman who had interviewed me was a Mr Smith, a pleasant but not striking man. I only learned comparatively recently that some time after I left the company and after the death due to cancer of R.J. Mitchell, chief designer responsible for the Spitfire fighter, Smith took over Mitchell's mantle. He was then responsible not only for vastly improving the aeroplane but after the factory was blitzed he organised Spitfire production in other factories, including that of Austin Motors.

I gave notice to Thorny's and by December I was in Super's drawing office, drawing bits of the first production 'Spitfire'. In the New Year I was moved up and, nominally under R.J.Mitchell who was already a sick man, I had Shenstone as my 'patron' and worked directly under a Mr Sherval. He was primarily in charge of fuselage and hull design; a powerfully built and serious man, he was a little forbidding but he was very good and tolerant to the rather jumped-up me and helped me greatly in early days, and I think he came to trust my judgements.

On one of my first days there I was wandering round the building hangers looking at the three types of flying boats under construction. These were twin radial engined 'Scapas' and 'Stranrars'. This latter had the new sleeve valve Bristol engines. There was also the single engined 'Walrus'. The 'Walrus' development(which later became the 'Sea Otter') was only just started and was still largely on the drawing boards of the technical and drawing offices, (some of it on mine!).

In an odd corner of one of the hangers I saw a small mono-winged fuselage surrounded by scaffolding. Nobody was working on it at the time and I climbed up and had a good look at it. This was the prototype Spitfire- not named at that time- just a P.V.(Private Venture), designed and being built to the latest Air Ministry specification for a high performance multigun monoplane fighter. It was built to use the latest Rolls Royce aero engine, the twelve cylinder V bank 1200hp liquid cooled 'Merlin'.

Hawker's were also competing to the same specification, and their plane later became the 'Hurricane'. The Spitfire was certainly influenced by the Supermarine S6 and S6B Schneider Trophy racers and World speed record holders. Mitchell was primarily responsible for these, the fuselage being very similar, and it is my opinion that credit for the wing design belongs to Shenstone, and this made the machine what it was.

What struck me most forcibly about the Spitfire was the seemingly immense strength built into the all metal wing, which had a root thickness which must have been nearly a foot. The main spar was built up from corrugated stainless steel rolled sections, through which protruded the barrels of eight Browning machine guns, four in each wing. Other striking features were the retractable undercarriage and the elliptical plan shape of the wings.

Some months later this machine was transported at night to Eastleigh Aerodrome and on the evening before it was scheduled for its maiden flight I went to Eastleigh with some other volunteers from the Technical Office. The aircraft was on its back on some trestles and we stacked the wings with a heavy carefully distributed load of sandbags and measured the deflection (Bending) of the wings, simulating the stresses of pulling out of a dive, so that they could be compared with the calculated stresses.

The next evening after work- it was summer time- I rode my motorbike out to Eastleigh and watched our test pilot 'Mutt' Summer taxi the machine along the runway once or twice. And then with a most impressive roar from its mighty engine and its fixed pitch, two wide bladed wooden airscrew, it took off with apparent ease and circled the airfield a few times at perhaps 2000ft, never out of sight or sound. It then let down its wheels and made a perfect landing.

That was a day of greater significance than any of us onlookers realised!

*

The office in which I worked was at the top of a largely steel and glass structure of about the same height as a 5 storey building. This was situated about a quarter mile upstream of the floating bridge ferry on the River Itchen. It faced down the river and overlooked the concrete slipway area in front of the factory. Mutt used to scare us in the offices by taxying down the river in a Walrus, turning round and then, waiting for the ferry to get out of the way, he would take off and head straight at the office block and at what seemed the last moment would pull up and roar over the roof just above us.

In those days aircraft were simpler creatures than they are today, and in my office we were not assigned to definite tasks. Apart from the men (and in our case one woman) who were involved with calculation and stress checks and analysis, the rest of us were liable to have any problem or design job thrown at us. This made the work really interesting, sometimes challenging and if you got it right, very satisfying.

One of the first challenges I got was to try to find a practical solution to one of the problems with the Walrus. Some of these aircraft were carried aboard H.M. Cruisers and were launched by crane for take off and reconnaissance. At a later time they were launched by catapult.

The aircraft were difficult or impossible to recover except in calm conditions and when they had to come down in the open sea they were taken in tow by a destroyer with the crew of four men still aboard. The problem was that under a fast tow- and destroyers were not meant to go slowly-the Walrus had a bad habit of digging in a wing tip float and with the high engine position they would then roll right over, sometimes trapping and drowning the crew.

My solution was in effect to squash the float to make it wider and shallower and, using the existing mounting strong points on the wing in a different way, to move it outboard about two feet.

The idea got the approval of the stress people and I designed the float and its attachments. One was mounted on one side of a Walrus and it passed a sea test and then became standard on both the Walrus and the Sea Otter. (During the War I had occasion to go to Cowes and was happy to see a whole park of Otters equipped with my floats).

By a curious coincidence some thirty years later one of these floats turned up at my floating home as a 'toy' for my son Simon who was then about eight or nine. It was made by a good friend of ours, a Colonel Tracey who had been a flier in the interwar years and had picked up the float in some scrapyard! He had turned the float into a petrol engined airscrew driven trimaran, a hole cut in the top of the float for a cockpit and the vessel stabilised by two cylindrical outriggers. Simon pop-popped up and down the river sitting in front of a real airscrew, great fun!

In the two or three years or so that I was with Supermarine I was involved in quite a variety of jobs. The engine nacelle and cowling of the Sea Otter (which unlike the Walrus was a tractor instead of a pusher plane)was considerably cleaned up aerodynamically. And I worked too on the geometry of the retractable landing gear. At that time all calculations were normally done with the slide rule although an electric calculator was introduced into the office during my time and I learned to use it when I was given the job of working out the mass balancing of the ailerons on the new twin engine 'Stranrear'. I must have had quite a lot of help on that job. It involved calculus and I had left college with a pretty poor grasp of that subject; however it is easier to do something when you can see its practical application and use, to-day I would have no idea even where to begin!

I got a reputation for being good at designing and fairing up shapes, fuselages, hulls, nacelles, floats etc, and the one job which may have stuck was the fuselage of a twin engine fighter we were working on in the office. For some political or commercial reason beyond my ken all the work we did was passed to Westland Aircraft at Yeovil.

For a time I was involved with the installation of four Orlekon Cannons in the nose of my beautiful fuselage! These guns were the first of the shell (explosive bullets about half inch in diameter) firing guns in aircraft, and it was calculated that the combined recoil thrust was greater than that of the airscrews! This aeroplane or a derivative of it was produced during the War in the form of the 'Westland Whirlwind' with the four Orlekons sticking out of the nose, (which had been shortened because of the blast damaged it was sustaining,) and twin engines, I think Merlins.

A squadron of these machines were for a while stationed on a small grass field near Ibsley north of Ringwood in Hampshire, where I was working for a time in the summer of 1940; it was rumoured that they were not the easiest plane to fly and that several were lost accidentally training was very brief in those days.

I am something of a pacifist now and sometimes wonder how people can bring themselves to work on the design of better, more efficient, more lethal weapons systems, whether nuclear or conventional, in time of peace: and yet in my younger days I was doing just that without a thought- just interesting problems- one did not really give any actual thought to the practical effect for which they were designed. In relation to what is being designed to-day for killing and destructive purposes our systems were not much of an advance on the muzzle-loading musket, but the morality was much the same.

Mr Sherval was working on and off with the preliminary design of a four engine monoplane flying boat. This, from memory, was remarkably like the Sunderland, and I had something to do with the nose and tail gun turrets which were being made by the firms of Fraser Nash and B.M.W., both of which were basically in the motor car business, one in England and the other in Hitler's Germany. At that time -1936- there seemed to be no secrets between the two countries and a certain section of the British 'Upper Class' were on very friendly terms with the German régime.

Of course in other ways too, Britain and Germany were still very close. The 'Bremen' and the 'Europa' were German transatlantic liners shuttling across the Atlantic carrying mail. To speed the delivery they each carried a twin engine seaplane on a catapult, these being launched in the Western Approaches. They then landed off Southampton Docks, taxied up to moorings by our works and the crew and mail were brought ashore in our launch. The pilots were greeted in a very friendly manner, and appeared to have the run of the works!

'Supers' was wiped out in 1940 and Spitfire building was dispersed all over Hampshire, in garages and bus depots, anywhere there was the covered space.

*

Late in January 1936 I had a crash on my motorcycle while riding home one very dark wet night. I believe I hit the kerb while trying to avoid an unlit cyclist. Anyhow I was knocked unconscious and came to on a stretcher in a corridor of my old hospital- Southampton General- with a friend of ours, Honor Lister, standing beside me. Honor was a very nice girl, a clever and athletic person handicapped by a slightly defective palate so that her speech was nasal, but this did not seem to worry her. I do not know how she knew I was in trouble but, as always, when 'coming round' it is and was wonderful to see a familiar face.

I wasn't badly hurt, just a little concussed and bruised, and was kept under observation for a few days. I think it was the next morning when Maud came in to see me and gave me the stunning news that she was four or five months pregnant! I could hardly believe it, we had only barely consummated our 'marriage' but the foetus, later to be my son Tyl, was evidently determined to exist! And of course I have always been glad that he did arrive. In middle and old age respectively he and I are now very close and intellectually alike.

At that time, however, I had not given any thought to marriage, except to Peggy! That was a rather hopeless and romantic idea, she was I felt too good for me. I now know that she was a remarkable woman but we would have had much in common...

Maud's news brought me up sharply to reality. As supposedly a 'gentleman', there was only one right thing to be done and as soon as I was out of hospital I borrowed Ivan's car and Maud and I motored to Southsea where I bought a modest platinum and diamond engagement ring.

I do not know what the Cooke family thought about this but I am afraid my own family were none too pleased. I was only a very young 23 earning £5 a week, which wasn't much even then. Maud was seven years older than me, too big a difference . However, we went through the usual formalities and arranged to get married in March at Winchester Registry

Office. For a few days before our wedding I lived by most kind invitation as a guest of Mr and Mrs Robinson who lived almost next door to the Cookes.

And then, with minimum fuss, we were duly married. We visited the Cathedral before returning to Hamble for a small reception laid on by Mary Cooke. My 'best man' was Hugh Arnold, a friend and fellow draughtsman at Super's, (my family always called him the kidney man, he only had one and this was of course before transplants were invented.)

*

Up to this time I was still corresponding with Peggy in India and knew that she was due back in England with the rest of her family on Home Leave, and that she had an address outside Oxford. I wrote her there that I was engaged to be married- I don't remember in what terms- and arranged to visit the family one Saturday. I borrowed Nick's Renault, by chance the same bull nosed model-with the radiator behind the engine- as the one in which I had driven with Peggy about six years previously.

I think I expected some sort of miracle, perhaps that Peggy would rush into my arms and beg me to change my mind. I don't believe it ever entered my head to try to see the situation from her point of view, if per chance she had actually been in love with me over all these years and that I might be hurting and embarrassing her.

About that I will never know. She died in 1980.

In Oxford I found her to be a grownup young woman, beautiful and self assured after living in India as the eldest daughter of an important civil servant. I must have seemed somewhat gauche to her but she and her mother and brother and sister were very nice to me. We played tennis. They put me up for the night and I took the three young people into Oxford in the Renault and we went to a cinema in the evening. By what seemed to me a trick of fate the film was Noel Coward's "Bitter Sweet", and that never to be forgotten song "I'll see you again, whenever spring breaks through again..."

I was in some sort of mental agony the whole time I was with them. Peggy did probably give me the chance to talk to her, but I was totally incapable of doing so, and I drove back to Hamble the next morning in great distress, really hoping I would never get there.

In Hamble Maud had destroyed all my letters from Peggy which was a natural but cruel thing to do. The die was cast so to speak. I could not accept it and never really did. This was my crime against Maud, that I never really accepted that I was married to her. Although I do think perhaps she could have made it easier for me and might have won me over had she tried to see my problem in the early days of our marriage and been a little warmer and less influenced by her reading and theories.

For our honeymoon we went to an hotel in Midhurst by train, only a short distance. It was an area well known to Maud from her younger days and not having any transport we did a lot of walking locally and also visited Petworth by bus. The March weather was not too kind to us.

Maud had found a cottage to rent near Cadnam on the north side of the New Forest, lovely country of heathland and forest. We moved in with a minimum of furniture and possessions immediately after our honeymoon.

The cottage was really the gate lodge of the Crossthwaite Eyre estate. It was of reasonable size, being two storey with three small rooms up and down stairs. There was electric lighting but I cannot remember much plumbing! Water was gained from a proper well with a wind up bucket in front of the house. There was a small garden behind.

We did quite a lot of work on the house and garden and Maud made it attractive inside using her artistic abilities. Shortly after we moved in Maud's assistant at her embroidery work came to live with us, to help about the house and, until the arrival of our child, with Maud's work

From the very first Maud made the mistake of putting us in separate rooms and this to me unsatisfactory state reigned for the next eighteen months. In English bourgeois society of that period the matter of sleeping together or not went through phases, and this time in Maud's mind was one of the Not phases! But the arrangement was not my idea of marriage, not simply from the sex point of view but because coming from a very warm family, closeness was most important where love was involved.

Maud never had any idea of how poor we really were and during most of the time we lived together she had domestic help. Having had an Indian upbringing I suppose this was natural to her, and she was always much better at getting her own way than I was! I had the nerve to ask for a raise soon after I got married, I had only been in the office for about three months and was smartly told that I did not get a rise just because I got married!

Our baby son was born without trouble at Lyndhurst Cottage Hospital on the 26th of June- a good time to be born- and I drove them home after a few days in an ancient MG that I was tinkering with. Maud chose the name Tyl for our son, with the O'Brien thrown in to keep it in the family. Tyl because Maud was at the time reading the life story of Tyl Eulenspeigel, a Flemish nobleman of the middle ages, an unofficial court jester and practical joker. As far as I can remember from the story he was also a sort of Robin Hood but apparently went too far with some of his pranks against V.I.P's and lost his head!

My Tyl is also a bit of a comedian at times and very uninhibited.

I was very happy to have a son, it was a good summer and the happiest time of the marriage in spite of the frustrations. Maud called our home "Three Bears Cottage". She adored her baby and I think was very happy at that time.

Living in Cadnam meant I had a 12 mile ride to and from work, through an area now vastly built up and through Southampton town itself, the old town with it's historic 'Bar Gate' through which the trams had to pass going up and down the main street. Hitler sorted this problem out by levelling some of the surrounding buildings, and in the rebuilding the street was re-routed on both sides of it. However I was young and as all who have done it know, riding a good motorcycle is a pleasure or a challenge in any weather.

For a time after Tyl was born Maud had as a domestic help an Estonian girl as an au-pair. The girl had virtually no English, was a real peasant with no charm whatsoever, continually wanted to get to the city lights, and we were not sorry when she left us.

It was at about this time that there occurred the Abdication Crisis when Edward VIII wished to marry the divorcee Mrs Simpson, causing an unprecedented constitutional problem. People generally were very divided on the issue. Maud and I and most of our friends were rather pro-Edward, considering ourselves broadminded. With hindsight I know we were wrong. Edward was a weak man and was inclined towards the extreme right in Europe...and I don't think there was much good to be said for Mrs S either.

At that time we got little information in the papers we read about what was really going on in Germany. We knew little of the fierce nationalism worked up and worked upon by Hitler when he became Chancellor in 1933, his flouting of the clauses of the Versailles Treaty in relation to rearmament, nor of his effective crushing of the left wing parties, particularly the Communists, after the Reichstag fire. This was thought by many, and probably rightly, to have been the work of Goering precisely with that end in view. Unfortunately for the world Britain had rather weak right-wing governments at the time and certain of the upper classes in the country were favourably disposed to Fascism in Italy, Germany and in Spain.

IN THE Summer of 1936 I competed for what was probably the premier award in the dinghy world at that time, The Prince of Wales Cup for the International 14ft class dinghies. One of the rules for this race was that it should be sailed in the open sea and in a different location each year. Prior to the P.O.W. race itself there were several days of racing within Falmouth's large and beautiful natural harbour.

I was only able to compete because Tom Thornycroft, Peter's father, carried 'Dawn' down to Falmouth and back on the deck of his large motor yacht 'King Duck'. He had a dinghy of his own and was a pretty good helmsman too.

Nick agreed to sail with me and to drive us down to Falmouth in the old Renault with camping and sailing gear. The drive down was a bit nerve wracking for me at times. The top speed of the Renault in gear was about 45, but in neutral its terminal velocity was almost infinite and some of the hills in Somerset and Devon were long and steep. I still have a vision of Nick crouched over the steering wheel thoroughly enjoying himself, only just managing to keep the car- which was directionally very unstable at speed-on the road, myself sweating gently and nearly pushing my right foot through the floor, praying that we might reach the bottom of the hill before we met any traffic coming up.

We had a great week's sailing, camping and socialising as far as our limited finances permitted, most of the other dinghy owners were comparatively wealthy people. These boats were very expensive. Most beautifully built of Honduras mahogany, they were finished and all varnished to the smoothness and gloss of very expensive furniture. Mostly built by the inimitable Uffa Fox at Cowes, and a few by Morgan Giles of Teighnmouth in Devon.

Giles had been one of the world's top designers and builders of centreboard boats and a number of the class boats he designed are still sailing in many parts of the world, including Bombay, (about which more later in my story) and on Ireland's Shannon the Shannon One Designs, 18ft completely open boats.

We had no great success but always managed to beat a few boats which was as much as we reckoned we could achieve but we did learn a lot. And Uffa Fox was just as free with his advice to us as to any of the people sailing his own boats. I always considered him a friend of mine, I had met him on his floating home a year or two previously, and bought all the books he produced before the war: they are still a wonderful record of particularly British and American sail and power craft of the period.

At the time it was always a bit of a mystery how he managed to get the various designers to hand over their plans for him to publish. I'm sure it wasn't with money because I don't think he ever had any! But he did have great charm and must have used that instead!

He was at one time described as the uncrowned king of Cowes but not by 'the best people'! In his youth he was a bit of a prankster and a thorn in the side of the local police, he loved shocking people and exposing their hypocrisy. After the war Uffa became quite a friend of the British Royal Family and taught the Duke of Edinburgh and others how to sail.

He had also been quite well known to the Yachting fraternity in Dun Laoghaire in pre-war days, when he sometimes lectured at clubs there. There are stories of one lecture he gave- perhaps his last-! when he told of some of his funny experiences, which were not generally considered suitable for mixed company, and some of the ladies got up and left the room, and Uffa was not invited to lecture there again!

The last time I met Uffa was when he and I were judges in Ireland's first boat show held in Dublin's Busaras in 1961 or 1962.

The Prince Of Wales that year was won by Peter Scott (later to be the famous ornithologist) and John Winter sailing 'Lightning' jointly. It was also the first occasion in competitive dinghy sailing when the Trapeze was used... and in that class it was promptly banned! We saw it first from Dawn as a man in a boat ahead of us apparently standing horizontally on her side! He was of course suspended by a wire, invisible to us, from the mast.

*

At that time the famous clipper 'Cutty Sark' was languishing and deteriorating on a mooring in the harbour opposite Falmouth, and one free evening we sailed over to her, got permission to climb aboard and then, at our own risk to go aloft. I bet Nick I could touch the truck of the main topmast before he could do the same on the foremast. I don't remember who won the bet but it was a risky venture, most of her cordage and ratlins were rotten and we had to climb mostly by the standing rigging, and I had finally to shin up the top-mast which was a completely bare pole about twenty feet long and ten inches in diameter.

A few years ago I happened to be near Greenwich and walked down to the graving dock where 'Cutty Sark' was permanently berthed, and as an old man I gazed aloft and said to myself, "I don't believe it, it must have been a dream!"

*

Soon after this Falmouth trip I bought the only 'sports car' I have ever owned. It cost me £27 and it was an M.G., or at least it had the badge and the radiator of that marque. Basically a 1927 Morris Oxford, the car was an open tourer with a hood, red painted wire wheels, and a windscreen that folded onto the bonnet. Under the bonnet was a more or less standard Morris side valve engine, with a very modest power output: but then it was far from young, and did at least produce a very satisfactory sporty exhaust note and carried my small family round the Forest and over to Hamble occasionally.

My old Triumph motorbike came to its end around this time. I set off one saturday afternoon to have a sail in 'Dawn', which I was then keeping at a small boatyard near Totton at the top of the tidal estuary of the River Test and where Nick kept 'Wanderer', the boat he has had nearly all his life, an Itchen Ferry Punt. These 'punts' were small sailing fishing boats about 21-22ft long. They were peculiar to Southampton Water and the Solent from the turn of the century onwards, they were quite fast and made excellent small cruisers.

On the way carrying the sails and my gear on the motorbike tank in front of me I pulled up at a shop in Cadnam and immediately the engine burst into flames between my legs! In my haste to get off I lost the balance of the bike and it fell over on the road. I just managed to get the sails and gear away from the blaze, only a little scorched, before the fire really got going with the petrol leaking out round the filler. By the time a passing motorist managed to put it out with an extinguisher the bike was a total loss.

For a while I used the M.G. to go to work but it was relatively expensive to use. However I had recently bought a badly crashed but almost new 600cc twin port Norton from a garage for £5 and was already rebuilding it from the ground up. This turned out to be a magnificent machine and I rode it for the next two years and only had the one crash!

(Due to singing, reported elsewhere!)

*

Our nearest and best friends at the time we were living in Cadnam were a young couple, the Weares, Tony and his wife whose name I cannot remember. They had a cottage on the edge of the common at Lyndhurst and were both competent professional artists, she concentrated on portraiture and he was more general, making his living principally with a strip cartoon he did over quite a few years for the London Evening Standard. It was a 'Western' and concerned a certain Matt Marriot who I think historically was a real character. Someone else wrote the story and Tony illustrated it. I had no idea these strips involved so much work until I saw Tony at it. His studio was full of 'props', saddles and bridles and guns of all sorts. There were stetson hats, gunbelts and general clothing and if he happened to be working you were liable to be dressed up for some scene he was drawing. His drawings were quite large and in great detail, he said that if the details were not accurate some wise guy would write in and complain! The advantage of this work was that he could work hard for several weeks and get well ahead of requirement and then take time off.

Tony was quite a character, he was in his mid or late twenties at the time and had been in the British army for a spell some years previously. He and a friend whom we also met decided that they wanted to learn to ride in the proper military manner and went to the Recruiting office in Southampton. There they told the sergeant on duty that they wanted to serve their country! But only in the Scots Greys, the cavalry regiment. The sergeant was not too sure about that but in the end they were enlisted into 'The Greys' and stayed with them for a year or so until they reckoned there was little more to learn about riding and then bailed themselves out!

After that Tony teamed up with a couple of professional tramps to get a line on another side of life and lived rough with them. He knew they were a couple of rogues and robbed him without embarrassment when they could. The three of them carried all their possessions in a little hand barrow, including some pictures supposedly theirs, which Tony painted for them to spread on pavements or lean against walls beside their begging bowl.

One of these pictures, devised by Tony was double sided, one side was clean, the other had a painted wet stain down it.Then when a lady with a dog following her passed by they turned the picture round and called out, "Oi miss look what yor dawg's done", pointing to the picture, when hopefully she would say 'oh my poor men I'm so sorry'and put a half crown in their bowl!

THE WINTER of 1936-37 was uneventful, working a six and a half day week at Supermarines, while at home the infant Tyl was at the centre of things. I was very happy at work but was not settling into domestic life and when early in 1937 I read in an advertisement in the Daily Telegraph of a prospective Antarctic expedition seeking suitable personnel for the team, I applied. I later went for an interview in London and was accepted as expedition handyman and ships carpenter in the British Antarctic Expedition of 1937, to be called up in due course. This did not happen until the following September.

I still have the leaflet setting out the very ambitious objects of the Expedition. We were only to be paid pocket money, except for myself as the only married man in the team apart from the Commander. I can't remember what my wage was to be but it wasn't much. Reward was to be a share in the profits from films, written matter and commissioned survey work. It was expected that we would be away for about two years, without the home leave that air transport has made possible now. I don't know what Maud thought about it, but she probably felt it might get some of the restlessness out of me, and she did not raise any strong objection.

For part of my summer holiday from 'Super's' I planned a solo cruise in my dinghy 'Dawn'. The idea was to go as far west as time and weather would permit. However, an International 14, a completely open and somewhat overcanvassed boat was not an ideal cruiser but I made a canvas foredeck for her to keep out some of the spray and a large, long, low, more-or-less watertight box in which to keep spare clothes, sleeping bag and food.

It was in late July when I set sail from Totton and in perfect conditions sailed down Southampton water and then westward down the Solent to Hurst Castle and up the Milford Haven creek, a distance of about 26 miles. There I spent the night afloat very happily on a Li-Lo airbed on the bottom of my boat with only the sky above. The next day was equally kind to me, and with a fair wind and tide most of the way I sailed into Poole harbour in the afternoon, another 25 miles. My only problem was sunburn, I had no hat and had taken no precautions, my face and particularly my lips were badly burnt and took a long time to recover. I had no means of getting a weather forecast except ashore, and so was not aware that the weather was about to break, and that I had got as far as I was going to get.

However, the matter was settled in another way. When I sailed into Poole Harbour I found that another class of dinghies of that period, The National 12-footers, were holding their annual championships and sixty or seventy of them were racing round the buoys. (The National Twelves were a restricted class like the Fourteens, so anyone could design and build them, and they both gave great scope for experiment and innovation. I designed and built boats to both classes later.)

I was drifting about with reefed mainsail as the wind was freshening and rescued the crew of one capsized dinghy and towed their boat ashore, and then we decided to all go out in Dawn and watch the finish of the race. Sadly, now with a full mainsail and three people sitting out it was too much for my beautiful hollow spruce mast, and it collapsed, which put an end to my cruise.

By pure chance when at the Parkstone Yacht club in the evening I met a distant cousin of mine, a Dr Hamilton who had a practice in Bournemouth. He had just chartered an ex-Brixham trawler of the type known as a Mule for a cruise with his wife and twin sons who were aged about twelve. So, being rather short handed he invited me to join them for a few days.

Mules, and why so named I never found out, were big heavily built fishing vessels. They were 50 to 60 ft long and cutter rigged, and this one had an auxiliary engine. The sailing gear was very heavy and not very efficient.

We motored out from Poole Quay the next morning, intending to make for Weymouth, and hoisted sail after passing through the narrow entrance crossed by the Swanage ferry. With a beam wind and in the lee of the land we soon passed Swanage and were in the open Channel. We then found that the Mule was a very poor performer against a strong wind and quite a big sea. After tacking backwards and forwards for a couple of hours without being able to weather St Albins head, and with nearly all of us seasick, we gave it up and turned east and headed for the Solent. We entered the Lymington River in mid-afternoon.

I knew this river to some extent from dinghy sailing there and offered to act as pilot. Unfortunately we met the Yarmouth ferry coming out. The tide was ebbing and this car and passenger ferry both pushes a lot of water in front of her and sucks it off the muddy banks. I had not allowed for this and in giving the ferry room, grounded 'good and proper'. They put me ashore with the dinghy to catch the train to Brockenhurst and so home, feeling somewhat mortified! My last view of the Mule from the Lymington Pier station was of her laying over at a most awkward angle with the family still aboard and several hours to wait for the tide to come back and float them!

Late that summer when back at Supers, I had a letter from the Leader of the Antarctic Expedition explaining that he had got on free charter a 2,000 ton steel auxiliary sailing ship "The Westward" which was lying in the Thames Estuary off Southend. He wanted me to join her and work to prepare her for sea and help get the necessary certificates for carrying the 80 or so first class passengers she was arranged to accommodate. His idea was to do a World circumnavigating cruise to make money and take the expedition stores and team to New Zealand. There he was arranging to take over a small timber ship the "Penola"- strengthened for ice- on her pending return from another expedition.

The truth was that the Leaders were having difficulty with sponsorship, and were not getting on too well with the Royal Geographical Society, the Scott Institute and other possible sources of finance, and this charter offer seemed the answer to a prayer.

I was genuinely very keen to go to the Antarctic, having been brought up on the heroic and historic tales of Scott, Shackleton, Amundesen and others. I also had the urge to get away from domestic life. On the other hand I knew I was a fool to throw away a very interesting job in which I had good prospects- but then I was only 24 and not very wise!

I handed in my notice at 'Supers' and I hope explained my reasons for leaving to Mr Shenstone who had been so good to me, (he was having domestic trouble himself), and a week later I packed up my books and instruments, and a few days later set off for Southend on the Norton. This involved a ride through London from west to east, a journey which I did many times over the next four months as we generally had weekends off.

Leaving my bike at a garage I took the little train to the end of Southend Pier, reputed to be the longest in Britain. From the end of the pier I had a good view of "The Westward" about a mile away up the estuary, painted light grey with white deck houses. She had four masts, and was rigged 'fore and aft' -like a yacht- and with only a square sail on the foremast, and a long bowsprit over her clipper bow and figurehead.

I was a bit ahead of my appointed pick-up time but the weather was fine and the pier was crowded with trippers to watch. After a while I saw a lifeboat pull away from the ship and come down rapidly on the strong ebb tide, being rowed by four of my shipmates to be, with the man acting as expedition secretary steering. Being designed basically as load carriers lifeboats generally are most unhandy craft and very heavy to row. In trying to avoid being carried past the pier by the tide they missed the landing stage and were carried under the pier and got mixed up with its legs. It took them a long time to get clear and pick me up, and it then took the hell of a long time to get back to the ship, even though they took my advice and rowed up along the shallow water out of the tide and then cut out across it. We learned later to use the tides to our advantage as do all old hands.

On climbing aboard I was met by Mr Walker, who I suppose reasonably had given himself the title of Commander and met all the fourteen or so people aboard which included Mrs Walker. Apart from the Walkers and the second in command Mr Kent we were all treated as equals although some of us were qualified scientists and specialists and some just aspiring explorers! The total complement for the Expedition was to be 23 men, the rest to join later.

I was allocated quarters in a first class cabin and given the task with one helper of putting the cabins in order. This consisted of freeing out literally hundreds of cupboard doors and drawers which were made of white european oak, kiln dried, and as they had never been used since the ship had been converted to passenger carrying, they had swollen in the damp atmosphere. I was also told to inspect the eight lifeboats and repair them as necessary. It did not take me long to realise that virtually all were beyond mere repair and would never pass Board of Trade inspection. But the one we were using was just about serviceable, and I did some work on it.

My mate Welfar -I don't think we ever knew his first name and just called him Welf- and I filled cabin after cabin with shavings as we worked along the accommodation decks, and became great friends at the same time.

Welfar was about my age and the son of a Norfolk fruit farmer, he was also the amateur welterweight boxing champion of East Anglia. He was the caricature of a boxer with a broken nose and cauliflower ears, but he had the sweetest nature of any man I have ever met, and completely without a temper.

We set up a 'ring' in one of the holds and he and I used to spar in the evenings, he taught me a lot and of course could have knocked spots off me had he wanted to, but I was able to give him a little practice and exercise and keep myself fit too. I never forgot him and a few years ago tried to track him down in Norfolk, and eventually located two of his sons, two rather tough young men making a living hiring out fruit crates to growers. They told me their Dad had been dead for some years-cancer again.

For the first month or so the weather was good and we had tripper launches round the ship all day, quite a lot of whom we invited to come and see over the ship for a small contribution towards the Expedition funds. There were also picture postcards of the ship with signatures of the Expedition members on them, which we the other ranks were supposed to sell. But because we were always broke, one of us took an unofficial photo of the ship, got prints, signed them and forged the officers' signatures and sold them for our beer and baccy fund!

Some of us grew beards, -unusual then, got pretty suntanned and put on the act of being tough explorers, in spite of the fact that I think only one had ever been near Antarctic ice, even Walker had only experience in Northern Canada. One of my special friends Frank Shuttleworth, an engineer, was an experienced high altitude climber. He was made chief engineer of the Westward, his job like mine was to get the ship ready for sea as far as the engine room was concerned. The two early type diesel engines had been long out of use and he did not get them running until after I had left the ship. However he did get the generator going so we had light and also the donkey boiler which was required for heating and even for cooking - steam was used for heating the cooking ovens- electricity for the hot plates.

My other special friends aboard were Hubener a seaman of Dutch origin who had been to the Antarctic and Buckinghan, Buck for short. He was a huge young man who made his living by being an extra in films where large men were wanted, and he had also worked with some oil exploration company. There was also another seaman Franklin who was on the fringe of our 'clique'.

We had only been aboard for a couple of weeks when the "the management" decided that the "crew" should not be in the first class accommodation and should remove to the forecastle. The forecastle was in a very bad and dirty state, so we were ordered to clean and paint it up.

At some previous time in the ship's history but since the conversion, some of the accommodation cabins had been stripped out and a small fish meal plant installed. There had apparently been some scheme that the ship would be used partly for shark fishing and would produce oil and meal from the catch. The plant had never been used and the furnishings and plumbing fittings were removed and stacked in one of the holds. Most of us felt somewhat bloody minded about the move, we had not signed on as crew in the ordinary sense and the cabins we were moved from were not required. But we set about making a real job of the forecastle refit.

We dragged up from the hold everything we needed to make it quite luxurious, dividing it into two-berth cabins with running water, curtains etc, comfortable bunks and heating. Somebody's girlfriend while visiting the ship painted some suitable pictures on the bulkheads! And we moved in. But from then on the atmosphere on the ship changed and it was them and us!

It dawned on us quite early that the owner of the ship, I think he was one of the major tea importers, knew what he was doing in offering the free charter because he would get his ship back in seagoing order, and the effect on the 'Expedition' was that a large amount of the expedition funds began to disappear into the "Westward". But we did make progress with the fit out and actually repainted her topsides from the lifeboat and plank seats slung over the sides.

Walker had engaged an old sea captain with sailing experience, but unfortunately he had spent most of his life on the China Station with all coolie crews, and he was not very tactful with us! Consequently we were always taking 'the micky' out of him. Painting from the lifeboat was a bit of a pantomime, it was far from calm weather at the time and as a big swell was running up the Estuary the boat was going up and down the ships side like a lift and when the Captain was on board we managed to see that he got liberally splashed with grey paint. He also decided- quite rightly- that the ships sails which were stowed in a hold should be brought on deck for his inspection.

The three gaff headed mainsails were huge and extremely heavy and were rolled up into giant Anaconda snakes and should have been hoisted on deck by means of the steam winches which were used to hoist them up the masts, but they were all unserviceable at the time and anyhow the donkey boiler was untested for high pressure. It required nearly all hands to get them on deck, climbing companionway ladders with sections of the sails draped over our shoulders. We opened them up and restowed them straight down the hatches and I never saw them set.

At first we were made welcome by the Southend Town Council because we were an added attraction for the trippers and they issued us with free passes on the pier railway. On the whole I think we were well behaved when ashore. However one night when I can honestly say I was not there there was a serious bust up with some of the local lads in a pub and a certain amount of damage done to personnel and property and the passes were withdrawn- probably the season was just about over anyhow.

It was about that time that I got into a serious fight on board. Walker engaged two casuals who claimed they were seamen. Welshmen, they brought aboard some welsh brand of Poteen which we all sampled, but I don't think it was the cause of the fight as it was in the daytime and in my cabin. I do not remember what it was about but I got into a quarrel with one of these men and he suddenly drew a knife, and I completely lost my temper and somehow got the knife away from him and then proceeded to nearly murder him. He kicked up such a row that some of my friends came rushing into the cabin and managed to rescue him, although they were all on my side. This was followed by a sort of courtmarshall and the two men were discharged...the last I saw of my adversary was of him standing up in the boat as they were rowed ashore, shaking his fist at me standing on deck and swearing that if he ever met me again he would cut my throat!

*

I set off most weekends on the Friday evening for the long ride home. I quite often took Buck with me on the pillion of the Norton as far as the West End of London where he had a girl friend.

At that time there were still many streets in the East End of London with trams and consequently tramlines which a motorcyclist had to treat with the greatest respect! The East India Dock road is particularly memorable as a long straight stretch of wet cobbles and tramlines.

With Buck who must have been nearly twice my weight looking over my head it was very hard for me to steer the bike as I wanted and not as he wanted in dodging the tramline points, crossings and all the traffic...but we never did have a fall.

One night when we were belting along the open road between Southend and London, I became aware thro' my leather helmet that Buck was swearing at me and shouting at me to slow down, and as soon as I did a police car passed me and forced me to stop, I thought he was going to charge me for speeding -which I am sure I was- but no I was making too much noise! (I thought the bike made a lovely noise and not all that loud !)

"Have you taken all the baffles out of those silencers" asked the policeman. I strongly denied that I had because I hadn't, he didn't believe me and produced a steel tape measure and pushed it up first one silencer and then the other, too obviously there was absolutely nothing inside! He seemed very nice about it and a little amused and took my particulars, suggesting that I might hear more about it and I thought he would let it go but he didn't.

I was fined later!

WHILE I was away on the Ship, for reasons never made clear to me, the Crossthwaite Eyres terminated the lease which Maud had made with them. This must have been on a monthly or even a weekly basis, but anyhow Maud moved out and into lodgings in a house on the southern outskirts of Lyndhurst, not far from the Weir's. And so it was to this house that I returned at weekends for the remainder of my time on the Westward.

Winter was now setting in on the Thames Estuary and with it came fog, - in pre Radar days the dreaded enemy of the mariner and still of the small boat yachtsman- and the departure of the trippers. We got our share of it that winter, really dense stuff that made shore going impossible. One shore party did get caught out on coming back in the half light and fog and with the tide going up the Estuary they missed the ship. And this in spite of the fact that the bell that was rung at two minute intervals- a statutory requirement at all times in fog, - and an unpopular duty that fell to each of us in turn. The shore party got completely lost and only returned next morning when the fog had cleared, having spent a very cold miserable night in the open boat on a mudbank somewhere up the Estuary.

A small dinghy was acquired and this made it possible for small parties to get ashore and we became a bit more practical in dealing with fog and tides using a small compass to give us sense of direction and getting back to the ship at a definite time so that those aboard could make a lot of noise and keep an oral watch.

*

Some of us on the Westward were to the Left politically, and were very concerned with the way things were going in the Civil War in Spain.

The Popular Front, which had won the election in early 1936, looked like being defeated by the Fascist forces of Franco. He had military and material support from Hitler and Mussolini in ever increasing measure, while the treacherous French Government forbade arms sales to the Republican side and the British Conservative Government blockaded the Spanish Atlantic ports. They also tried to prevent British subjects from volunteering to fight on the Republican side.

Meanwhile Hitler was able to test his latest aircraft in battle. He had already heavily bombed the city of Guernica and was ferrying Moroccan troops into Spain in his transport aircraft.

People from Ireland who supported the Republic formed a unit in the International Brigade and lost about 59 men, considerably more than half the volunteers. Irishmen supporting Franco, known as The Blueshirts, never saw front line action.

The Republic was only finally defeated with the fall of Madrid about four months before the outbreak of World War 2. The Spanish and the International brigades were the first people to put up a determined resistance to the advance of Fascism and Naziism in Europe, and received virtually no official support from the Democracies or the U.S.

During the course of this war the majority of the media in England made little of it and of its implications, just as it made little of the terrible things which were already happening to the Jews and the political left in Germany and Italy. About this time somebody lent me a book about the situation in Italy called "Fontamara". This painted a terrible picture of the true situation there and advanced my political thinking.

My reading generally of current affairs up to the end of 1937 was, if anything, to the right of centre and it was only Shuttleworth and other people on the Westward who made me begin to think more broadly.

I do now strongly believe in keeping history alive and am today depressed by how little is known by the young about how the last war came about and how few take any real and intelligent interest in World Affairs. I was as bad myself as were most of my class and generation, which made it possible for terrible things to happen at the other side of this mist-this wall of ignorance and indifference.

*

As Christmas '37 approached a feeling of frustration began to arise among the 'Crew' many of whom had given up good jobs to join the Expedition and one by one they started to leave the ship. And of course there were many who had never actually come aboard.

A section of us even started to think about setting up a a small scale expedition on our own.

There was a timber built auxiliary brigantine 'The Waterwitch' available at that time and we reckoned she could be strengthened for ice. For finance we hoped for sponsorship- not so readily available in those days as it is now- and by just sailing her round the British coast and begging from port to port we hoped to raise money. The plan came to nothing.

We knew the Ship would have to be dry docked for a Hull Survey, so arrangements were made to have her towed up to Gravesend pending docking. I missed the actual move and I found her gone from her old mooring off Southend when I returned. But I knew where she was going- onto fore and aft moorings in mid stream off the P.L.A.(Port Of London Authority) pier at Gravesend- and I rode back there via Tower Bridge and found her laying off in a sluicing ebb tide. This was impossible for the dinghy and I had to wait for near low water before I got aboard again.

The Gravesend Reach of the Thames was (and it probably still is!) a pretty dreary part of the river, particularly in winter with its frequent fog and smog. Even then it was an area of industry, particularly paper mills, which were supplied with the necessary wood pulp from Scandinavia.

The buoys we were on were frequently used by Norwegian and Finnish ships awaiting docking and they came alongside at all hours and we had to turn out to assist mooring. We were able to fraternise with their crews in so far as language would permit. Most of the ships were old British freighters, very rundown with very poor crew accommodation and pay, even the officers were very badly paid by British standards of the day.

These Scandinavian countries were then very poor, a great contrast to their state to-day, where both have a very high standard of living. Norway now has one of the biggest and best merchant fleets in the world and Finland is building some of the most advanced cruise and merchant ships, with a standard of workmanship and finish second to none.

Little old Ireland has been left far behind in all these things and it is a sad reflection on the people of an island nation.

*

I had been thinking about what to do in the future and soon after the start of the new year (1938) I quit the Expedition. Not without regret, because I had been very keen to get to the Antarctic, but there did not seem to be any future in that direction. I was living partly on my capital and made up my mind to do what I really wanted to do- design and build boats!

I said goodbye to my friends on the Westward and went off and did some scouting along the Hampshire- Dorset coastline and picked on Poole Harbour as the most likely spot to start a small business. I was totally ignorant of business, of book keeping and balance sheets etc and just thought that if I could build boats, - which I could- I could make a living for myself and my small family.

I set about finding a site near the water. I borrowed about £750 from my Aunt Vi and bought the end house of a terrace in Hamworthy, on the west side of Poole Quays but without direct access to them. The nearest access to the harbour itself was past the Hamworthy and Bournemouth Sailing Club. I believe it is a Yacht club now but was generally known as the Ham and Bone Club then! The club had a very nice club house, a dinghy slip and offshore moorings.

The house being an end one had a garden of a little over a quarter of an acre and I assembled at the back of it a 24ft by 12ft pre-fab timber hut I bought, adding in extra windows.

Instead of redecorating the house and moving into it Maud found a small newly built bungalow to rent, on what was called the Lake Estate, about a mile from my 'yard'. Its only attraction was its situation on rising ground at the top end of the estate. It should have had a good view of the Harbour and the Purbeck Hills beyond but this was blocked by the rather miserable remains of a wood of small fir trees.

A little garden had been left by the builder full of rubble and brambles which we never got cleared up in the fifteen months we lived there. The bungalow was square in plan with just four rooms and bathroom, the two front rooms became our bedrooms and as I was fully involved with my 'business' all my waking hours, Maud and I did not see much of each other.

We were both selfish or self-centred in our different ways. I felt that Maud might have lived in the terrace house -it could have been made quite nice, although on a fairly busy terminal road- and learned to help with office work. I was also aggravated by the fact that she had a daily morning help which we could not afford. Maud in turn no doubt felt I took too little interest in our baby, our home and her interests. I did however always have a car of sorts, first the old M.G. and then an almost equally ancient Alvis, also an open tourer which was an ex-police car. If driven fast for a few minutes, this suddenly boiled its cooling water and blew the contents of the radiator straight into the air. This blinded the driver and sprayed the passengers with very hot water. To get to and from work I used a rather sporty bike with racing handlebars for economy and exercise.

I did take the family for drives and visits most weekends because Maud had no friends in the neighbourhood and she never ever learned to drive.

We did later become friendly with a near neighbour who was a portrait artist of some note. He specialised in prominent local personalities such as

Lord Mayors and Masons, and then me!

This picture was commissioned by my Aunt Evey and it hangs to-day not in the Royal Yacht Squadron but in what was my grand children's play room in East Sussex! A head and shoulders portrait, I am shown wearing a white sailing smock. This in years to come will, I expect, be mistaken for a surgeon's operating gown and I will have become a famous surgeon!

*

The sort of ill wind that blows somebody some good blew up just after all the yachts and 16ft "Snipe" class boats had been launched at the beginning of the sailing season. It blew me a great deal of repair work and the chance to build one of these Snipe- which were the local one design class. It also introduced me to various members of the "Ham and Bone Club" of which I became an active member and this gave me the courage to borrow some more money and start building a 60 by 40ft permanent workshop and install some woodworking machinery.

I just called myself SMALL CRAFT, cut out the letters in blue Perspex and mounted them across the front of the building.

I never established the business as a limited company as I suppose I should have done, and from the beginning my finances were generally in a pretty precarious state.

I well remember one visit to my bank when the manager remarked in a fatherly way "You know Mr Kennedy you are in business to make money"! I don't know what I said to him but to myself I think I probably said "Good Lord I never thought of it in that way!"

I just wanted to design and build boats and being paid for it was a secondary consideration! Indeed my wife used often remark 'that is why you never made any'! Too true I'm afraid.

I had another stroke of luck when I was building the main shed. The Southern Counties Agricultural Show was held at Wimbourne that year- not far away- and somebody told me that after the show was over all the stands were sold off by auction. I went to it and came back with a lorry load of excellent red deal flooring, only a little muddied on one side. I sorted this out, used the slightly knotty timber for a splendid loft floor - which I painted matt black for drawing on- and put the rest aside for a "Dragon" class yacht I was hoping to build at the time.

*

Small Craft existed for just about eighteen months before England declared war on Germany. Certain things stand out in this part of the film of my life.

For one thing I met Peggy.

I heard that she was staying with all her family in The Mayflower Hotel in Lymington. It was summertime and they were home on leave from India, I phoned and asked her to come sailing with me! I knew she knew something of sailing as an uncle had a yacht on the Lymington River and to take her sailing was something I'd dreamt of doing since my days with 'Rusheen' in Ireland.

If I considered Maud's feelings on the matter I rode rough shod over them. Peggy agreed to come and I drove over to Lymington in the old Alvis and collected her. We drove to the 'Ham and Bone Club', rigged and launched 'Dawn'. And I sailed away in a dream!

It was a perfect day and we sailed right round this rather lovely natural harbour with its islands, creeks and mud banks, stopping only once when we noticed a sign at the end of an old jetty marked TEAS!

The 'Tea House' was on the Arne Peninsular on the north west side of the harbour. It was just a simple country cottage where we had a lovely homely tea. What we talked about that day I haven't the least idea, it wasn't I know sentimental but I still have a feeling we were both in a very happy dream without reality.

When we came back to earth and ashore we drove up to the bungalow but Maud wasn't there so we drove back to Lymington and I met all Peggy's family - I had never met her father before- they were all very friendly but I suppose they couldn't really have approved of me. Peggy came out to see me off and we shook hands, that was all, I drove away without looking back. I never saw her again but have never forgotten her or ceased to wish her well on life's journey.

*

One morning in the early spring of '38 when walking down Poole Quays I noticed in the distance a large sailing vessel coming up the harbour under tow. It suddenly dawned on me that she was a 'four master' with a squaresail yard on the foremast and that her hull was light grey, she could only be the Westward! She let go her anchor in the main channel of the harbour, the only place where she would have enough water to swing in.

That evening I met my friend Frank Shuttleworth ashore and learned the history of Westward's travels since I had left her. Frank had remained on as Chief Engineer, and with the last of the Expedition funds Westward got her passenger certificate and a cruise to the Azores was advertised. She sailed with 20 to 30 fare paying passengers- probably less than half her capacity.

The cruise had turned into a disaster when the engine room staff mutinied and refused to run the main engines because the lack of ventilation in the engine room made conditions impossible. They were by then only in the Western Approaches and they attempted to continue under sail. Progress was so slow that the trip was abandoned and they turned for home only to meet head winds and to find that Westward could barely make any headway against a fresh wind. They were left tacking to and fro off the south Irish coast with food and particularly drink rapidly running out!

She eventually made Plymouth, many days after she was due back, with very indignant passengers aboard. She came to Poole where apparently harbour dues were believed to be modest, to lay up but it was soon found by the harbour authorities that she was causing the main channel to silt up and she was told to clear out. I never heard of her or Frank again.

*

The eighteen months of Small Craft's existence covered two summers. I was too busy to get much sailing, except for a little handicap racing in 'Dawn'. This was usually crewed by Jack, a friend I had made when buying old mahogany furniture and table leaves from the furniture shop he was running with his elderly mother- the cheapest way of getting good seasoned timber for certain parts of the boats I was building.

Jack had reluctantly taken over that rather rundown business after his father died and loved to get away from it whenever he could. I once went with him to an auction of the furniture of a big old house and was somewhat shocked at the way in which the elderly owners were to all intents and purposes cheated by the dealers 'fixing' the auction between them.

That first summer I also crewed 'off and on' on a Twelve Metre yacht belonging to a Bournemouth surgeon, a Mr Adeney. This was mostly in port to port passage races along the south coast.

The yacht 'Iruna' had a professional skipper and usually only two or three amateurs to man her, a very small crew for a yacht of this size, over 70ft on deck. Winches for sail handling were only just coming in then and it was very hard work in any strength of wind. What I enjoyed most was bringing the yacht back to Poole after the races, usually at night and because I did not much care for drinking I was left alone at the helm, the skipper coming on deck occasionally to see that all was well.

There is a great thrill and satisfaction in sailing a large fast yacht in the dark, a great spread of sail above you powering the ship along, the bow wave peeling off and the foaming water streaking past below the steeply slanting deck and the boat obeying your every movement of the helm.

In the winter of '38- '39 I built several small dinghies, one 18footer I called a Camping Cruiser (of which at least six were later built by George Bush in Ireland) and a 'Dragon Class' yacht. This class is still going strong in many parts of the world, including Dublin Bay. The one I built was for the proprietor of the Royal Bath Hotel in Bournemouth. I rather unwisely accepted another yacht as initial payment and there was to be a balance in cash on completion. I think the contract price was £250 complete and even then that was too cheap. I had no cash in hand on the job and then the client got himself killed in a skiing accident. And it was found that he had left no instructions about the Dragon with his family -he was a bachelor- and they did not want to take the yacht or pay the balance.

I managed to sell the other yacht, an old but rather beautiful small racing cruiser designed by Charles Nicholson, an old man then, principal of the firm of Camper and Nicholson at Gosport. I was unable to sell the Dragon because of the war crisis situation. I raced her in her class in the Bournemouth Regatta that year - 1939- and won the premier award, a magnificent bowl of Poole Pottery (which I lost later in the London Blitz).

In the end when Poole harbour was cleared of yacht moorings to make way for the operation of Sunderland flying boats I sailed her over to a creek on the far side of the harbour, anchored her, and sent a note to the Hotel saying where she was and that I took no further responsibility for her. The war followed and I never heard of her again.

Perhaps the most interesting boat I designed and built in '39 was 'Fuss'. The origin of the design was her commissioning by an architect, a member of the Parkstone Yacht Club. He had the idea of starting a smaller and cheaper class of dinghy than the Dolphins, the sixteen footers which were already a strong class in the harbour.

The suggestion was greeted with considerable antagonism, particularly in the Parkstone Yacht Club, and caused such a kefuffle that my client named her 'FUSS' on launch. Fuss quickly proved herself in handicap racing but the world situation was such that she was the only boat built to the design before the war. Post-war boats to the 'Fuss' design became one design classes in several places under different names. Principally the IDRA 14's in Ireland, Waldringfield Dragonflies in Essex and REB 14footers in Durban in Natal

Her near relation, the Yachting World Day Boat is in many places. Basically Fuss was a clench built International 14 but much heavier and with reduced sail area.

The last boat I built almost entirely with my own hands was 'Hiltraut', from the name of a German girl known to her owner Noel Jordan who was a member of the Edgbaston Sailing Club near Birmingham. She was an International 14footer, and perhaps one of the most beautiful boats I ever built. Hiltraut's racing career was interrupted by the war, and I lost touch with her but I heard that she was a successful boat after the War. I certainly put all I knew into her and reckoned I achieved a standard of craft and finish on a par with the dinghies built by Uffa Fox, though perhaps not quite achieving his depth of gloss even after nine carefully applied and rubbed down coats of varnish.

On the other hand I later heard that Uffa got some coach builders in Cowes to apply the final coats, (by coach builders I mean the men who built and maintained State horse drawn coaches), and it was said that they applied the final coats not with brushes or sprays but floated it on with their hands.

I delivered Hiltraut to Edgbaston on the day war was declared, Sunday the third of September, towing her behind the old M.G. on 'Dawn's' rather high and unstable trailer, and very nearly crashing the whole outfit when I got into a speed wobble on a long downhill somewhere on Salisbury Plain. We rigged her immediately on arrival and had a short sail, and then everyone went into the club house and heard Chamberlain tell us over the radio that we were once again at war with Germany.

We left the clubhouse in a very sombre mood, gazing aloft at the hundreds of barrage balloons already up over Birmingham.

It is hard now to recall one's feelings at a time like that. At Trent the then so-called Great War had been close to us with the school roll of honour, and there had been a propeller from one hero's plane on the wall of our dining room. The school library was full of bound copies of *The Illustrated London News* of the first world war period, and this had brought home to us the horror and destruction and carnage of war... and now it was to start all over again. One had a dreadful sick feeling, a sense of unbelief, and a sense of fear too.

I drove straight home, and registered at the labour exchange the next morning. I was there to seek temporary work. I had very little money in the bank as usual! And no income or work for 'Small Craft'.

I was immediately told to report to the big National school in Poole where I was set to work making the timber shuttering for underground air raid shelters. I had only been at this for a few days when I got a message from an acquaintance of earlier dinghy days. John Coste told me that his wife was secretary to Norman Hart, a naval architect with a London office.

Hart was working on a design for the Fairmile Organisation of Cobham in Surrey and was looking for another ship draughtsman...

*

Maud had joined the Peace Pledge Union in the summer of '38 and this led to us meeting a Quaker family, father and mother and two daughters, aged about 19 and 25. Father was the proprietor of an Engineering Works in Ringwood Hants, and a Labour Party supporter. Mother and daughters were all members of the British Communist Party.

We met this family first at a weekend seminar held at their home ourside Ringwood. The weather was fine and the event was all held outdoors in the garden.

I don't know in whose name the seminar was called but it was certainly of 'The Left' as were most of the participants, although many of them including us could have been described as Parlour Pinks! The principal speaker was the journalist Claud Cockburn, best known by the name he used at that time, Frank Pitcairn. He was the producer of a news sheet called 'The Week' -it had been in production since 1933- produced I remember on buff coloured paper and only available by subscription. This was very 'Left' but had an extremely wide readership, of whom Churchill was said to be one. Frank had ears and eyes everywhere it seemed, and access to inside information available nowhere else. He was also a very good speaker and had recently returned from Spain where he was war correspondent for the Daily Worker, the British Communist Party's newspaper.

Frank was no lover of the P.P.U. which he strongly suspected was being used by the forces of the extreme right in England to discourage standing up to Hitler. Most issues of 'The Week'- to which I became a subscriber after that weekend- carried some inside information about what he dubbed 'The Clivedon Set' headed by the Astors. Some members of that family had strong Nazi-Fascist connections.

I have a book of his dispatches from Spain, vividly describing this very one sided war practically from the front line and have also read several of his extremely witty and historical books. He wrote some eighteen books post-War, probably most of them in Ireland living near Youghal- where I visited him shortly before he died in 1981.

Claud -his real name- had at one time been correspondent for the London Times in Berlin and Washington, and finally wrote a weekly column for the Irish Times; Graham Green has described him and G.K.Chesterton as the two greatest journalists of the twentieth century.

Back to the seminar. On a personal level a friendship grew up between our two families, partly because Mr A. was also a boating enthusiast and was converting an ex-RNLI lifeboat into a cabin cruiser so I was able to give him some help, and also because Maud got on well with his wife. Although Maud was not interested in politics, apart from being just anti war, this friendship turned out to be significant later.

We exchanged visits occasionally and in the early summer of '39 organised a weekend picnic with them near Wareham in Dorset on an inland part of the Arne peninsula.

This peninsula was at that time mostly heathland, a nature reserve of some significance. It was beautiful and peaceful with a few scattered cottages- hardly a village. I heard during the war that this delightful place was being used as a battle training area by the army and had been devastated. Now I believe oil has been discovered on this land and that oil rigs are being set up.

It was a scorchingly hot day and after the picnic lunch Maud stayed talking to the parents and the younger daughter D and I a strayed a little apart and under the shade of of a tree got into a most serious political discussion. D had recently returned from a conducted tour of Moscow and Leningrad and was full of enthusiasm for all she had seen and heard of socialism in the USSR. She was already a communist and was well versed in the literature of the subject.

Like most of us she was ignorant of what was really going on behind the scenes and of the ruthless regime which produced the impressive growth of heavy industry in particular. Of course it could be argued that it was this which in the end made it possible for the Red Army to defeat Hitler's armies and so save Europe from even worse pogroms and bloodshed.

D was completely committed but I also noted how physically attractive she was in every way, with her mass of near blond hair, bursting with good health and energy (she was nineteen or twenty at the time). She was quite unconscious of her attractiveness, being so absorbed in convincing me in the rightness of Socialism! This in time would inevitably be followed by communism and eventually (when mankind had been transformed!) by anarchy. It was all Pure Idealism of course, but heady stuff then to many young people. Just as she herself was heady stuff to me!

She made me promise to read Marx's *Das Capital*, plus some of Lenin's works and also those of Frederick Engels.

I hadn't needed much converting and I am a slow reader and a slow absorber of ideas and facts...but nonetheless I joined the communist party as a card carrying member soon after the outbreak of war and in spite of everything I have never regretted it.

I JUMPED at the opportunity. The very next day I went to London and met Norman Hart in his St James West End office, his organisation consisted of Yvonne his secretary and Eric Rouse his hardworking assistant and draughtsman. Norman had been responsible for the design of a number of very attractive motor yachts in the 70 to over 100ft class, these mostly built of steel in Holland. He engaged me to start as soon as possible.

The Admiralty had commissioned the Fairmile organisation of Cobham in Surrey -manufacturers under Reid Rialton of the Rialton sports car- to set up an organisation for the designing and construction of a new class of coastal defence and general purpose boat of about 120 to 130ft. Fairmile then engaged Norman to design the prototype, while Woodnuts of St Helens on the Isle of Wight were to build it. Norman had recently patented a hull shape which eliminated compound curves and so could be built by wrapping flat sheets of steel or plywood round the frames of a vessel. He persuaded Fairmile and the Admiralty to use this method for the prototype and produced the plans for a rather narrow vessel about 120ft on deck, with two 800hp Hall Scott engines.

When I joined Norman's office the basic design was fairly well advanced and my work was mostly on engineering and general details and then in acting as liaison with Woodnuts and working there on the drawing board, shuttling between London and the Isle of Wight. When working in London I lived with the Costes in their Esher home, a much appreciated arrangement. Yvonne and I commuted to town together while John kept more leisurely time at Lloyds Underwriters. Later he got his papers and joined up, being already in the RNVR.

London was then a rather depressing place under its cloud of barrage balloons, with the blackout, the absence of children and, that autumn, the smog. By contrast the Isle of Wight was unchanged except for the blackout and there I found a home with a charming elderly left wing couple, the

Elliots, friends of the A's of Ringwood. They lived in a very original bungalow which they had designed and built themselves, overlooking Bembridge Harbour and Woodnuts boatyard which was only ten minutes walk away down a steep path.

While at Woodnuts I became very friendly with the yard foreman- I wish I could remember his name. He was a most skilled shipwright and the prototype Fairmile grew almost as fast as he got the drawings. He was also a very keen model yacht builder, building really beautiful models to his own ideas and designs and to a strictly controlled one metre class, even in those days radio controlled. We used to sail them and race other similar yachts on the artificial pond at Ryde on Sundays.

It was on one of my spells in London I joined the Communist Party of Great Britain, and became a member of the Westminster branch. It was at about the period known in some circles as the 'phony war', - with only a few skirmishes at sea and in the air. Then the French Government under Deladier arrested all the Communist MP's. This had the effect of confirming in the minds of all those of the 'Left' in the country and especially in London that Hitler was going to strike East against The Soviet Union and would have the tacit blessing of Britain and France. There had been indications in the past that this might happen, and there were certainly many people in high places who hoped for it.

Anyhow the C.P. in London called a public meeting in Hyde Park on the following Saturday and a huge gathering assembled to hear various left wingers speak from the platform (Harry Pollit and Palme Dutt were certainly among them) and a march on the French Embassy was set in motion to petition the French government to immediately release the MP's.

I went to this meeting with D and we marched together. The march was held up at Hyde Park corner by foot and mounted police and a series of scuffles took place in one of which D managed to dismount one of the mounted men, we did not molest him- he was quite young and we gave him back his helmet and helped him remount! The whole thing was comparatively good natured but we were prevented from going to the Embassy; however someone was allowed to take the petition there and the march certainly gave publicity to the arrests and gave some inkling as to what was to come later in the debacle of the French Military when Hitler struck.

At that time the most popular meeting place for all sorts of people of 'The Left' was The Universities Labour Club in Percy St, off Tottenham Court Road. It had a bar and was always packed with people and rumours, many of the people were refugees from Hitler's Germany and it was also frequented by some of the intellectual Irish in London. It was there that I met Sean Dowling, then freshly released from Franco's prison camps and somewhat bitter about how the International Brigade had been run.

The Soviet-Finnish war was also still being fought, a war about territory close to Leningrad (near where coincidentally in 1988 I spent two weeks in a Soviet Guest House). This is land of no value economically, being all sandy soil and lightly afforested. But it is on the Gulf of Finland at the eastern end of the Baltic, strategically very important to Russia.

Mannerheim a close associate of Hitler was at that time in charge of Finnish affairs and of the Finnish army and probably with Hitler's backing refused what was a very fair exchange of territory. And so the Red Army took it after fighting a war which should have revealed its weaknesses. Britain supported Finland even to the extent of giving her some R.A.F. support with Hurricane fighters. And this at a time when we were supposed to be attacking Germany on behalf of Poland, building up the British Expeditionary Force in a comparatively leisurely way while lyric writers wrote ridiculous songs such as "We'll hang up our washing on the Seigfreid Line" etc (The Seigfreid Line was the German equivalent of the Magenot Line in France) and waited for war to commence!

*

About this time I bought a used 500cc Velocette motorcycle, a splendid machine which I rode throughout the war and covered many thousands of miles in government service

Norman had been asked by The Admiralty via Fairmile to prepare plans for a more conventional round bilge boat. This he refused to do maintaining that his design was the best. (Only some dozen of these original Fairmile boats were built whereas hundreds of the Admiralty designed Fairmile 'B's were built).

With the conceit of youth and knowing this, I started work in my own time on a a new design unknown to Norman. I still think it was a good design and had some bright ideas in it, such as carrying a Hurricane on a Gyroscope controlled catapult for merchant fleet protection in more sheltered waters against bombing.

Anyhow, thinking that Norman might be interested I had the temerity to show it to him one day. He was not receptive to say the least, would not even look at it and dismissed me from his office. This was, in fact, probably the beginning of the end of my association with him. A strong conservative, he and Eric were probably fed up with my political ideas so ardently expressed! Sometime in the early part of 1940 I was transferred to the Ministry of Shipping in Berkeley Square.

By this time John Coste had been called up and as it was not 'proper' for me to stay on with Yvonne I moved into temporary bed and breakfast lodgings in a house overlooking Earls Court District Line station. My room was the smallest possible with room for little else than a very uncomfortable bed, breakfast was an equally cramped affair shared with numerous other inmates. And there was the almost continuous noise of trains just below my window to keep me awake. However with the bike I was able to get away at weekends. Maud or I then found a flat in Richmond and she moved up from the New Forest with Tyl, then about three.

I think we were there for only a few weeks when things began to happen in Western Europe and Maud who was pregnant again decided to go to Ireland, to Galway where she ended up in a tiny primitive railwayman's cottage on a level crossing of the defunct Clifden Railway. Here, in the hamlet of Leam, she lived until some time after the birth of Finn in January of '41. He was delivered by the local midwife in front of the open turf fire.

We had camped in this village some time before Tyl was born so Maud had arrived with some contacts. The people of the village were extremely poor, the children going barefoot most of the time, as did most of the kids in the west.

On one occasion on this earlier visit we left our tent and camp to go for a drive in Mother's Austin Seven, which I had borrowed for the holiday and on returning it became obvious that the tent had been entered and a certain amount of our tinned food had vanished. When we asked the children in a neighbouring cottage if they knew anything about this they said that cattle had been round the tent and must have stolen the tins! We had to accept this explanation, feeling that since we obviously had more than two of everything, they were almost entitled to share it with us.

*

My job at the Ministry was that of a ship surveyor, in this case the 'ships' being mostly small vessels of all sorts which were being taken over by the Government- requisitioned- and records had to be made of their condition so that at the time of handing back to their owners only damage in Government service would be made good.(It was known as an 'on survey'). It was quite an interesting job and took me all over the Thames dockland as it was at that time.

Most of the craft were tugs, lighters and miscellaneous small vessels based on the Thames and due to be got away to safer ports. As indeed they were just before the Blitz. I used to hire a taxi in the morning and keep it moving from place to place, while I clambered on and into dozens of boats, and on the way learned quite a lot of the Lightermen's craft, the skill with which they navigated the Thames in these clumsy powerless lighters, using only the tide and a long pole to take I suppose up to 400 tons at a time up and down its tidal waters.

The Ministry building was a large red brick one and must have housed a great many people and I was there when Hitler attacked in the west. We had frequent air raid alerts and hundreds of men and women filed quickly down into the basement complete with gas masks and brief cases. Most of the time I was out and I don't remember any actual bombing, only heavy anti-aircraft fire.

About this time too my little workshop at Poole was requisitioned and became the fire station for Hamworthy and I suppose some small rental was paid into my bank account there.

Also the 'powers that be' caught up with me in two ways. First they found that I had aircraft design experience and then that I was an open member of the Communist Party. I received a message at the Ministry that I was to go for an interview at the factory of the Airspeed Aviation company at Portsmouth aerodrome. This I did, being taken on immediately as a Draughtsman. While there I met George Errington their chief test pilot whom I had met before the War. He was about to deliver a new twin engine Airspeed Oxford to one of the R.A.F. fields defending London and offered me a lift for most of the way back to the city!

My memory of that flight is that because we had no parachutes to sit on we had to sit on our coats, that it was heavily overcast, that without any ceremony we were climbing steeply through thick cloud and then came out of the top to see the clouds standing on end until we levelled off! A half hour flight in the sunshine, a little chat on the radio and we plunged steeply down again and out the bottom of the clouds and into what seemed to me a fierce height loosing sideslip, a level off and we were down and almost immediately the plane was taken over by the ground staff and taxied out of the way of the mostly Hurricane fighters...and then we were driven in a staff car to the nearest station for London.

Things were very tense.

The Dunkirk Evacuation was about to commence when I packed up at the Ministry next day and took a train down to 'Pompey'. I went briefly to Airspeed where I got the address of possible digs and a taxi to get me there. The house was on the northern outskirts of the town, not far from the aerodrome. The digs there were with two firemen and their wives, both of

(Above) The author's mother, Ruby Alice (Mullaly), around 1910
(Right) Nancy, Brien and Doreen Kennedy, c1924

(Below) The author with his mother and his sisters Nancy Abercrombie Kennedy (on left) and Doreen Leigh Kennedy, around 1917

(Above) Steam threshing , Co Wexford, 1916. Children at front are (l to r) Joan and Jack (Plews), Brien, Doreen and Nancy (Kennedy). Miss de Momerancey (governess)

(Above) The author's father, Frederick Alexander Kennedy

(Right) Auntie Vi, Violet Gertrude Mullaly. (d.1958)

(Below) Family picnic at Carnsore, Co Wexford, 1916

(Above) The author with local doctor's coachman at Bellevue, Bray, around 1915

(Left) At Glenade, Manorhamilton, Co Leitrim. G.A. Mullally (author's grandfather) drawing hay

(Below) Knockranny, Kilmacanogue, Co Wicklow, around 1925

(Left) Trent College, Derbyshire, England

(Below) Trent College Library, built by Brien Kennedy and other pupils around 1927

(Right) The author's first self-built boat, Rusheen, on Lough Melvin Co Donegal, 1928

(Below) Transporting 'Rusheen' in author's father's Chrysler, 1927

Supermarine Vickers Spitfire design team, 1936-37, the author at bottom right.

(Previous Page) The author, 1930's. The J.I. Thorneycroft Shipyards at Southampton, and docks from deck of the 800 ton 'Trenora'

(Above) 'Small Craft' premises at Hamworthy, Poole, 1938-39, built by author.

(Left) A 'National 12' building, at Small Craft.

(Below) 'Hiltraut' building, at Small Craft.

(Top Left) The dinghy 'Evolution' at Cowes, 1934

(Top Right and Below Left) 'Fuss', the first of all the 14's

(Bottom Right) The first Dublin Bay IDRA 14', in the Liffey, now demolished gasometer in background

(Above left) Positioning device for centreboard, Hiltraut

(Left) Hiltraut, rear view

(Below) Launch of Hiltraut

(The day 2nd World War was declared!)

(Above) Maud Cooke, the author's first wife

(Right) Tanya and Tyl Kennedy

(Below) Peggy

(Above) Christine Kennedy, at Lymington, in 'the boat I first learned to sail in-how I loved her!' (Written on back of original)

(Below) 'Maia', the author's houseboat at Lymington, a 69 foot ex ASR boat built by Thorneycrofts

(Following page) The author with Christine Wilkinson, his second wife, on board 'Maia', 1947

whom were very pregnant! I had high tea with them and got settled in and then just after dark the sirens went and the men departed at the run and left me with the women. It was one of the worst nights I had in the war. The men had hardly left the house when we heard ack ack in the distance and then all the local guns and the guns on the few ships in the dockyard opened up. We had no air raid shelter and the women would not leave the house to go to a public one, so I had to stay with them and pretend not to be scared.

Soon the noise was undoubtedly that of bombs. The house shook and the doors and windows rattled and cracked -they were taped up- by the state of the women I wondered what sort of a midwife I would make. It seemed a horribly long time into the small hours before the all clear sounded, The men did not return until just before I left for the factory. That was the first serious raid on the city and did a lot of damage.

*

During the short time I had been in the factory the previous day a call had gone out for people competent at handling small craft. I had given my name then and I had only been in the office for an hour or two the next morning when the chief draughtsman sent for me. Thinking I knew what it meant I went excitedly to his office. But he asked me to sit down opposite him and then gave me perhaps the biggest shock of my life when, apparently reading from a letter in front of him and half apologising, he told me to collect my things immediately and leave. He gave me no explanation and it only slowly dawned on me that someone probably at the Ministry had reported me as a communist, and at that time in spite of the communist anti Nazi-Fascist record we were treated as security risks.

There was obviously no room for argument, I think I was given my fare back to London, I collected my things at the house and got the train to London. I did not get a chance to see George again and felt very embarrassed about that. (George was killed test flying an early post war passenger airliner, the Airspeed Ambassador).

In London I went to the flat of Sean Dowling. He had fought with the Irish contingent in the Spanish Civil War, and was temporarily out of work and on the dole. The address was a flat over a grocer's shop on a corner on Theobald's Road in the city and on the 4th floor up a steep wooden stair. There were two other flats besides Sean's. One was that of a young bachelor probably Jewish -a hospital worker- and a definitely Jewish girl known as Topsy who lived with her Alsatian dog and from time to time shared the flat with various female refugees. Topsy was a lovely person, almost grossly fat but everyone, including me, came to love her.

The first morning I was back in London I went along to the local Labour Exchange and signed on for the dole and for four or five weeks was without work, being sent to various prospective jobs, the only one I can actually remember was the drawing office at Hanley Page's the aircraft firm, in Cricklewood. There I was immediately taken on, given a board in the hanger like drawing office overlooked by the chief's elevated room...and within half an hour fired again! It was the same everywhere, I was black listed. It never occurred to me but I could probably have claimed Irish Citizenship and gone home.

For a time Sean and I pooled our dole, I sent what I could to Maud and we lived on the balance which was so little that we had fierce arguments over what Sean spent on 'fags' I was a non-smoker and Sean would rather smoke than eat!

Various people passed through those flats where I was bored and broke! One girl I remember well, a Polish refugee, she was a singer in opera before the war and when she was staying with Topsy borrowed my overcoat to go for an interview with Sadler's Wells Opera Co. She got taken on and we were good friends for a while, she gave her name as Anna Polak. I have a recollection of leaning out of an upstairs window on a sunny evening with Anna listening to distant gunfire and talking about ourselves, and the prospects for the coming night. Holborn Tube station was our nearest refuge. I met Anna once after the War. But then she was one of the stars of opera. And she hardly deigned to know me!

*

Sean was not on the dole for long before he got a job as an ambulance driver. My problem it seemed was that because I was supposed to be in a reserved occupation I could not be allocated to one outside my sphere!

I had been keeping up correspondence with D who was doing an arts course in Oxford and she came to see me in London, and having the idea that her father might be able to employ me she rang him, and after this long and frustrating stay in London I was offered a job as a machine tool fitter in Mr A's factory in Ringwood. Mr A was a Quaker and would not directly make armaments but only machines for what purpose he wasn't supposed to know! He was more or less free to employ whoever he wanted.

The night D was in London turned out to be one of the worst fire bomb raids the city had experienced up to that time. D and I took some blankets down to a lower level of Holborn tube, and while we were lying on the platform with hundreds of other people we felt the blast of air as The Bank

Station took a direct hit from an HE bomb which collapsed the upper levels of the station with great loss of life.

Soon after that Sean came down looking for us and persuaded us to go up and see the city burning! Sean did not know what fear was. (He later applied for and got into the RAF and, as he had insisted, as a tail end gunner in a bomber. And he still survived the War!) For perhaps half an hour we three lunatics walked the streets, streets covered with debris and running with water from numerous fire hoses which snaked everywhere while buildings blazed above us and the sky was lit by searchlights and bursting shells, and our ears were battered by the din of the madness.

A few days later and just after I had gone down to Ringwood, leaving most of my worldly possessions, my books and some pictures and my push bicycle and most of my clothing - I had left the Velocette at the place we had had temporarily in Richmond- the shop was burned out and I lost the lot.

The only person in the flat that night was Topsy. She could not take her dog down the tube and would not leave him and the two of them, both terrified, stuck it out in the flat. But then she was forced to leave by a fireman who came up to her flat dragging a hose to fight a fire across the street, and when fire spread from an adjoining building, she got out in what she stood up in, she and the dog and an old tennis racket!

My memory of that flat in Theobalds Rd is of the almost overwhelming smell of coffee which must have been ground in the shop.

Topsy who was a hospital worker got another flat in London and for a time she most amicably shared her bed with me when on several occasions I visited London!

THEN BEGAN what was I suppose the second phase of the war for me and perhaps the happiest and most fulfilled time of my life.

For a time I lived in lodgings in Ringwood Village, and my friends were Francisco Molina, and Mary who was a local teacher. Shc was also a Communist and we spent a lot of spare time together. One Sunday walking with Mary along a country road across heath land to the north of Ringwood a Heinkel bomber came in low and let go a 'stick' of bombs parallel to the road and not 100 yards away from us lying in the ditch. It then climbed away into the distance leaving a cloud of dust and smoke drifting over us- we learned later that there was a large ammunition dump hidden on that heath and wondered who had reported it to the Luftwaffe.

Francisco worked in Mr A's Engineering Works as a jig and tool maker, he had previously been similarly employed in the Spanish Hispano Suiza aircraft engine works. He was a communist and refugee from the Spanish Civil war, as were several other employees, and he was only beginning to speak a little English. He claimed to have been the Lightweight boxing champion of Spain at one time and he was certainly a tough young man and very handsome and attractive to the girls...so not so popular with most of the men! I worked beside him for some time and he taught me a lot, so that I was soon able to do some of the skilled work of precision machine building.

I also worked besides Hal, a different type of man. He was quite old and had spent most of his life in the U.S.A., spending time in jail and doing just about everything during the depression period. He too was a skilled machine tool fitter and a most entertaining workmate as we worked on rebuilding big machines from Woolwich Arsenal which had been damaged by enemy action. Hal was also a real rogue, a poacher in his spare time, and full of unrepeatable stories!

Some of his experiences were very interesting as when he had joined an organisation - Anarchists in a sense- who refused to work for other men's profit the IWW (I won't work). They were the original bums and hitch hikers, covering America on freight trains and living on their wits and without money. Hal said every social type belonged to what was really a brotherhood. When you wanted to get from A to B you walked along the track towards B and when you came to a gradient which would slow the huge freight trains you waited for a chance to scramble aboard. Then, when it came towards evening you watched for another up gradient and also for any sign of a glinting in the woods near the track. This was from bits of mirror hung up to catch the light and tell the traveller that there was a camp there. You hopped off and sure enough would find a camp with perhaps a few men in it. Maybe there'd be no-one but there would be a rough shelter and the making of a meal and a fire place. The unwritten law was that before you left the camp you left it as you found it, so you snared a rabbit or stole a chicken and perhaps some bread if you could not beg it, and cleaned up, after first leaving your 'catch' cooked in the pot.

*

My second son Finn or Fionn was born on the 3rd of January in 1941, and I got leave to go to Ireland early in the spring. There I spent a few days with Maud in Leam. She seemed happy with her very primitive life, Tyl was already going to the little school only a few yards down the boreen and Maud seemed to have been accepted into the small community and had made one or two lifelong friends, particularly Kate Nee and her large family who lived on a hillside across the valley. I was also able to have a day or two at Knockranny before returning to Ringwood.

I was invited to the A's houses quite often in the evenings and weekends and began to enjoy a life of some culture - music and literature and meeting interesting intellectual people. (Up to then, due to my passion for boats and sailing, I had allowed many things to almost completely pass me by.)

They then invited me to PG with them and I moved as one of the family into this very comfortable house with its garden, tennis court and small swimming pool. While living with the A's I met a number of interesting people, one of whom was the painter Augustus John who lived near Ringwood. He was surrounded by admirers and his talented and very Bohemian family and in his old age rather basking in the attention.

About the same time I voluntarily joined the local Home Guard unit and since I had a motor cycle became the brigade dispatch rider! It was of course a very critical period in the war, the Battle of Britain was being fought overhead and invasion was expected at any time.

Although we were quite well equipped with Canadian army rifles, plus Brens and Spiggot morters I don't think we would have lasted very long against the Panzers, or against the airborne troops who might have landed in the New Forest area. However, I hadn't been a Home Guard for very long before I was called before my genuinely embarrassed commanding officer, - who was a friend of the family- and ordered to hand in my rifle and equipment and accept discharge as being a potential security risk! I did not hand in my bayonet but hid it and some ammunition in the roof of an outbuilding which I know is now demolished.

I sometimes wonder who found them.

*

D came home from Oxford two or three times and we were openly very friendly. And then came a time when I met her in London on a quiet weekend and we spent the evening with Sean and Elsie, a red headed Irish girl whom he was living with and later married. There were only two rooms in that modern flat near Euston and when it came to bedtime D and I were left with mattresses and bedding in the living room!

And so began for me the most joyous time of my life and I think perhaps hers too. The next morning we took the train to Southampton and hitched to Ringwood on a truck with a friendly driver.

*

Now looking back after many years I am in a deep quandary about whether or not to commit to paper my feelings and experiences of that time, because of causing hurt. I have done many things in life for which I feel guilt and regret but of the real affairs of the heart- which have been very few- I feel no guilt. In fact I feel a sense of joy that they did happen in this my life which is now rapidly passing away.

We were so much in love that I think we believed everyone must have been aware of it and accepted the fact. Morality, right and wrong, even honorable behavior on my part went by the board.

Mr and Mrs A slept out in an open summerhouse during the summer months, so that when D was at home we were usually alone in the house and our bedrooms faced each other across the landing. At first we just met in our nightclothes on the landing, talked and listened to the drone of enemy bombers and sometimes the crump of bombs in the distance. The sounds of war getting nearer and nearer as the bombers followed the line of the Avon valley.

Before long we were lovers who shared beds and no beds whenever and wherever we met. The fact that I was being unfaithful to Maud and betraying a trust at the same time carried no weight, I even convinced myself that the A's were aware of the situation and accepted it, we made no attempt to hide our feelings for each other.

There were occasional charity dances in Ringwood which we all attended and D and I were both very energetic people and danced wildly together for most of the evenings, apparently without raising eyebrows! At weekends we walked for miles and explored much of the Salisbury plain using my bike - quite illegally- to get there. Among the places we visited was The Miz Maze, a maze cut in the turf and miles from anywhere. If I ever knew its history I have forgotten it. It was a beautiful summer's day and we had the maze and the world entirely to ourselves.

*

In June Hitler launched his attack on The Soviet Union. We are only learning now that we "Fellow Travellers"- as Communists and Russofiles were called- had been completely deceived by the propaganda coming out of Russia. We believed that all was well there and that it really was a union of soviet socialist republics, when in fact it was a total dictatorship controlled by Stalin who had greatly weakened the Red Army by his execution of many of its senior officers.

From that day- 22 June 1940- the British attitude to Russia and to the fellow travellers changed. D and I started selling the *Daily Worker* in Ringwood and the surrounding country in the evenings and at weekends. I built a knockdownable stand to sell Soviet propaganda in the market square on market days and we supported the campaign to open a second front to relieve the pressure on the Red Army. Churchill promised as much support as possible in the form of military equipment, resulting in some heroic Northern convoys and loss of life and ships.

One Sunday I was walking on the high ground near the A's house alone- D was away- when I saw a lone Heinkel Bomber flying straight towards me at low altitude and just after it had passed over I saw two small bombs and then two large ones drop from it and disappear behind trees down towards the town.

They were presumably aimed at the railway station and the factory where I worked but they fell a few hundred yards short and completely demolished the Vicarage, a lovely old house known as 'Old Stacks'. It went up in a great column of smoke and dust and debris, the debris being largely the vicar's collection of books and valuable pottery. Miraculously the elderly vicar, Mr Errignton, and his wife and the old maid who were all in the house at the time were blown out onto the lawn and survived, badly shaken and bruised.

*

Mr A's peacetime work at the factory, besides general engineering was flour mill engineering. This was a long established business which serviced many mills -principally water mills- throughout Britain and Ireland and specialised in the manufacture of vertical shaft turbines. I, as a sort of general handyman with my own transport was sent out on several interesting trouble shooting jobs.

One of these was to a beautiful part of the west country, a big farm on the edge of Exmoor. A small river running through the farm had been dammed in a valley 3 or 4 hundred feet above it and, via a pentstock down the hill, it drove a turbine and generator which lit and heated the house.

This was entirely automatic in operation and had been running for nearly 20 years with a minimum of maintenance but was now running out of the control of its governors and I had to discover why and put it right!

On the second day by mere chance I spotted why, a furred up hydraulic slave operating water pipe. I put it right and, as I was living as one of the family -friends of the A's- I was very happy.

A less pleasant job was at a very big flour mill and bakery, assisting a diver- proper one with a huge helmet and an air pump who was to place a new bottom thrust bearing at the bottom of a water filled pit, while I with the assistance of lifting gear and men from the mill lifted the turbine. This job was deep underneath a huge brick built mill.

The unpleasant part was that the mill was where the water of the River Test drops down to the tide on the northern outskirts of Southampton. It was night time when the mill was normally shut down and there was a very heavy air raid in progress and the brickwork of the mill seemed to be shuddering something horrible! As it happened I nearly got killed on the was back to Ringwood when in the dark I ran into a herd of stampeding New Forest ponies and finished the journey bruised on a damaged and lightless bike!

*

Then quite suddenly life for me changed again and my comfortable life in a country town and house ended. I was apparently considered a good guy again! I had letters at about the same time from The British Power Boat Co of Hythe Southampton and from Vospers of Portsmouth, both offering me jobs on similar projects, Motor Gun Boats -M.G.B's- and Motor Torpedo Boats- M.T.Bs-.

I reported to both companies meeting at British Power their chief designer Fred Cooper, a man and designer I had admired for many years. Cooper, a very quiet unassuming person, had been responsible for the design of most of the pre-War British record breaking speedboats. He offered me a job in the drawing office right away but I then went on for an interview with Vospers, where I was interviewed by John Rix, manager of sub-contracts. He was a man of about my own age and was to end his career many years later as Managing Director of Vosper Thornycroft Shipyard in Southampton - my old firm.

For some reason which I cannot recall I opted for Vospers and started at Vospers Porchester Yard a few days later, having moved my residence to Hamble and the house of Maud's father and stepmother, a most kind Scots woman and WREN.

My first immediate boss was a Commander Summerville known to me as one of the early offshore yacht racing skippers and owner of the ex Bristol Channel pilot cutter "Jolie Breeze". He was at the time overall Production Manager. His office, a fairly large room, had for wall paper most elaborate charts and graphs covered with colour-headed pins. Sitting opposite him across his desk he noticed me looking somewhat overawed by all this and said cheerfully 'don't let all that worry you it's mostly for show'.

He then set me the task of sorting out a tangle of equipment and bits and pieces salvaged from the bombing of the main works in Portsmouth and particularly to try to assemble sets of the dual steering gear, mechanical and hydraulic, and of the gun control mechanism for the M.T.B's. I apparently did this job satisfactorily and was even congratulated by Commander Peter Du Cane who was M.D. and also Chief Designer of the firm.

I then became assistant to Rix and having spent some time in the workshop getting to know all about the boats and what went into them (it is perhaps interesting to note that many of the actual boatbuilders were women) and after a day or two at Morgan Giles boatyard at Tinemouth, Devon, going on a sea trial of one of the boats building there under contract to Vospers, I was packed off to Glasgow.

GLASGOW SEEMED a rather ugly city of tenement houses. And my flat was in one of these, up a rather smelly dirty cement staircase. But it was in a pleasant enough part of the city near the University, and the flat itself was quite spacious , well furnished and comfortable. This became my base for about nine months although I was not there very much, also having a room in Belfast and a bed in Hamble when I was back at base.

My memory of much of this time is that it was winter and a pretty severe one with a lot of snow. My work left me quite a lot of time to myself as I was not working regular hours. I had to keep in touch with Porchester and the three yards I serviced with information and plans and also go on all sea trials of the boats built by them and keep all the performance records. I used my spare time to get around on my motorcycle, explore middle Scotland and do some solo climbing.

On the Clyde and the sea it was sometimes extremely beautiful. My first trial run was from the yard of McLeans of Renfrew which is some way up the Clyde. It was foggy and cold when we started down the Loch in the early morning with a mixed crew of yard and naval personnel. Officially the M.T.B. was still the responsibility of the yard and of Vospers whom I represented. As we approached Dumbarton the fog began to clear, with Denny's shipyard to starboard. Dennys had built many of the cross channel ferries of the pre war period including our own pre war Holyhead/Dun Laoghaire Mail Boats, the fine steam turbine steamers Hibernia, Scotia, and Cambria.

But then in wartime all I saw there were the grey hulls of destroyers and corvettes on the slips or fitting out afloat. Then we came out into brilliant sunshine, and open blue water with shining snowy mountains to the north. Soon the throttles of the three twelve hundred horsepower Packard converted aero engines were half opened and the roar of these mighty engines added to the drama. The water broke away from the transom as we half planed on the glass smooth water as we headed for the boom defenses off Dunoon, passing Gourock to port and Kilcreggan to starboard between the sea loughs of Gare and Long (now NATO submarine bases). There were numerous war and merchant ships about, these from the trans-Atlantic convoys at that time bringing over 'Lease Lend' military and other supplies.

We had radioed ahead and the anti-submarine net boom had its gate open. We passed through between the big buoys from which steel nets were suspended and out into unrestricted water where revolutions were pushed up to 2,000, and the boat was up and planing. I stood on the extreme stern holding onto the ensign staff with a fine curtain of water and spray high on each side of me turned into rainbows by the sunlight, the unforgettable smell of high octane aviation spirit in my nostrils and my ears deafened by the roar of the exhausts...all adding up to an experience I shall never forget.

These boats when fully loaded carried nearly 4000 gallons of this highly volatile aviation spirit. This was contained in five tanks, covered with a thick cellular rubber blanket which was supposed to make bullet holes self sealing and prevent fire. However, in combat the situation of the engine room crew between two sets of tanks cannot have been a very happy one. The boats also had two Ford V8 engines of about 80hp each, and these could be clutched into the wing propeller shafts as auxiliaries. These engines were very carefully silenced and were used for night approaches to targets or when landing parties on enemy held shores. If it was a torpedo attack, as soon as they were fired the main engines would be started and the boat would beat a hasty retreat!

On this first of my trial runs we headed for Aran Island and the measured mile on its eastern side to make a series of timed runs, taking averages at various throttle settings and maintaining them for so many hours. If all was going well we would work up to full speed at just about 40 knots. Usually each boat ran about three trial days out, sometimes incorporating torpedo firing and gunnery trials as well. The guns were heavy twin, powered- turret mounted machine guns -very noisy!

The measured mile we normally used was some way up Lough Long. On one occasion there doing the U turn at the end of a run the Naval officer on the helm made the turn towards the land instead of seaward. He was perhaps not aware that the boats made a tighter turn one way than the other and that at full speed the turning circle was well over 100yards. More by luck than judgement we just cleared the off-lying rocks!

On another occasion and after we had completed the final acceptance trials and were proceeding back to base -either Clynder on the Gare Lough or Renfrew- at slow speed in rather heavy weather, I and most of the crew both naval and civilian were sitting in the forecastle celebrating on Navy rum - I had just been handed a mug full of it without realising what it was! Then there was an almighty crash right behind my back and a hole and daylight appeared just above the waterline. (It was just as well for the yard that at the time we again had a Naval officer on the helm.) What had happened was that in going through the Dunoon Gate not enough allowance had been made for sideways drift in the strong wind and we had hit one of the Buoys of the gate. We got home safely as we were entering sheltered water but repairs considerably delayed delivery.

When the return was to Renfrew it was usual for Naval inspectors and non-essential civilian personnel to disembark at Greenock. We would proceed back to Glasgow by train after topping up at the station bar, this added to the navy rum meant we were a somewhat noisy party on the train. These however were non-corridor trains and we generally boarded an empty compartment, the only snag being that there was no toilet and we had to relieve ourselves one at a time by partly opening the door!

*

McLean's yard was beside Fairfields who were building the Steam Gunboats, the SGBs of which Peter Scott (later to be Sir Peter) got the first. These were intended as the answer to the German 'E Boats' which, nearly twice the size of the British M.T. and M.G. boats, were faster in rough weather, and faster in any weather than the smaller Fairmile Patrol Boats. In fact in most of the inter boat scraps there were not many casualties, gunnery on small boats at sea was somewhat inaccurate! A considerable proportion of the small British naval craft were manned by men from the occupied countries, particularly Norwegians and Dutch, and I met quite a few of them, very bitter and committed men. There were also a lot of foreign sailors off merchant ships in Glasgow and Greenock and as there was no restriction on alcohol there was a lot of street fighting at night, the local lads being the chief culprits.

The other yard in the Clyde area which I serviced was McGruer's at Clynder on the Gare Lough. This in pre-war times had been a famous yacht building yard, a fact fairly obvious by their standard of workmanship and finish. James McGruer was the Managing Director and Designer in peacetime and I found him a rather dour little man, in contrast to his brother John who was business manager and very forthcoming.

*

The third yard I serviced was Harland and Wolfe's in Belfast. To get there I usually flew over from a small airport near Paisley. The planes were De Havilland biplanes, either two engined Dragons or four engined Dragon Rapides, very noisy. The planes flew quite low and had their windows blacked out so it was hardly a pleasure trip but I found the backmost seat on one of them had a window which did not fit properly and I could wedge it open a little with a screw of newspaper. From here I'd have a tolerable view of the Clyde and the sea and all the shipping.

Belfast at that time, never a very attractive town, had suffered very severe air raids and was a very depressing damaged city. (By pure luck I missed all the major raids on Belfast and Glasgow and only saw the aftermaths.)

Harland's found me digs on the southern suburbs of the city, which I shared with a young Naval Lieutenant of about my own age. This was within a short tram ride of the Yard. Harland's were of course a major builder of Naval ships. At that time there was an unnamed aircraft carrier and a cruiser, The Black Prince, on the stocks besides smaller vessels. The M.T.Bs were being built in the Boat Shop, a huge shed in which they were building several boats at the same time.

My main memory of trials from Harland's is of a run in fair weather when we were diverted from our usual course to the measured mile somewhere along the north coast of Belfast Lough, by a radio signal requesting us to cover the minefields - as we were shallow draft- so that shore stations could check their underwater signalling equipment!

We were not too happy in case there was a mine too near the surface!

I also remember that we had aboard one of the first Radar sets to be tested at sea- very secret! We all got a sight of the tiny cathode tube screen and the vague image on it in the little radio cabin in the middle of the ship. (The 'Array' on the mast did not rotate in those early days as they do now.)

*

When I was first sent up north the US was neutral in the war and trading to some extent with both sides, but 'Lease Lend' had been contracted, and this included making over certain islands to America in exchange for some rather obsolete destroyers for convoy duty. Two bases were being built on the Garelough in connection with lease lend. One of these with American labour and equipment, the other by by the Royal Engineers.

The contrast between the two 'works' was most impressive, the Engineers were doing the work with picks and shovels while the

Americans were using dynamite and equipment we had never seen before, bulldozers and diggers and graders, and the toughest gang of labourers imaginable. What struck me most forcibly about the Americans was their ability to improvise.

The works involved literally tearing down the hillside and pushing it out into the lough, levelling and immediately erecting huge hanger stores. The whole area was a sea of mud, churned up by half-tracks, trucks and jeeps of every sort...even jeeps were a novelty at that time.

In the evenings the pubs in Rosneath and Clynder were taken over by the construction gangs and there was never a woman to be seen! The site managers and gangers of the work squads, although in 'civvies', were believed to be US Army officers. Then in December came Pearl Harbour and America was in the war on our side.

*

Shortly before the US entered the war I was crossing to Belfast by steamer, the ship as usual full of men from the labour gangs who had got leave over Christmas and were heading home. They virtually took over the ship, and the few women aboard were advised to lock their cabin doors! On this occasion I too was locked in my cabin, but for different reasons.

On going aboard everyone had to show their identity cards, passing in front of a uniformed intelligence corps officer sitting at a table with two armed sergeants flanking him. I placed my card before him and he began turning the pages of a file, stopped at one page and ran his finger down it for a moment. He then looked up at me and said "Mr Kennedy please go to your cabin with the sargant, someone will come to speak to you later".

Sometime after the ship had sailed the door of the cabin opened and a plain clothed man came in and very politely and in a cultured voice proceeded to quiz me about my Communist leanings and activities. At the time it all seemed quite ridiculous and still does. Besides questioning me about my job- about which he probably already knew- most of his questioning related to my background, family, education etc and I answered perfectly honestly and frankly. I felt I had nothing to hide, but I also felt that if I had, this man was not really expecting to find it. I don't know how long the interview took but in the end he stood up shook my hand and said " I don't think you will hear any more about this Mr Kennedy" and I never did!

I have always presumed I was interviewed by MI5 or MI6 and since the spy affairs of the early Cold War period, with Philby and McLean et al, I have thought how crazy the secret service was. Because of my background and the 'oldboy' network I myself must have been considered above serious reproach, as indeed at one time were these spies.

*

One of the advantages of my job was that when I went over to Belfast I could get through what I had to do by midday on the Friday (or sometimes even on the Thursday!) and could catch the afternoon train to Dublin. These trains were usually full of Southern Irish workers going home for the weekend. They were all making good money working in the shipyard or on construction work for the American Army and Airforce. Numerous camps were being built, and also aerodromes for land based and water based aircraft. (In recent years I was at Killadeas on Lower Lough Erne which had been used by Sunderlands of the RAF. I walked down to the shore and looked at the foundations of the hangers, the concrete slipways and hardstands. Although still intact they were moss grown with trees and shrubbery beginning to encroach. It was very still and in my imagination I saw all the activity of fifty years before, the big flying boats being hauled up on bogeys by tractors assisted by men in thigh boots, the growl of Bristol radial engines revving up and taxying away to the buoy- marked runways on the open lake. And I thought of those which never returned...a strange experience.)

On the wartime Belfast to Dublin train parties broke out in the open carriages as soon as it left the station. Bottles came out from luggage and in a short time everyone knew everyone. Between Newry and Dundalk there was a stop for a sort of security check, the showing of identity cards and passes, and there were also customs formalities. But it was all a bit casual though of course then the 'Border' was virtually open, as it still is... and in any event intelligence either way was unlikely to go by train!

The train arrived in Dublin to a city all lit up, as were most of the passengers! It was a delight and the shops seemed well stocked although there were some severe shortages and hardships for the poor of the city. In the South the war was known as the Emergency, some things were fairly plentiful but fuel of all sorts was in short supply, particularly petrol which was severely rationed. (At that time my parents had a little Austin Seven and were able to do the shopping and get about a little.)

After arrival in the city it was then another train to Bray and a joyous five mile walk to my old home of Knockranny. My parents and Aunt Vi were rather lonely in those days, with Nancy in India and Doreen in the ATS. So my brief visits were welcome to them and a great pleasure to me.

THE WALK back to Bray station was always a sad one, my parents were getting old and I never knew when I would see them again. Apart from shortages, the war really only barely touched them, although two magnetic mines did land by parachute quite near Knockranny. (They were detonated by bomb disposal parties). As to their family, Doreen in the WAAF stationed in Dover and myself travelling about Britain were in some danger but it was slight, and Nancy was in India and far from danger.

The South of Ireland did not entirely escape the war physically, some 80 bombs were dropped, most of these not far inland along the east coast, from the end of 1940 to the end of May '41. Up to ten people were killed and some damage to property was sustained. Then on the night of May 31 1941 (whether by accident or design) a heavy raid was made on N.E Dublin causing much damage and leaving 28 dead and some 90 injured.

It has been generally accepted that most of the bombs dropped were not aimed at specific targets but came from aircraft which had got lost in the night and wanted to get rid of them and head for home. The Dublin raid would require a better explanation.

The return journey to Belfast was never a happy one, leaving the land of light and peace if not of plenty. Nothing purchased in Eire (as it was called at that time) could be taken into the North and through stupidly putting it in the rack instead of wearing it I lost at the border a very nice raincoat which had just been given me by Mother, leaving me coatless...now I believe I could have reclaimed it. One of the principal products which people tried to import was butter and all sorts of dodges were tried. Large bosomed women were suspect! And to quash this method it was said that as the train neared the border the carriage heating was turned up!

After one of these trips to the south and on my return to my lodgings in Glasgow I found instead of the hoped-for letter from D, a letter from her mother G, a person for whom I had the greatest affection and respect.

On reading the letter I was really shattered, she had discovered that D and I had been lovers throughout the war, and was exceedingly bitter about this, particularly as it had occurred in her house.

I could not blame her, from her point of view I had behaved attrociously and betrayed a trust. She had been a friend of Maud's but did not know how basically unhappy was my marriage.. D and I had made no secret of our love and were always together whenever possible, and without ever really thinking about it we assumed that everyone was aware of and accepted it, there had never been any indication of disapproval.

I was quite stunned and felt that if only from a humanistic point of view G was unjust, to the extent that at the first opportunity I rode down to Ringwood and visited G and her husband H in their home.

They accepted me and we had a quite civilised talk, I cannot remember the gist of it but I felt that H was sympathetic but that G would never forgive me. D and I continued our relationship until after the war.

We met in all sorts of odd places, I being mobile could get to where she was, and we could pillion ride to places where we could have long walks and perhaps nights together (it was of course illegal to use petrol for purely personal travel).

D had several wartime jobs, one being with a company, Wessex, who made distress and parachute flares for illumination purposes and for many others. Nearly all the employees were women. For a time D was in the red flare department where it was impossible not to get any exposed parts of the body dyed bright orange, and on one occasion I collected her from the factory after work when her face was that colour, it was considered to be a badge of honour. The women were not left long in the department but were moved round in the various departments.

While staying with my in-laws in Hamble I met a most remarkable young Polish woman who was also a PG in the house, she was an R.A.F. Ferry pilot attached to Air Service Training Ltd (AST Hamble) who were operating one of the biggest repair and rebuild factories for Spitfires and Lancaster four engined bombers. After the machines were passed out they had to be delivered to airfields all over Britain. This young woman not only flew Spitfires but also single handed flew Lancasters. She went in all weather and to places as far away as Scotland and with the minimum of navigation aids or guidance, returning to base either by public transport or by air. She had a fighter pilot brother also in the R.A.F. The mechanics in the hangers really worshipped this woman, would do anything for her and were deeply concerned about her safety. I never heard if she survived the war.

Another and famous woman pilot Amy Johnson, famous for early long distance flights solo and with her husband Mollison was lost on a delivery flight somewhere in the Thames estuary, neither she nor her plane were ever found.

My work in connection with the subcontracted MTB's was coming to an end with the near completion of the programme, and as Maud was agitating to return to England, I applied to be transferred to a drawing office job with Vospers.

Maud had been in several places since the birth of Finn in Connemara, sometimes leaving the two boys in charge of strangers. On one occasion when I visited her she was staying in the house of Sean O Faoilean, a well known Irish writer, on Killiney Hill. It was there that I confessed my infidelity. Although I did not love her I found it a most distressing thing to do.

Maud duly returned to England and for a short time occupied the flat in Richmond we had occupied at the beginning of the War. She then moved to Hampsted to another flat near friends of hers, I visited there once or twice and it was about that time that my daughter Tanya was conceived. The next move was to Hamble where we rented a furnished bungalow on the Crowsport estate, a rather jerrybuilt house with a flat roof, not really intended for family living. It was in that house on May 30 1943 that Tanya was born.

One of our neighbours was Jack Wyatt, a photographer living alone at the time. He and I were old friends I had built him a National 12 racing dinghy at SMALL CRAFT before the War. Another of our neighbours was an anti -aircraft gun, a rapid fire Bofors. But this only had occasion to bark once -very noisy- when shortly before the invasion a cheeky German fighter machinegunned the main hanger at AST.

I was transferred to Vospers drawing office in 1943. This was situated in a large house near Fareham, standing in its own grounds. Here I met again some of my old friends of Thornycroft days and after my rather lonely time of travelling enjoyed the camaraderie of a drawing office with about ten draughtsmen, women tracers and secretaries.

The house also served as the office of Commander Peter Du Cane, credited with the design of the Vosper MTBs and also of the Admiral who was chairman of the Company. Although at this time the War had still over another year to run, we were not under very great pressure of work. So, sometimes staying late in the office I did some designing on my own and produced the design for what later became the Slipway 5 Tonner.

It was the time of the massive daylight raids (and of course continuous night raids by the R.A.F.) of the US Airforce over Germany. We used to see the so called Flying Fortresses passing over in what seemed like hundreds at a time in formations, perhaps 500 engines droning heavily overhead on their way to wreak destruction and death.

It was also the beginning of the Flying Bomb period. We knew they had been doing damage and creating some panic in the London area but I very well remember the first time we experienced one. I was lying awake in bed early one summer morning when I heard what I thought was a Spitfire- they were overhead on test every day and all day- flying low and with the engine misfiring badly...suddenly I felt my hackles rise as I realised what it was, it seemed to pass directly overhead and continued on growing fainter until it stopped, the silence followed by the detonation. We heard later in the day that it had landed in open country and done no damage.

This was the first of many aimed at Southampton. Shortly after this I was conscripted into the Home Guard (in Ringwood I had volunteered and been discharged for being a communist!)and our main task when on duty, as the possibility of invasion was long past, was reporting night and day on these 'nasties' we called Doodlebugs. We had to phone in a compass bearing and estimated distance from our location to assist with rescue.

Our unit of the HG was armed with Stenguns, a most basic and apparently crude firearm but a most effective automatic and practically jamproof, unlike the modern infantry weapons which look as if a few grains of sand would put them out of action.

Watching the flying bombs approaching at about 300 mile per hour, by day appearing as a small aeroplane and by night as a flaming object was not a little nerve wracking when the line of flight was going to pass over you and the cut out might happen at any moment. In fact I never did have one land near me but they caused considerable damage and casualties in and around Southampton.

Later work ran out at Vospers and we draughtsmen were dispatched to other plants and I found myself at AST Hamble. This was most convenient, working among some old friends on modifications to American aircraft Mustang fighters and Mitchell bombers to suit the R.A.F.

*

I was at AST for two summers and for holidays I and several other draughtsmen volunteered to work on the land. We found ourselves in a lovely part of Cornwall. The men lived in tents and the women volunteers in the nearby mansion, this was right on the coast near Portscath with it's own beach. The weather was very hot and the work really hard for us softies, and we were bossed by professional Land Girls, big sunburned lassies as tough as they come.

After a lot of potato picking racing against tractors, we spent a day weeding a 10 acre field of Pyrethrum growing in orderly rows, this meant crawling on our hands and knees between the rows for which job we had to wear hats. The first day at this I found myself crawling up a row next to a young woman...so we kept pace and chatted as we went.

We found we were both married, her man in the Army and for the rest of the two weeks Sylvia and I were great friends. Whenever the call went out where is Brien or where is Sylvia the answer was always 'where ever the other one was'! But it was all really great fun and we had the evenings off and could get transport to a local pub, but were turned in early. Some of us went again to the same place the following year, and it was equally enjoyable.

*

Also while at AST I was called up as a volunteer to do a bit of Naval service. I became a member of H.M. Royal Navy Supplementary Volunteer Reserve! Reporting to Portsmouth I was allocated to a 52ft Harbour Launch based at Yarmouth on the Isle of Wight. This was a type of boat I had worked on as an Apprentice!

I was issued with a pair of heavy serge pants, a blue jersey, and a bedroll plus a travel pass. I duly joined my 'ship' at the end of Yarmouth pier.

It was still winter, the weather was rough and our job was ferrying fresh meat and mail to American Liberty Troop Ships anchored in open water south of the island. Officially I was the mate and usually acted as coxswain, the CO was a yachtsman with in my opinion little seagoing experience. There were two other hands and an engineer. Getting alongside these lightly loaded ships in a heavy sea was not easy and when we got there, heavily protected with fenders, we were going up and down her sides like a lift.

We were no sooner alongside than the rail of the ship above us was crowded with very bored G.I.'s and we heard shouts of "want any cigarettes Limey," and cartons of 'Camels' and other cigarettes came showering down, also packets of nylon stockings. After a few days of this, and failure to make any headway with the snobby WRNS in the signal station at the end of the pier, we were ordered to return to our base which was in the dockyard right under the stern of Nelson's Victory.

My naval service which I think was only for a month anyhow was terminated when I was ignominiously discharged for being absent without leave. I had slipped away for Maud's birthday and was reported missing! My CO did not like me anyhow!

*

I don't think I was entirely a bad father. I made toys for the boys, and what I still think was rather a nice little buggy in which Tanya could be pushed or pulled. (This was made entirely of wood including the springs which were laminated and also formed the armrests...the handle telescoped and there was a small 'boot' for the shopping.)

I found an old genuine canadian canoe and rebuilt it fitted it with a outrigger which acted as ballast or buoyancy. This could safely take the three children canoeing without lifejackets which, in any event, were not readily available in those days.

I also bought a little three wheel car, a J.M.B. of which I think very few were built. The concept was quite good, a single cylinder 600cc Norton engine driving the single back wheel from its horizontal position under and between the seats. This could just accommodate Maud and I in front and the three kids squashed in the back. I was not satisfied with its stability or front suspension and partly rebuilt it, getting it lower and generally much improved so that I used it regularly for going to work when I was working in Fareham.

My first outing in this little buggy ended ridiculously.

When I had rebuilt it I naturally wanted to give it a trial run! It was of course untaxed and uninsured and running on petrol allocated for my Velocette and getting to work. Anyhow I set off for Bursledon, only three or four miles away, along a bridle path through woods after a half mile of quiet side road.

I planned to visit Adlard Coles, editor of the Yachtsman.

So to keep my machine out of sight I pushed it into a field and behind a hedge. I had tea with the Coles and walked back to the field where to my astonishment and dismay I found a large policeman standing beside it! I was so taken aback that when he said "does this belong to you sir" I admitted it, instead of saying "so what, it is not on a public road."

So of course out came his notebook, where did I live, I could not have pushed it from Hamble so where were the documents ? And from where was the petrol, it was a fair cop. Then I asked him how he came to know it was there? He replied that a lady saw it as a strange object (painted bright red!) possibly hostile and reported it. It turned out that the lady in question was a friend of the Coles and was horrified when she heard of the trouble she had got me into. It was trouble, I was quite heavily fined and temporarily lost my driving license.

*

After I had the car taxed and insured and with legitimate petrol coupons which I stretched to the limit I made several long journeys in it without mishap. One was the first visit to that Cornish landwork camp. The second was to South Wales, to see D.

During the War, conscripts in certain age groups if conscientious objecters were given the choice of going in the non-combatant Pioneers -labour gangs- or down the mines with reasonable pay after training.

The mines near Merthyr Tydfil were perhaps the biggest training centre and a lot of young men were housed in specially built hostels and to attempt to keep them happy various entertainments were laid on by concert parties and drama groups etc. D's job was to assist in organising this entertainment, living herself in staff quarters isolated from the main hostel.

At that time I was living in Hamble with Maud and family, but with her full knowledge as to where I was going, I took off in the little three wheeler one week end; it was one of my most callous acts against her and I regret it to this day because I really think I wanted to hurt her.

*

It may be that what I am writing now should never be published, that it is just being written to try to clear my own conscience, but I don't think I could do that. Perhaps I am writing to my children to try to explain why I did not want to marry Maud in the first instance and that when I did, I never really wanted to live with her. And thus give an explanation as to why in the end I deserted my family to a very large degree.

Maud, not now being able to give her point of view or refute my accusations, which means that the story is not a balanced one. But I can only say that I am telling the truth in the most factual way I can.

To a considerable extent I am repeating what I have already said about my meeting with Maud and perhaps the whole affair of my early personal life is purely academic...perhaps it is now of no real interest to anyone and that even I should forget it. However the fact is that I am still in love with a dream, a dream that Maud tried and failed to banish, and a dream that will die with me.

My fault was and is that I am rather a weak character and that Maud was a strong and determined one. I do not believe that at the beginning of our affair she loved me. She was seven years older than me, which made her nearly thirty when we first met. I don't think she was an experienced woman but in theory she was well versed in sex, having read the works of Havelock Ellis and 'Married Love' by Marie Stopes (whose works have recently been republished, reviews are critical of her and her beliefs).

Maud met me when I was living alone in my houseboat, rather defenceless and virgin myself. She brushed aside my love for my far away Peggy and managed to get me to give her Peggy's letters which she destroyed. After knowing me for only a short time she set about seducing me. I think there was something very wrong about Stopes's idea of married love and that Maud accepted it and that it caused me great frustration when I might in other circumstances have come to accept the fact that I was married to her. I of course admit that my dream was only the dream of rather romantic young man and that Peggy and I had we had a chance of getting to know each other better might not have hit it off. But from what I have learned from her sister recently (1995) of the sort of woman she was in war and peace I think it might have worked.

In any event, from the time of my visit to D in Wales my marriage to Maud continued to break up.

*

The build up for the invasion of Europe was literally going on all round us. London was suffering the rocket bombardment which I experienced on some weekend visits to London. People were quite fatalistic in this. The things arrived before their sound, unlike the flying bombs which heralded their arrival and made people jittery!

I joined the Ranelagh Sailing Club at Putney and raced a National 12ft dinghy at weekends, riding up on my bike. I was generally crewed by Hank, an American GI journalist who was living with Maud's cousin Enid in a flat in Chelsea .

He eventually married her and they emigrated to New Zealand soon after the War. Sadly Enid was killed in a car crash leaving three children. She was a lovely person in every way and very different from her cousin.

The Hamble river began to fill up with small military craft of all sorts. Troop, vehicle and tank landing craft mostly. Out in Southampton water strange floating objects appeared, enormous reels which turned out to be coiled steel pipe to carry fuel across the Channel. There was no enemy air activity noticeable.

Then came the day of the invasion and we all waited anxiously for news of how things were going and watched the weather which was quite stormy. White painted ambulance planes began to arrive on Hamble airfield. But the true story of the invasion and the battle for Europe is well documented, we just felt that it meant the beginning of the end and did not realise how far away and how hard the battles still to come.

I worked on at AST and led an unhappy domestic life. VE day arrived with all its celebrations, and a General Election in which I as a communist worked for LABOUR with a huge full length sign over my little car. It was a landslide for LABOUR and a blow for Churchill.

I cannot remember now at what stage we were turned loose from AST but I think it was not until after VJ day and the cruel and, in my view, unnecessary bombing of Hiroshima and Nagasaki.

For what seemed a long time we in the drawing office had virtually nothing to do, a nightmare state as far as I am concerned. Some attempt was made on work connected with converting the main wing of the Lancaster bomber as a wing for the Avro York, which for a time after the war was a major passenger plane.

But nearly everyone in the office was thinking about their future and either making plans as I was, or actually making things as were one or two of us, making jewellry from small sea shells they were able to collect on the shore of Southampton Water in our lunch break. This work was carried out in the the big plan drawers under our drawing boards. Spray painting was done with toothbrushes flicked with a small piece of metal and the results threaded on coloured ribbons and nylon cords for necklaces plus ear decorations with purchased out clips, they seemed to find a ready market via some of the office girls. The residue of dozens of wrecked aircraft were stacked behind our offices after they had been stripped of anything that could be reused and we found some useful pickings there but never enough to build a Spitfire!

Eventually it all came to an end and we were all looking for jobs or something to do to make a living.

I MADE an attempt to restart Small Craft in the upper part of a boat shed overlooking Southampton water. I had sold my old premises to Dorset County Council and this time round had my old friend Bert Bellenie of Thornycroft days join me.

It was almost impossible to obtain timber in the normal way but there was a great deal of pillaging from plants which had closed down, and I think it was from the Power Boat company at Hythe that we acquired some plywood which allowed us to build two double chine 14ft dinghies which I designed on the lines of the 14footer I had built just before the war.

While carrying a mast for one of these on the windscreen and open hood of my three wheeler along the lane to the shed on a very windy day my attention was distracted for a moment by two girls I was passing! The mast went over a branch of a tree and the car collided violently with it and that was the end of the little car, leaving me with a quite badly cut scalp and forehead.

At this time I was in a psychological mess.

I wanted to get away but at the same time hated to leave the children, and my future employment and source of income was a problem, as was where to live. I advertised in yachting publications for a partner with some capital to start or buy into an existing yachtyard where he could be the manager and I in charge of design and building.

This resulted in my meeting Ian Carr, an officer just discharged from the REs. He had a yacht in Lymington and a house near Beaulieu in the New Forest, and was married with two small girls. Ian had begun tentatively investigating a small boatyard and engineering works above the bridge on the Lymington creek. It was called the Lymington Slipway and Engineering Co. We investigated it together. It was not ideal because of the bridge and also because it was very tidal.

The location suited Ian and he decided to buy it anyhow and offered me the position of designer on a salary. I was suffering my lifelong handicap of having no capital worthwhile except my own ability so I agreed to this. In the meantime I was living in an unfurnished room over a Drawing Office supply shop which my draughtsman friend John Hayward had just started. It was in half a house, the other half and most of the surrounding area having been levelled by Goering's boys, and rebuilding had not yet been started. It was all very depressing. I only had a small table and a camp bed.

D visited me there accompanied by a young man she had met at the Slade in London and whom I think she married later, but he left her with me and we spent what cannot have been a very comfortable night in the camp bed!

The only asset I had was mobility with my trusty Velocette, but I was only in this 'accommodation' for a few days before I arranged to live on an old first war ML, converted to a houseboat. All 80ft of it was lying in a mud berth in the territory of the boatyard.

Here I was visited by D.

I met her at Lymington Station where she rushed into my arms with her usual enthusiasm for everything. I was dreadfully saddened because I felt this could not go on for ever, the possibility of a happy marriage with the bitter opposition of G seemed remote, and I felt I had little to offer her.

I was feeling very depressed.

We spent the night together on the old boat and made the bitter sweet parting in the morning. But I did I keep track of D and unknown to her I visited her home in Bara in Wales without letting her know. And when I was about 75 I wrote to her to find out how life had gone for her. She replied and I have her letter still. Maybe I'll write to her again at 85!

I have only had three loves in life. And two are gone forever.

*

Maud visited me unexpectedly while I was on the old M.L. and stayed the night aboard. I felt very sorry for her. She was trying to win me back but I had become very hard towards her, and when she tried to sleep with me I rejected her absolutely, but did agree to have the children to stay from time to time.

I settled down in what was to be for three or four years my drawing office. This was a timber building behind the main workshop. I arranged for my original workshop at Poole, which I had retained, to be shipped to Lymington and did a deal with Ian for a site for it in the yard. About a third of this was divided off for use as an office, and this left me a 16ft workshop. I then bought an ex Air Sea Rescue launch without engines which was on the beach half converted in Chichester harbour, getting one of the Lymington fishing boats to tow me back. We put her nose to the bank quite near to my office and moored her aft.

I was now very self contained, I had a workshop, office, home and transport. I began to recover my equilibrium and improved my home somewhat. News came from Ireland that Nancy and Morty as we called her colonel husband, plus three children, were on their way back from India. And then that they had arrived in Ireland and had taken a bungalow at Portnoo in Donegal for part of the summer.

Maud wanted to take our three to Maam Cross in Connemara so I sold my trusty bike and bought a rather pretty little Riley Nine sports car with a four seater body. It had a high mileage for those days and looked more sporty than it was but it was a nice British Racing green and made an agreeable noise and never let me down.

With this I took my family plus dog to Connemara to stay in a little cottage on the hillside with Mrs Kate Nee, she who had been a great support to Maud in the country during the War. I then went on to Donegal to meet Nancy and for the first time her family. I had with my young Stafford bullterrier bitch pup Sally, who inconveniently came on her first season just before I left Lymington, and to attempt to counter this I had bought a bottle of a preparation called Anti Mate; unfortunately this got broken in my luggage after I left the family and everything stank of it, and as I said jokingly I had no romantic successes on that trip!

To add to all this, in the excitement of the meeting I forgot all about the dog, she was next seen halfway up the hillside with a retinue of half the dogs in the village. (Later I had the horrid job of drowning the new born pups). Actually I nearly lost Sally when she was a delightful fat little pup herself. She was following me up the gangplank of the ASR -which we later called MAIA and my first Merlin Mercury- in the half light one evening when she fell off into the deep low water mud in which MAIA sat and disappeared. I went straight in after her, nearly up to my thighs, and fortunately found her almost immediately. I fished her out, scrambled up the bank, ran up the gang plank and down below to wash her poor little face, nose and mouth, helped by her sneezes!

The firm built the first of my five tonners which proved immediately successful in local racing, resulting over a period in 18 of them being built. I also designed and got building in my little workshop a Merlin which was a type of restricted class 14footer which had just been introduced. This boat turned out to be, I believe, the best allround boat of the period and I won many races and one or two championship races in her with different crews. With a beam of only 4ft, a 25ft mast and no trapeze, Merlins were hard and exciting boats to sail.

While at "The Slipway" I was more than just a draughtsman. I spent a lot of time in the building shed developing ideas and was on very good terms with all the staff. Steve Biggs was in charge, he had been with the firm through the War when the place was more a machine shop than a boatyard (I discovered an area of ground where steel and iron machinings had been thrown which grew me the most magnificent vegetables!)

The boatshop foreman Mr. White was a great friend of mine and wrote to me later when I went to India. Muriel Ladler who was the firm's accountant was (platonically!) a good friend of mine, a very modest and quiet and I think rather lonely young woman. We occasionally went for walks together at weekends and enjoyed serious conversation.

The firm had several other directors besides Ian. One of these was another R.E. ex-officer whom I think was running some sort of racket in connection with the disposal of Miliary equipment and scrap! An immense quantity of this was being shipped back to England, dumped in woods and waste ground and auctioned off. This chap disappeared and we were joined by Charles St. John, ex-Spitfire pilot of fame. He crewed for me in some Merlin championship races but we always seemed to be dogged by gear failure when we were in the lead, which was probably my fault. We did win one marvellous race at Burnham on Crouch in the second Merlin I built.

I joined the Royal Lymington Y.C. and raced some of the Slipway 5's. The firm built six Swallows to my working drawings. These were 26ft keel boats which were to be the two main boats in the forthcoming first post-war Olympic games. We also built six 14footers to the design of "Fuss", the original pre-war boat, and these were shipped to Durban Natal where they were known as the REB 14s. Another class grew up around this design in Norfolk, these becoming known as the Waldingfield Dragonflies.

About this time I was invited to Dublin to meet some Dinghy enthusiasts who wanted to start a new national dinghy class, and also liked the Fuss design, which had been published in one of the yachting magazines.

I duly crossed to Dublin and had lunch in Jury's Hotel, which was in Dame Street in those days. There I met Douglas Hurd whom I knew from pre war dinghy days, and the Drs Mooney, Billy and Jimmy, father and son. Jimmy sailed for Ireland in the Olympics, once in Finns and once in Dragons. Also around at the time were Ronny Baskin (who became our accountant much later), Laurie McLelland (who also much later became with his family great friends of ours), and Hugh Allen who became the owner of the first Irish built boat if I remember right.

They gave me a good lunch , which I probably didn't taste!

We came to an agreement and The Irish Dinghy Racing Association was born and from that the IDRA 14 dinghy, and they are still racing.

25

ON THE last night of 1947 I met Christine Wilkinson. Christine was to become my second wife, and we were to share an active and productive marriage of 45 years.

I had first set eyes on her in the summer, sailing up the Lymington river alone in her 16ft sharpie. And I immediately thought that she was my sort of girl. Following on from that we must have seen each other many times out sailing on the river and beyond. She was more often than not alone in her boat, and I too often alone in my Merlin.

*

I once very nearly drowned myself from that boat. I was out on the Solent sailing alone in a breeze in which I could just about hold up the 25ft rig when I sailed into a group of dolphins and got so excited that I flipped the boat. The Merlins, having wide side decks, could float high on their sides without taking in water but in this case I slipped over on the windward side and before I could grab anything the boat started to blow away from me at a surprising rate. I found myself swimming furiously after her and for a horrid moment I thought I was not going to catch her and that I would be left swimming far out in the Solent.

In those days very few dinghy sailors wore life jackets. We were all good swimmers and on this occasion I was not wearing one, and had it been otherwise my swimming would have been so obstructed that I would have lost my boat and probably my life. With a supreme effort I did catch up and, after hanging on on the lee side until I had recovered my breath, I scrambled up and over onto the centreboard. I pulled the boat up and sailed home, another lesson learned!

*

Apart from seeing her at a distance, the actual meeting with Christine took place at the New Year's Dance at the RLYC in 1947. I had never seen her close to, and at first was not certain that the tall and somewhat shy looking girl in the light blue dress and moonstone earrings was the girl in the Sharpie. She seemed to be on her own, and I plucked up courage and asked her to dance.

We seemed to hit it off. She scoffed at my freakish boat and I scoffed at her old tub! It was hers for the use of, and she had got it from the uncle on whose yacht she had been living the previous summer. (She had then been actually convalescing from a long illness which dogged her all her life).

Christine had read all the Arthur Ransom books and having a boat of her own was a seventh heaven. Her uncle was the retired chief engineer of Napiers, the aero and marine engine builders and his yacht was a big Dutchman "Seven Bells" which had a professional skipper who had taught her all the practical aspects of small boat sailing.

We danced together practically the whole night, for which I was severely ticked off by Ian Carr the next day! Christine was staying with her uncle again but in a house with a housekeeper a few miles across the salt marshes, and when we parted for her to take a special bus home, we arranged to meet again with our dogs in two days time in the middle of the marsh.

The weather was kind and we had a lovely walk and told each other all about ourselves. I was afraid that this would be the beginning and the end, my being married with three children, but it was only the beginning of nearly half a century together.

She came to tea on Maia a few times in what were her college holidays, (She was taking a degree course in Science at Brighton Tech,) sometimes alone and sometimes with her friends Boo Batten or Carol Philby, a very sweet coloured girl.

Chris as she had now become was at first living in lodgings in Brighton and later rented a caravan in a park east of the town. I bought another nearly new Velocette and used to pick her up on Sundays at Chichester station and then we would go for long walks on the South Downs. We were extremely happy together but not lovers in the accepted sense until much later in the summer of 1948. By this time Chris had dropped her studies to come and live with me on Maia.

Rather naturally, this caused a huge rumpus in her family. Her uncle cut her off completely, so much for genuine love, and her father was very disappointed with her for abandoning her career. But at the time her wish was to be with me above every other consideration. I think that in later life she had some regrets because she remained intensely interested in biology and would I think have made a naturally good scientist.

*

About the time I first met Christine a young man walked into my office one afternoon, introduced himself as Rex Stuart-Beck, qualified aircraft engineer, aerodynamacist from the Miles Aircraft College. Miles who at one time produced quite a range of light single and twin engined aircraft of which the Magister was perhaps the best known. Rex had just come from the Isle of Wight where he had been living for some time in a beach hut with a fisherman. He had formerly been a ballet dancer, and seemed to have the look of a dancer, but he said he had to drop that as a career when he broke an arm and it did not set properly.

Now he was looking for a job. I took him on as my assistant. He was a good draughtsman and had ideas but he was a bit scatterbrained and drove me mad at times.

For a time he lived with me on Maia and one day I got an invitation to a party in a big barn converted to a dwelling owned by some Swedes and took Rex with me. I came away unscathed but not so Rex who a few nights later brought home a young Swedish woman whom I gathered was married to an elderly Professor! This was Barbro who was a little older than Rex at about 23.

I allowed them to move into Rex's small cabin with its single bunk! It was winter time and my dog Sally who was then nearly full grown moved in with them so they all kept warm! Problem was getting Rex up in the morning, but this was solved by my calling Sally who promptly jumped out of the bunk bringing most of the bedding with her!

Rex eventually married Barbro and they went to live in Sweden where they had two children, her family were wealthy shipowners. I doubt if Rex did any more serious work in his life, a pity because he was highly intelligent. After Rex left me I employed my old friend Johh Hayward but could not pay him enough to cover his travelling expenses from Southampton. And then finally I employed Tim Hobbs, brother of Bill who had been so good to me in my earliest days in Hamble. Tim remained with me until I finally packed up.

The last design I did was at the request of Edward Haylock, then editor of the 'Yachting World'. This became the Yachting World DayBoat, and at the time of writing this some 700 of these boats have been built and it has a strong class membership.

When Chris came to live with me she soon set about getting a job locally and because of having some training in metallurgy and work with microscopes she got quite a good and reasonably paid one with

Wellworthy just outside the town.

They were at that time one of the biggest manufacturers of vehicle pistons, rings and liners. Chris's job was assistant to the chief of the research and quality control department. Ian had broken his agreement with me as an employee but had given me the use of my office free and also a contract to design him an offshore racing yacht. My first design was for a 42ft aluminium alloy boat (the 42inch half model of this yacht hangs above my head as I write!) On costing it seemed it was going to cost more than Ian could afford, so this was changed to a boat about 34ft overall which was built in timber and became "Binker" which won the 'Channel Race' in 1949. When not sailed by Ian, Binker did very well in other offshore races before to my great disappointment he sold her to a man in Portugal.

One of my greatest triumphs was winning the famous Island Sailing Club's Round the Island Race, (about 130 starters at that time). I think it was in `'48 with a Slipway 5 Tonner which wasn't my boat so I didn't receive even for a minute the Crankshaw Gold Bowl! I also won the night race round the island, that time with Chris in the crew.

The owner of one of the six Swallows we built failed to take delivery. I had a British passport at the time, being a British subject and an Irish citizen, and was eligible to represent Britain in the Olympic games if I could qualify. So it was suggested that I should be lent this boat for the elimination trials of the Solent division.

With the well known dinghy sailor Richard Creagh-Osborne as crew, we survived the Solent trials and went to Torquay and Brixham for the finals which Stuart Morris won. He went on to win the Gold in the Olympics. Richard sailed a Finn class dinghy for Britain in the next Olympics. Stuart was perhaps the best British racing helmsman of all time in round the buoy racing, a most likable fellow, a bit older than me and with a great sense of humour.

*

I badly wanted my parents and my Aunt Vi to meet Chris. We decided the cheapest way to travel and the most exciting was by motorcycle. It was summertime and my recollection is that we had good weather for the whole trip. We went through lovely Wiltshire, then across Wales via Brecon to Fishguard and Rosslare. I was in some trepidation about this meeting, my parents (particularly Mother) had not approved of Maud but neither did they approve of divorce. However on meeting her they did seem to like Chris in a subdued way.

And Mother made sure our bedrooms were on different floors!

We spent at least two lovely days walking in the Wicklow hills. We climbed Lugnaquilla and being alone there made love in the heather. We also walked south west from Sally Gap to a little hilltop tarn where we stripped off and plunged in and out again as quickly as possible! It was freezing and we had no towels and just ran about to get dry.

On the way back to Rosslare going by a rough coast road, we had a rather ridiculous accident. A woman suddenly drove out of a private entrance and to avoid a collision I braked hard and skidded round almost stationary, allowing Chris literally to step off the pillion. Unfortunately I could not get clear and my left leg was trapped under the bike. I was not in trouble until the woman panicked and instead of stopping, she was going very slowly, drove her car on top of me and the bike with her front wheels. When I was 'released' nothing was broken, just rather painfully bruised, but the bike however was damaged beyond immediate riding. The lady was of course really mortified and Chris and I had to comfort her! We all went into her house, her husband turned up, and after a rest he drove us and the bike in a trailer to Rosslare from where we finished the journey by train.

*

Maud had moved back to Hampstead with the children, who came down to Lymington to stay with Chris and me several times, on one occasion we took them to the Island and had a great walk on the downs west of Yarmouth.

Chris and I, now 'living in sin' on Maia, were frowned upon by certain hypocritical members of the RLYC. This did not worry us much, it was just that we were too open about it, little would be thought about it today, but we did want to get married and I asked Maud to divorce me. She reluctantly agreed and the whole thing was set in train with our solicitors. I had to go through the somewhat farcical business of getting a witness to declare evidence of my infidelity. It was arranged that Chris and I would be found by a pre primed chambermaid in bed together in a London hotel!

For my part I promised to continue to support Maud and the children and also to buy them the little house which Maud had found at Lower Heyford in Oxfordshire.

This meant that I would have to find a reasonably well paid job. This turned up in the form of an advertisement I saw in the Telegraph for a naval architect in a Bombay shipyard. Following an interview with a Mr Gidwani in a London office, I was offered the post at what seemed to me to be a reasonable salary... but with no accommodation or extra living allowance.

Chris and I discussed the proposition in a somewhat agonised way. I was in a small way on the crest of a wave as a designer but yacht building was still in something of a doldrum. On the one hand the Indian opportunity would give me the chance to start a new life with Chris in a entirely new environment, but on the other it meant me virtually saying good bye to my children for long periods, and also leaving my ageing parents to my sisters' care.

In a way there wasn't much choice unless something else turned up, as I had no money. I signed up for the job and my air passage was booked. This was in early October. Ian was furious but I was not very sympathetic in that direction as he had broken our employment agreement, and his selling 'Binker' out of the English racing circuit had lost me my best advertisement, although the 'Slipways' were doing very well. From the point of view of my career going to India was of course a mistake, but I had no means of knowing that within a year the boat business would be booming.

I had to hurriedly sort myself out. I sold boats and my other possessions and left Chris to live alone on Maia with the dogs, my Sally and her redsetter Patsy!

The worst of all was that we had to accept that we would be separated until the divorce was made absolute and we could get married in Bombay. We were deeply in love and did not even know how long those wretched formalities would take. On top of that her passage out, which would have to be at our expense by sea, would take nearly a month.

*

I travelled to Ireland to say good bye to my people. Mother and Dad drove me to the morning boat as they had done so often in the past. I remember seeing them from the upper deck, an old couple plodding up to the car park. My father then was like me now, very lame and very old.

The tears flowed freely.

Three

INEVITABLY the day arrived. I nearly missed the train at Brockenhurst and possibly the plane at Heathrow. Fortunately Charles St J was there to drive me to the station in his Allard, (a very fast machine).

Anyway, my farewell to Chris was cut pretty short.

The flight to India was in an Air India Super Constellation, a very successful and elegant machine in its day, its four propellers driven by big radial engines.

It was my first long distance flight in a big machine. The weather was good and as we approached Switzerland we met some magnificent cumulus clouds at about 20,000ft. They had sharp edges and looked absolutely solid even close up, the plane at that stage was obviously being flown 'hands on' and as we wove our way down to Zurich through gaps in the cumulus one felt that if we touched one there would be a severe bump! Of course in reality there is generally considerable turbulence in these clouds. Glider pilots who can get great lift under them have to be careful not to get sucked up too violently, and of course all sense of attitude without instruments is lost in their dense moist interiors.

The stopover at Zurich was brief, I used it to start writing to Chris. The next stop was Cairo. I remember lots of men in white nightshirts and red fezzes, heat and frenzy. We left the plane for a short time and were then off again for the long flight to Bombay.

Flying relatively low by present day standards and in clear weather it was most interesting to see real desert. By no means flat, it was in fact mountainous and looked quite impossible for an emergency landing. One could just make out camel trails and camel caravans. After some hours we were over the Indian ocean and then the Indian coastline. Then it was down and down over the incredibly green post-monsoon countryside and the sprawling city of Bombay.

This was to be my home for nearly ten years.

Stepping out of the aeroplane was like stepping in to a mild turkish bath!

I was almost immediately met by one of the Varuna shipyard's employees. He spoke good English and escorted me through immigration, (I had of course had all the necessary antis injected into me in England), and he then drove me in a large American car through the shanty towns on the outskirts and into the city of multi-story flats and other buildings. My hotel, fairly modest, was at the southern end of the city, not far from the renowned landmark, the Gateway of India.

When I arrive in a strange city my first move is to find out where I am and if possible acquire a map. I set out to find the 'Gateway'. I wanted to see the harbour and what yachts if any were afloat there. (I was pleased to see that there were quite a few yachts on moorings, mostly half decked boats, and four or five keel yachts.)

This was only a few streets away, and I made note of a prominent building as a land mark for my return. I was dressed in long cotton pants and a white cotton shirt and thought I looked like nearly everyone else but in no time I was surrounded by small children demanding annas, having 'no mamma no pappa'!

Then I was approached by a little man wearing a round black hat, a white cotton jacket and a doti, with a little black leather pouch over his shoulder. He came up beside me and after saying something to me that I didn't understand, he grabbed me firmly by an ear and before I could do anything about it he had a sort of probe up my earhole!

I was paralysed and kept perfectly still while he made soothing noises to me about having found a stone! Then, to prove this he magically produced a very small pebble on the end of his probe, at the same time implying that he had saved my life or at least my hearing!

I managed to escape him a few annas poorer, before he could grab my other ear!

*

I found my way back to my hotel by a different route and into what was the main thoroughfare, the Colaba Causeway. This was lined with small shops and even smaller pavement vendors' stalls selling everything that the people of Bombay could possibly want.

The population was incredibly mixed. Hindus, Moslems of different sects, the men and women dressed according to (as I found out later) their different Indian districts. There were also Parsees, a people with whom later we found most affinity. Racially and religiously connected to earlier

Persians, the Parsees then made up most of the professional classes in Bombay.

Then, on returning to my room at the hotel I made the acquaintance of the most numerous of all the populations...bed bugs and cockroaches! Despite this, I had quite a good first night with a big punkah fan blasting down on me.

*

I was duly picked up the next morning and introduced to the 'shipyard' and its staff. The yard was at the top of a wet, *ie* a tidal dock known as Guncarriage Basin, the name no doubt arisen from the days of the British Navy or even of the ships of The East India Company. There was no proper 'Hard', the whole yard being just natural earth, compacted under the roofs of the workshops.

My drawing office was up a flight of timber stairs in a big room, a small office for me off it. I had two assistants. One was an American-trained qualified Naval Architect named Dhumal who was a Gugerati. The other was a draughtsman named Fernandez who was from Goa, still Portuguese in those days.

These were both very good men and we made a very friendly office. Another good man was the boatbuilder foreman, Saimbi, a Punjabi and I think a refugee from the new Pakistan. They were all good at their trade and could speak pretty good English. We also had a Hungarian engineer named Rudi, competent with diesel engines and good at getting things done.

The management were all Sindis, refugees from Lahore which was by then the capital of Pakistan. There they seemed to have had a thriving agency for General Motors...and consequently they drove huge ugly Buicks and Chevrolets. On the whole they left me to get on with my job. This involved the preparation of designs for tenders and, when orders were forthcoming, getting out the working drawings.

I found lodgings with a middle aged Anglo-Indian lady who fed and looked after me quite well. I stayed with her until Chris arrived.

*

I arrived in Bombay with an introduction to one of the Jameson family who were our near neighbours at Knockranny. He was resident at the Royal Bombay Y.C. and he invited me to lunch at the club.

Not being well up on the etiquette of these clubs, I turned up dressed in clean white shirt and pants. I was shown up to his rooms by an immaculately turned out servant in gold decorated jacket, (plus red turban and cummerbund!), who made no remark as to my dress. But when Jameson saw me he gave me a look of horror. His "how do you do" and shaking of hands was quickly followed by "But you can't go in the dining room like that".

He loaned me a jacket and tie and I was able to take lunch in the hallowed dining room! At that time, although already three years after independence, the R.B.Y.C. was strictly For Europeans Only. By the time Chris and I left India in 1960 we had seen the club pass through all the phases of transition and the Commodore was an Indian, a Parsee friend of ours, Kerse Naoriji.

I think that Mr Jameson thought I was 'beyond the pale' and I don't remember meeting him again! But he did give me an an introduction to Ian Bagshawe (who had a 16ft sharpie sailing boat of unknown type) and we became good friends. He invited me to spend a weekend in his shack across the harbour at a place called Mandwa. This was the beginning of quite a love affair with that place.

*

On my first journey there I remember the wind was very light and by the time we had covered the 8 mile voyage it was nearly dark. We were ferried ashore by the Indian caretaker of the little shack clubhouse, a very pleasant young man called Mardeo.

(I am finding it strange how all these names are coming back to me, me who normally has a very bad memory for names. The brain has an incredible capacity for storing information, most of it useless!)

Ian when we knew him was working for I.C.I. chemicals and dyes division. He had a part time servant of his own whom he seemed to be able to warn of his coming by bush telegraph or something, but he had been in the Indian Civil Service under the Imperial regime and had perhaps learned some of the mysteries of the east!

Anyhow we had a meal under rather a dim oil lamp so as not to attract too many flying beasts, all quite harmless but rather trying. After our meal we walked over to another shack, much more permanent than Ian's, which was only a framework of untrimmed timber covered with woven palm leaves and thatch of a sort.

This belonged to Mario and Luochi Levy, British nationalised Italians. They and later their son Sonny were to be our greatest friends in India. Mario had come to India before the war as a specialist in flooring, marble terrazo etc., running a successful company called AFCO. During the war they started building boats for the British Indian Navy and when I arrived on the scene at Varuna they had nearly a monopoly of modern boat building in Bombay. So, in effect, we were friendly rivals, particularly for Government contracts. As they were long established and Varuna were newcomers we didn't get too many!

*

When I arrived at Varuna they were just completing a big timber motor lighter designed by my predecessor, an Englishman. When this was completed I volunteered to take it to its destination, Goa, with a native crew, one of whom was to be the engineer and also interpreter as he had some English. The weather was good for the trip of about 280 miles but it was shortly before the Monsoon was due to break on the Indian west coast and although there was little wind there was a heavy ocean swell breaking. I had 10 or 11 crew, really with nothing to do, and all went well and every one was happy until we sighted the string of small islands ending in the Vengurla lighthouse.

The normal and shorter course for smaller coastal traffic was between two of these rocky islands and according to my information the correct passage was buoyed and as time was running out for arriving at Marmogoa in daylight I was going for the shorter course. However, as we drew near, no one could see any buoys. There was a very strong tidal current running with us and we had to decide pretty quickly which was the gap to go for and not dither! I was steering and had full responsibility, and made for what looked the most likely passage, rash but by then there was no alternative. Due to the tide we were going much faster over the ground than I could have wished, when suddenly I and everyone else on the boat saw right in front of us in the deep tough of the wave ahead and for a brief moment the wet surface of rock. I didn't let go the wheel and scream (only inwardly) and apparently calmly gave her full port helm, waiting for a hideous crunch as we dropped in the next trough; it never came and in another minute or two we were out in the clear again. The passage we went through was the widest and may have been the correct one but perhaps to one side or the other, I shall never know how near I came to loosing the vessel and drowning us all in that sluicing tide. (The buoys had been removed prior to the Monsoon!)

I did not want to spend a second night at sea but of course I was not familiar with the entrance to the Panjim river in Goa, and the location of the channel across the bar was a bit vague. Leading marks and lights were indicated on the chart but as we closed with the coast we could not identify them and the light was going so I decided the safest thing to do was to anchor off until morning knowing that it would be an uncomfortable night with the swell running over comparatively shallow water and the chance of the anchor dragging. We had just let the anchor go when we saw a small launch coming out over the bar and signalling us to follow her in. So it was up anchor and get behind her. The only trouble was she was going faster than us, it was almost dark and the only light she carried looked like a candle in a jampot! The surf was so big and steep that she kept disappearing in the troughs and was hard to find again. It was an exciting ride as we surfed forward and then fell back into the troughs, and the possibility of a broach and a capsize was very present. Then quite suddenly we were in a lagoon in front of the lights of the town and proceeding into the river until we were directed where finally to anchor. We had been expected and I was ferried ashore and parked in a small hotel where I stayed for a couple of days. It was all very Portuguese in architecture but almost a military camp - the Indian Government was threatening to annex it and did so some years later. The population was very mixed race, the Portuguese freely intermarrying with the local Indian women and the result produced people of considerable beauty, particularly the women.

Gidwani came down by train and we returned to Bombay the same way. This though did not end my involvement with Goa. We had a contract to build two trans river self propelled vehicle and passenger ferries. The preliminary work on the design had been begun by my predecessor, so I had no choice of method of propulsion. This was by Hotchkill Cones and I thought rather low powered Thornycroft diesel engines. They were successfully built of steel rivetted construction and delivered to Goa - one by Gidwani himself, it was in the fair season but must have been a slow trip.

*

Chris and I had been exchanging at least one letter a week. Nearly five months had passed before the Divorce was made absolute, and before Chris was able to book her passage. She had in the meantime moved back to London and her parents. Maia was let, and I was able to help my sister Nancy bring her children over to England from Ireland and get them made wards of court. (There had been rather a violent break up of her marriage in Ireland, a sad story.)

Chris and I had in an odd way a piece of luck in England shortly before she left, in that our tenants in Maia somehow had a major fire aboard.

Fortunately Maia was insured and was considered a total loss and this realised five to six hundred pounds, a big boost to our finances!

Nonetheless, soon after I arrived in Bombay I realised that I could not both afford reasonable accommodation on my salary and also meet my commitments in England....so I decided to build somewhere to live!

I wrote to Chris asking her if she would live in a caravan if I built one.

Of course her reply was yes so I set about designing a big caravan, suitable for the climate. I found and bought the front axle of a Rolls Royce with serviceable tyres. The whole of the structure was native teak including the main chassis members. The roof was of the lantern type, allowing maximum ventilation. By the time Chris arrived the framing was nearly complete.

*

At last the day of Chris's departure arrived. She was travelling second class on an Indian owned ship, the 'Jalazad'. She had Sally, our dog with her, and as I learned later she was sharing a cabin with three other women, and the food was mostly Indian. The captain of the ship was British which made the voyage more pleasant for Chris.

In the meantime I got permission from Gidwani to put into commission a motor launch of about 16feet with an Austin marine engine of about 25hp which had been designed and built by my predecessor. It had quite a useful turn of speed at about 20-25mph with two up. I had it launched on the morning the Jalazad was due and met her well out in the harbour and circled her until I attracted Chris's attention!

Then I left the boat in the charge of the boatmen of the Colaba Sailing Club, hired a taxi to the Ballard pier where the ship was due to berth, and we had a marvellous reunion which included a somewhat bemused Sally.

I had made all the arrangements for our immediate wedding, without any frills I'm afraid, at a registry office. My two best men were my assistant Dhumal and a Danish friend Moerner. After the formalities we had lunch together, dumped Chris's luggage at my digs and went sightseeing with Sally on a lead. When we eventually got back to the digs we found my landlady had imported a double bed for our benefit! I think we must have spent the evening talking at the digs because I remember at least two young men called to see if Chris had really got married!

Our wedding night was not without it's funny side. We had not been in the bed for very long when we realised that we were not alone. Lots of little black bugs wanted to share the warmth and we spent a lot of time remaking the bed and reducing the insect population!

Our landlady was horrified when we told her about our experience and the bed was changed for the remaining night we were there.

I had been befriended by Bill Williams, then Bombay Port Harbourmaster. He lived alone and invited me and my bride to stay with him while we built our home. Bill lived in a very large and somewhat gloomy house surrounded by trees. These, some form of fruit trees, attracted what we at first thought were large black birds but they were actually Fruit Bats, sometimes called Flying Foxes.

We moved in all our belongings and, shortly after, we went on our honeymoon.

MANDWA was an idyllic venue for a honeymoon, I had told Chris all about it in my letters. We set off from Gateway with our food, bedsheets, and spare petrol.

Normally deserted during the week, Mandwa woke up at weekends. Friday evening saw various yachts arriving with small parties aboard. They picked up moorings and were ferried into shallow water by Mardeo and paddled in from there carrying their supplies.

Mandwa was on the southern shore of Bombay's great natural harbour, it lay under a little conical hill surmounted by a white tower. Lining up this tower from seaward with the main lighthouse gave a safe course inwards to the harbour. But to us that day it marked the location of a five months dream, and we slithered towards it at speed on flat calm water.

*

I think I must have told Mardeo the last time I was there that I would be bringing a wife on about that day. In any event he had spotted us on the way over and he came out in the club boat to meet us. He was quietly welcoming to Memsahib and later they often prepared meals together on a very smelly old paraffin stove and primus in the rather gloomy 'kitchen' at the back of the club.

Club was a rather grand name for what mostly was just an open space with miscellaneous beds dotted about under the trees! There was really no privacy and while there was some shelter under a tin roof from the very occasional rain, the sleeping area was just covered by matting sunshade.

The beach was silver sand with black streaks which were believed later to be of mildly radioactive sand. The sea was very shallow with a moderate tidal range and at low tide when the fish traps were exposed the women and children from the village inland came down to collect what were usually very few and tiny fish. Watching them collect these fish and knocking barnacles off the rocks gave us an idea of how poor these mainland people were. But they did seem happy and in later years when Simon arrived he used to disappear, at three or four years old, up to the village for hours. He would go 'fishing' with them and help drive their cattle. They accepted him and he seemed perfectly at home with them, soon chattering away in their tongue! Some of the Europeans who came to Mandwa did not approve of him going with the local people but we did, also of his going stark naked on the beach!

Our honeymoon holiday was a thoroughly lazy one, going for evening walks and exploring some of the neighbouring creeks in the launch ...and playing with Sally on the beach. While there we socialised with the weekend visitors, principally with Mario and Luchy (who became quite a friend of Chris's), and also with Ian Bagshawe.

I climbed up the ancient iron rungs on the inside of the round tower, wondering who had built it and when; it was probably the East India Company. The tower was built as a hollow ring, in such a way as to allow painters to drop down the outside whitewashing. There was an impressive view from the top.

*

The time went all too quickly and soon we were heading back into the smell and heat again. I cannot now imagine living in an Indian city which was not on the sea with somewhere to sail to on holidays and week ends. For us it was always a joy to leave behind all the noise and smell of the great city of Bombay. Having a boat of some sort made life for us worth living.

For the next five or six weeks, while we were living with Bill, Chris came to Varuna nearly every day and worked in the heat on the caravan and I joined her after my day's work.

No doubt we were a strange phenomenon in Bombay, an English couple working manually in the heat of the day at building their own home!

But we finished it and moved on to the site within the yard which Gidwani had kindly allocated to us. This was out of the main working area and arranged so that we could extend an existing roof to give us shade and protection from the monsoon rains.

*

While still at Bill's house, a lone long distance yachtsman called Adrian Hater arrived off Bombay from Aden. He was escorted into a dockyard berth by Bill personally, and then brought as a guest to the house. He was physically in a very poor state. This was the time of the Monsoon and his voyage had been difficult. He was in what was a very small yacht, a little yaul called "SHEILA" under 30ft overall. (The yacht had come originally from Dun Laoghaire in Ireland).

Adrian was half starved and covered with salt water sores. To quite an extent Chris took him in charge, helping to clean and clear up the yacht and get all his clothes washed and so on. Bill refitted the boat as necessary for nothing. He stayed on after we moved to the caravan. Adrian had virtually no money and in fact rather overstayed his welcome! He wrote a book ("Sheila In The Wind") when he eventually reached his New Zealand destination,

We lived in the van for about two years, very happily if unconventionally. Essentially we were in a native village, a village of fisherfolk which had been absorbed into greater Bombay when the causeway was built. On one occasion they invited us to be guests at one of their festivals, providing us with chairs to watch dancing while everyone else sat on the ground. The dancing went on and on and it suddenly dawned on us that it was for us! They were dancing specifically for us and they would go on all night if we did not get up! So expressing our appreciation as best we could we got up and left.

This time was of course not long after the mass migrations of the Independence period, the Assam earthquake had also displaced a great many people. There were many thousands of refugees in Bombay and one of their shanty settlements was hard by us, so that we were almost overlooked by them, which did not worry us. We were partly screened off and it gave us an interesting view of Indian life.

More than once I had to go into the water to fish out a toddler who had fallen off the wall and hand it over when its mother came round for it. We also had the interesting spectacle of young women washing their saris in situ, unwinding, washing and drying whilst starting to rewind it on again and so proceeding until it was all washed... and nothing had been revealed!

*

To get a bit of mobility I bought a very well used Morris Oxford saloon, and we were thus able to visit friends... apart from our best friends, many acquaintances refused to visit us in our 'squalor'. Returning late at night we used to find the streets near the yard strewn with sleeping bodies, all male, some on string beds called charpoys (four legs). Chris had to get out of the car and wake them. They never complained and helped us through very good naturedly.

Soon Simon was on the way and as we did not trust Bombay (buffalo) milk except when boiled, we decided to get goats and become a bit more independent! We had no personal servant at that time but one of the older workmen attached himself to us and became in fact our servant for all non domestic duties. This was Pandoo, a dear ugly old soul with extremely bandy legs. We asked him about getting a couple of pregnant nannies and in due course they turned up. They were nubian goats, a breed without horns and with hanging down ears. The problem of feeding them was solved very conveniently when we got permission to let them loose on some enclosed waste military land on the right hand side of the basin. In the wet season there was tons of grass and in the dry they fed on the leaves of the scrub trees with a little hay which Pandoo bought for us. We soon had nearly a dozen goats and had plenty of milk which we could trust. Pandoo wanted to do the milking but as we were a bit fussy about hygiene Chris or I did all the milking.

Perhaps the saddest thing that happened to us in India was the death of our dog Sally. She started behaving in a very odd way, as if she were a bit drunk, and it suddenly dawned on us with some horror that she had Rabies. It was the dumb variety, she was completely docile but we were very careful in handling her, it really was heartbreaking to see her, she still knew us and feebly wagged her tail when we spoke to her. There was only one thing to do- take her to the Kafkine Institute which dealt with Rabies so we drove her there in the Morris. They put her in a small compound by herself and from outside we said good bye to her. We were both in tears, it was such a dreadful end to a marvellous canine friend who knew us to the end.

We all three of us had to report to the Institute. The heavy injections into the stomach muscles was most unpleasant and for poor little Simon a torture.

*

I had been missing dinghy racing very much and we decided to build a Merlin on the same lines as Mercury. At the same time we got Sonny Levy interested in building and several other people interested in owning, including Gurth and Joan Kimber. Gurth was at that time the British Resident High Commissioner and it wasn't a bad idea having him on our side!

And so a racing dinghy class was born on Bombay harbour. Sonny built seven at AFCO to an Ian Proctor design and we built two to mine, and they turned out to be pretty evenly matched. The problem was where to keep them. Afloat they would get heavy and possibly grow worms as they were built of cigar box type cedar and not teak, and if kept ashore they would dry out and leaking would always be a nuisance.

The first solution for all boats except ours was a manually operated hoist on Ballard Pier and a special shed there. 'Nick' as we called ours was out a long time before the others and we kept her under cover beside the van, and launched her along a rollup slipway rather like a rope ladder. This was an ideal arrangement and allowed us to go sailing at almost any state of the tide. There was usually quite a good offshore breeze at night and we frequently made use of this. Sometimes it was strong enough to get us up and planing which in the dark made thrilling sailing.

I remember one night when we caused an incoming ship surprise and confusion when we sailed across her course. Wanting to know what we were he switched on his searchlight and we were pinned on the end of the beam, dazzled and unable to escape until we turned back towards the ship and sailed down her portside where the beam could no longer bear on us.

*

I was kept pretty busy at Varuna and we turned out a number of timber launches and one high speed craft for Bombay Police. One day I received a surprise note from the general manager of another and much bigger yard, Alcock Ashdown and Co. Ltd., to the effect that he would be pleased to meet me at his office if and when convenient!

So, unknown to Gidwani, I went along to Alcocks and met a Mr Gumley, who there and then offered me the job of naval architect at a considerably higher salary and with accommodation. When I said I had a contract with Varuna he said he could look after that. It was very tempting but after discussing it with Chris I turned down the offer simply I suppose on moral grounds.

One of the people we met at Mandwa were the Godrejes, Novel and Soono and also their friends and I think relatives the Naorojis, Jenie and Kerse. Novel was managing director of probably the biggest employer of labour in the Bombay area and Kerse was the personnel manager. They had a modest but properly built bungalow at Mandwa. Novel and Kerse were Parsees and both keen sailors, men of about my own age. They ordered a Merlin from AFCO. Novel's firm was Godrel and Boyce Ltd, they had a very mixed output, machine tools, typewriters, refrigerators and locks of all sorts. Also they provided excellent services for their employees, clinics and kindergartens, etc.

Chris was now pregnant and we were lucky in finding a very good doctor, McKenzie by name. He was attached to what had been the European hospital at Breach Candy, where there was also the well know swimming pool. This was Europeans Only when we first arrived but later it was opened to all wealthier europeanised Indian citizens. McKenzie kept a check on Chris's pregnancy and Simon arrived by caesarian section at Breach Candy on 27-10-54, and was soon installed in the van.

*

As the Bombay Sailing Association now had a number of dinghy sailors the club was invited to send a team of eight to compete against The College of Military Engineering on the river Mullah at Kirkee near Poona. Chris and I were in the team and for transport we went with one of the Indian members in a large American car. It was our first time up the Ghats and the driving frightened us somewhat. The CME at that time was commanded by a British Brigadier of Engineers, and there was a very pleasant small clubhouse with a balcony overlooking the river, this being about 50 yards wide at that point and slow flowing. The only hazard was the occasional buffalo swimming across!

The club had ten 14ft undecked dinghies with gunter rig and in the racing each side had four boats but we were not really racing as a team which I would have preferred, as it makes tactics much more interesting. Chris and I won the first race beating the Brigadier which was not quite the thing to do but he took it very well! We sailed two races splitting up crews and on points the CME Won. It was only during tea after the race that I heard someone refer to the boats as 'Wags', and then of course I recognised them as Dublin Bay Wags, claimed to be the oldest one design class in the world, my father had recently built one! They had been introduced many years previously not only to Kirkee and to many other places where the British Raj ruled.

After that we visited Kirkee many times and it was always most enjoyable, particularly the social side with evening dancing. On the return journey, a convoy of several cars including ours, we always stopped for a meal together at a sort of roadhouse at the top of the Ghats. There were no mosquitoes, only myriads of fireflies in the trees, and it was delightfully cool and the Indian food very good.

(These visits also lead to my being invited a few years later to design a new class of boat for Kirkee and for further afield. I will come to that later.)

The Merlins were now well established. Merlin Rockets they were now called, due to a merger with the similar Bruce Banks Design, the Rocket class. They raced regularly and when it came time for the Monsoon to break, instead of laying up the boats and forgetting about sailing for about three months we all decided to start racing on what was known as Back Bay, a partly enclosed artificial lagoon on the southern and ocean side of the city. This was exposed to the full force of the monsoon wind, usually about 20-25 knots, also to surf only slightly less than on the open coast.

We were sailing off a lee shore so getting afloat was not easy. Men and women were sailing in shorts or bathing costumes and the water was warm, and the technique was to fully rig the boats, then launch them into the surf with the crewman holding the bow into the waves. The helmsman on board shipped the rudder and let a little centreboard down and then, at a precise moment between waves got way on, the crew turning the boat and scrambling in over the stern.

The first boat away took out the buoys which were to mark the course, usually a triangle, and the last boat in the race collected them. Once afloat there was great sailing with a planing wind all the time, and at the finish we raised the centreboard, the rudders hinged and we surfed right up the beach.

Some members found this a bit too strenuous, so we moved the whole fleet up to Vickroli where Godrej had his factories and where there was a large creek with plenty of wind and rain but no waves.

I WAS INTO my third year with Varuna when Gidwani got an invitation from Burma Shell to quote for a very big storage barge. I refused to design or estimate for it, feeling we had neither the means to build nor launch it. Giwani would not accept this and, on the entirely false charge that I had been exchanging information about another tender with Sonny Levi, he gave me notice and re-engaged my predecessor.

This was another naval architect, older than me, and he apparently quoted for the barge. The yard got the order and started building , which had to be to Lloyds rules and built under Lloyds supervision.

Building went ahead using the heavy plating specified and predictably the ground began to subside under the weight! The work of plate welding went ahead without realigning and the whole thing became distorted. My friends at Lloyd's said rather unkindly that whenever they wanted a good laugh they went to Varuna to see how vessels should not be built! In the end the half built barge was abandoned, Varuna went bust and closed down and the barge was cut up for scrap.

We were not even offered our passage home, so I went to see Mr Gumley, this time rather 'cap in hand' and in a weak position. We agreed conditions, not as good as the original offer but including free accommodation. I also managed to persuade him to to buy our caravan as a mobile 'on site' office for very considerably more than it had cost us! Gurth the High Commissioner fixed things so that we got everything due to us and a second class passage home in a P&O ship. This was the 'Stratheden' in which, as it happened he and his wife Joan were also sailing. As the sailing date was nearly a month away the Kimbers most kindly offered us accommodation free in their residence, which had been the palace of Jinna, the creator of Pakistan. And it was a real palace! I can still see Simon in my mind's eye, aged about three, wandering about these marble halls with lots of brilliantly clad servants keeping an eye on the bewildered little boy, bewildered by the transition from caravan to palace!

The passage home was as good as a cruise in a very informal atmosphere helped by the Kimbers inviting us across the class barrier for socialising and for meals. We called at Aden and shared a taxi for a trip inland to the strange town of Crater built within what seemed to be a huge crater and entered, if I remember rightly, by a tunnel. Then it was the Red Sea where I spent some time on the bridge with the 2nd officer studying wind charts to see what would be the best time of year to sail north through it (we had been discussing possibly building a seagoing yacht in Bombay).

Then we berthed at Suez, where the Gulli Gulli Man (a magician) came aboard to entertain the children and adults. He was let loose in a space in the main first class saloon and soon had chickens and doves all over the place produced by magic, he was very good. I went ashore for a short walk in the bazaars of the town. Then through this man made waterway about which there was just then a dispute between the Canal Company and the Egyptian Government as to who should own and control it, leading to its closure a couple of years later for quite a period. A brief stop at Port Said and then we were in the Med. Our course was past Crete and the Captain took us very close in to the steep shore and and pointed out over the public address system places of interest from the lost battle for the island in the last war. Then through the Straits of Mesina and close up to the volcanic island of Stromboli, which managed a little puff of sparks for our benefit! Next between Corsica and Sardinia and then to Marseilles. Here I watched the docking of the ship with interest. It was in full daylight early morning, we approached the completely deserted quay, and just when it seemed we had not been noticed a man rode onto the quay on a scooter at just the time a light line was hove ashore, he hauled across the main warp, put the noose over a bollarad, rode to the other end of the ship and did the same. In the meantime another man drove a self propelled gangway up to the ship and in a very short time with no fuss or shouting the ship was berthed and the officials were aboard. The comparison with the dockings in India and Egypt was most remarkable for its quiet efficiency.

It was wintertime and the Med was quite stormy and cold. We were soon through the Straits of Gibraltar and turning north for Biscay and home, to dock in Londons docklands. Christine's father met us with a chauffeur driven car on loan fron his accountancy firm, and so to her home.

We spent some time at Chris's home in Hendon and also went to my parents' home as a married couple with a very charming little boy. I think that in both families we were favourably accepted.

I also briefly visited my first family now living in Oxfordshire, and promised Maud that I should be able to let her have a little more money.

I had only allowed myself a leave of three to four weeks and as we agreed that Chris should have a longer break, we were faced with another separation of several weeks which was going to be hard as we were still very much in love.

A that time it was possible to fly India in stages by BOAC and I was very keen to experience Jet travel so I arranged to fly first to Rome where I had a full day to explore a little of the city and its night life when the proprietor of the small hotel I had booked into suggested we joined forces with two BOAC air hostesses who were in the same hotel and dine in an interesting restaurant he knew. This was agreed and the place which was in the catacombs under the city provided very good food and even better music, to my ear really marvellous singing and traditional songs, it was obviously a place frequented by the people of Rome, we were the only outsiders, and when I remarked to our 'host' that there seemed to be a lot of family groups he explained that that was so, a custom of the Romans to show off their families, the real object being potential marriages. After the meal our 'host' engaged two horse drawn open carriages with hoods when required and we men each took one of the girls and in convoy toured some of the city.

I don't know how the others got on but me and my girl enjoyed the tour and our company and no more!

The next morning I was due at the airport to fly direct to Bombay by DeHavilland Comet Jet. These machines had only recently come into service, and their main route at that time was Rome, Bombay, Calcutta. I was travelling on a first class ticket and was right forward in the aircraft. The whine of the turbojets was much the same as the turbo prop Vikings and Viscounts we were used to, but on take off the lightly loaded machine had a much more impressive climb and went up to over 30,000 feet as we slowly turned east over the sea and southern Italy. The flight was very smooth but we were flying over haze nearly all the way and I could only see the land far below. The first class cabin was used as a crew rest space and I always say and without hindsight that I did not feel very happy on the flight and also that there was stress noticeable in the crew. We landed safely and on time in Bombay.

A matter of a week or two after that a Comet crashed near Calcutta without any warning, at the time it was put down to a freak electric storm. Soon after that another crashed in the sea soon after take off from Rome, again no warning. No doubt there was worry but the machines were not taken out of service. Then came a final crash close to the location of the second. I was naturally interested. The planes were immediately taken out of service and a massive search was taken on by the British Navy and the wreckage of one was located and most of the wreckage was salvaged and taken to Farnborough. The biggest and most expensive detective operation ever undertaken on a crash got underway. A full report was later published by H.M Stationary Office, I got and still have the report. The planes were exploding due to internal external air pressure differential at a certain approximate altitude and the failure of the fuselage shell at the corner of a small dome in the roof. It is almost certain that the plane I flew in was one of the three!

I ARRIVED at Alcocks to find that Gumley had not yet found suitable accommodation for myself and the family. I was installed in the works 'chummery' which was cheap and convenient but not exactly luxurious as there was only a kind of bed sitting room and a common room which I shared with two bachelors.

My work office was rather depressing, air conditioned but windowless. I shared this with the chief draughtsman, an Englishman in charge of the structural side of the business which in fact was the chief money earner. I had two good draughtsmen, the best being Mathre, a great help to me for the next five or six years.

My first task was to do a basic drawing for a new fire fighting and salvage vessel for the Bombay Port Trust to a general specification and prepare an estimate, not a easy task to start on. However we did get the order and then I really had to design it. It was rather outside my field, but it got designed and built. About 90ft overall with two 200hp medium speed propelling engines and two 400hp similar engines driving five stage pumps. These could be used to supply 16 fire hose outlets and/or two foam or water monitors mounted on deck, and 8 suction points, (all this supplied by the German firm of MAN). The vessel had to do 11 knots and was to be built under Lloyds survey.

It was of all welded steel construction and of double chine hull form, a type of form which has almost become my hallmark. She did meet all requirements. After that from my point of view we met a doldrum. Too many tenders unsuccessful and I think some interesting designs but too pricey because in my opinion our managing agents put on too high overhead charges. We did eventually get an order for four seagoing tugs which I designed.

*

One evening Sonny Levi rang me and invited me to dinner at his parents' house, they were away somewhere, after dinner when we had a drink or two Sonny suggested we visit the part of the town known as the Cages, the red light area of which I had of course heard.

We called a taxi, and Sonny first took us to a rather superior place standing in a garden. The large entry room had lots of gorgeously sarid girls sitting round, they greeted Sonny as an old friend! Apparently the girl he wanted was not there and so we went on to a much less glamourous place up flights of stairs.

On Sonny's advice I picked the prettiest girl and she led me to a small room with a clean bed but walls spattered with the the stains of beetle nut, as are so many walls in public places. I took off my shirt and she her sari and we lay down together.

I took her small naked body in my arms and literally just wanted to give her my love- I felt I could no more possess her much violated little body with its rather dried up breasts and shaven pubic hair than fly.

This was not virtue or not wanting to be unfaithful to Chris physically which I never was but because I have always hated the idea of prostitution. She of course could not understand why I did not get on with the 'jig a jig', I could not speak to her but I think she got the message. We stayed together for a long time and I gave her all the money I had brought with me which on Sonny's advice was not much. When I left in the small hours Sonny had gone. On reaching the street she called a farewell to me from an upstairs window. I still think of her and all the other little slave prostitutes and what would have become of her.

I was lucky to find a taxi to take me home.

*

Chris and Simon flew out to Bombay in a Super Conny, as they were affectionately named, and I met them at Santa Cruz airport. I had a company car and we drove straight to Alcocks and installed ourselves in the rather restricted accommodation. This did not worry Chris, she was so happy we were all together again. It was only for a few days and then we were moved to a first floor furnished flat in a new block. It wasn't very grand but we made the most of it for a few months and while there we (almost exclusively Chris) built a 13ft speed boat. We had been instrumental in starting a small skiing club and had undertaken to build the tug and two pairs of skis, somebody else provided the outboard engine.

We built it to my plans in one of our three rooms and kitchen, knowing it would have to go out the window somehow. It meant taking the whole window out and without permission we carefully sawed the window out of its frame one night but leaving it in situ until by arrangement with one of the junior managers we had a works lorry come round at midday siesta time bringing two long planks. It was then a case of quickly take out the window, shute the boat out, down the planks and away... then I put the window back, secured it as best possible and puttied and painted the cut parts. It turned out to be a great little boat and much fun was had out of it mostly on the aforementioned Back Bay.

*

Mr Gumley was replaced by a Mr Campbell but shortly before he retired he sold us a little yacht for a song. I had got my eye on this boat, which was lying covered in dust and dirt in a corner of the big building shed. It seemed to belong to nobody and nobody seemed to know anything about it and I made plans for its restoration.

When Campbell arrived he arranged for us to change flats in the same building and we moved to the top floor where we had as an extra quite a big roof area, which made all the difference. We were able to make a roof garden in boxes, but still not satisfied I managed again without permission and as quietly as possible to make two rooms into one with an arched opening. The rooms had been rather pokey and this made a big improvement!

Though I can't remember what we did with the rubble!

Campbell did remark to me one day that the landlord had received some complaints about noise from our flat but nobody came to see what had been going on! We remained in that flat until we went on our next home leave.

We called the little yacht Cinderella. Cinderella was 26ft long, about 7ft beam and with a very shallow dishy hull, she was a centerboarder and had her rudder in a trunk also to lift. In a way she was ideal for Bombay harbour and its creeks and for coastal sailing in fair weather. She had no sails and her mast which we located in another part of the factory was a crude and heavy thing which I rejected.

Time for our home leave was approaching and we had begun to think about the more distant future when my employment contract would be up. I was fairly sure that the Firm would offer to keep me on, but would we want to spend the best part of the rest of our lives in Bombay? For various reasons the answer had to be no, but what then?

I don't know what put the idea into my head, but I suddenly thought of The River Shannon as something I would like to know more about and I wrote to my Mother asking her to try and find a book or anything else about the river.

She sent me a copy of "Green and Silver" by a Mr Tony Rolt.

We both read the book which was well illustrated with photographs, and we knew what we wanted to do!

Start a Hire Boat Business on the Shannon!

This time we flew home and broke our journey for a day in Rome and again in Zurich. My dominant memory of Rome is of Simon squatting on the pavement in front of a toy shop window where an animated toy monkey was performing, and had him, a little blond 3-4 year old laughing joyously and completely oblivious of the crowd of Romans gathered round him enjoying his delight! We also did some sightseeing without going very far from the centre, which included a conducted tour of the Vatican. It seemed to have little relationship to our ideas of Christianity.

Zurich was a disappointment. We had hoped to see something of the Alps and booked a coach tour but in the morning the cloud ceiling was right down on the Lake so we just went up into the clouds and somewhere up there was the museum of the Swiss railways, where we saw a splendid model of the complete railway system of the country complete with mountains, lakes and towns. Trains running all over the place on a 24 hour cycle of about 15 minutes night and day. It was certainly a model worth seeing.

*

It was a winter leave, and the main thing we wanted to do was go to Ireland and visit the Shannon. We were soon at Knockranny and borrowing Mother's Morris Minor. We set off in this, the first of its type, to explore the river from the land.

Using Tony Rolt's book with its maps and notes to guide us, we started at the proper place, the source of the river known as The Shannon Pot. After a few miles the river flows into Lough Allen, gets lost on that big open lake and is reborn when it flows out near the southern end. The flow from here is artificially controlled by a weir and big sluice gates operated by the Electricity Supply Board (ESB).

The Navigation proper did not begin until Leitrim Village in those days. It has recently been extended into Lough Allen and much more extensively through to the Erne waterways and Enniskillen.

From Leitrim Village we went to Carrick-on-Shannon where there was a stone quay with mooring bollards and other signs of commercial traffic. We then diverted to the beautiful Lough Key where there was a semi-derelict lock allowing access to the lake, this then in the private hands of the King Harman family.

We were very attracted to the village of Jamestown with its weir, a rather nice stretch of river, a stone arch in the middle of the street and above all the stone quay and the five arch granite masonry bridge. We saw a rather intriguing big converted dumb barge moored to the quay. Jamestown seemed to us certainly to be one of the places to note as a possible venue for future operations.

We met a Mr Mathew Burke who occupied the house of another semi derelict lock at the eastern end of the canal known as the Jamestown Cut. This was the Albert Lock, the first of only five locks on the Shannon Navigation which wends its beautiful leisurely way down the centre of Ireland. At the major lock at Ardnacrusha the river then drops to sea level. The lock into Lough Key is the 6th but strictly is not on the Shannon at all, but on the Boyle River. Most of the work of building the bridges, quays and locks was carried out in mid 19th century as famine relief work.

From Jamestown to Rooskey there was not much road access to the river and I think we missed the very attractive Carnadoe waters off to the west into Co Roscommon. Rooskey did not seem to offer us much and we went on to Tarmonbarry where below the weir the Royal Canal enters the Shannon after passing through Richmond Harbour, a very attractive basin which we thought had much to offer as a base if we could get any domestic accommodation there.

Then we came to Lough Ree, a great stretch of water I had never seen before. We spent quite a lot of time viewing the lake from vantage points on its west side and it looked most attractive, in spite of the fact that it was a bitterly cold winter's day. Chris, Simon and I must have spent several nights away on the Shannon but I have no recollection of where. Athlone at the bottom of Lough Ree we found to be just a big and not particularly attractive town. From there we next met the Shannon at Clonmacnoise, the very interesting ancient Christian settlement with the river winding past it and through water meadows all the way to Banagher and beyond. Before we got to Banagher we visited Shannon harbour where the Grand Canal from Dublin joins the river. This seemed to be a ready made boat building site with the big shed and a dry dock. However it was a commercial port at the time operated by CIE, Coras Iompair Eireann, and it did not seem to be available. Another factor was that it was two locks up from the Shannon and therefore not really suitable as a hire boat base.

We visited some places on Lough Derg, nearly 30 miles of it, undoubtedly a marvellous cruising lake particularly for sailing cruisers. Killaloe was already quite a big base for private craft. On the whole we decided we would set up on the upper Shannon if possible.

With our minds made up that we would start our next 'life' building and operating hire craft on the Shannon, we went to see several people we knew who had an interest in the Shannon as a private river. These people were encouraging but from their selfish point of view they had no wish for commercial developments. We were advised to discuss our ideas with the Tourist Board, Bord Fáilte, there we met with considerable enthusiasm and even vague promises of financial help when we explained that we would not have much capital to invest. After the exploratory trip I returned to Bombay, as usual going ahead of Chris and Simon to give them longer with her parents.

I FLEW back to India, making two stopovers, one being in Athens where I 'did' the Parthenon on a bitterly cold early March day, snow on the mountains to the north. I had the place entirely to myself except for a few goats, it was rather nice as the city was completely free of tourists. The second stopover gave me a day in Beirut, a quite peaceful city in those days. I booked in at an hotel where I was picked up by a rather friendly and attractive Spanish girl. In my innocence I did not immediately recognise her as professional and I even think that we might have managed a strictly platonic friendship. This idea was not put to the test because my carrier TWA suddenly paged the hotel saying they had changed schedule and were leaving at midnight. Suez was at the time closed and the airlines were ferrying out a great many mid eastern folk who would have normally travelled by sea.

I abandoned my room and my girl and was bussed out to the airport and took off in one of the big prop driven Douglas A/C of the period. This was packed with people, children, masses of luggage and parcels of every description. We flew out over the sea but failed to climb and started to circle quite low over the water which was made more alarming by the fact that there was a thunder storm in progress! There was a full moon and we could see we were circling because the moon kept passing the windows!

I must admit I was not feeling too happy about the situation.

The second officer was trying to pull up cabin floor panels obstructed by luggage and it was a full half hour before the Captain came on the public address and in a strong American accent announced that the undercarriage could not be retracted. We should have to fly round until sufficient fuel had been used to allow the heavily laden craft to land back at Beirut. The passengers were all very worried, they probably didn't want to fly anyhow, and could not understand a word said!

I found the eventual landing somewhat nail-biting as I didn't know if the wheels were fixed down or not. VIP's (like myself!) were ferried back - but sadly to another hotel! After two hours sleep we were woken, and flew off again for Barrin and then Bombay.

On reporting back to Alcocks I was delighted to to learn that we had been allocated another flat. This turned out to be an old time flat with big airy rooms, marble floors and a balcony from which we could just see a corner of Bombay Harbour. It was also quite close to 'The Gateway', within easy walking distance.

The place was to be redecorated and I had quite a battle with Campbell and his 'number one', Mr Bielby, to let us choose the colour scheme. They use the silly argument that the next occupant might not like our ideas!

I said, in effect, F the next occupant.

So we got our way and were well set up there in our final three years.

Around this time I also acquired a new and slightly livelier car, a Rover 'Sportsman's Light Fifteen', with a six cylinder engine and free wheel. Chris had learned to drive in the normal way, ie, not taught by her husband!

Her teacher was an Indian Airforce Squadron Leader, Lalkaka, Lally as we called him. A pilot instructor flying Hawker Hunter jets, he was also a keen sailor, which was how we came to know him. He became very fond of Chris and kept up a correspondence with her for quite a time after we came home.

*

As soon as we were properly settled into our new home we started really working on Cinderella, in particular building on a rather nice little coach roof. Due to the shallow hull this barely gave me sitting headroom but it did give some protection to the primus when we were camp cruising and also made a little cabin for Simon. I made a more efficient centreplate, a hollow mast and boom...and Chris made the sails from the best cotton we could get locally. All this meant a great many spare time and sweaty hours in a very dusty and dirty building. I recall returning one Saturday evening in the (recently acquired and much used) Rover and on the stair to our flat meeting one of our neighbours and his wife who were well known dance band leaders...they were in full evening dress while we were really filthy with sweat and dirt! A good laugh was had by all!

Social life was now good, centred very much on sailing and sailing people. We had dinner dances at the Royal Bombay YC which was by then open to Indian Nationals. Bombay was and I think still is a 'Dry' city. Europeans and some Indians for medicinal reasons (!) could buy alcohol based on a coupon rationed system, but we could not afford to drink and so passed our coupons to others. Liquor was of course available on the black market at a price and at considerable personal risk, risk either from the preventative police or from buying Scotch which turned out be to high priced tea! One of our acquaintances spent some months in jail after his flat was raided during a party and excessive amounts of alcohol were discovered, he was quite an important English business man, no quarter given!

With Cinderella now afloat we raced her occasionally on handicap against other miscellaneous yachts, but the close Merlin racing was much more fun. For cruising as a small family Cinderella was ideal. On one national holiday (lasting several days) in the winter-dry season we planned and carried out an interesting and very pleasant cruise round the main island north of Bombay. This, named Thana, is a high hill or a small mountain, and an island only at high water. In order to circumnavigate it the tides and the wind had to be carefully studied and worked out. About half way up the creek on the east or inside of the island is the point of the watershed, where the tides from north and south meet. If you can reach this point at high tide going up with the tide and can get over the top and catch the ebb on the other side you have the current with you all the way.

We took our Tindal (native crew man) with us as we thought he would be useful if we did get into difficulty, such as getting stranded on a falling tide a long way from shore, though this was unlikely as we only drew a few inches with plate and rudder up. We arrived a little late at the watershed but with the wind behind us and steering with an oar went over the top and then down a cataract of shallow rocky water on the other side. Lucky to get down with only a few minor bumps we then drifted virtually windless on for a few miles and anchored for the night a few hundred yards above the railway bridge.

Nights were so mild that after a shared meal in the short twilight we put Simon to sleep in the cuddy, Chris and I slept with most of our clothes on under a light blanket on the cushioned side seats and the Tindal slept curled up on the foredeck under his blanket. In the morning we successfully negotiated the bridge on the last of the morning ebb.

To some people tides are an enemy but properly understood they are much more the sailor's friend, and can be used to his advantage as a current or to dry out his boat between tides for scrubbing or repair. In old days ships were 'careened' on a suitable beach for the same purposes.

We were towing our tiny 6ft pram dinghy which could just about carry the three of us in fair weather, but was once seen to carry six of the club tindals all in fits of laughter and with zero freeboard! It had a dagger board, a rudder and a sail added later for Simon. A few miles beyond the bridge our tindal - whose name I regret I have forgotten - took Simon ashore at a coastal village to buy some eggs. After that it was plain sailing back to Bombay with a light thermal onshore breeze down what is at that point the Arabian Sea.

One other memorable mini cruise was an inland one, again using the tide to take us up one of the creeks which extend far inland east of Mandwa and over a watershed with another return outlet. This time we were alone and spent the night aground in the firm bottom of the creek after pushing the boat from behind as far as we could go.

On the way we had an amusing race with one of the quite big (35-40ft) native fishing boats on a beat in which she was faster through the water but, like most lateen rigged craft, if they try to tack head to wind as does a yacht, then on one tack the sail is against the mast with so little drive and speed that steerage way is lost. This particular race ended when, being unable to tack, the boat sailed deep into the mangrove trees, we could imagine the Indian cussing and swearing while they extracted themselves and we sailed away!

It was a memorable night, absolutely still, with distant drums beating and dogs barking and above us the myriad bright stars. We woke with our blankets wet with dew. At one point on our return another way we tied to a grassy bank and after a few minutes had a swarm of small boys and girls looking down on us chattering excitedly at the very strange sight we must have made to them.

*

We once cruised in company with three of the 21ft Seabird Class boats, spending the night dried out on the sand in the lee of an old Portugese fort. On another occasion when son Shane was on the way I sailed alone with our tindal to the very minor port of Alibag which is some miles down the coast. There's a river running out of it and consequently a sand bar. We arrived at low water and with a fair swell running, so it was again steering with an oar and being carried in on the crest of a wave. We anchored off and went ashore in the dinghy.

The tindal went to the town and I wandered into the jungly woods past overgrown ruins, where I suddenly became aware of the most hideous noise, a screeching and groaning which might have been human! For a moment it really stopped me but I decided to investigate and found myself at a big well with two blindfold bullocks plodding around it. They were rotating a great timber beam which in turn, via primitive wooden cog wheels, operated an endless rope with dozens of Dalda (cooking fat) tins attached. This brought up water and tipped it into a trough of large split bamboo stems, and from there it was directed into runnels in the ground to irrigate a plantation. The noise was caused by dry timber binding on dry timber, occasionally it was deadened by a small boy throwing water over the bearing.

Living in Bombay

(Above) The caravan at Varuma Shipyard, Colaba

(Left) Christine working inside uncompleted caravan

(Left) The caravan in 1951

(Below) The yacht 'Tyr'

On following page

(Above) View of part of Varuma shipyard, showing beach, and caravan in shed. Large boat is a 72 wartime HDML

(Below) Christine (pregnant with Simon) and goats at Varuma

(Left) Prototype CBK Dinghy, Christine and Ken Stiffle sailing

(Below) Christine and Brien Kennedy sailing at Lake Khadakvasla in Western Ghats, near Poona.

(Above and Below) 'Cinderella'

(Above) Group of sailors from Bombay and College of Military Engineers at Khadakvasla, Brien and Christine 3rd and 4th from right, Major Ken Stiffle sitting 2nd from left

(Below) CBK design, built at Kirkee under supervision of Christine and Ken Stiffle. This became an Indian national class!

(Above) Author designed tugs at Alcock Ashdown factory, Bombay, 1958 (4 built)

(Below) Car & Passenger ferry for Panjim, Goa, designed by author (2

(Left) Putting out Inis Cealtra, Killiney Hill, 1960

(Below) St Brigid as bought, above Ardnacrusha, 1961

(Bottom of page) Mr Carthy, original owner, in author's field as bought, 1960, 2 acres for £250!

(Following Page) Jamestown Quay, first base of K Line, 1961. St Brigid, with Inis Cealtra and Plover alongside

(Above) Pontoon in original state at Shannon Harbour, Simon Kennedy, Seamus Woods, Brien McClelland, Ms McClelland

(Below) Dry dock, Shannon Harbour, 1964, John Weaving's boat

(Top) Simon and donkey Johnnie aboard St Brigid

(Above) Christine Kennedy 1960

(Right) 'Ice Yacht' at Shannon Harbour, 1962,

(Above) 'Waterwitch', building for Dr Hennesy, 1969
(Below) Jim Foley working on backbone of Curlew, Shannon Harbour

(Above) Launching K Line 'Grebe'
(Below) 'Curlew' off to Boat Show at RDS, mid sixties

(Above) Inismore and Inisbofin, pictured at Dublin, Christmas 1962
(Below) Brien and Christine on K Line 'Mallard', Jamestown Quay

(Above) Curlew & Inismore on Lough Ree, 'K Line' boats, built by Brien Kennedy at Shannon Harbour, c 1970

(Opposite) K Line Mallard 1968

(Below) 'Catavan', built Shannon Harbour 1972, Pat Kelly Rogers aboard

(Above) Inis Cealtra towing the pontoon on River Barrow, this later forming the hull for (Below) the K Line base, pictured 1976, Christine coming ashore

I only had one mishap with Cinderella when during a race in a moderate breeze we were 'reaching' with our big spinnaker up. I wasn't steering but warned the helmsman to expect a stronger puff coming out of the Naval Dock and not to luff up into it, which is the natural thing to do, but rather to turn away from it. He did the natural thing!

Cinders had rather low free board and put her side under. I was too late letting the sheet go, we filled and sank, all but the bow where the air was trapped under the deck. There were three of us aboard and we were all left swimming with me trying to keep from loosing floorboards and miscellaneous gear. The tindal who could swim like a fish was the most frightened and was trying to climb onto about 18ins of nearly vertical bow from which air was escaping!

Christine who was on the committee boat saw what had happened and immediately took off in a dinghy to the rescue. In the meantime a big seagoing Dutch tug's skipper also saw the capsize and as he was already 'under way' and not far off, he immediately headed for us. My first thought was oh God he will plough into us and do serious damage but he carefully drew up to us bow on. The Dutch skipper himself leaned over and offered to take us in tow. My second thought when it seemed we were going to sink was that I wasn't insured. I shall be obstructing the fairway and will have to pay for salvaging a wreck. When the Dutchman offered help I shouted up to him, submerged to my neck!

'Is this a friendly offer?'

Of course it was - he pulled away and then backed up most carefully and dropped me a rope. I managed to dive and make it fast around the base of the mast. In the meantime Chris was standing by and collected the flotsam. I gave the signal to go ahead as slowly as possible, the huge propeller began to revolve in front of us very slowly. Even so, it put us who were hanging onto the boat as she began to lift under stress, and the mast to bow horribly with the strain of the mainsail which was still hoisted. The tug pulled us as slowly as was possible but her speed plus the slipstream tore the sail to ribbons and bent the mast beyond repair. We were manouvered alongside the committee vessel and all the available tindals helped to make her fast to that vessel. We got the mast down and then moved the two boats into shallow water where we dumped Cinders and bailed her out when the tide went down. All I could do was wave my thanks to the tug. A new mast was soon made in the glueing jig which I had fortunately retained, and Chris made a new mainsail and repaired the other sails.

FOR THE rest of my stay in India I was kept very busy at work. We tendered and got the order for four seagoing Lloyds Classed tugs to my design.The four tugs were all under construction on the slipways at the same time but at different stages, and it gave me much pleasure to see them grow. It also gave me the chance of a solo trip to the UK, this had a double purpose and being of only two weeks duration I did not get to Ireland. The purposes were first to inspect the tug engines which were big slow speed Ruston Hornsby diesels, and secondly to learn how to electrically weld aluminium alloy so that I could teach our welders the techniques. For this I spent about ten days with Northern Aluminium (now amalgamated with one of the other big firms) which I found most interesting. They went to a lot of trouble to teach me welding and showed me half inch plates which went into the P&O ship Canberra then building.

I had occasion to visit London and there occurred one of the most extraordinary chance meetings of my life, a chance which would seem so remote that it could not possible occur. I got on a bus at Hyde Park corner heading for Piccadilly. I went forward and took a seat next a lady: she was my former wife Maud!

Both of us were astonished! We exchanged a few words about our children and she left the bus. Maud was living in Oxfordshire and would rarely have visited London, and I was only in London for one day. It cannot be explained, same day, same place, same time, same bus, same seat.

Back in India, life went on. In addition to my work at the shipyard. I carried out a number of private commissions. Novel Godrej commissioned me to design him a 42 ft ketch rigged yacht, this to be built by Alcocks in teak throughout, with a bronze centreplate through her finn keel and a diesel auxilliary. The Yacht was duly built and launched and christened 'TIR' meaning arrow, she had a good performance but was not built to race, rather to cruise safely and in some comfort and I believe she fulfilled the bill. Chris and I sailed in her many times. (More than forty years on I know she is still in service although sadly her owner is dead).

The Commandant of the C.M.E. at Kirkee asked me to design a new class of dinghy which could be built by their carpenters in their workshops, both for their club and for other Indian clubs. So the C.B.K. 15ft class was born.

During my employment with Alcock's we had three local holidays, the first we spent at Marbleshawar, a hill station well known to the British of old.

We only had Simon at that time and my memories are of pony treking and walking through the woods in the comparatively bracing climate of the Western Ghats. Next time we decided to be more adventrous and I borrowed one of the works jeeps, and obtaining some maps plotted a tour of part of these same Ghats. It was in the dry season and very dry and very hot but quite an adventure. Without leaving roads entirely and taking to the bush we travelled sometimes on mere tracks and reached considerable altitudes and places with magnificent views. We did not camp but managed to find hill stations, or semi derelict hotels one of which was still run by an old and rather pathetic anglo Indian couple who like most of these people had a dream of being able to retire to Blighty as they still called England. Every day we got more and more sunburnt, and at the end of each day we were caked in the red dust of the region.

Lastly when Shane had come on the scene we visited Materan another well known hill station, this time taking our ayah and bearer and travelling by train and then by the little narrow gauge mountain railway up the minor mountain to this very much a hill station. We rented a small furnished bungalow under some trees and with a corrugated tin roof over which monkeys thundered from time to time and who gave Simon much amusement. The mountain railway really was rather fun as it zig zagged up the hillside. There were times when the tailend of the train was directly below the front end and apparently going in the opposite direction! At one point when it was impossible to make a hairpin the track had a branch into which the whole train went and then reveresed out and proceeded across points and on up the track backwards. The pointsman lived in a little hut beside the track, he was a lowly but very important person and obviously took his duty most seriously.

During the latter part of our time in India, The National Defence Academy was built. This incorporated all three of India's defence services, Army, Navy and Airforce. It was a vast complex incorporating an airfield. The Navy utilised the neighbouring lake of Khadakvasla, on which they had quite a fleet of small naval craft such as cutters and whalers. They also had two types of modern sailing dinghies, 14 footers very similar to the Merlins I had introduced but heavier, and a 16ft boat of a more stable type. These had been both designed and built by Sonny and AFCO, and again the Bombay sailors were invited to take part in their regattas.

Chris and I were always in the teams and at one time were guests of the Commandant of the N.D.A.,Brigadier Habibulla. We stayed in his beautifully situated bungalow overlooking the lake and surrounded by gardens. We met Nehru there briefly. The lake itself was artificial from earlier times, though it seemed perfectly natural and very beautiful, extending many miles into the Western Ghats, hills partly covered with jungly woods where peacocks crowed. (A few years after we left the dam burst and for a time the lake must have been a sorry sight.)

In the distance from the commandant's bungalow was the Mountain of Torna which I climbed in the Monsoon with a party of young army officers on a navigation-map reading training course, made realistic because the mountain was in dense mist. There was a mule track to the top which had been fortified in a much earlier period. How they got the laden mules up was a bit of a mystery, some of the track was formed of steps cut in the rock; I suppose it's even more amazing how they got them down!

I went on several of these treks at week ends and Chris on at least one. They were most enjoyable, if wet! The young officers we found to be the most pleasant young men, most of whom could speak good English. They were delighted when Chris was on the hike - it was most unusual to have a woman with them. The officer we were most friendly with at the C.M.E. was a Major Kenneth Stiffle, an Anglo Indian with an Anglo Indian Wife and a resident officer and in charge of the workshops. He also looked after the sailing club affairs and after we left India was for a time Secretary of the All India Sailing Association. Kenneth managed to get Chris a horse and riding kit and she - who hadn't ridden for some years and then not a great deal in Hendon - took part in one of two jackal hunts with the Poona's. I followed with a camera but was not too happy about it as it was during the dry season, when the terrain was bare and rock hard, stony and full of nullahs - dry ditches - but she took it easy and, well shephered by Kenneth, thoroughly enjoyed herself and came to no harm.

After I had been commissioned to design a boat for the C.M.E. I got down to it in the evenings and came up with a set of plans which Chris had been following and we discussed it as it went along so when they were finished it was arranged that Chris would interpret them to Kenneth and his workmen.

We, including Simon now 5 or 6 drove up to Kirkee in our Rover and after a day or two, Simon and I left Chris to carry on, staying as a guest with the Stiffles for about two weeks until the first boat was well advanced and Kenneth was able to take over.

When it came to naming the new class I think it was Kenneth's idea that it should be the CBK, and so it became. The large C being for Christine enclosing the smaller B for Brian and the small K for Kenneth. We knew this but officially the K was for Kirkee! Kirkee built 12 of these boats while we were there, I believe many more were built for other places later. They were all fitted with English metal masts and sails.

I suppose inevitably Kenneth fell seriously in love with Chris and she not a little with him. He being more British than the British and being naturally a thorough gentleman told me of his love which he knew was hopeless. Chris too admitted it but we somehow managed to keep things under control and remain friends until we left India, when for several years Chris and he kept up a correspondance.

*

Our second son, Shane arrived on the 9th of October 1957 at Breach Candy Hospital. We had been using the very nice swimming pool there since first coming to Bombay and when Simon was two or three he was very soon able to swim or dog paddle and never had any fear of water nor of heights. By the time he was four he was climbing the 10 metres to the top of the diving platform and jumping in, coming up spluttering...then he'd paddle in and do it again.

"Tir" was completed and launched, not without a slight unfortunate mishap. I had organised the erection of a platform from which the launching ceremony could be carried out. I was on board ready to give the ground crew the signal to winch her back into deep water - she was already surrounded by water a few feet deep - and could not really see what was going on below the bow. Soono Godrej named her and said some prayers and put flowers on deck. Thinking that was it, I gave the signal and the boat almost immediately moved away from the platform. Precisely at the same moment another lady dressed in a beautiful sari was leaning forward with a garland! She fell into the water and was fished out unhurt, but rather spoilt! I did not even know about this until Chris told me when I came ashore later and I sent my most humble apologies to the lady via the Godrejes.

The first Tug was duly launched in the proper big ship manner down greasy slipway at a carefully calculated declivity, and she floated as we hoped she would. This is always a most anxious moment for a designer, "the moment of truth". Had I got my calculations right, both as to draft and trim, fore and aft... the paint line is there for all to see?

I had, and I went home happy!

*

I had one more job which gave me a bit of a jolt. Campbell called me into his office one morning and told me about a big 10 -12 thousand ton Pakistani freighter. The Captain wasn't too happy concerning her stability when light, she had recently been fitted with additional above deck cargo-handling gear. He wanted an inclining experiment carried out so that he could correct his hydrostatic graphs.

In theory I knew how to do an inclining experiment from my student days but had never before been asked to do one. Campbell gave me an introduction to the ship's captain, and after hurriedly refreshing my mind from a text book, I went down to the docks to make preliminary arangements.

Really it is quite simple, and on most new ships it is carried out automatically as soon as she is launched to check the position of the vertical centre of gravity of the ship against the postion estimated from the plans and weight distribution. It consists of (from a position about midships), hanging a long plumb line down a hold on the centreline, the bob swinging in a shallow water filled box - to dampout occillation - a batten across the box marked on each side of its centre in inches. A known weight, in this case sand filled bags, is first stacked exactly midships, then moved a known distance to each side of the ship in turn. Down below when the bob settles the number of inches each way is recorded as is the length of the plumb line. With these figures the angle of inclination can easily be calculated. The weight of the ship at the time can be got fairly accurately from her draft marks and tables kept on the ship, but also required is the waterplane area and lines plans are not often kept on a ship in service so it has to be guesstimated.

Before all this is started all tanks, water, fuel, oil etc have either to be drained or pumped up tight, all objects which might move have to be fixed and all personnel not involved to be off the ship. Well, the Captain (a very knowledgeable and pleasant Pakistani) and I did it together to his satisfaction and he was able to make slight modifications to his hydrostatic curves and satisfy himself that his ship was safe for sea in light condition with the ballast he already had aboard, and I saved my honour!

*

Our time was now nearly up and we had to begin packing up and selling off what we could not reasonably take home, these items being principally our car, our boats and our Corgi dog!

We had decided to make our return passage (by air and at the firm's expense!) as interesting as possible. We sent the heavy luggage by sea and booked with Aeroflot from Delhi to Moscow. There had been a plan to go on a pony trek, organised by Major Stiffle, in the eastern part of the Himalayas. This was frustrated a few weeks before take off by a small border war in that region between India and China. In place of this it was arranged that we would have a cruise in TIR from Bombay to Karachi with Novel and Soono, our mutual friend Kerse Naoroji acting as Captain.

A great send off party at our flat was attended by all our many friends. They presented us just before we flew out with a silver plate inscribed with their signatures.

It now hangs here on the wall of my home at Jamestown Bridge.

*

The cruise started at night - to suit the tides and convenience of some crew members. Our party included Russi Cama, a delightful character weighing nearly 20 stone. (During the cruise he was not allowed on deck because although a swimmer we felt that if he fell overboard we would never be able to get him back!) All in all there were seven of us, including the professional crew, the tindal Balia.

A fine night, we motored a bit to clear the harbour. However, nobody had bothered to phone the Met Office because it was March and we expected only thermal winds but, unknown to us a small depression had built up in the Arabian Sea and we sailed into it that first night. By morning we were travelling fast with a portside beam wind and quite a sea building up.

Tir was carrying all plain sail, she was a powerful yacht and had only a moderate sail area. Sea sickness soon came aboard and stayed with us for about 36 hours. Soono was very bad and did not fully recover until we were nearly in Karachi. For the rest of us from the second day on when the wind had practically disappeared and the sea gone down it was a real pleasure cruise. At one point, north of the Gulf of Kutch, when we were motoring through lack of wind we saw against the horizon a school of whales, really big ones disporting themselves. Had we been sailing we might have got closer to them but with the motor we hadn't any hope. When we arrived in Karachi we found the yacht Diana Cassidora moored off the yacht club. She had recently been built by AFCO to an Aitken design for Mr. Achevarious, the architect of the then 'New' Delhi. Diana was about the same lenth overall as Tir but was a finer lined vessel with a bigger sail area - a real ocean racer. Achevarious had built her with the idea of sailing her home to America, and as far as Aden with his wife and two young children aboard.

Before she sailed for Aden Chris and I were aboard her several times and were very friendly with them. The voyage to Aden nearly ended in tragedy. When in the middle of the Arabian Sea they suddenly discovered that the main petrol tank was leaking badly and nearly all this highly volatile fuel was in the bilge, a bomb waiting to go off.

Besides Mr and Mrs and the two children there were two young American men aboard. Somehow they managed to bale out the petrol and the petrol vapour without igniting it with a spark, it must truly have been a terrifying experience. I had not realised she had a petrol motor, Tir had a Mercedes diesel, much safer. We spent a couple of days in Karachi as honorary members of the Karachi Y.C. Chris and I were lent one of their boats in a regatta. We won our race and I have the rather nice mug here still.

*

Chris and I flew back to Bombay, successfully disposed of car and boats, said final and sad good byes, paid off our small staff of ayah and bearer, with whom we later kept in touch for some time, in fact until his death.

We flew up to Delhi, and caught the Moscow flight the following morning. The flight was in a TU 104 which, since the disastrous failure of the Comets, was probably the only jet aircraft in regular service anywhere in the world. I think their capacity was 120 to 150 passengers, propelled by four jets in two pairs. Their wings were swept back and were rigid with considerable anhedral or droop, which is common now in most military aircraft but unusual then.

We found that we were the only non-Russians on the plane so were objects of considerable interest and kindly attention particularly from a young man who was a professional interpretor. The machine climbed powerfully towards the western Himalayas, which we crossed at about 35000 feet so that although the mountains were perfectly free of cloud they seemed almost insignificant. I was able to photograph them through the cabin window. Our first stop was Tashkent, which is the home of the Tupolov aircraft factory and there appeared to be dozens of the 104's parked round the aerodrome. We left the plane for a time and sat in the warm sun, noting that the winter snow was only now melting from around the airfield.

The next stop was supposed to be Moscow but for some unexplained reason we were diverted and made an unscheduled stop at Baku, flying in over the Caspian sea. By this time Shane was due for a feed but there was no milk available which caused great consternation among the other passengers who obviously considered we were their guests! The aircraft had no sooner come to a halt when our interpreter opened the cabin door and jumped to the tarmac, shouted 'milk for the baby', and went running to the airport building.

We all got off the plane and went in to the canteen where our 'host' insisted in plying us with food, mostly tinned, we had hardly time to eat before we were called back aboard. The last leg was flown over cloud and then the slow let down through cloud which I always rather dread, the engines almost silent and the machines in a steep glide. Then suddenly fir trees and snow covered land quite close and we were coming straight in to land smoothly and then swinging in to the airport buildings. As usual in Russia the children are given the best of attention and Simon and Shane in his push chair were taken off our hands by special hostesses while we attended to our luggage and passport business. The next thing was accommodation for the night. We were booked on an Air France flight to Paris via Warsaw the following morning. We had to carry our overnight luggage to the airport hotel which was some distance away along a snow cleared road and Simon who of course had never seen snow before was much intrigued with the stuff and managed to fall into a snow drift, and was extracted by a rather grumpy babushka. The hotel was far from four star but we got a room to ourselves and ate in a kind of canteen, it was full of airport workers who were sleeping in the corridors. The country had far from recovered from the Great Patriotic War as they called it.

The next day we went for a short walk but it was very cold particularly for us and we later hired a taxi. The driver was terribly anxious to show us everthing of interest in his city and gave us a lightning conducted tour aided by a Russian-English phrase book he kept referring to. He then drove us out to the airport and on the way was stopped for speeding. He jumped out of the cab and ran over to the cop and ran back and drove off furiously having obviously told some story about English people already late for their plane! We flew to Paris with a short stop at Warsaw.

*

At Paris airport I tried to buy some francs with my travellers cheques...only to be told that they were not correctly made out and were unacceptable. Fortunately I had a little sterling which, turned into french money, enabled us to take a taxi into the city and book into an hotel for the night.

The next morning, expecting a long stint for me at my bank, Lloyds, Christ went to the Louvre which was not far from the hotel. I arranged to meet her at the entrance later but, this being my first time in Paris, I knew nothing about the geography of the place and when I eventually got there I realised that it was immense and had several entrances!

There was not a sign of my family so I set about searching the building more or less at the double, ignoring all the masterpieces I passed on the way. They were nowhere to be found and, in some despair, thinking how are we going to meet up again, I stood in the entrance facing the Seine pondered what to do. Then I saw some small figures in the distance along the bank. My family.

That was my experience of 'doing' the Louvre!

*

Four

I WAS BACK in my native land, aged fifty, after many years away. Knockranny my childhood home had been sold. Too old to live so far out my parents and Aunty Vi were living in a pleasant conventional bungalow in Foxrock. It was from there that my very dear aunt had gone shopping in Dublin and never returned.

Maybe she had a premonition that she would die a violent death, I certainly remember her saying that she always liked to be sure she was wearing clean underwear when she went to Dublin so that she would be respectably dressed in the event of an accident! Almost totally deaf, she stepped in front of a bus right outside the G.P.O. in O'Connell Street.

I moved in with my parents, they called me the bed and breakfast man! My first task was to find somewhere for Christine and myself to live, with somewhere close by where we could build the cruiser I had already designed. I also started checking to see what Bord Failte could come up with in the way of financial assistance, and I set about locating old friends, particularly the Denhams, Peter and Maureen and their three children.

At first I sought accommodation near the Shannon.

I did consider and looked at a house in Drumsna, near where I am now. My first cousin Henry Kennedy came on the trip. He had himself just set up a photographic business in a Leeson Street basement. In the following years he gradually worked this up until it became a major business on Tallaght industrial estate.

We decided that the house, although cheap, was too big and needed too much repair. So we then visited the land which Chris and I had earlier picked out. I determined to come back and see if I could purchase it. Bord Failte was a big disappointment. No direct financial help was available. The best they could do was to get a guarantee from the Minister for £10,000, and this I could use to get a loan from a bank or other finance house. We ourselves had only a few thousand.

All of these goings on took me several weeks. Chris, who was sharing a house near Oxford with my sister Nancy, was getting very restive. So somewhat in despair I rented a rather odd little furnished flat, consisting of two rooms one over the other via an open spiral stair.

This was situated right on the top of Killiney Hill, right behind The Druid's Chair pub! When I was negotiating the rental with 'the landlord', an elderly woman artist, I asked her if she knew of any building where I could build a large boat. She showed me a stable yard she owned which was very close to the flat, really its only merit, it being was just a cobbled and far from level space between buildings.

I decided I could make a temporary shed of timber and polythene in this space and took it at a very modest rental. This settled, I called Chris to come over and she arrived speedily!

It was by then early summer.

We settled reasonably comfortably into the flat. I had bought a small used Triumph Estate and with it drove alone to Jamestown with the idea of buying the field by the bridge which I had set my heart on.

Mr Clyne, in charge of the weir and sluice gates at Jamestown and whom we had met briefly three years previously, put me on to the owner, Mr John Carthy. He lived in a very run down thatched cottage on the other side of the road. Very overweight, and not particularly old, I feel he had health problems. In any event he did not live much longer after we met. He agreed that he might consider selling, at least part of it, if we could agree a price but we needed a referee.

He said he would meet me on the field at three.

So on a glorious afternoon the three of us sat against the hedge, the same hedge where I now have my gate!

I offered two hundred pounds.

He wanted three!

The referee suggested I make it two fifty.

I did.

The bargain was struck. We agreed on the boundarys, to be the road and the bridge, and a line which would still allow his cattle to water at the Shannon. My area was a little under two acres but, more important, included about a hundred yards of river bank facing Jamestown Quay.

We agreed to leave the legalities to solicitor Walsh in Carrick on Shannon, and I drove home feeling pretty happy.

Things were going our way.

*

The temporary boat building shed in Killiney was soon constructed.

Fairly sheltered and fairly waterproof it was adequate for our purpose although the sloping cobbles made an uncomfortable floor.

I bought some electric tools (after organising an electricity supply!) and a small saw bench. I then hired a carpenter, willing and interested but with no boatbuilding experience.

Eugene Byrne, (the harbourmaster at Shannon Harbour on the Grand Canal) also worked for us for a time. Drinking a fair bit, he was not in good psychological state, having just lost his only son a boy of about 12 in the lock basin at the harbour. We somehow made room for him in the flat and I really believe the therapy of having a job saved his life.

Christine helped as much as she could while looking after the kids.

And Inis Cealtra grew and grew!

*

While we were building Inis Cealtra, CIE (the state transport company) decided to close down its water transport operations. Whilst bad news for the canals, this was the greatest piece of luck we could possibly have wished for.

The company announced that they would be auctioning off about 25 Canal Boats, 60ft by 13ft- and also two of the bigger Shannon barges, the St Brigid which was 86ft by 16ft and the St James, about 75ft by 14ft. All these craft were self propelled but to us the really interesting craft were the big boats.

I first inspected the St James, tied up at Portumna. There was no one aboard but her engine was running and in gear. This was standard practice with all the C.I.E. boats as they all had hot bulb ignition semi diesel engines. These required quite a performance to start, (as we found out later!), so they were left running in gear to give the engine something to do and to keep the bulbs hot.

On deck over the engine room I found myself bouncing to the rhythm of the engine, a pretty massive two cylinder. This excessive vibration at tick over speed disappointed me in the boat.

I then went in search of the St Brigid which I was told was in Limerick. I found her there in the lock to a short 'by canal' and, like the other boat, tied up with her engine running. This engine was a three cylinder and, though probably as powerful, it was smaller and practically vibrationless.

The engineer Michael -who later became quite a friend of ours - was aboard and I told him that I intended to bid for her or St James at the auction. He agreed that the St Brigid was a much quieter boat to live aboard.

She was actually leaving for Shannon Harbour in about half an hour on her last trip with C. I.E., and he and the other crew members were to be paid off there.

It was the end of an era.

I waited to see her leave Limerick. She was given quite a send off, some of the older women actually crying to see her go. I waited for her to come up the Ardnacrusha lock and took a photo of her underway with 'a bone in her teeth' (we later timed her doing 9mph on Lough Ree); and then I went back to Killiney determined to buy St. Brigid if we had enough money.

*

The auction of all these craft took place at James Street Harbour, a covered dock just beside the Guinness Brewery in Dublin. No longer in existence, the harbour was where the assembled barges had once loaded their cargoes of barrelled porter.

Chris and I went to the auction in the greatest excitement.

£750 was our absolute limit.

The possibility of a splendid floating home was in the balance.

The Auctioneer started off with the St. Brigid, and there seemed to be only two other people interested. A man withdrew at about £200, and a woman (Mrs Denham bidding for a friend) took the bidding on to £300.

I firmly bid £320, my heart beating like mad.

Mrs Denham shook her head!.

Christine and I were delighted.

This was the most wonderful moment we ever had together, we had become instant owners of an 86ft motor barge in good order (complete with hatch boards!) for half of what we had been prepared to pay.

Our future home on the Shannon was assured.

We stayed on for the auctioning of the Canal Boats and bought one! Number 52M, if I remember, for £120!

This was also complete and in good order.

We paid for the two boats and went back to Killiney in high spirits.

Next day we were down at Shannon Harbour inspecting our new home to be; well satisfied we straightaway began planning the layout of the conversion and accommodation.

The main CIE shed at Shannon Harbour caught our eye as an ideal location for working on the St. Brigid. The conversion would be done in winter and the second bay of the shed being over the water meant we could work in all weather. The shed would also be a perfect place to start building more hire boats.

We knew there was someone else interested in the premises, someone we knew. But I'm afraid I rather went behind his back and got the lease, I really felt our need was much greater than his!

*

In the meantime we had a message from CIE that we were required to remove the other barge, 52M, from James' Harbour. So one lovely late hot summer's day we went to collect it. The idea was to take it down to Ringsend Basin, - one lock up from the River Liffey- until we could get it down to Shannon Harbour.

We knew in theory how to start the engine!

This was a single cylinder Bolinder, the most basic of engines, built in Sweden and much favoured by Scandinavian fishermen. To start, firstly a paraffin burning blowlamp had to be used to heat the Bulb on the cylinder head until it was just beginning to glow. Then the flywheel was vigourously rocked, (using a handle which retracted into it when released,) so that you were bumping the piston against the compression at the same time as fuel was being injected.

She would suddenly come to life and fire.

But, being a two stroke the engine could rotate either way and if you wanted to go forward it had to be the right way! If not the trick was to stop it by holding back the injector pump lever until you saw the flywheel bouncing the right way and instantly releasing it. The boatmen had this trick to a fine art.

We did get 52M going (and by luck the right way) and set off up the canal. We made our way through several locks and on clearing one the Keeper waved his arm and said cheerfully "Now you're away to the west." But we were supposed to be going east!

"We don't want to go west , we want to go to Ringsend", I cried.

"Well you're on the wrong road, you're three locks up from your turning!"

We were forced to continue to a place where we were able to turn her and go back. The main canal is parallel to the road on the south side of the City, (the branch line we had come up is now filled in as a park), and we had missed the turning which was immediately before the first bridge and lock. In our anxiety to get the boat into the lock without damaging anything we just had not seen the turn. Bearing in mind that these boats have no brakes - the instant reverse available in normal boats - and being pretty heavy even when empty they have to be given plenty of room to stop.

This section of the waterway was heavily weeded and after going a few hundred yards the engine was labouring so badly with the weed on the propeller that I declutched...upon which it immediately ran away, the very simple governing known as 'the hit and miss system' failing to miss! (This system accounted for the unique and most attractive exhaust noise of these boats when heard approaching from a distance on a calm sunny day).

This was now really quite alarming, the engine roaring and vibrating like mad, even when the cylinder head gasket blew out releasing flames and smoke the revving continued. I climbed down to try to stop it before it wrecked itself and succeeded in cutting off the fuel. The engine died leaving itself without any compression, and we were stranded. We tied to the bank and walked back to James St, and motored home somewhat downhearted, deciding we would have to man haul it to Ringsend on the morrow.

The next day was another very hot sunny one and I had the crazy idea of getting Christine to start the pulling while I steered. I guessed that if I did the pulling I would be pulling alone all day, whereas if Christine started then some gallants would turn up to give a hand. So the scene was of a poor wretched woman hauling a 60ft barge with a rope over her shoulder while her shirtless husband stood on the after deck smoking a cigarette and steering.

I don't think we had moved more than fifty yards at a snails pace when a young lad on a bicycle came along, pulled up beside Christine and, looking at the scene, said, "why don' t yer man do it?"

I never heard what Chris replied... but can well imagine!

But anyhow the bicycle came aboard and Chris had an assistant. And then a few more, as the canal seemed to collect young men with nothing else to do but haul barges. We were soon making good speed and locking down to Ringsend where we tied up. I went off to a pub and brought back bottles of Guinness for the helpers and then, having done no work, I left Chris on the boat and walked back for the car. In those days there was an engineering works near the Brewery who were specialists in these barge engines, and as there was no serious damage they soon had it running again.

*

INIS CEALTRA in Killiney was now ready to meet her element. C.I.E. were hired to do the loading and transporting, and then the launching into the Grand Canal. But first we had to get her out of the 'workshop'.

We knocked down the wall.

And then with the enthusiastic help of the whole Denham family, using a car as a tug, we pulled and skidded her out to a back road where the crane and low loader could operate. While this was going on Douglas Hurd who lived just up the road, and whom I had known in my early dinghy days came out to me and said "Thank God she is finished, you've been ruining my television reception with your electric tools." (Hurd owned an Uffa Fox designed fast cruiser and a boat on the Shannon, he and his wife Ruth later became very good friends of ours).

Our intention was to move the boat to Shannon Harbour as soon as she was afloat, and then move into her ourselves, in spite of the fact that it was now late December. Everything we needed to live afloat was already aboard.We dumped the rest of our possessions on my parents, paid off the rent, and arranged with a builder to repair the wall!

*

On the day of the launch, Chris, Shane, Simon and myself in the Standard followed (shopping for provisions on the way) the convoy of low loader and crane to Sallins on the canal. After she was successfully dropped into the water, with some of our friends as onlookers, we moved aboard with Shane and Simon. And the friends came on for a little celebration!

One of these onlookers was one Barney Heron, later a good friend. He had heard of us and of our proposal to operate a small fleet on the Shannon. There and then he offered us his very elderly converted RNLI lifeboat 'Charles Whitton' at a price which seemed reasonable.

Chris and I discussed this, knocked him down a little and bought her. Now we had two cruisers and one canal boat which we and some of our newly acquired friends brought up from Ringsend. We planned to make for Shannon Harbour in convoy with the barge towing the other two boats.

Before we left my father, now a semi-invalid after a stroke, was brought along to the canal to show him our somewhat mixed collection of craft. He was to die not many years after in a nursing home in Greystones. I was with him when he died. In memory now I realise the great moral support he gave in all my ventures, not to mention the practical mechanical instruction in long gone childhood.

Extra hands for the journey were made up by my cousin Joan Plews, by Brian Denham, a medical student, and David Laing, a steam and inland waters enthusiast. This made five people for three boats, a bit of a skeletal crew, particularly with about 32 locks to negotiate, each one twice. It was going to be hard work, and it was. But it was also quite an adventure for all of us. David and I took it in turns to steer 52M, Joan and Brian were on 'Chas' (as she came to be known), and Christine was aided by eight year old Simon on the combined canteen-committee boat, Inis Cealtra.

The voyage took perhaps a week. Sometimes we travelled well into the winter's night and, with no spotlight to help us on the barge, we found it surprisingly hard to keep in the middle of the canal, shadows and reality merging. Much like now as I write, memories merging with all the half forgotten days.

We had some serious engine trouble on 52M in Tullamore.

Brian and Joan had to leave us there anyway to get back to work and they went off on his small motorbike which we had brought along on the barge. I don't think Joan had ever ridden pillion before(she told me afterwards she was terrified and very cold) but she was a good sport. And a good sportswoman too. A radiologist by profession, she was an experienced horsewoman and sailor and played hockey, tennis, badminton. . . she never married.

At Tullamore we contacted an engineering works which was familiar with Bollinder engines, and left the barge there. We carried on with Inis Cealtra towing Chas until we ran into cat ice on the canal. This was cutting into her stem and bow planking but we spotted it before it had done serious damage. So, as Chas had a much sharper bow with a good brass band on it, we set her towing Cealtra. This worked perfectly, Chas cutting a channel like an icebreaker without damaging herself.

It was late evening when we passed through Rahan and came out on that long level through the big Bord Na Mona (Turf Board) bog operation which supplied the power station near Ferbane. We carried on into the night. In the distance we could see the power station and across the flat land which might have been sea it looked all lit up like a ship. I remember saying to Simon, "Oh look, there's the Queen Mary".

We moored up near Ferbane, knowing we could reach Shannon Harbour on the morrow. And the morrow was Christmas Eve of 1960 when, with Charles Whitton's two cylinder Thornycroft Handybilly petrol engine chugging away, we moved through thin ice into Shannon Harbour and moored up alongside St. Brigid.

We had really arrived.

*

Shannon Harbour had been for many years the point for the transfer of cargoes and passengers from the canal to the Shannon. The passengers would have been mostly emigrants from Dublin and the Midlands carried on the horse drawn 'Fly Boats', as the faster passenger boats were called, and surprisingly fast passages were indeed claimed for them. The emigrants would have been heading for Limerick where a passage might be had to America. To cater for these people in transit there was a substantial hotel at the harbour which was still standing but derelict.

There were two pubs in the place and even a practitioner of the oldest profession, - even inland sailors seek female comfort betimes! There was a post office and a shop selling the basics. The Harbourmaster's house was two storeyed and up a flight of stone steps. Here Mrs Byrne was living with her daughter, Eugene the harbourmaster had not returned at that time. There was also a semi detached three storey house one half of which was lived in by the local capenter and his wife, the other half was derelict. Then there was a small National School. Simon attended here for a time but as a Protestant and/or stranger was not well treated by the local kids, although he did make one rather rascally friend!

Leading off the canal basin, which was several hundreds yards long by about 25 wide, was a dry dock big enough to take the St. Brigid. As the canal at this point was banked up to be above the level of the surrounding country, this dock practically worked itself. It filled from the canal and emptied onto the land below, no pumping required. We used it extensively later and in fact we considered it to be included in our lease!
A 4 ton crane overhung the canal, less its hoist chain which we soon replaced. And there was a semi derelict workshop with all sorts of interesting bits of engines, much of it useful to us for the two types of

Bollinder we owned. This was next to the big and relatively new steel and corrugated asbestos shed. This was about120ft by 60, with a useful office. Overhead were tracks carrying two electric hoists which we never used, their capacity being too low, though we did use the tracks with chain blocks and travellers we had made, and grossly overloaded the roof structure by lifting 5 ton boats! There were three waterside doors and one door to the road.

As a workshop the shed was not ideal. It was really too big, terribly draughty and impossible to heat. Nonetheless, in it we built six of our 'K Line' boats and four for James O'Connor's Flag Line, also several private boats, besides a lot of repair and alteration jobs on private cruisers.

The overshed was a godsend. At first we had to keep it as a freeway for passing boats but one day Chris had the brainwave that the part of the canal basin outside the overshed, almost solid with mud and weed, could be dug out and used as the navigation. The canal engineer in Dublin was Mr Dalton, we knew him well and asked him to get one of his draglines to clear it out.

The job was done in a couple of days work. This now meant that we were able to house our own fleet in winter and charge for private boats when there was space, probably illegally as the overshed was strictly not part of our lease.

Further on at the Harbour we also had access to some of the original brick built warehouses, one of which had a tin roof and was weatherproof and lockable. This became our garage and twice a ballroom for a local ceili! Beyond was the first of the two locks down to the Shannon.

This was our domain!

*

INIS CEALTRA was to be our home for about three months, and quite a cosy home it made too. The boys Shane (three) and Simon (eight) slept in the for'd cabin, Chris and myself in a pulldown double bed in the saloon, with a spare quarter berth. We had a most efficient turf briquette burning solid fuel stove which also heated water by means of a jacket tank round the flue, and there was a small gas water heater.

And now began a period of pretty intense activity. It was hard and interesting work and quite a lot of fun.

The first thing done was to sort out the boats and berth them under the overshed before they were all frozen in. St Brigid went in first with Chas outside her. Inis Cealtra remained half under cover so that we could get ashore without going through the shed.

One day Chris and I decided to start Brigid's engine. (I had been shown how by Michael). This Bolinder was relatively sophisticated, it had gears and starting was by compressed air. But the three cylinder bulbs had to be heated with three blowlamps, quite a business in itself. The flywheel had to be set exactly on certain marks, and a little fuel had to be hand injected into each cylinder when the bulbs were deemed to be hot enough, and after a suitable prayer the compressed air lever was pulled very briefly. We did all this and on pulling the lever the engine started immediately, emitting as onlookers said a great mushroom cloud from the vertical exhaust. It revved up in a manner reminiscent of the other Bollinder and fearful of doing damage I shut it down!

We moved her under the shed with manpower!

Later I went up to see Michael who lived in Banagher about what I should have done.

"Oh you shouldn't have stopped her, he said, put her in gear, that would check her engines... anyhow flounders are female! But you should have properly moored the boat first."

*

A little back down the canal another family were converting St Patrick, a barge almost identical to St Brigid. Jean and Ronny Kersley were ex-circus people, she the 'Rosinback' and he the Ringmaster. They had a little girl about Simon's age and we naturally became friendly.

St Patrick was being turned into a floating mobile hotel, and later they converted two more big boats for the same purpose. For some years they seemed to be doing well but after marriage difficulties the business seemed to collapse.

The problem of our own money was beginning to raise its ugly head!

I had taken my piece of paper from the Minister to my bank manager, but he wasn't interested in lending money for a venture like ours. This bank didn't have a branch in Banagher and I had been cashing cheques through The Bank of Ireland. One day I mentioned to the manager there that I had this guarantee and he said his bank would be interested.

We changed banks!

Nonetheless, by present standards this was still only marginal help unless the business was going to be pretty paying. We had £10,000 to spend, less interest and the term repayments. We also took a loan of £5000 from the Guinness Workers Development fund. We then made ourselves into a limited company and managed to get some of our friends - those whom we thought could afford to risk loosing it- to buy some shares.

Labour was also a problem.

Jim Foley was taken on as working foreman. He had been building GP Fourteens in Bray and we'd heard of him when in Killiney. We also took on local carpenter-farmer John Feary, and one other local handyman, but these latter two had of course no knowledge of boatbuilding.

We bought a 19ft half decked centreboard sailing boat from a friend of a friend, Walter Levinge, himself a gentleman farmer and boatbuilder of repute. The staff were set to converting this to a little sailing cruiser with a Seagull outboard engine, this becoming 'Plover', later to prove an ever popular little three berth boat.

We roughed out plans for St. Brigid, and this conversion was largely carried out by amateur labour. There was David Laing, Philip Trevelyan, my two sons Tyl and Finn, plus myself and Chris and John Feary. For the first two years we only converted part of her, leaving the original small wheel house, making a galley, a living room, two cabins on the same level and a bathroom on the level of the hold floor. This left a useful workshop area in which we built a "Fireball", most of the work being done by an apprentice Seamus Woods under my direction. The old forecastle/crew accommodation was cleaned up and painted and became the very popular guest cabin with a double bed.

As something to go on with we bought cheaply a two berth semi speed boat with an outboard engine. All this time, some six weeks, we were completely frozen in, the ice on the canal a full foot thick. Water and sanitation were a problem, the village pump was about a quarter mile away. But Chris somehow managed to feed our amateur workers who were also paid pocket money.

In our first full year at The Harbour we built two 32ft cruisers, capable of sleeping eight persons. These boats, Inis Mor and Inis Bofin, had the popular turf burning stoves and were powered by B.M.C. one and one half litre diesel engines.

We also produced two conventionally built timber motor sailers, 26ft overall and with the same diesel engines. These were "Mallard" and "Curlew", four berth boats which were ever popular and usually booked solid.

*

K LINE Cruisers, as we called ourselves, was the first hire fleet operated full time on the Shannon, and certainly the first to have built most of its fleet.

Other people were also thinking of starting up in 1961. And there were already several individual boats for hire up and down the Shannon, mostly elderly converted ships' lifeboats with petrol engines.

Dick McGarry had some boats built by Hickey's of Galway later that year and several other people began to investigate the possibilities, including Guinness who sent Mr Dereck Dann to interview us.

Other starters were a Mr Collins at what is now Carrick Marine, Dominick Mitchell in Carrick with Mitchell Marine, and Captain Axford at Cootehall. There were others down south at Banagher and Killaloe.

K Line started with an early season booking for Inis Cealtra.

It was exciting to see her head out into the Shannon from the lower lock, even more exciting to actually pocket some money after about a year of spending. We were now living on St Brigid but had earlier had one brief winter cruise ourselves on Inis Cealtra as far as Lough Ree.

It all seemed beautiful and I remember the lake teeming with wild fowl. Today a brace of mallard is quite a rarity.

Too many hire boats?

No doubt, another of life's ironies!

*

Inconveniently two locks up from the Shannon, Shannon Harbour was also rather inaccessable to public transport and so we decided in April to move our hiring base to Jamestown Quay.

We built a small two comparment timber hut there with the assistance of John Weaving whom we had recently taken on our pay roll part time. John and another man had been hiring out two elderly boats from the Dublin office of a business they had in shop and exhibition fitting.

We commuted to Jamestown each Friday to do the Saturday change over. And before and while the hut was being built - it later became my drawing office - we got permission from the owners of a big barge ("The Gilaroo" which was moored at the quay), to live aboard her at week ends. 'Gilaroo' was becoming semi-derelict and it was a little difficult to find a dry place to eat and sleep under! One night the two tier bunk Chris and I slept in fell through the floor and capsized! However, the accomodation served its purpose, and once the hut was built we had a proper base, even if not very imposing by present day standards. One recollection of that hut was how in a severe thunder storm the quay right in front of us was struck leaving a tiny patch of steaming wet grass. Chris had been out there only a moment before.

*

Our second winter at the harbour was just as severe as the first, probably even more so. All the surrounding meadow land was flooded and rapidly froze over and, as often happens, this trapped two or three Mute Swans which sadly we were unable to help because the ice was too thin. When we did get to them they were dead and we found they had broken their wings trying to free themselves.

There was a jam of ' icebergs' on a bend below Shannon Bridge which would have looked at home on a Canadian river. And someone drove a car right across Lough Ree to Hodsons Bay!

Nonetheless we were quite snug on the Brigid, to some extent being kept warm by the water under us, this of course being above freezing. We had a good turf stove and a connection to mains electricity.

On the day after Christmas 1962 I made an ice yacht.

Three skates, two pieces of timber crossed, one with a sitting area on it, and then a dinghy's spars and mainsail... an ice yacht!

Simon soon learned to sail it, after being thrown off it once or twice when it luffed violently -turned into the wind. The winds were light but even then we reckoned it did between 20 and 30 mph. There were literally square miles of shallow ice to play on, the only hazard barbed wire!

An elderly friend of ours in Banagher, (a former pilot in the Royal Flying Corps who had never grown up) heard of this 'yacht' and asked to be let have a go. This he did, despite his daughters disapproval, and had a great sail and thoroughly enjoyed himself. But what none of us knew was that his sail was being filmed from afar for Telefis Eireann, and the next night with father and daughter sitting in front of the T.V., there he appeared!

'Oh look at the old gentleman on the ice yacht!' he is reputed to have said.

One of our early bookings was for 'Plover' from people called Stimpson. Later to become friends and employees of the Company, they weren't too friendly when they first arrived and found that 'Plover' wasn't ready. Although we had worked furiously we hadn't overcome one problem. She was an old hull and the planking had shrunk so that she leaked badly before 'taking up'. So, much to the Stimpsons' disgust, we sent them off in the little outboard engined speedboat!

We promised to bring Plover to Lough Ree behind the Brigid in about three days. This was Brigid's first time out and, thinking it wise to have some professionals aboard, we had both the late skipper and the engineer, both called Mick, along as far as Athlone.

We carried a miscellaneous cargo, including a crate of ducks and on the small foredeck on a bed of hay a young donkey which Chris had recently acquired.

Plover in tow, it was an exciting moment when our home St.Brigid moved down the two locks to the Shannon.

We noted again the pneumatic chisel marks on the sides of both locks, Eugene had told us the history of these previously. It was during the War that CIE bought the St Brigid and the St Patrick in England, where they had been the Avon Queen and the Avon King.

Shortly before they were due to arrive up the Shannon one of the CIE engineers came down to The Harbour to check that everything was in order. Eugene recounted how he and the engineer went to the upper lock to measure it with a tape, and Eugene holding one end saw a sudden look of dismay on the engineer's face.

While someone had measured the barges' beam, and presumably also the locks, they would not fit, and by a margin of nearly two feet!

It took them over six months to carve down the granite sides of the two locks and make and fit four new gates!

*

Once out on the Shannon Chris and I were allowed to steer, with the Bollinder running like a dream below us, practically vibrationless, being effectively a six cylinder, its clean exhaust making a lovely rumble.

Rated at 80hp at only 800rpm and with a two to one reduction gear, she had great pulling power and had been generally used as a tug, loaded herself and pulling a loaded canal boat. Some years earlier in a storm on Lough Derg she had tragically pulled under one of these barges loaded with Guinness, with the loss of two men. (This boat was salvaged with difficulty by a friend of ours, Donagher Kennedy, from 100ft of water in the late 60's).

We locked up at Athlone and when the upper gates opened the two Micks left us and wished us a trouble free run up to Jamestown. I had been well briefed on managing the engine, which did mean I had to spend quite a lot of time in the engine room on all our Shannon trips, leaving the steering mostly to Chris and other people. On this first trip I think we had David Laing with us.

It went well. We had a most enjoyable trip up Lough Ree, successfully meeting the Stimpsons off Rindoon point where they switched boats as promised. (They were delighted to get sailing, the rather tubby little Plover sailed remarkably well).

We spent that first night at Tarmonbarry, stopping the engine with some trepidation in case of problems in the morning when starting again. In fact as the air bottles were well charged (charged by using one cylinder with fuel cut off as the compressor- about 350 psi), and as we went through the routine of properly mooring the boat and heating the bulbs and so forth she started immediately and we were on our way rejoicing!

Two more locks brought us to the Jamestown Cut and then, back in the Shannon, we were faced with turning and docking at the quay. I did a dummy turn before attempting it in the open water upstream. It requires a certain nerve because the river is carrying you down to the bridge sideways. (I got in bad trouble once when trying to turn her from the far bank and finished up with St Brigid firmly held sideways against the bridge). Nonetheless that first time we did it successfully without too much barge language!

*

St Brigid then became our hire base for the season, and I commuted between Jamestown and Shannon Harbour where I lived in a borrowed caravan, rather ancient and just about weather proof.

Myself and the four employees worked on the construction of the two 32 ft motor cruisers, two motor sailers and an 18ft sailing boat with an inboard two-stroke petrol engine. (That engine gave us more trouble over the years than all the other engines put together!)

During the building of the first of the 32 footers John Feary was bending in the first chine, a long piece of timber 2" by 1" with a sharp bend into the stem. He hadn't done this before and I was watching him from a distance. I suddenly decided that the way he was going about it was going to break it, so I walked over and said "I think you had better let me do it".

"Right you be sir". He stepped back.

You guessed the rest!

John was delighted and said "ah, the right man done it, the right man done it"!

This expression became part of our family lingo!

*

In addition to building craft for our own fleet, we built four for James O'Connor's Flag Line. (I also designed two bigger boats which were built for him by Crosshaven Boatyard). We also built a 30ft auxilliary yatch for our family doctor, Dr Hennessey. And for a well known character of the time, Jack Kelly Rogers, ex wartime transport pilot for Churchill, we built a 'Catavan'. A good friend of ours, this was Jack's idea. It was a twin hulled craft with twin diesel engines, and with an extra wide caravan-type body fitted on deck. Relatively cheap, 40ft long and very roomy, this was quite fast at 11 knots and very manouverable. I had great hopes that this type of craft might become popular but Jack's was the only one ever built.

IN EARLY October we brought St Brigid back from Jamestown to Shannon Harbour. The voyage was something of a saga.

The crew was mixed!

David Laing much involved in the classical music world, (organising concerts in great Irish houses), had with our agreement invited three members of the Radio Eireann Symphony orchestra along for the trip.

We had the first and second flute, Andre Priour and Patricia Dunkerley, plus Anita Dunkerley, Violin. There was also a French couple, Henri Bourguet and his wife.

Henri, an engineer, had driven them all up to Jamestown in his Triumph Herald.

The weather was good but the river was in spate. This, when going with it, can make things a bit hairy at times, particularly when approaching locks, most of which have a weir beside them with a strong pull away from the lock entrance. There was also one very narrow bridge in a swift flowing part of the river above Lough Ree.

We got off the a good start, the engine obliging by firing on the first puff of air. Casting off, we headed into the Jamestown Cut, that length of canal which bypasses a loop of the Shannon.

Halfway along this the engine sounded a bit rough and the external silencer cum funnel appeared to be very hot with the paint burning off it!

We entered the lock and tied up, leaving the engine running, but suddenly it let out a loud squark and stopped. Henri and I went down to investigate and found the engine seized, but why? We tried barring the flywheel and after a few minutes it came free. As the engine was still very hot we set the flywheel in the start position, gave her a puff of air and away she went.

We loaded Henri's car, which his wife had driven to the lock, on the after deck and when the lower gate opened I pushed the gear lever forward as before.

Brigid backed smartly into the upper gate!

Then the penny dropped, the engine being of the two stroke variety had started backwards first time and I had forgotten that to go forwards one pulled the lever back!

After that not so much as a hitch as we continued on our way, everyone enjoying the cruise and the countryside and I not being too troubled by the current apart from over running one or two marker buoys due to not being able at our considerable speed to wind the big wheel quickly enough!

At Lough Ree and found we had time in hand before landing the car and our party at Athlone lock, so we decided it visit the Levinge family who lived in a lovely old house above a small lake connected by a cut to the inner Lakes off Lough Ree proper. We had no problem on the way in because we could go slowly against a considerable stream and wind.

Half way along we came across a cruiser tied to the bank, on board Jem Sullivan, whom I knew fairly well, with his wife and two dogs of the chow variety.

At the sight of Brigid's bow about 8 ft high approaching there was panic aboard as they prepared to defend themselves with fenders, but in fact we were just able to slip past without making contact but near enough for the chows to board us and get thrown back!

The little lake was just big enough to enable us to turn Brigid with the aid of the little speed cruiser we were towing back to The Harbour but the water level was right up to the lake margins and was really in the middle of a meadow. The whole Levinge family came to meet us and boarded via the speedboat. However, the musicians were due back in Dublin for an evening rehearsal so we could not stay long. Brigid had stayed running nicely with her nose pressed against the bank, and Jem had brought his boat up to give us a clear run out. The cut was by no means straight and I put David on the bow with a big pole to help steer that end round the bends. It was impossible to go slow enough and after bouncing and being pushed off the banks several times we ran hard aground on one bank, I was going ahead and astern and had just wriggled her off when the engine seized again. This time it was final and solid. We pulled her backwards into the little lake with the speedboat and managed to get our passengers ashore but were unable to get Henri's car off.

They phoned for a taxi in to Athlone and somehow made the rehearsal.

Our home was now in an unforseen situation, however we were with friends and the boys were quite happy. Chris and I decided to get Inis Cealtra up from Shannon Harbour and tow her back there. Jim Foley came for me in the Morris which he was using - we had by that time acquired a short wheelbase Land Rover- and I was back next day with two long heavy planks on the roof.

We then set about getting the Triumph ashore. The stern of the Brigid was about four feet above the field which by now had an inch or two of water on it. Jacking and packing we somehow got the car facing steeply down the planks with all four wheels lined up, I started it and fearing getting bogged in the field drove it full tilt down the planks and keeping going fast reached dry land, and drove it to the Harbour.

I returned with Inis Cealtra and when at the lock explained our situation to Percy Hewett the lock keeper, a friend of ours, and asked him to have the upper gate open and keep a lookout for us after I had phoned him our ETA.

It was going to be somewhat dicey coming into Athlone and the lock with the strong current with us and tending to move us sideways onto the powerful weir with no brakes and virtually no steerage way on Brigid.

So with me alone on Cealtra and Chris alone with the boys on St Brigid we left the little lake and going as slowly as I could we gained open water without grounding and then swinging out into the main lake headed down stream for Athlone. It was really the most tricky towing operation I ever undertook and it was our home I had on the string!

I was really tense as we approached the railway bridge, trying to go as slowly as would still give Chris any steerage way, - we had arranged to keep as near the moored craft on the right bank as possible and hopefully keep out of the water going over the weir. I shortened up the tow and gave just enough pull to keep Brigid going slightly faster than the water.

It was great to see the gates open and Percy and his assistant ready for us. I entered the lock just as Brigid began to feel the weir-going current and her stern began to turn out of line but the bow was in. She made contact with the pierhead of the lock entrance but not heavily, this took the way off her and I pulled her easily into the slack water of the lock. I think it maybe took a year or two off my life!

We thanked and paid Percy, and went into the town to get some supplies. Leaving Athlone we were making a good 6mph over the ground until the wind began to increase as we neared Shannon Bridge, more than halfway home but the weather ahead began to look really bad and it began to rain in torrents. About a mile or two before The Bridge there is a long straight stretch of river and the wind was blowing straight up it against the current and soon Cealtra was bucking.

Twice I was blown off course and Chris dashed forward to give me more rope. I was on full throttle and barely able to keep moving through the water. We had run into something quite exceptional. I was also very cold and half drowned as the cockpit roof was off for towing purposes.

Brigid drifted towards the left bank and we could do nothing about it. Quite suddenly an extra strong gust caught Cealtra on her port side, turned the boat right round and blew her sideways agaist Brigid. I switched off the engine, let the tow rope go, jumped onto Brigid's side deck and tried to make her fast but failed, and in the now half light she blew away into the gloom.

Chris meantime was trying to secure the dinghy and loose articles on deck, Brigid now being firmly ashore, but fortunately on a soft muddy bank. The wind was now at near hurricane force, for that was what it was, and we could do nothing about our situation, but we were safe so we went below, I changed into dry clothes and Chris cooked a meal while the storm roared over us.

Sometime later with the wind still a fury I felt our situation had changed somewhat and on looking out into the pitch black night realised we were now aground on the opposite bank. With the noise of wind and wave we had not felt the change of position. Soon after midnight the wind began to ease and by two am the sky cleared a bit and I made out Inis Cealtra in the reeds on the other bank some way up stream. Deciding all was safe I turned in quite exhausted, the others already asleep.

The morning was fine with little wind, we launched the dinghy and I rowed accross to Cealtra, and she started immediately. I had no trouble getting off the bank. I went down to Brigid, took up the tow rope and bridle and with full throttle pulled her into the stream and with Chris at the helm we were soon turning left into the canal entrance and by mid afternoon had turned her and berthed her in her usual position half out of the overshed.

Sometime later I tackled the engine and found after removing the heavy flywheel that the forward crankshaft bearing had seized and literally broken up due to oil starvation when running in reverse, I was amazed to see the double row of tapered half inch diameter rollers in bits. SKF were immediately able to supply a replacement, the parts being common to some of the dockyard cranes.

*

One of our problems at The Harbour was a water supply. There was a supply of good drinking water at the village pump but as that was over a quarter of a mile away we used it only for drinking. The canal was considered to be somewhat polluted and with very little flow, so I decided to harness rain water off the huge expanse of roof. The drains from the valley between the two roofs came down inside the building and as it happened the nearest one to Brigid was missing its down pipe, the water just running down the wall and into the canal. I rigged up the crajiest Heath Robinson arrangement consisting of a filling funnel led with string to the stub pipe from the gutter, this was about 16 feet up a ladder and to this I joined a length of garden hose by a short piece of intermediate hose all jubilee clipped together and leading to the ballast tank in Brigid's stern where it could settle out the dirt. From there it was manually or electrically pumped to a gravity tank on the back of the new wheelhouse we had built. It would have worked perfectly but for the large quantity of moss on the roof which quickly filled and choked the filling funnel and I had to be constantly removing and cleaning this. Sounds easy but it was at full stretch balancing on the top of the ladder with the water overflowing on to me and when I got it off, the full flood of the water trapped in the gutter poured over me and even up my sleeve and found its chilling winter ice way out my trouser leg! Those were the days before wet suits, and I never did find a satisfactory way of doing it without getting) very wet, but never fell off the ladder!

IN EARLY 1964 one of our early hirers was the American Military Attache in Dublin, Col Bradford Butler Jr, and his Italian wife. Brad seemed to take a liking to us and told us he had recently bought a 27ft fibreglass Prout sailing catamaran and intended to sail it to America via the Canaries and West Indies.

He invited us to join him, but before that for me to inspect the craft and assess it for the voyage proposed. We couldn't leave our business for that long but we agreed to sail with him to Crosshaven, and I agreed to go as far as Vigo in Spain. Chris wanted to do that trip too, but I vetoed it because I thought the risk element rather high. She was furious but I wasn't too impressed with the craft and especially with many of its fittings which I considered not much better than those for a day sailor.

We sailed with him to Crosshaven, quite a pleasant trip in good weather, but we did form the opinion that Brad was not a very experienced seaman. He did all the cooking on the little voyage and we consumed a great quantity of scrambled egg and porridge!

Very reluctantly Chris left us at Crosshaven, and we started to seek a third hand. This turned up in the form of Ian Miller, a well built youngish man who had just come into the port on another yacht, and was prepared to go all the way to America with Brad.

We made up water and stores and sailed one evening without so much as seeking any weather forecast. I was concerned by the look of the sky and by the fact that on the way out of Cork Harbour we met a number of trawlers coming in!

As it got dark the wind began to get strong rapidly, we reefed and reefed again in a very rough sea, waves thumping up against her bridge deck with a violence which worried me. As we had a good offing from the land I suggested we take all sail off and let the boat look after itself while we took watches in case of being run down.

I don't know about the wind speed but a very severe little depression passed over us and most violent seas frequently broke right over us. Ian took the first night watch and I the second. Changing in the small hours I had just scrambled into the cockpit, Ian had unhooked his lifeline and I had not hooked on mine when in the pitch dark we were completely overwhelmed by a breaker which knocked the boat over, completely filling the very large cockpit. For a moment we both thought we were in the sea and were attempting to rescue each other!

The boat surfaced but leaving the cockpit full to the brim and draining so slowly that we started bucketing it out in anticipation of the next big breaker. But it didn't come, that was the last bad moment and as dawn broke in my watch, me sitting soaking wet inside my oilskins, the sea and wind began to moderate. Thinking back I don't think I was frightened during the experience, possibly the worst in my sailing lifetime. I think I just took it philosophically. What must be must be!

By midday we were well into the Bay of Biscay, the weather was fine and clear, we were under full sail with a fair wind, and were heading in the general direction of Cape Finisterre on the Spanish N.W. coast.

We tidied up the ship which was in a hell of a mess down below. She had taken a lot of water in both hulls and nearly all our stores and much else was in the two bilges. It was fortunate that we had not far to go because we were now short of many things, particulary I remember sugar, though someone had given Brad a large jar of honey which had survived and this took the place of sugar for the next two days. (I had commented to Brad about the stowages in Crosshaven because they were all open fronted with just a little lip; he had said "but catamarans hardly heel at all!")

That night was peaceful, travelling down The Bay under a starlit sky, the sea beneath us full of phosphorescence and of illuminated fish and their wakes. Numerous big fish seemed to charge at us from all sides and although never making contact it was quite alarming.

The second morning we saw the outline of the Spanish coast. We passed Finisterre in the late afternoon and then, using the outboard engine, we turned into a small fishing port. Inside it was a shallow lagoon, partly surrounded by the village, which immediately reminded me of India; it had the same architecture as Indian coastal villages influenced by Spanish invaders, there were even women and girls carrying pots on their heads.

Evidently some sort of fiesta day, there were many young people out in small boats singing and playing guitars and other instruments. Many of these came alongside. They tried to make conversation, and succeeded in selling us a fish!

A calm sunny evening, it was all quite idyllic.

Ian and I wanted to go ashore but Brad wouldn't let us as we were not cleared for entering Spain and there were obviously no such facilities at this place. We were very piqued but had to accept that as he was an Important American he had to observe protocol.

After a peaceful night we sailed down to Vigo, passing near the great inhabited rafts of mussel cultivators in the bay. We moored up near the yacht club, a most impressive building but very run down. A bar about 40ft long but with little stock, few members and a gentlemen's changing room of huge proportions with about a dozen showers. Each producing only a trickle of cold water!

My most pleasant memory of Vigo was of sitting under the trees at a restaurant on the waterfront in the evening listening to what I thought was an extremely good band particularly a trumpet and a male singer, we all agreed they could have made a living anywhere.

I left Vigo before the others sailed but in the meantime spotted on the moorings one of my Slipway 5 tonners, and via one of the boatyards met the owner. He came to the yard in an impressive car, and turned out to be a well known surgeon of Brazilian extraction He took me for a long drive into the country and then wined and dined me in a seafood restaurant. He seemed very pleased to have met me, and was obviously very proud of his little boat.

I said goodbye and bon voyage to my friends. (As I shall relate Ian and I were to be shipmates again.) They reached Barbados less one bilge board and one rudder, and told me in correspondance that the night off the Cork coast was the worst of the whole voyage. After an interesting and amusing train journey from Vigo to Paris, I flew to London and then it was the train and boat and train again back home.

*

We sold our canal boat quite profitably for conversion after chartering her to a contractor on the Shannon estuary, and then bought another canal boat, a privately owned boat (known as a 'by trader') which was called 'Peter Farrell' after her owner who had retired.

She was in reasonable running order but her forward accommodation was absolutely alive with bed bugs! We had to completely strip it out to the bare steel, fumigate and paint it and then build in new bunks etc, most of this work was bravely done by a young friend of ours Brian Mc Lelland, now a Dublin doctor.

We converted her to a work boat by literally uprooting a small crane from one of the old warehouses at The Harbour and mounting it forward on deck and for a time we employed John Weaving to operate her. The work being mostly making concrete sinkers and placing floating channel markers (ex anti-submarine boom net buoys we had bought cheap) under the guidance of Mick Madden who was in charge of the Shannon Navigation for the OPW and John Carthy in Dublin.

After about six months we sold Peter Farrell to John Weaving for a nominal sum and he (plus his dogs) and the Peter Farrell gradually became a legend on the Shannon.

*

SOME TIME very early in 1963 Mr Barry, at that time Offaly Co Engineer, borrowed Inis Cealtra and with the assistance of Jack Kelly Rogers and another man towed a 60ft pontoon from The Harbour up to Clonmacnoise, the famous ecclesiastical settlement. Here it became the landing platform for boating visitors.

On returning our boat he asked me if a similar pontoon would be any use to us, and the idea of a floating base at Jamestown was born. We bought it for £100.

It was on the Barrow river off the navigation above the town of Athy. It was actually sunk in the river bank with trees growing out of it! Mr Barry promised to pump and clean it out with the use of his Fire Brigade .

The hire season had not yet begun and so we set out en famille in Inis Cealtra in early March, via the Grand Canal to the Barrow branch for Athy.

Jack Kelly-Rogers had asked if he could be involved and we had agreed to let him know when to meet us in Athy. At this time I had taken over my mother's Morris Minor and so that our movements would be more flexible on the trip we brought it along. Driven alternately by Chris and myself it followed Inis Cealtra on land, going ahead to open locks and do the shopping and so forth.

The weather was pretty cold, but no ice, just very heavy weed which would have been a serious handicap or even made the voyage impossible were it not for the tailboard built into the boat. The whole transom dropped down to within about 6" of the water. Great for bathing, it also allowed us to carry a dinghy in the cockpit instead of towing it.

On this trip we removed it altrogether which allowed us to lie down and reach under to free the propeller when it became so balled up that it no longer provided propulsion; every mile or two we had to stop engine and repeat this performance.

It took about four long days to reach Athy but it was still enjoyable,

Simon was capable of steering for short spells and whoever was not driving the car could have a walk.

Below Athy the Barrow Navigation becomes a canalised river, the actual Barrow itself. On arriving we had a good night in a quiet part of the town and locked down to river level early in the very misty morning.

While we were making preparations for the tow, fitting the oak towing beam across the forward end of the open cockpit, so that the boat could be steered when there was a strain on the towrope, and making up the bridle, Jack arrived and we set off upstream. We went under the bridge, passing through the relatively narrow centre arch which was going to be our main worry on the way back.

We had brought a Seagull outboard engine and I had made a bracket for it, this not for propulsion but to give the pontoon a modicum of steerage. The plan was that Jack would sit on the back of the pontoon on a butter box and steer with the outboard.

I put Cealtra alongside the pontoon facing downstream, attached the bridle-tow rope to the front corners. Jack nailed down the bracket, untied the pontoon from two trees and we were on our way into midstream. To keep full steerage way on Cealtra I had to go appreciably faster than the stream which meant we were approaching the invisible bridge at least 5mph - much too fast for comfort considering the pontoon had no brakes and very little steerage.

The bridge emerged from the mist about 100 yards ahead with the middle arch fortunately more or less where I had hoped it would be!

There was just enough time and space, Jack obeying my hand signals, to make the necessary corrections and we passed through without touching. Had we hit one of the piers going downstream at perhaps 5mph over the ground the very heavily built pontoon (weighing roughly 60 tons) might have done considerable damage to the bridge and to itself.

Immediately below the bridge we had to do a turn of about 170 degrees to enter the canal which joined the river at an acute angle. This proved easier than I expected because the flow of the river did most of the work, with the help of Jack's 'rudder'. I let the pontoon pass me and turned upstream and pulled hard. The pontoon turned gently in the stream and I was able to enter the canal and we manhandled the pontoon in without difficulty. The pontoon took up the whole lock so it was double locking all the way home.

Before leaving Athy we put the Morris aboard the pontoon - we were able to get it on and off at any of the locks- Jack decided to stay with us for the day, very good company and a considerable help.

As we had passed through the canal the previous day the prop did not need clearing quite so frequently but the pontoon with its deep square front 13ft wide scooped up immense quantities of weed on some sections of the canal. Clearing this was hard work with a boathook and progress a snail's pace until we met the main line at Lowtown and turned west, when we were able to make a slow walking speed. We did not meet another boat under way in the whole trip. We said good bye and many thanks to Jack after the evening meal, driving him back to his car in Athy. He was one of these boys who never really grow up.

Like myself!

The morning after we got back we put the pontoon in the dry dock to clean and paint her and start to turn her into our vision. There was beside the dock an unused steel bow section of a Wartime 'Emergency Boat'- these were used pricipally for carrying turf from the midland bogs to Dublin- the main part of the hull being timber.

This we hoisted and jacked into position and welded onto one end of the pontoon, calling it the stern, adding 11ft of useful deck space. Next we built the deck structure which, starting from the front end, included a covered, glass fronted foyer open at both sides, an office cum reception room and toilet, a linen and general storeroom, a workshop and, under the stern canopy, petrol and diesel pumps with tanks below deck. There was also a stainless funnel shaped water tank on the roof. Everybody worked on the pontoon and it was ready to tow up to Jamestown early in the season.

*

Early one morning we loaded Johnny Donkey and Rani a piebald pony which Chris had recently acquired. This was for Simon, but I have photographic evidence that both Chris and Olive Stimpson rode her. We also had a crate of bantams, a nanny goat and , of course, our permanent resident Tara the corgi.

Having signed on a considerable crew, including Laurie Mc Lelland, his wife and son Brien, also Brien Denham, we started Brigid. We were getting better at it and had fitted gas burning torches instead of the old blowlamps, these instantly lit and were much quicker. We took her through the upper lock and manhandled the pontoon through. We then towed to the lower lock, pleased to see that with the bridle she behaved properly, keeping in the middle. When Percy Hewett brought us up to street level -we could get both vessels in the lock- we caused quite a sensation with all the animals on a what looked like a floating petrol station!

And then we were away to Lough Ree.

The weather was very kind to us. My memory is helped on this because I have photos of us all landing by dinghy on Quaker Island in the middle of the lake, the two vessels anchored peacefully in the background.

We were able to do the whole voyage in one day. The only excitement was when we arrived at Lanesborough Bridge. Here we had an appointment, not to stop, but just to speak with Maureen and Nuala Denham and Dooley their dog- famous stud of no particular breed!

We were nearly up to the bridge when it seemed that one of the bigger hire cruisers was going to enter it from the other side, a big crunch up was only avoided by Nuala warning them off in no uncertain manner! I was steering at the time and could not have stopped without having the pontoon pushing me on. No sooner were we through the bridge than Dooley, spotting Brien Denham on our deck, jumped off the quay and swam out in front of us. I thought I would run over him but he bumped along the side and Brien was able to reach over and fish him out.

It was evening by the time we passed under the railway bridge near the Albert Lock. This is the lowest fixed bridge on the river, the lifting span now fixed. Going under was always a touch and go affair with St Brigid's new wheelhouse, no strain going up river because it could be approached very slowly with a fixed pole up front, but very nail biting going down in winter when we weren't quite sure of river levels and there was a strong flow. This time there was a cross wind on the approach to Albert Lock and at slow speed we were blown into the reeds and had some trouble getting in.

But we did. And later when we tied up at the west end of the Jamestown Cut we were well satisfied with our progress. The three hoofed animals were landed and walked to our 'estate' and the party broke up. The next day we took St Brigid to her berth on our side of the river and then brought the pontoon down to her prepared anchorage off the end of the jetty which John Weaving had built for us. Using Inis Cealtra as a tug once again, successfully turning this very heavy article above the bridge. As a base it was a great success. And about the same time we constructed a hauling out slipway, partly cut back into the river bank and partly pushed out into the river.

I had acquired three very long rolled steel joists, H section, 14"by 8". These came from a convent in Rocommon and I collected them with our heavy trailer, an ex anti-aircraft gun carriage, a dreadfully awkward thing to tow behind the short wheel base Landrover, but I and Chris too towed it many miles, including two trips to London Boat Shows.

One of these joists we had cut in half professionally and used this to extend the others to about 44ft by welding, these were then fabricated on land into two parallel channels with R.S.Js between, spaced about 6ft apart and partly decked with 3" oak planks. Using a wet suit and a snorkel I cleared the bed of the river of large stones and then from the far quay using a pulling machine we winched the pre fab into position and cemented it into the concrete slipway. It was rather steep but we were able to haul all our boats out.

*

Sometime after our return from India, Ireland's first proper Boat Show was held. I think this was organised by the Irish Yachting Association with Coras Trachtala, in any event it took place in Busaras, the Dublin bus station.

There was a prize for the best boat in the show and the judges for this competition were three 'distinguished chaps', Uffa Fox, Jack Tyrell, and myself. In earlier days Uffa had been a good friend to me and it was good to meet him again.

The Dublin show was in fact the first time I saw an all glassfibre boat. And it must be said that myself and the other judges were a bit sceptical about their future! (We may have been 'distinguished', but not prophets!)

I can't remember who or what won the prize in question, but the show itself led sometime later to the periodical Irish Yachting and Motor Boating, sponsoring (backed by Coras Trachtala), a design competition for a small, about 27ft, sailing yacht suitable for construction by Irish boatyards and aimed principally at the export market.

I won the competition and the cash prize.

I had been given the impression that a prototype would be sponsored but somehow Coras Trachtala never came up with anything in that regard, though they did pay for a stand at the London Boat Show the next year.

I myself financed the prototype and was fortunate enough to sell it to Mr Gerry Callinan, although this sale only recovered part of the outlay as I had to make plugs and mouldings for all the glassfibre parts.

This little yacht became the 'Kerry Class', of which eventually 24 were to be built. (I deal with this later in these pages).

*

We had several very busy seasons but our economics were not working out right!

It was somewhat galling to see newcomers on the Shannon getting grants of one third of the cost of their imported boats from the government via Bord Failte. We applied for assistance in retrospect but rather unjustly they would not pay.

Christine took immense trouble with the bookeeping, guided by a very friendly accountant Ronnie Baskin, but with so much borrowed money we could hardly win.

And we didn't!

I formed a new company in my own name, financed and directed by the Dock Milling Company of Dublin, (Nial Higgins. was M.D); this company was expressly to put an all GRP Kerry into production.

Earlier Chris and I had bought at a knockdown price the redundant Drumsna railway station store, a large stone and slate roofed building.

We also got the signal box!

We had been using this store for wintering our cruisers after we had finally left The Harbour. Some two miles from our self-built slipway at Jamestown, it was quite a performance putting them away and getting them back again.

The end of the hire business overlapped to an extent with the new boat building venture but, in any event, this station building became the Kerry workshop.

DONAL CONLON and another young man Eamon Hennessey were our first employees at Jamestown. Donal had been working for Dominick Mitchell, proprietor of Mitchell Marine (one of the early hire companies at Carrick), under a man whose real name I never knew, he was always known as Davy Jones - claimed he had a cat that could play scrabble!- he had Donal making Mirror dinghies from kits, but Donal had also on his own initiative built some lake fishing boats.

Eamon was younger and had little or no experience of boats or boatbuilding at that time but was always plesant and very willing to learn. Now about 30 years later Donal has his own Marina and has built and played a major part in the building of a great variety of craft from big cold moulded ocean racers to the plugs for the famous glassfibre (G.R.P). Shamrock 30ft half tonners, and Eamon is a leading hand with The Emerald Star hire company in Carrick.

We later sold the railway store to the new company (called rather grandly Kennedy International Boat company). This was virtually owned by the Dock Milling Co with myself as Technical Director. Now with adequate finance we transformed the old stone building into an efficient boatbuilding workshop, removing the railway platform, which was a bigger undertaking than we had anticipated as we found solid rock under the timber decking.

Having removed this we had a level floor which was then concreted. We also built in a mezzanine floor which accommodated all the woodworking machines and which had a walkway extending from it at the level of the Kerry's deck of which at one time we had three or four under way at the same time. We also built a lean-to full length on one side of the building which housed the stores, toilets, a canteen and store for fibreglass and resin. Onto one end of the building we built a timber block which included a drawing office, manager's office, an office for our secretary, and a toilet.

Neil and I were not very clever in selecting managers of whom we had two in the five year period we were in business. Both from England, neither had much practical experience. It might be said that at that time men experienced in running a business building glassfibre boats were very scarce, technology and materials have improved considerably since those times and of course it is now big business and it would be hard to find a manager for a timber boatbuilding business!

We were however a little unfortunate in that we ran into the period of the oil crisis which greatly inflated material costs, and we were for some time selling boats at about cost. Nonetheless, the story of the Kerry lasted about seven years in all.

In the meantime Chris was doing more than her share of running the Hire business. I should really say 'running it down' because we could see that 'K Line' had really had its day and we could not afford to buy or build new boats, so we began to sell off those we had.

I was on a salary with K.I.B. which brought in more money per month than the hire business ever did, and it allowed us to send Shane to Limerick University to take Electronics, I felt that that was his bent and was the future, and it is proving so to-day.

Now (1997) Shane has got his teeth and brains into something which with any luck has a future. After a year or two working more or less on his own building small computors to do specific jobs he has now got a backer for more advanced work and a salary to go with it .

He often tries to explain to me how computers work but does not understand that he talks a language I do not understand and now never will!

Our other son Simon had his education rather broken up with our moves. He was also very handicapped because he had no Irish which in his time was an essential subject in any school certificate exams. A trained Scuba diver, he thought of working for a degree in Marine Biology, but was discouraged from taking it up by the professor of that subject at Galway University, principally because he thought the profession was going to be overstocked. He then decided to take up fishing and went to the fishery school in Greencastle, where he failed his eye test for the mate's certificate, but has now been fishing his own boats for some years.

Both sons Simon and Shane had been boarders at Sligo Grammar School during most of the time of our hireboat business. Due to age difference I don't think they were ever there at the same time. Chris and I used to take them out for mountain walks near Sligo on Sundays, weather permitting, otherwise it would be to an evening meal in the town. They and we became very friendly with an American family the Cripps whose mother Ann was the widow of a pilot who killed himself crop spraying: she brought her family of three girls and two boys to Ireland and sent them to the Grammar School, our two families shared many interests, riding, sailing and canoeing.

Ann, largely to her own plans and with her own hands, rebuilt and extended a cottage right on the inner coast of Ballysodare Bay. They all eventually filtered back to America.

Also at Sligo Grammar were two other young people Guy and Wendy Marsden who with their mother Hazel also became close friends who had similar interests, Guy crewed for me several times on Brainstorm and was later for a time in the British Merchant Navy on Tankers.

*

It was decided that I should go as a salesman for the Kerry on a tour to Norway, Sweden, Denmark, Germany and Holland.

I had no business or selling skills, and nothing but a sheaf of simple brochures in English, and I was travelling to countries all of whom were well known boatbuilders!

Coals to Newcastle!

I had no contacts in any of these countries except a note from my brother-in-law Reggie Cooke, he had a contact in Oslo. And of course I could not speak the language of any of the countries I was to visit!

For me it was a most interesting tour, but for the company I'm afraid it was a waste of money.

I flew to Oslo in mid-March, approaching over the thawing fjord. Having booked in at a modest hotel and arranged by phone a meeting with Reggie's friends, I explored a little of the city and its marinas (yachts were kept from freezing in by air bubbled from underwater pipes!) This was a weekend and all the young and not so young people were heading for the hills with skis on their shoulders. I was surprised to note that the police were all armed.

Reggie's friends turned out to be somewhat 'stiff necked upper class'and not able or willing to be of much help...certainly not optimistic of my chances of selling. I failed to make any useful contacts in Oslo and took a train to Karistad in Sweden near where lived my former draughtsman, my friend Rex.

The atmosphere was somewhat depressing as the thaw had started with that characteristic heavy mist hanging over everything, and so it turned out that in both Norway and Sweden I saw nothing of the countryside except snow and birch trees!

On the train to Karistad I found myself sitting beside a very heavily intoxicated Swedish carpenter (a bag of woodworking tools beside him) elderly, rather nice and quite harmless, but terribly talkative and quite unable to understand that I could not understand a word he said until one of the other rather embarrassed passengers managed to explain the situation to him. I understood he was going home to his wife after for some time working in Norway. I wondered about his reception when he got home!

Rex met me with a car at the station and drove me out on roads which were feet deep in frozen snow. Double rows of long rods with reflectors on top were the only indications where the roads were on this snow and birch tree wilderness of a landscape.

Situated above a frozen lake, Rex and his wife Barbro's house was very warm and comfortable. Rex did not seem to have any serious employment except working on plans for a man-powered flying machine! (At that time someone had offered a big cash prize for the first such machine to fly a figure of eight course of a minimum duration.) Barbro was the daughter of a wealthy family and that apparently sufficed!

I spent two relaxed days with them, my stay including a visit by road to The Albin Factory where there seemed to be literally hundreds of finished yachts, many of Kerry's size, covered and standing in the snow.

It made my feeble efforts in Sweden seem slightly rediculous.

Leaving Rex and Barbro I took the train to Stockholm. (Somehow when I was away in India Rex and Barbro had got to know my East Sussex family, and from them I heard news of the couple. They later had two children, and Rex died quite young, but of what I know not).

Stockholm I found a little depressing, I cannot now remember why. Perhaps the lack of pubs as we know them, combined with a lot of drunks on the streets!

I did some photography in the harbour area and arranged a flight to Copenhagen having decided after my stay with Rex that I had no hope of selling boats in Sweden.

I had one friend in Denmark, Sommer. He had been my best man when I married Christine in Bombay. Before contacting him in Slagelse (in the centre of the island on which Copenhagen stands) I decided to have a look round this city, and also took a hydrofoil trip to Malmo in Sweden, a short trip across the sound which separates the two countries. I just went there and back because I was interested in this type of craft and its performance.

The next day I took the electric train to Slagelse and located Sommer. He and his English wife put me up for the night and took me for a drive round the Island. Ninety nine percent cultivated, the few small wooded areas remaining were strictly preserved for picknicking! Altogether I felt the country to be on the surface at least just too well behaved and the towns too immaculate. To drop a cigarette packet or to step off the pavement at a pedestrian crossing before the lights changed even with no traffic in sight were major offences! I once stepped off before the lights and earned a stiff reproof from another pedestrian! What these Danes must think of us Irish I hate to think!

As for business in Denmark, I did meet a yacht chandler and broker but failed to enthuse him, I think he only thought of the Irish as being Denmark's rival in the production of bacon and dairy produce!

I then took a train to Hamburg, quite an interesting trip, it included a ferry crossing in the train. At first I felt pretty lost in the great seaport city, but as it was late in the day I booked in to a rather lowly hotel and did not go out until the morning, a map to guide me.

The dock area was immense with canals branching off. Right in the city there was a big lake on which were numerous small craft and even what appeared to be quite a large fleet of Dragon class keel yachts. As there was a commercial Irish attache in Hamburg I contacted him and went to his office and explained my mission. He drove me personally to the only likely person he knew of, a yacht chandler who was an agent for some craft. He showed interest in the Kerry and later ordered two boats through our Dublin office on some financial arrangement I had nothing to do with. We duly shipped him two boats but they were only partly paid for, and then we heard that he was bankrupt!

BESIDES MY failed Scandanavian efforts we shipped a Kerry, "Kerry Mist", to a yacht agent in Lymington and Chris and I followed it. Lymington had been a home to us in the late '40s and we hoped to pick up some old connections but twenty five years is a long time and we found all our young friends dispersed.

We took over the Kerry and showed her off at The Royal Lymington Y.C. and then went for a pleasant demonstration cruise - at the firm's expense- to Weymouth and Yarmouth on the Isle of Wight. We visited my old haunts of Hamble and Bursledon, and then went back to the agent in Lymington who if I remember right did eventually sell her. This was before inflation, nevertheless our price for this well equipped and very seaworthy little cruiser with a good performance was at about £4500 ridiculously low.

*

An earlier sales trip had been to London. This was before the company had been formed with the Dock Mill, and I had personally taken a Kerry to the London Boat Show, largely at my own expense but with some help from Córas Trachtala (the Irish Export Board).

Chris and the two boys went with me in the short Landrover towing a dreadfully awkward four wheel trailer which tended to steer the Rover, we had some dicy moments on icy roads. The trailer had once been an anti-aircraft gun carriage!

It was just after Christmas. Somewhere on the M1 at about 10pm we pulled off the road. Chris and the boys bedded down somehow in the back of the Rover and I stretched out on the front seats. We started off again at about 2am without waking the boys. Arriving in London at Marble Arch and thinking to save some distance I drove into Hyde Park (no commercial vehicles allowed!). Of course I was stopped, but the policeman said 'I see where you have come from and know where you are going', and he gave me some instructions on the best route and waved me on.

Kerry's pitch on the mezzanine floor of the Exhibition turned out to be a rather out of the way place. Nonetheless we climbed aboard and got on with the job of making her as presentable as possible inside -we knew she would have to be exhibited in an unfinished state hoping that any knowledgeable yachtsman would appreciate her beautiful lines and possibilities! While working we were approached by some union men who rather half heartedly told us we were breaking arrangements made with the management by working in the building but they did not attempt to stop us.

We stayed at a modest hotel which was not too far away, this was to be for over two weeks and so represented a hefty dip into our exchequer. However the visit was to some extent a holiday for the boys, with visits to places of interest with Chris and to her parents. Chris had also to do a stint on the Bord Failte stand selling our own and other peoples holidays on the Shannon, as she had done in previous years.

I don't remember that we actually sold any boats or kits but we did make useful contacts which paid off later. We had Sir Francis Chichester and his wife aboard making appreciative noises and this gave us good publicity. Two week shows are a very tiring bore but we met many old friends from pre-India days, and of India days too.

John and Pat Baker whom we met again were now building boats in Devon, the very first of which had been based on a little ten footer I built in India. That was clench built of cigar box cedar and so light we called her Bubble. John's G.R.P. production boats became Otters. He ran quite a successful business for a number of years, building to other peoples designs including Ron Holland's.

I have no recollection of the return journey from the Boat Show but we brought the Kerry back to our Drumsna factory and finished her off. We launched her down our Jamestown slipway and Chris and I took her for her first sail on the Shannon, only bumping her a few times, her draft being 5ft. We then took her to Dunlaoghaire for demonstration and photography and sold her to a friend Gerry Callanan. After several years sailing he lost her off the Saltee Islands in very heavy weather when for reasons never made clear she sprung a bad leak and foundered. Fortunately Gerry and his companion, dressed in wet suits, were able to inflate the dinghy and after a long time were picked up by a French trawler.

There was rather a strange sequel to this loss.

I happened to be crossing to England on the Rosslare Fishguard route. I found when I got to Rosslare that I had some time to spare and I motored to the nearby fishing port of Kilmore Quay. It was an unpleasant wet afternoon but I got out of the car and was gazing out at the Saltees when I noticed that I was standing beside part of a boat, just about six feet of bow, but more or less intact.

I suddenly realised it was the bow of that Kerry, Gerry's Margaret! I immediately went over to one of the trawlers and asked a crewman if he knew who brought it in, he told me who it was and said if I liked he would lead me to his house, which he kindly did. The skipper involved, a young married man, was very interested to meet me and hear the story. He said he had only picked it up in his trawl a couple of days ago and was relieved to hear there had been no loss of life.

The whole thing was quite a remarkable series of coincidences, of time and place, that I who had literally built the boat was at a place many miles from home a few days after it had been brought in!

After selling the first Kerry we started another composite boat, GRP backsone keel (Filled with lead and cement) and her special stern - pattern made by me.

Córas Trachtala were now looking for financial backing for the venture and introduced me to The Dock Milling Co and M.D Nial Higgins. Soon after that the Company in my name was set up.

*

To convert my original drawings to proper working plans and building schedules, I engaged a young man, Tom O'Donnell.

Tom had been working for some time under a friend of mine at Thomas Thompsons at Athy on G.R.P fabrications, and also on a Proctor designed 15ft sailing dinghy, which never really took off.

The time had been reached when a new class of boat had very little chance of getting going unless it was sponsored by one of the yachting periodicals. This was the case with several classes of boat built by Jack Holt, notably the Mirror and the Enterprise - many thousands built - and my own Day Boat of which about 700 have been built although I have never built or even sailed one! (I left for India about the time I designed it). All these boats and many more were sponsored by Group Captain Edward Haylock, at that time (late '40s) editor of the Yachting World and a good friend to me.

Tom was a sailing enthusiast and came to us with an O.K. sailing dinghy he had very skilfully built himself. He was in his mid 30s and was an extremely nice chap, also a very good and innovative draughtsman. But, as I had been warned, he had a problem with alcohol and a psychological one also which dominated his life. He had had several visit to St Patricks Hospital in Dublin. We treated him almost as one of our family and I know that Chris in her great efforts to try to help him fell more than a little in love with him.

She bought a 'Flying Fifteen' - a keeled dinghy - and sold him a half share in it in the hope of breaking these evil spells but it did not succeed. I also had him crewing in my yacht Brainstorm on several occasions and was as tolerant as possible with his works timekeeping. In the end I attempted to give him a dressing down about his behavior in the hope that this would have a good effect because he seemed to respect me.

I was quite wrong.

He went into a violent temper and walked out of the job and went to Dublin where Chris met him several times but I don't think he was capable of accepting love from anyone at that stage. He had two good jobs in Dublin, living in lodgings. It was from the landlady of one of these that one morning Chris had a call telling her that Tom had not come home that night and she was worried for him.

Chris knew immediately where he would be found and got onto the Dublin Garda and told them to go and look for him up the neighbouring Three Rock Mountain. He was found there dead in his car.

For a time after this Chris herself was quite 'off balance', principally because knowing his state she felt she had failed to save him. He was a sad loss to me too. Basically a very intelligent and when normal a very pleasant man, but I think that when he came to us he was already beyond recovery.

*

In the middle of all this Kerry business I had a letter from a man we had both known quite well before we went to India, Colin Moody had been then working in Laurent Giles's office in Lymington. (While we were away he had built an interesting little yacht, 18 or 19ft overall. This was 'Soprinino' which he and another young man sailed to America and started a mini offshore class of racing yachts there.)

Colin was also involved in the design and actually took part in an attempt to cross the Atlantic East to West in a hydrogen balloon. The story of this heroic effort was written up in a book called 'Small World'. After a hectic three days aloft they were forced to ditch and sailed three quarters of the crossing to Barbados arriving half starved. Colin had designed the gondola which saved the lives of the three men and one woman -Colin's wife- the third man was the leader's son.

In the intervening years Colin had become a highly successful yacht architect specialising in really big and luxurious vessels.

His letter came with some drawings of a proposed Currach for Tim Severin. (Severin would later make his St Brendan voyage to the 'New World' in this). He wanted to know if I would build it and the letter was followed soon after by a visit from Severin himself. I had the means to build the boat but was not paticularly interested. I just had too much work on hand, but I did agree to inspect the work as it went along and make any suggestions which might help the project.

She was built in the Crosshaven Boatyard Cork by some of the shipwrights in their spare time. I visited the work several times. The 35ft craft was launched by Bishop Casey of later notoriety! Severin introduced me to him at the reception, a rather jolly and pleasant man. After the initial launch she was trailed up to my place, had some foam buoyancy built into her in our big shed and had another coat of evil smelling animal grease applied to her hide skin. She was then launched into the Shannon here at Jamestown, and towed down to Lough Boderg by a borrowed Emerald Star cruiser. There she was rigged and sailed for the first time with me aboard, and I must admit that the crew seemed to me to be somewhat ignorant of the basics of sailing!

Severin in his book never mentions the help given by Chris or myself in his book "The Brendan Voyage". When they eventually reached Newfoundland after some months in the Faroes, he sent me an autographed photo of the St Brendan looking rather a wreck, however she had made it and one cannot help admiring his determination in making this and several subsequent long ocean passages in replicas of other ancient vessels.

EARLY IN the Kerry building, in fact when we were building the prototype of the all GRP and beamier version, I suggested that we should enter it for the second Round Britain and Ireland race, in 1970, and I said I would race it if I could find a suitable crew.

This was agreed by the board and we made a provisional entry. I knew it would be a tough race and I was in my sixtieth year, but I was confident in the boat and of its performance. Thinking of a crew Ean Miller came to mind and as I had an address for him in Scotland I wrote him, and although he was running a business of his own he was prepared to leave the running of it for a few weeks and agreed to come.

I knew he was a good seaman and navigator. He had been a Buccaneer pilot in the Fleet Air Arm, invalided out after a crash , due to flame-out on a carrier take off. He came over to discuss the project, I took him for a sail in a little cruiser we had with us to see what his abilities were as a racing helmsman, and was rather critical which rather rubbed him up the wrong way! We took him out to dinner at a Carrick hotel and he surprised us by asking for his coffee "black like my daddy". He was rather dark skinned but very good looking, tall and well built.

I learned his history later and have no reason to doubt it. He was born in China of a black missionary father and a Scottish mother. They got involved in a local fracas and were killed, the infant boy was delivered to the British Embassy in Shanghai and shipped to his mother's mother in Glasgow. She brought him up and he went to one of the Naval training ships and so into the Navy, later volunteered for flying duties and finished as a Lieutenant flying instructor.

In any event, he returned to the UK and it was arranged that he would join the Kerry in England before the race. I myself was to sail the boat down to Plymouth with Christine and my son Simon as crew. Of course all this in turn had been preceded by a hectic rush to build, fit-out and equip Kerry for the race. She was launched into Ringsend Basin Dublin by crane and by Bill Fowler (as there weren't any wives or even women around on Tuesday, June 23 about midday) and sailed at 06.00 on Thursday.

Our only engine was a Yamaha outboard carried on Kerry's quarter and this pushed us out of the Liffey and halfway across Dublin Bay, while we cleared up the mess below. Suitable sails were eventually found, unpacked and hoisted as we went along. We cut and removed the engine off Killiney, and with a fresh off-shore breeze headed south in good spirits close to the shingle shore and with the lovely Wicklow Hills as a backcloth. The hills in which I grew up and knowing so intimately.

Somewhere at this stage we realized the Avon Redstart was still in its packing case in Bill Fowler's Office, also the Sailor Radio and RDF set did not seem to be working too hapily. So into Wicklow we went and were made at home by Neil and Rosalind Watson while we 'phoned Dublin and waited for Bill and Mr. Turney whose knowledge of Radio is second to none in Ireland. Strolling back to Kerry, Simon noticed that her mast seemed to be falling overboard to port, and a check revealed that the shrouds had not been equalised by the rigger, however, the screws just permitted correction.

Off again about 17.00 and round Wickow Head into a backing and freshing wind and rising lumpy sea. Kerry perfectly happy, full main and No. 2 jib, but not so the crew, mal-de-mer having come aboard and did not leave until after the Lizard. Fortunately it did not quite get me, although I was not too happy trying to cook or navigate, but on the second night still beating south when we were 20 miles south of the Smalls, in a falling wind, good visibility and little shipping, I lowered all sails and slept for a few hours because I couldn't stay awake any longer. The next day, Saturday, with light headwinds we reshipped the OB and motored for about 6 hours before the breeze came in again from the SW preceded by a heavy swell. Christine took over in the evening and steered most of the short night in a rising wind and sea.

By morning (Sunday 28th) we were reaching fast in a very big sea, with the Scillies somewhere to starboard in the murk and rainsqualls, and much shipping coming into view and disappearing as we went up and down like a lift. Made out Cornish hills, fine on port bow about 0700 and from then on navigational worries due to lack of recent experience and self-confidence were over.

Passed Longships close to, and the Lizard so close in that the Trinity House boys apparently never recorded out passage, possibly because there was a Helicopter - Lifeboat exercise going on. As we had a day in hand for our deadline on pre race scrutiny in Plymouth, we put into the delightful Helford river for the night, which I remember as a dull and rather a cold one. We blew up the river and landed in a tiny National Trust village, and when looking for milk were given it, with payment refused, something I now only associate with Ireland, but in these days it is a most friendly gesture anywhere. A good night's sleep and then away in the morning for a glorious reach roaring on port tack averaging 6 1/2 knots to Plymouth, arriving about 1600 to be met off the Millbay Dock by the secretary of the Royal Western Y.C. of England, Captain Shaw, in a Dell Quay Dory. Captain Shaw and his wife were the chief organisers of the race, and a more pleasant and helpful couple we have yet to meet. We were towed to a berth in the non-tidal dock, and found ourselves among our competitors, and a mixed and strange collection they were, ranging from the huge Ocean Spirit, eventual winner of 1st boat home and Binkie, smaller than ourselves and winner of the handicap race.

Internally Kerry was far from finished and we spent four hard days trying to improve arrrangements below and stow everything properly. With two days to go we were joined by crew Ean Miller, straight down from Glasgow, armed with more charts and a sextant. Press was much in evidence, but being small and ordinary we did not attract much attention; we did, however, get quite a lot of free canned food from the lady rep of Cadbury-Fry, and later we found these two-part cans made a quick nourishing meal. Little rivalry of a commercial nature was noticeable then or at any time during the race, and fraternising at the ports of call was the most pleasant aspect of the race, as of course was the reception we got from the locals.

Suddenly the race was upon us and all the months of hard work and anxieties were in the past. Somehow, I never really believed I would sail this race, and there were times when I was appalled at the idea, knowing my own comparative inexperience as a navigator and sailing an untried boat. Ean, my crew was however a very experienced navigator being an ex naval flier and also had made some exceptional ocean passages. But as it turns out was not so happy with a coast-line never far away. It was this latter fact which makes this race a very hard one, because to do well corners must be cut and chances taken, and with only two of a crew and no self steering gear it was hard going all the way. As skipper-designer I was asleep or awake - acutely conscious of how the boat was or was not going, so that real sleep in the short 3 ½ - 4 hr. breaks was never possible. The biggest problem for me in the night watches was to keep awake and to keep up strength. Nourishing food such as Complan or Horlicks was too sleepmaking and at night I found I could only take coffee, sweets, biscuits and caffeine-containing pep pills.

Saturday morning July 4th, found us milling about among Tris, Cats,

Proas, and Monos of all shapes and sizes, under a cover of helicopters and small press planes, and surrounded by boatloads of cameramen and well wishers, one of which was Christine. Then we were away to a rather ragged start and heading for the west end of Plymouth breakwater, which we just failed to weather, having been caught with a light reacher up when the wind headed and freshened just after the gun. Also just after the start Trumpeter, the huge racing tri and probably the fastest boat in the race streaked through our lee, going at least twice our speed.

Setting a close-hauled course for the Eddistone L.H. away in the haze, the 25 boat fleet rapidly scattered accordingly to their speed and pointing ability and we were pleased to find ourselves pointing as high as the highest and footing faster than our near rivals. We passed Binkie to weather going so much faster that Lt. McMullen shouted joking 'turn off your engine'. We in fact had no engine of any sort on board, although we had a bent oar which was to serve as a Yulah.

At Eddistone we seemed in the middle of the fleet and with many bigger boats behind us or to leeward we were pretty bucked. I believe we made our first mistake here in tacking round the lighthouse instead of standing well out into the channel. All afternoon we tacked west in a moderate wind and sea gradually losing sight of competitors.

The wind freshened in the night, and by morning we were off the Lizard in pretty thick fog with an uncomfortable sea and far too much traffic invisible but audible. Sometime in the night our remaining spinnaker boom was washed overboard, we had lost the first on the way down, this was rather inexcusable. Wind eased to light westerly as we approached the Wolf Rock where we saw an unidentified yacht ahead. Then a painfully slow beat out to and round the Scillies, with the Bishop L.H. abeam about midnight. The next morning we were bound N.W. for Crosshaven with light and at times non-existent winds from south and south-west.

We were rather badly handicapped through lack of a spinnaker boom, for a time we used our Yulah until it broke. This was perhaps the pleasantest and most interesting part of the race, the weather was fine and we had other boats in sight all the time, but usually too far away to be identifiable until we began to converge on Crosshaven on Tuesday 7th when we found we were among many boats who were giving us time. On the final run in to the line we dropped the mainsail to try and get the most out of the boomless spinnaker and finished at 1435, 3 days 4½ hours out of Plymouth and very well up on corrected time.

A very pleasant two days in Crosshaven, though the weather was rather wet and windy. Crosshaven was the only place where we were in at the same time as all the other competitors; from there on we became more than two days behind more and more of the faster boats, until at Lowestoft we only saw about six others. Christine drove down from home base with two more spinnaker booms and helped restock the boat, and other friends helped physically and with advice. Several yachts dropped out at Crosshaven including the extraordinary proa Sidewinder which had gone into Crosshaven only about half an hour ahead of us, and was having structural troubles, also the big cruising cat Tahini.

Escorted to the line off Roches Point by Robert Fowler, Mrs. Fowler and Christine in Sogndal we started alone this time, on the long haul to the Hebrides and Castlebay. Started with spinnaker set and just drawing nicely when 'bang' the wind suddenly came in from the S.W. and fresh, so that it was a hectic down spinnaker and reef mainsail, set No. 1 jib and commence a hard slog for the Old Head. We had been beating hard and wet for an hour or two when I suddenly noticed that the port upper shroud was no longer attached to the spreader. This was rather a bad moment but we just kept going on starboard tack, brewed a cup of tea and considered the matter.

Ean was prepared to climb the mast and try to sort things out, but in the rough sea I could not agree to take the risks involved at that stage of the race, nor with some 450 miles of North Atlantic to cope with did I think we could make a satisfactory job of securing the stays. It is somewhat fightening to see how flippy an aluminium spar is without proper staying. We dropped the mainsail preparatory to tacking and sailing for the shelter of Kinsale when suddenly I noticed that the shroud had somehow got back into its notch on the spreader end, and I yelled at Ean to grab it which he did and lashed it into the mast as high as he could reach. This lashing and the fact that the halyard had got forward of the spreader and was trapped meant that we could not hoist the main again so we beat into Kinsale quite successfully under No. 1 jib. Kerry will go to windward extremely well in a blow under jib only, tacking easily when required which is a most useful asset. We anchored in the little nook at the west of Kinsale entrance, made a job of the shroud and had a quick meal as we had anyway lost the tide round the Old Head. When sailing we passed John Westell's Trixia heading back for Crosshaven with some trouble from which she retired; she is a small Tri which sails under headsail only and very well at that.

Rounded the Head in the night of Thursday 9th having lost some 12 hours over the shroud trouble and probably about six places. The next morning found me steering close hauled in a moderate breeze off the West Cork Coast, a coast I have never visited by land or sea, though I would very much like to, and here I was trying to get past it and the Fastnet as quickly as possible. In the late morning we saw a yacht on the starboard tack heading out from Galley Head. This proved to be Hurrying Angel, a boat of about our own size from Thames Marine, she tacked fairly close in our wake and we then slowly left her behind and by the time we made the Fastnet Rock, she was out of sight. The Fastnet looked as it does in photos, but from some angles very ugly with all its concrete work, it was a pleasant sunny afternoon with a short period of calm.

The weather forecast was not good and as we rounded Mizen at nightfall the wind began to freshen. The leg to the Bull Rock was a beat. Steering alone, I remember well a strange black cloud vaguely in the shape of a hand reaching towards us from the west; it looked so solid and real in the faintly lit sky that I was quite frightened, and relieved when it began to break up. I think I was beginning to feel the strain and lack of sleep. Ean took over in the small hours and at first light on the 11th we were some 2 miles off the Skelligs, and saw Blue Smoke (second boat on handicap) away inside us and apparently rubbing her sides against one of these somewhat daunting fangs rising from the foam at its base; she gradually dropped to leeward and was lost to sight in the poor visibility. She was the last competitor we actually saw at sea for the rest of the race, which gives some idea of what a lonely sail against time and fatigue this race was. At this time we must have been very close to Binkie again but we never saw her.

The fading Kerry mountains was the last we saw of Ireland as we headed out into the Atlantic, anticipating that the wind would veer and head, which it never did. On Sunday 12th it gradually freshened to F5 or 6 westerly. In this dull period of the race with 10/10 overcast sky and every shipping forecast warning of gales in our area we reached, perhaps too cautiously, with reduced sail for mile after mile. The reach later became almost a run for Barra before a heavy but not dangerous sea, in a wind which may have touched F.7 occasionally but never more. Cooking and resting was difficult with the somewhat violent motion of our little ship, and we were two pretty tired men when we rounded Barra head in the evening light on the 13th and headed north for Castlebay. It was a grim night with black clouds and vicious rain squalls off the islands, lights seemed non-existent and we could only find a small-scale chart though we knew we had a plan of Castlebay. So the beat in was slow and cautious under mainsail and echo-sounder, and as we arrived at 0130 there was no reception committee or anyone to tell us where to anchor. We crept in among the dim shapes of the other yachts and let go, only to drag our 40 lb. Danforth; got under way and dragged again; only on the third attempt with all chain out did the anchor hold, and with frayed tempers we went below and slept a glorious sleep, 4 days 12 hours from Crosshaven and 450 miles by the most direct route.

Most people seemed to be spending their time repairing their boats, or in the care of the Services having their boats, steering gear, etc repaired for them. We were rather pleased we had virtually nothing to do. A high proportion of the competitors were young service people, Navy, R.A.F., Marines and Army, and interservice competition was keen. There is not much to be said for Castlebay as a town, very little in the shops, because everybody appears to shop in Glasgow by post or phone and the goods come over in the daily plane, which lands on the beach at the north end of Barra, or the steamer which calls several times a week. The total road mileage is only the few miles round the island but the town seems full of cars, any one of which can be borrowed or hired. The people speak Gaelic among themselves, and are nearly 100% Catholic. The Parish Priest offered me a pair of warm ex-army trousers and I regretted on the the next leg of the course that I did not accept his kind offer.

Rosemary Smith arrived in the Austin Maxi by steamer, at the end of her drive from Crosshaven in the second stage of her race against the boats.

We were the last in and so the last away from Castlebay, but instead of being only an hour after the boat ahead (the trimaran Renew) we overslept due to alarm clock failure and left on July 16th at about 0530 instead of 0130. The weather had continued stormy and wet while we were at Castlebay which is pretty sheltered from all winds, but offers poor holding ground and is somewhat reefbound. We got away in the light breeze, ran to Muldoanich Island and tourned south for Barra Head; soon it became a beat with a S.W. wind bringing in fog so thick that we lost sight of the Head and eventually rounded it very close, only seeing the base of the cliff, white with gulls.

From Barra Head we headed for the St. Kilda group and were not sorry that Rockall was not included in the race! St. Kilda was a place I had never expected to see, but it has had a fascination for me, and I would have liked to stop and land. We had a fast reach out steering by R.D. bearings and dead reckoning, and picked up the island as it was begining to get dark. It had been a sunless day and it was a dark night, the island and its off-liers dark menacing shadows rising from the sea and disappearing into the clouds; it was impossible to judge distance off under these conditions, and during my night watch I know I was uncomfortably close; I was very glad to get clear of the group with its mountain not seen but definitely felt. We sailed round in a force 5 breeze with a moderate sea running, and headed into the dawn on a course to pass west of the Flannan Isles.

During the morning of the 17th the wind fell light and fog patches developed, in one of which the Flannans must have hidden because we neither saw nor located them as the lighthouse has no D.F. beacon. From here we were on a long leg in the open North Atlantic, 230 miles with the wind aft and varying from F.5 to 7. It was very cold, and lonely on watch under a sky which never cleared until we were round the northern point of the Shetlands.

The only company were the seabirds of which there's always hundreds in sight, gannets with their yellow necks and long bodies and fulmars over curious of us the intruder and surely the most perfect fliers of all birds with their effortless gliding flight. Also little storm petrels flitting about over the waves close enough to snap up the minute sea creatures thrown up in the spray. We had earlier seen shark on the surface and probably shark tearing about under water in the night leaving phospherescent wake like torpedoes.

The only thing of note on this leg was picking up and passing Sula Sgeir, a lonely barren rock like a great whale, which must be given a wide berth to clear offlying submerged rocks and reefs. We wondered about its history as a wrecker of ships and also about the monks of long ago who had lived in the beehive dwellings, the remains of which could still be seen on the skyline. Sula Sgeir disappeared into the falling night, and we rushed on with full sail a heavy following sea and nothing to steer by except the wind and the luminous compass card. By now I had every confidence in Kerry, she ran fast and steadily and a few heavy dollops of water which had come aboard aft quickly cleared - she never looked like getting pooped.

The night in this latitude in July is very short for which I was glad as it is easier to keep awake in the light and it was very cold during the few dark hours. All the third day we ran almost dead before the wind and I seem to remember more than one accidental gybe which even in F.6 was comparatively harmless with our short boom and kicking strap. This is, however, not appreciated by the man below! Occasionally one wondered morbidly how long it would take to get rescued out there if you had to take a liferaft for we saw no ships and the sky remained low and completely overcast.

About 1400 we sighted land, the high peaks of Foula Island to the west of Shetland and we altered course slightly for Esha Ness L.H. which lit up and was abeam at nightfall. Ean steered us round Muckle Flugga, the northern most point of the British Isles in the early morning.

The sun came out for the first time for many days as we turned south feeling that we had really broken the back of the trip. The islands looked beautifully green, not heather-covered like the Hebrides, marred only by the cupola of the early warning radar on the hill-top. We sailed south with a fickle southerly wind, and tacked around the Outer Skerries L.H. about midday and it took us 11 1/2 hours to sail the remaining 20 miles to Lerwick, working along by virtue of draughts from vast black rainclouds which periodically deluged us, and left us stationary and dripping in a flat calm sea. We finally entered with the last of the light and a nice little breeze, being signalled in over the line by car headlights at 2310, 3 days and 18 hours from Barra.

A tremendous welcome ashore in the harbour in spite of the midnight hour, with invitations to meals, baths, clothes, washing etc. Our stay in Lerwick was to me the highlight of the trip and I should much love to visit these islands and people again. I believe the best time to go there is May and June and one could spend a summer exploring the islands by boat. Everyone seems to be boat and sea minded, and Lerwick is a tremendous place of the fishing fleets of all northern people, and prospers on this and tourism. The people are very definitely Shetlanders and a race apart, largely of Norweigan stock though now very loyally British. We bought warmer clothes which we never needed again!

We had made up quite a lot of time on the Barra-Lerwick leg and were no longer last away. We left on the Tuesday 21st at 23.20 for the longest leg of all to the tooting of car horns and flashing of headlights. For the first night and morning we had a pleasant fresh westerly sailing in the lee of Shetland mainland and then of Fair Isle. Orkney was out of sight to the west. Navigation by radio fixes was easy in this area. Winds F3 to 4 S.S.W. which set us too far to the east and we tacked short and long to keep within 40 to 50 miles of the Scottish coast in fair weather and easy seas but progress seemed slow after the long runs and reaches of the previous legs. Somewhere here Ean had a whale nearly alongside but he said nothing to me about until I came up to take my watch and I regret I did not see it.

On the 25th there was a beautiful but lurid sunrise and it was a warning of what was to come. Just before the 0640 forecast, which said nothing about gales, I heard an A.A. report of high cross winds on some northern roads. I felt, correctly, that we were in for something. Sailing some 30 miles east of the Humber and homing on the Dudgeon L.V. the westerly wind started to freshen rapidly that morning and by the time I came on watch, at 1500, we were broad reaching S.S.E. in F.6 gusting 7 and steering was getting a bit wild in the steep seas caused by the comparatively shallow water. In spite of Ean's protest, I insisted in shortening sail from full main to double reefed and No. 2 jib.

Conditions rapidly got worse until by 1800 it was blowing a full gale and we were broad reaching under No. 2 jib only, in the worst sea we had experienced during the whole trip. Really steep breaking seas and motion so violent that even Ean had to admit he could not get a radio fix, though we were homing on the Dudgeon but without any precision of bearing. Visibility due to driving rain was less than 1/2 mile. While Ean was holding onto the mast and peering ahead for a sight of the Dudgeon, Kerry broached on a breaker and she was rolled over until her mast was horizontal. I can see Ean now, lying along the mast and a great trough below the boat. The crest passed and we came upright again, having shipped no water and only a little more mess that usual below!

We were now back on course but somewhat lost and running fast into an area of sandbanks unknown to us and most unattractive-looking on the chart. I decided the safest thing to do was to down all sail and let her run slowly under bare pole and lashed helm in the general direction of Cromer where the water was clear. Our speed by the log was just over 1 knot so we had quite a lot of sea-room and time.

We felt the blow would only be a short one, but it was not until nearly midnight, and after enduring the anxiety of our position, the violent motion and the occasional crash as a breaker came aboard for some 6 hours that the rain stopped, the wind began to ease and we began to see lights we could identify; we were in fact in our estimate position some 4 miles S.S.E. of the Dudgeon, which we must have passed pretty close. From there on through the watch and down to Lowestoft was easy sailing in a wind which fell so light that we could hardly stem the tide past Great Yarmouth. We entered Lowestoft harbour at 12.40 on Sunday 26th, 4 days, 13 hours from Lerwick, a straight line distance of 470 miles.

We were towed to a mooring and taken ashore to the most hospitable R. Norfolk and Suffolk Y.C. We were a small party now in Lowestoft, perhaps a dozen crew-men enjoying the hospitality of the club; there was anxiety here for Renew, the tri which arrived nearly 2 days after us. She was caught in the same gale as ourselves, and driven far out to sea, but suffered no serious damage. Just before leaving Lowestoft we got the news of the only real disaster in the race, when the cat Apache Sundancer one of the largest boats in the race was capsized off the Isle of Wight and later became a total loss. The crew were picked up in good order.

All too soon our two day rest was over and we set off on the last leg, which proved to be the slowest, although the shortest, and least eventful.

It took us 24 hours in the light southerly to reach Deal off the Kentish coast. The wind freshened and brought rain and visibility as we passed Dover. Off the western entrance to this harbour, we heard the tremendous roar of an approaching Hovercraft and out of the rain at 50 knots an S.R.N. 4, apparently heading straight for us. She was in fact making a crabwise course with the wind on her beam and swept across our stern and into the harbour. It was evening by the time we reached Dungeness and we tacked slowly for most of the night past this vast brilliantly-lit atomic power station. The next day was fine but very hazy and we only saw the coast with its many seaside towns on our inshore legs.

We managed to scrape past Beachy Head in the early afternoon, for once having the tide in our favour. Then began the slow slog against light to moderate S.W. wind to Selsey Bill, I was feeling at a rather low ebb when I handed over to Ean to take the first night watch. The next morning (31 July) we were off St. Catherine's beating against a foul tide, and making nothing west until the tide began to slacken. Then 6 hours of hard winds but favourable tide and we just failed to get round St. Albans before the tide turned.

We had a disagreement here. I wanted to short tack right inshore in the comparatively slack water, which I considered safe in the light conditions and knowing the Head of old; but Ean who had just come on watch refused to do this and we tacked out and were carried back a long way before we tacked again to head slowly for Portland Bill. The wind died right away in the night, and we spent it anchored in the mist, not far from the Shambles L.V. In the morning of August 1st the tide was against us, the wind too light to attempt to round the Bill, so we crept slowly into a little shingle cove on the east side of what really is an island connected to the mainland by the Chesil Bank.

We blew up and launched the Avon and paddled into the beach, climbed the zig-zag path in search of water and other things which were running low; we also phoned Captain Shaw to say we were on our way and doing our best. On return to Kerry we used our oar, an oar we had acquired in Lerwick, and which was made by Marvins of Cowes at the close of the 19th century, for a steam yacht's gig. A beautiful ash oar as good as the day it was made and as springy.

Sculling slowly over the stern we worked out into the tide, and with hardly steerage way were carried round the Bill, which now appears to be a vast caravan park. The Bill on this occasion was as calm as it could be, but in spite of this the tiny tide-making breaking waves made a sound of rushing water. We gradually lost sight of all and, as we drifted out into Lyme Bay in the haze of a hot sunny, almost windless day. I always find a boat will move where she is pointed so west she was kept pointed for the next night and morning. At 1000 we began to see craft, power and sail, passing towards Torquay and Brixham, obviously returning from Plymouth after the start of the Tall Ships race. Shortly after this we made out Berry head and then - great thrill - Start Point. We felt we were nearly home. From there on the elements smiled on us, the haze lifted, the sun came out and a lovely easterly breeze set in. We dug out the big spinnaker we hadn't used since the Crosshaven leg, hoisted it and tore away over a sparkling sea off this lovely part of Devon, and being Sunday we had the company of many other yachts as we passed the entrance to the Dart and Salcombe. We covered the last 20 miles in under three hours and turned into Plymouth carrying the Spinnaker almost up to the Breakwater, where we completed our circle and headed for the finishing line among many Sunday racers. It was a great thrill to have got round quite regardless of our placing.

I had an added pleasure when I suddely heard a voice shouting 'Daddy' and I spotted two of my grown-up sons and a grandson in a small hired launch. They had gone out with no information that I was due but estimating that I might be had motored up from Sussex and timed it perfectly. We were met on the line by Captain Shaw and just made it into Millbay Dock before they closed the gates, 30 days away and 20 days at sea, and some 2,150 miles on the log, apart from the shroud with no trouble, and 6th on corrected time.

As a designer, I had learned a lot particularly on the layout and arrangements below deck. Only those who have sailed small boats know the difficulty of doing the simplest chore. Making two cups of coffee can be a major triumph.

We had been away for 30 days and had spent 20 days at sea, and we had logged 2150 nautical miles. When all the handicaps had been worked out we found we were only beaten by five boats. Kerry Mist had behaved perfectly and really deserved to have won that race.

For the fact that we hadn't I am sure she blamed me!

I contacted Chris by phone as soon as I got ashore, and she wanted to come over with the company's directors Higgins and Fowlers and their wives. To her annoyance I discouraged her, I cannot now remember why, but it was lucky because the others had a crash on a motorway with a runaway lorry and were all badly knocked about, their Mercedes car a write off. I didn't hear about this for several days.

While I was away Simon had qualified as a Scuba diver at the diving school at Fort Bovis, actually run by a good friend of Indian days, Jimmy Gill. The course had cost him nothing because he was employed as school boatman and accommodation was provided in the fort. A fascinating place built at the time of the Nepoleonic wars, the fort was on a small hill overlooking the harbour, a rabbit warren of tunnels, magazines and gun emplacements.

I stayed two or three days in Plymouth, Ean departed almost

immediately for Glasgow. I phoned for one of my erstwhile crewmen Colm to come over and join Simon and me in some south coast sailing, and hopefully some racing.

He was over in about 24 hours!

So with the idea of showing off the Kerry we set out, Simon, Colm and I, sailing eastward early with a fair wind. We were round Portland Bill just before nightfall with the last of the flood tide, so going through the 'race' when it was harmless. Simon was on the helm crossing Weymouth Bay and not having much experience of night sailing was having trouble in deciding the course of several other vessels in his vacinity and called me up to help him. There were several sets of navigation lights in view, all identifiable as power craft by their lights. The essential thing is that, being a sailing vessel, powered craft have to give way to you (except in restricted water when they may not be able to do so). Normally you must hold your course so that they know how to avoid you, if you change course you are likely to confuse, and holding your course is also essential if you are to judge speed and course of other craft.

By the time we reached St Albans Head the ebb - West going - tide was well away against a very fresh S.W. wind and we ran into this 'race' at its worst. It was really rough, every time the beams of the lighthouse came round they lit up a wild scene of steep faced breaking waves. Because of the strong tide we were a horrid long and anxious time getting through this, in spite of carrying really too much sail. Kerry took very good care of us, she steered well and shipped very little solid water, and we eventually ran into relative calm.

I should really have passed the Head a mile or two wide.

I know that now!

We sailed on east and entered Yarmouth on the Isle of Wight in the early morning, having made a very fast passage from Plymouth, averaging over six knots but with a fair wind.

At Yarmouth we found there was a regatta race that afternoon for boats in our class and requested permission to join which was given we thought rather grudgingly, even though we said we would not race at all aggressively and in fact would keep clear of other competitors. My interest was in seeing how Kerry would compare with boats of known performance.

As it happened we left it too late starting to get to the quite distant start line which was up against a strong Solent tide. We had no engine to help us and never did start the race but just sailed parallel to some chosen craft thus, our performance was very encouraging to me, specially because I knew that we were somewhat weed fouled.

We spent the night in Yarmouth tied up with the guidance of the harbour master. He was the only friendly person I remember there, although I was quite familiar with the port in the late 40's, perhaps our lack of welcome was because we were flying the Irish ensign.

The next day we sailed back to Poole, the port of my pre War sailing and building days. Mooring up at the town quay we went in search of a boat haulage company, having decided to road haul Kerry to Pwllheli in Carnarvan and from there sail home to DunLaoghaire, rather than tackling another long sail from Lands End. We were lucky to locate a small company prepared to do the job. Using a big American FWD four seater pick up truck and trailer, they arranged the loading and we derigged the boat, and phoned ahead to the boatyard about the relaunch.

We set off in the afternoon sitting with the very pleasant and competent young driver on the long haul through the most beautiful parts of England and Wales, Dorset and Wiltshire. I don't recall the Severn Bridge... perhaps it was not then open.

Then through Hereford, reaching Powys after nightfall. It was after midnight that we pulled up off the road. The driver turned in in his cab and we three climbed up into Kerry and occupied our usual bunks!

We were away again by 8 o'clock, through lovely country on a perfect morning. Arriving at the Pwllheli boatyard soon after midday we found the harbour dry, but to let the driver get away on his return journey we got the yard people to offload and park Kerry where she would float off at the earliest, and went in search of a meal and provisions for the crossing. I put out a call to Chris from the Pwllheli Post Office and much amused the girl there when she heard me trying to tell Chris where we were! The tide came in and Kerry floated, the yard stepped the mast with a derrick, we rigged her and bent on the sails, paid the bill and set off at about 18.00 in a light westerly breeze to sail the 20 miles to Bardsey Sound and then away for Ireland, or so we thought!

We only had a small scale chart of the Irish Sea and no Coast Pilot (book) but it seemed a straightforward trip in fair weather and we had R.D.F. for navigation. Perhaps the mistake I made was in not trying to get a weather report for the Irish Sea.

Though even if I had we would still have pressed on.

From my diary of the trip.....

"A pleasant sunny evening sailing on starboard tack, sheets eased to a light N.W. breeze past Abersock and inside the two small islands off the headland, Bardsey Island in sight. Harden in sheets heading for the end of arm of Caernarvon no allowance for tide which I reckon must be on the ebb by now. Our speed three to four knots sea calm. I plan a close hauled passage through the sound - no allowance for unknown tide - " .

Quite suddenly we become aware that the evening sun has disappeared behind what appeared to be low lying grey cloud, and then realise it is not just cloud but fog rolling in from the West, a grey wall with no fore runners. Bardsey Island and the end of Carnarvon disappear quite abruptly. Never mind, we know where we are and where the mainland and Bardsy are. I have a compass bearing which should take us through the sound and into the open sea. I put Simon on the helm with the course to steer. We sail slap into the fog wall and it is instantly almost dark with visibility about the length of the ship, a little unnerving. I switch on the navigation lights, on the pulpit forward, port and starboard, red and green. These only light the fog, can't see the masthead. I go below telling Simon to call me if he is worried, and stretch out on the lee berth. Been dozing for perhaps twenty minutes when suddenly a frantic call. I scramble through the hatch just in time to see a vertical wet face of rock reflecting our red port light before it disappears in the fog as Simon puts Kerry about!

What was that and where the hell are we?

If Simon had not been so alert we would have sailed straight into a cliff with deep water under it. My immediate decision to sail back on a reciprocal course for fifteen minutes and anchor. This I do, but finding the water so deep I have to add two extra lengths of warp before the anchor digs in. Then the boat immediately swings round and with the tide we seem to be making three or four knots through the water.

I spread the small scale chart on the cockpit seat and try with a torch to figure where we are and what it was we nearly hit. With this tide going South it must have been somewhere on the North side of Bardsey or possibly a rock shown a little north of the Island. With this somewhat vague information I put a cross on the chart for our approximate position, and settle down to wait for the fog to lift. After a time there is a slight lift, and for a moment long enough to get a compass bearing. I can see Bardsey lighthouse. As it disappears again I draw a position line on the chart and guess how far we are from the light.

It would now seem quite straightforward to sail due South, allow enough time to be sure of clearing the Island to the south and sail into open water. I have to haul the anchor manually, a hard job in this tide and with so much warp out but don't want to call the boys, and eventually have it on deck and am sailing fast over the ground with the tide and the wind aft.

I begin to hear the Bardsey fog horn somewhere to my right and it seems to be getting louder very quickly as though I were moving straight at it though I can see no light through the fog. Not knowing what is happning I panic and call Simon to come up and drop the anchor and the sails. The foghorn now extremely loud seems to be almost above us but we can see nothing in the fog and dark of night. We spend the rest of the short night trying to get some sleep in spite of the horrible noise. When we look outm in the very early morning the fog seems almost as dense as ever but we can just make out some rocks low in the water so we assume they are on the shore of the Island. The tide must now be on the flood, going north so if we are to round the island to the south we must allow for the tide. There is still quite a good breeze from the west so we up anchor and sail south until we can no longer hear the horn, then come close hauled into what must be open water.

The true wind is about N.W. so we stay on the starboard tack for Ireland and I get Simon to fix our position from R.D.F. The fog is as dense as ever and we are a bit worried about being run down. During the day we do hear two ships or trawlers pass near to us, but we have a radar reflecter up the mast so feel fairly safe. Conditions do not change all day and we take turns on the helm and cookup a good meal in the middle of the day. With the fog the light goes early. Simon has identified the Codling light vessel's radar signal and we begin to home in on that until it suddenly looms up right beside us.

Seeing a man on deck - he must have had a surprise - we shout "which way to DunLaoghaire!" and he shouts "thataway" and waves to the north before vanishing. We now home in on a radio beacon on top of Killiney Hill. It's really there for aircraft but will do us just as well. Making allowances for clearing Dalkey Island we head through the gloom seeing nothing.

Quite suddenly we began to hear goats on our port hand and Colm immediately says 'Dalkey Island'. A few minutes later we saw and passed close to the rocks at the northern end of the Island and just sailed on until we met the East Pier.

Home. Just about!

We had been incredibly unlucky to meet such a really exceptional dense longlasting fog in August. But that's the sea and sailing. At Dun Laoghaire we followed the pier round and entered the harbour where the fog was not so thick. We picked up a mooring close to the R St G YC. Sean the senior boatman had seen us and was soon alongside, and I went ashore to phone Christine and Niall Higgins of our safe arrival.

So ended an experience of fog which I shall never forget. And a lesson learned about blundering into a fog without adequate knowledge of tides and weather conditions.

CHRIS THOUGHT I drove too fast! And so, travelling round the country as consultant to the Irish Tourist Board (Bórd Failte) I usually went alone. The work involved the inspection of boats for sea angling and so there was little for her to do while I was working, so she would get rather tired and bored.

However I do remember one happy trip we made in the West together in a Hillman Hunter estate we had at the time, a fairly staid car, but one in which we could sleep. (One particular night was spent in the car, shared with two dogs, high up on the narrow road above Ballanakill bay in Connemara. We had no idea at the time that the little harbour of Derryinver would soon be Simon's fishing port).

On another trip which I remember we travelled down through Clonmel and over the pass through the Comeragh Mountains. We went for a climbing walk from the top of the pass, and there I had my first hint of the coming heart trouble, although I did not recognise it as such, I put the pain down to indigestion as so many people do.

After passing through Cappoquin we arrived in Dungarvan where there were several boat owners who were seeking financial assistance to fit out their craft to the required standard. It was up to me to enforce the standards if they were to feature on Board literature as recommended, and on my authority they could get limited assistance.

From Dungarvan we went west to Youghal where we hoped to meet Simon, then a deckhand on a big Dutch-built beam trawler with a Dutch skipper, married to an Irish girl in the town. But the ship was away on a several day trip. Hans the skipper was a very experienced fisherman and a fairly tough one, I think Simon learnt a lot about this type of fishing and boat handling, night and day.

After exploring the interesting old town we spent the night there and the next morning moved on to Ballycotton, a small attractive town over an artificial harbour with lifeboat station. Here I inspected several more boats, meeting their fisherman owners, all with great expectations for what they hoped I could do for them. These meetings were much lubricated by the fact that we had a fisherman son and I was a boatbuilder, not just a pen pusher from a Dublin office. I was well able to understand their problems and give them practical advice which I enjoyed. I also learnt myself from them.

We left Ballycotton after lunch and travelled through Cork, Killarney and Killorglin - where we bought a goatskin rug at a street market - to Cahirciveen. We then went over the bridge to Valentia Island where we spent two nights in a rather quaint old hotel, it was out of season and I think we were the only guests, and rather unexpected ones.

I inspected two more boats the first day and then we had a lovely walk up the hill behind the hotel and through the heather with Bunji our most beloved Stafford bull terrier. It was beautiful fresh weather, blue sea and sky, and we looked down on the lighthouse at the northern entrance to Cahirciveen harbour. I remember thinking that, in westerly storm conditions, it must be a boiling cauldron, though the harbour does have another entrance in the lee of the island.

Cahirciveen was at one time a very busy fishing port and landing place for fish, particularly herring. These were salted down in barrels by the women of the town, work extremely hard on the hands. It was for this trade that the railway from Tralee to Cahirciveen was built, a railway said to have been one of the most expensive ever built in the country. To follow its difficult line this would not seem surprising.

If any railway should be rebuilt as a tourist attraction surely it should be this one with its glorious views of Dingle Bay below it all the way, and some splendid railway engineering in the way of cuttings, viaducts and that long bridge into the town.

As a child of six I had travelled this line.

Different times!

*

Generally the seventies were a period of intense (if not especially interesting!) activity, Chris and myself busy at our own things.

She was involved with her own business, making boat upholstery, boat hoods and side curtains. This brought her in contact with a great many boating people among whom we established many good friendships. She was also involved with horses which she was breeding, breaking and training in a small way and selling to England via my sister Nancy in Oxford.

I can still see her standing in the middle of our small paddock with a young horse on a long rein and whip in her hands, happy, patient, gentle and completely involved with what she was doing.

*

My Mother died in 1971, on the first of February.

She died suddenly, after being in apparant good physical health, in a nursing home. She was eighty-five years old, the same age as myself as I write these words. Prehaps in places in these pages I have been rather hard on my mother. Basically a good woman, she was a marvellous mother to her three children, and a splendid maker of puddings, pasties and cakes! Essentially she was just typical of her time and class.

In January of that year I had a Kerry at the Earls Court Boat Show (and again for the last time on the following year).

My work as recorded in my diaries of the time show me always on the move. I was principally concerned with the Kerry building, selling and delivering. And gradually I was getting more and more involved with work for Bórd Failte as their marine consultant. I was now involved with the inspection of incoming hire cruisers, going to England to assess cruisers which new companies wished to import and which would be grant aided.

We wound up our own Hire Business, selling off the small fleet except for 'Plover', our rather favourite small sailboat which Chris took as her share of the company's assets. A very old boat even when we bought her, sadly Chris really had no value from her and she became derelict at the top of our slipway.

*

The pattern of my life at that time involved me with various overlapping enterprises. (To add to my other activities I started a CND branch in Carrick and took part in most of its activities and became the branch carpenter!)

One of the business enterprises was the assembly of spiral staircases, manufactured by my son Tyl in his business.

I assembled around twenty five of these, earning a useful amount doing so and getting quite a lot of satisfaction and amusement in the doing.

Usually these jobs were a kind of meccano assembly, everything being made to individual plans from more or less standard parts. Most of the stairs were in private houses round the Dublin area but some in far away places such as Tralee and even Inis Boffin off the west coast.

The range of stairs was quite astonishing and included the Belfast docks power station. I was helped by Simon on that but did the Stormont Castle one alone.

This was rather funny. At Stormont there was a lot of renovation work going on, including the installation of much communication equipment. And then myself, an elderly resident of the Republic, arriving more or less unannounced with a van load of knocked-down stair to go in the tower. The RUC saw to it that the van got nowhere near the castle!

The foreman (with a northern accent which I could barely understand) was highly suspicious. But I managed to borrow a student worker from him to help me carry everything in. Before the men knocked off for their lunch I had the centre pillar up and by working frantically while they were out of the building I dropped all the treads down it, fixed the top landing and lined up all the treads.

I was casually fixing the ballisters when they returned!

The reaction and change in attitude to me was quite astonishing, I was a kind of magician and the foreman, previously distinctly surly, now could not do enough to help me! The job was finished by the evening knock off, and I packed up and drove home, tired but content.

I had a very similar experience with a big industrial stair in the Hollister factory near Ballina in County Mayo. Here I had no help at all but had brought ropes and tackle with which I set up the large diameter centre pole. There was nowhere to work from on top when it came to dropping on the heavy and large diameter treads. Waiting until I had no audience at break time I managed a kind of spiderman act in the steel roof structure to get them on.

*

In '75 we had a visit from Jonathan George, second son of my sister Doreen. A Canadian citizen, and a very nice young man, he was working in the fisheries section of Canada's Wildlife Department, a very outdoor life. About that time poor Chris, who seemed to spend a lot of time in hospital, had a thyroid gland operation. It was found that her thyroid was not, and had not been functioning for some time. For the rest of her life she was on artificial Thyroid.

This was the time when I got involved in the St Brendan saga, previously reported. It was also the time when I began racing Brainstorm, (more of her in following chapters) which I did whenever I could. Sometimes this meant twice a week, Thursday evening and Saturday afternoons. I frequently drove to Dunlaoghaire, raced, and drove home again!

In the early days I had a most enthusiastic and efficient crew-sometimes including Simon - I took part in many offshore races but it was not until her third season that the boat was at her best, after numerous modifications. The first mast was broken and replaced, and modifications to the boat included building on a partial outer hull, making the forward rudder retract, lengthening the mast, changing the keel twice and getting some new sails, and a new engine...all involving much labour and plenty of expense!

By the time all this was done my early crews had all dispersed, three of them crewing the Shamrock class boat which won the World's "Half Ton" cup races in Trieste.

I HAVE ALWAYS found and to my disappointment, that the great majority of amateur sailors have no 'eye' for a boat in the flesh, and even less for a set of hull lines which they practically refuse to understand even when they are explained in the simplest terms.

A model is of course a great help and I have several about the house. Of lines plans I have drawers full, some I still like and others I think I should destroy, unless boats have actually been built to them and performed reasonably well. But, like a lot of other things I never get round to sorting them.

Generally what looks right on paper to a trained eye is right, but nothing made by man is or ever will be perfect. Christine used to chaff me because I was never satisfied - she herself at her work of making boat hoods, a most difficult operation, sidecurtains and upholstery, was most painstaking and never completely satisfied with her work. The material used was most difficult to handle and sew, on a heavy duty machine which she never used with its motor, preferring to pedal the thing!

When I eventually had a boat which was really my own I know I was always and continuously making alterations to it, spending far more time working on it in my shed or afloat than sailing it, and this was the 30 footer I called 'Brainstorm'. A rather ridiculous name but she was a sort of trial horse for so many ideas I had stored up in my head that perhaps it was not inappropriate.

In the middle of the Kerry building programme, when I was more involved with selling and demonstrating than any work on the drawing board, (we had a supposedly full time salesman anyhow), I asked permission of the company board to design and build a yacht to the "Half Ton" Royal Ocean Racing Club (RORC) rule. At that time the 'TON' rule for offshore racing had not been finally formulated. It was a very complex rule designed to be watertight so that bright sparks with computers could not find loopholes in it to design go-faster boats that were still within the rule, if perhaps not within its spirit!

I being really a mathematical dunce had difficulty in designing to the rule. However, although I hoped to build a fast boat the main idea was to try out a number of innovations, principally a forward rudder, which I think was unique at that time but has been seen since on some of the America's Cup boats.

In addition to the forward rudder, another innovation was the position of Brainstorm's mast, nearly amidships. I had always felt that the mast of a yacht should be very well back in the boat, and that the usual position only about a third way back was somehow a legacy of a bygone age. Current racing yachts of 1997, both inshore and offshore, are all light displacement shallow bodied boats with very fine forward lines, and in many photos it is noticeable that when on the wind they appear to be down by the bows and with the crew - for weight - very far aft. The designers of multi-hulled craft seem to have cottoned onto mast position already, and it was also noticeable in America's Cup challengers and defenders.

Brainstorm had to be built cheaply and, a double chine plywood boat, was built largely by my friends Donal Conlon and Bert O'Mahony in Bert's shed on Lough Key in Roscommon. There was much help from Chris, Tom, and myself in our spare time. We launched her sideways into the Boyle river after bolting on the fin and bulb keel. The bulb which weighed over a ton and a half had been cast very ingeniously in two halves by Bert. As her sails had not arrived and for fun with all the builders and several friends aboard we sailed her on Lough Key with Tom's O.K. mainsail and some small jib.

I then had to leave for a trip to England and asked Chris to take her through the lock and tow her with an outboarded dinghy to Jamestown with as much help as she needed. When I got home again, Brainstorm was on our pontoon but I found Chris on the verge of divorcing me, she was furious with me for asking her to the do this job - which I did in all innocence thinking she would quite enjoy the challenge but forgetting that Brainsorm drew six feet - and Chris had had a hell of a job constantly getting stuck with a struggle to get off and with a fear of damaging the keel- I had to eat rather humble pie to straighten things again!

Later we craned her out, trailed her to Dublin and launched her again by crane into Ringsend Basin, and from there after a day fitting out we sailed her across the bay to DunLaoghaire, having as one of the crew Drewry Pearson. He later sailed many races aboard both inshore and offshore.

She proved to be quite a fast boat when the wind blew but was obviously under canvassed and over ballasted. In one of my first outings at sea James O'Connor and I sailed her over to Howth, and on the way back in a fresh breeze and with a lumpy sea off Howth Head, the mast supplied by Proctors to their recommendation but which had always looked very slim, began to contort horribly and, just as we were watching, it suddenly collapsed about halfway up and the whole spar and sails were in the sea.

As more often than not the little old engine I had installed as a makeshift was unserviceable. But we were not on a lee shore or in any danger and were untangling sails and rigging prior to trying to jury rig with the idea of running up the Liffey, when we saw the DunLaoghaire Lifeboat heading for us. The Bailey Lighthouse keepers had seen us in some distress and although we had not shouted for help we were glad to accept it, and were soon back on our moorings. As soon as I got ashore I went straight to the pub frequented by the crew and found Eric Offer the cox'n and quite a friend of mine, to thank him and his merry men for the very welcome tow. He would not accept anything and I remember he said half seriously "we know you would do the same for us".

Proctors supplied me with another mast without charge, this one looked like a telegraph pole in comparison and even when I lengthened it later by about 6ft it never gave us any cause to worry.

I began racing Brainstorm which I did whenever I could. Sometimes this meant twice a week, Thursday evening and Saturday afternoons. I frequently drove to DunLaoghaire, raced, and drove home again!

A round trip of 200 miles!

In the early days I had a most enthusiastic and efficient crew- sometimes including Simon- I took part in many offshore races but it was not until her third season that the boat was at her best, after numerous modifications. The first mast was broken and replaced, and modifications to the boat included building on a partial outer hull, making the forward rudder retract, lengthening the mast, changing the keel (three times!) and getting some new sails, and a new engine...all involving much labour and plenty of expense!

By the time all this was done my early crews had all dispersed, three of them crewing the Shamrock class boat which won the World's "Half Ton" cup races in Trieste.

*

Brainstorm for ten or twelve years was perhaps my main interest in life, professional life anyhow, and the boat took up a major part of my spare time, I'm sure Chris thought too much. However as I had invested by my standards a lot of money in the boat, I wanted to make the most of her to demonstate some of my ideas and get in some pleasure sailing and cruising as well.

Our first cross channel race was from Howth to Holyhead, first rounding Lambay Island. It was a dead spinnaker run up to the island in a fresh breeze and Brainstorm, which was always fast off the wind, was right up with the fleet but on the inside relative to the island, and with a steel pylon beacon to leave to starboard. I was quite unfamiliar with this rock and had a crewman up forward to tell me when I was past it and able to turn to the East, I had other boats very close on my port side.

Just as I got the call "All Clear" we struck the rock.

I learned later that this projected well beyond the beacon!

We came to an instant stop, the jolt throwing us down in the cockpit. We were amazed that the mast did not go overboard and also that the keel was apparently still attached as we drifted clear.

The qustion now was, do we go on and hope the keel does not fall off in mid channel, which would probably mean the yacht capsizing ?

I calculated that we were not taking in any water. And she would right herself with the sails down , and if not we could let the shrouds off and the mast being deck stepped she would certainly right herself. I put it to the vote and the verdict was unanimous 'Go On!'

We followed the fleet, slowly dropping back so that we decided the keel bulb must have been knocked out of line. Arriving in Holyhead when most of the other crews were already ashore and leaning on the Club bar, someone suggested we had a look at the keel, so sailing up the harbour we sheeted both sails in hard and turned away from the wind laying Brainstorm over on her ear and leaning over the side we were able to see the keel which looked O.K. But the projecting bulb was buried in a huge mop of seaweed! This may even have softened the impact, and all we had to do to clear it was come head to wind and drift backwards. The keel was hardly likely to have fallen off as it was attached by four pairs of 1" diameter stainless bolts.

*

Brainstorm's keels went through several phases, I made four major changes in them over the period I raced her. The first change was to reduce the weight of the huge projecting torpedo. We removed the two halves, hoisting them vertically and with a big chain saw sliced nearly 1 1/2" off the inside of each. This was a somewhat dangerous game as the 'sawdust' consisted of lead pellets about the size of a .303 bullet discharged at considerable velocity. We collected these for remelt, and along with the two sliced pieces they were recast into fitted inside ballast.

Another change involved the ¾" steel plate which was the original keel being made into a proper foil with timber fairings.

The third keel was a disaster. This was a thick sectioned stainless steel hollow fabrication partly filled with lead poured in, and it was not until it was bolted to the boat that I noticed it had a twist from top to bottom of about 10 degrees, a psychological handicap as well as a physical one. That keel resulted in a disappointing season, including the ISORA week off Cork.

However we did have weatherwise a lovely sail home from that event!

It was a spinnaker run all the way to Carnsore Point and, going up the Wexford coast at low tide, we were inside the fully exposed sandbanks in the sunshine with the roar of the surf breaking on the other side in our ears.

The fourth and final keel was of solid lead, cast around steel reinforcing in a mould made from a pattern I most carefully made to a certain section.

During the period of the keels experiments I also made the forward rudder retractable (this rudder I think rather unfairly increased my racing handicap). To improve performance on the same rating I inverted the boat in my shed one winter and built on a partial outer hull, this allowing me to lengthen the mast and carry a lot more sail, and still maintain the same rating. Brainstorm's poor performance, particularly in the 3rd keel period, was so disappointing that some of my star crews gravitated to other craft and I never again had such a really keen and efficient one.

And then I had my heart attack in the middle of the '79 season!

Nonetheless, Brainstorm's sailing performance generally, especially on a reach, was disappointing. However, there are several (rather tarnished!) mugs about the house which bear witness to some successes.

We won the Howth Yacht Club's East and West cup in 1974 and in the St George YC's regatta a year or so later we won the prize for beating the greatest number of yachts in any class. This trophy was one of the splendid solid silver trophies which lived on the dining room mantlepiece at the George (until they were all stolen!) I was allowed to receive it and hold it for long enough for my crew to fill it up with a dreadful mixture of booze and pass it round the assembled company!

So we had our successes, and our disasters!

Our most successful race was quite early in Brainstorm's life when we finished third on handicap in the R.O.R.C. DunLaoghaire to Rothsea.

Our most disastrous race was a night race from Holyhead to Rockabill, finishing in DunLaoghaire. The start was inside the harbour and as we rounded the breakwater we were in the middle of a fleet of about 30 yachts of all sizes, Brainstorm being one of the smallest.

All bunched up when we met the considerable sea, all hard on the wind, leaping and plunging close together in the dark and very exciting until we began to spread out according to our speeds. I sailed the boat for about two hours and still had the navigation lights of a number of yachts in sight when I gave in to exhaustion and handed over to Joe Carolan and Colm O'Brolchain, the only crew I had, too few a number for any serious race, never mind a night race. Sailing a yacht at night close hauled at the best of times is not at all easy, and we had no instruments to help.

The crew took over willingly and I went to my bunk, asking to be called at first light. When I came up I found both the boys quite exhausted, not a sail in sight and the boat over canvassed with the big genoa and single reefed main. I decided immediately to down the mainsail and sail with the genoa only, being masthead and with a big overlap Brainstorm went very well to windward that way and the boys could leave the sailing to me and get some sleep. Joe went below and Colm lowered and stowed the main and I then asked him to winch in the genoa a bit, he had just started doing this when there was an almigty crash, the mast and genoa were in the sea and there was a large hole in the deck where the shroud plates and the bracket below should have been! Joe was on deck in an instant having just seen the sky above him!

It was quite rough and the boat without sails was rocking like a pendulum while we set about sorting things out and preventing the mast from punching a hole in our hull. Almost as usual we had no auxilliary. While we worked we planned to set up the boom as a mast and blow back to Holyhead. But before we got down to this another yacht in the race came on the scene and offered to try and tow us home using his engine but could not make any headway against wind and sea. We thanked him for his trouble and apologised for spoiling his race, just then a bigger yacht arrived and he too tried and failed. Then by the greatest piece of luck a big trawler seeing some trouble came alongside and offered to tow us to Howth, where he was bound for anyhow. Luckily I had aboard a long length of new nylon warp which being quite elastic is ideal for towing, and after a gentle start we were soon flying along at about ten knots and right through every wave which washed straight down the deck and over us, the boat was so steady at this speed that we were able to make coffee and have some biscuits to keep us going. In an hour and a half we were entering Howth and when we shortened up the tow Joe and Colm were able to talk in Irish to the trawler crew, all Aran men.

They cast us off in the harbour mouth and we free wheeled to a berth alongside another trawler and I made my way to our rescuers with the idea of seeing what was the score regarding salvage etc. I found Skipper and crew all having breakfast and when I broached the subject the reply was "forget it and have some breakfast" and a large plate of bacon and eggs appeared before me!

That episode ended that season!

*

The best cruise and race in all the time I had Brainstorm was the RORC race from DunLaoghaire to Rothesay on the Clyde - in the summer of 1974 - leaving the Isle of Man to port, Aran Island in the Firth of Clyde to Starboard and then through the Kyles of Bute. It was a race with a strong southerly wind all the way and very exciting with Brainstorm behaving beautifully, a good crew aboard and I may say good navigation or luck on my part when we ran into thick fog for a while in the Clyde. The best excitement of all was when we discovered we had finished third on handicap, only beaten by a very old boat with an age allowance and by a boat similar to ourselves which we actually passed in the fog. She was a Scottish owned boat and I guess her skipper knew the complicated tides in the Clyde area better than we did.

I had arranged with Chris that she and Shane would fly to Glasgow and find their way to Rothesay to join me and Drewry Pearson for a cruise through the Crinan Canal to Oban. There Drewry would leave us and my son Tyl would come up from the south of England to replace him, and we'd cruise to the Scottish Isles. The day after the race when the other three crewman had set off for home or joined other yachts for the sail home, I was delighted to see Chris and Shane, then about 15, walking off the splendid old paddle steamer, they had had a enjoyable and interesting journey and were in good form.

It was too late in the afternoon to think of going anywhere, Brainstorm was moored on the inside of the steamer jetty so we went aboard and sorted ourselves out in the rather cramped cabin, the only really comfortable places being the two quarter berths which Chris and I considered ours. Drewry and Shane had two of the cots over the rather narrow settees which had only bare sitting headroom.

Standing headroom too was somewhat limited!

I confess that in designing I had not given much consideration to comfort below deck and there wasn't much above deck either, plenty of sitting space but absolutely no shelter from the elements. To make up for this she was a delightful boat to sail, being very well balanced and responsive to the helm. She had a good gimballed cooker and galley and also a chart table, but the engine was practically in the cabin and (when it worked) was noisy. (The final engine was a little single cylinder B.M.W. diesel, but that came later than this cruise, when we had a two stroke petrol engine).

After a quiet night and breakfast we went up the town to do a little shopping and then got under way heading for the Kyles of Bute, where we saw the Jameson's yacht at anchor. Her crew were just going ashore for a climbing walk, so we decided to join them and blew up the dinghy and went ashore on the north side of the Kyle. There we had a lovely climb on a glorious morning and easily outclimbed the other party, taking a series of photos as we got higher and higher and Brainstorm got smaller and smaller. The weather on the whole of this cruise was most kind to us, I do not remember any rain, hard winds, or calms.

Leaving the very beautiful Kyles we ran before a fresh breeze up Lough Fyne heading for the Crinan Canal, on the way overtaking and running through a considerable shoal of Basking Sharks. They reminded us of a herd of bullocks met on a road . These massive fish are plankton eaters equipped with mouths adapted for the purpose, and are quite harmless except as obstructions which can be easily avoided in daylight as they are on the surface. Though we did wonder if they fed at night because to run into a herd at night would be a bit unnerving. Their length seemed to be about 15 ft. In my younger days these fish were hunted and slaughtered just for their livers off the Irish west coast, principally from Achill Island and the Arans. It always seemed a cruel and wasteful practice; they were hunted from currachs, trapped in nets and slaughtered with spears, then dragged ashore, their livers extracted for the oil and the carcasses set adrift to rot at sea, or to drift ashore to rot and stink.

We spent the night at Lochgilphead in a quiet berth.

Our little engine was temporarily out of service and as sailing through the canal was not possible I begged a tow from a larger yacht in the morning, and he kindly if I think a little reluctantly towed us all the way through to Crinan. There are a considerable number of locks up and down but not much traffic and the country is really beautiful, I have a good series of photos of that passage and would certainly recommend it to anyone cruising in that part of Scotland. On the passage I spent a lot of the time working on the engine and got it going, with the exhaust sticking out of the hatch!

There was a large basin at Crinan, then the home or graveyard for a number of large yachts of an earlier age which I would have liked to inspect, but we wanted to get to Oban before nightfall.

The next part of the voyage took us through the Gulf of Corryvreckan of ill repute. As one can see from the chart it is very exposed to the west and on an ebb tide a whirlpool builds up, this added to unbroken seas running into the funnel must create spectacular conditions, one cannot imagine why anyone would want to make the passage through under these conditions but I believe there have been many marine disasters there.

On the occasion of our own passage there was very little indication of anything unpleasant. On leaving the gulf we ran into quite dense fog and had to do some compass work and keep a sharp lookout for the several islands on the way up the Firth of Lorne. I seem to remember we went outside the island of Kerrera to enter the bay off the town of Oban. Pleased to see a Kerry anchored in the bay, we dropped our own hook near her, but her crew were ashore and we did not meet them until the next morning.

The Kerry turned out to be one we had sold as a kit to Frank Smith, at that time managing owner of the Bangor boatyard on Belfast Lough. Frank and his wife were aboard in the morning with another man and his lady friend. They were full of praise for their little yacht!

We put Drewry ashore and I went with him to the station partly to find out what train we might expect Tyl to arrive on, and to see Drewry my excellent crewman and good company off on his rather complicated journey home. Chris and Shane and I spent some time ashore exploring the town. By the time Tyl arrived it was late afternoon and we decided to put off our departure until the next morning. We had already agreed to meet up again with Frank at Tobermoray at the head of the Sound of Mull the next day and do a little cruising in company.

The next morning we set off up the Sound, passing very close to some rocks inhabited by many Atlantic Grey Seals, they took no notice of us. For lunch we turned into Lochaline, a very beautiful appendix to the Sound, and anchored almost under the beech trees on the bank. We must have had a fair wind as we made good time up to Tobermoray because we were there by mid afternoon finding the anchorage full of yachts and the small town and its bars full of yachtsmen and women, there was some club rally underway. We anchored some way from the quay and went exploring this treelined rocky inlet of which I have some lovely photos.

Tyl and I did go ashore and had a drink in one of the pubs but we felt we were strangers among unknown company, although there was at least one yacht whose owner I knew but he was not aboard, this was 'Sybil of Kumai' a 60 footer half shared by my old friend Nicolay.

Next morning we set off into the bay which becomes a fjord leading up to the small town of Srontiam. It was a pleasant sunny day with a light breeze, we sailed about taking photos and exchanging boats. It was then that I did one of those horrid thoughtless selfish things the memory of which never goes away. Chris had once in her youth spent part of a summer holiday with her parents on this Ardnamurchan peninsula, and she now wanted to sail up to Glenborrowdale a little way to the East, it meant parting from the Kerry and I wouldn't grant her request. Strange decision in a way, because I myself am very sentimental about places remembered from childhood, this cast a little cloud over the cruise which should not have been there.

In the event we did not in fact stay with the Kerry but put into a little bay on the North West of Mull for a peaceful lunch and then sailed South for Iona with the Islands of Tyree and Col fairly close to starboard. We found the Kerry anchored off the church and settlement on Iona and I put Chris and Shane ashore in the rubber dinghy and remained afloat with Tyl, which as it happened was rather fortunate for Frank who was ashore with his crew. I suddenly noticed that the Kerry was dragging her anchor into deep water and before I could start our engine she was well away on her own in a S.E direction propelled by a fresh breeze. We caught her up and Tyl scrambled aboard and I got her in tow. It took us quite a time to get back against wind and tide to where Frank was waiting thankfully in his dinghy.

A friend of mine, Billy Brown a mathematician and very successful amateur yacht designer, hearing of my intended cruise said if we were near we must visit an anchorage called Tinker's Hole on the South Western tip of Mull, so when I had picked up Chris and Shane we set off following Frank for this place. The entrance looked a little tricky on the chart which I had spread out in the cockpit while Chris steered. We were about two hundred yards behind Frank and suddenly noticed that he appeared to be heading the wrong way! We all started shouting and he suddenly realised his mistake and abruptly altered course and we were soon passing through a rocky entrance into a deep high sided and completely sheltered lagoon. We took a line and anchor ashore in the dinghy, dropped another anchor over the stern and we were nicely secured for the night, Frank did the same. The water was deep, right up to the steep hill side (we could almost have scrambled ashore from Brainstorm's bow). As it was still only mid afternoon we all went for a climbing scramble ashore, over to the next inlet where from a height we could see several seals both on the surface and clearly swimming under the clear green water. After a peaceful night we made a fairly early start southward, bidding farewell to the Kerry and her crew who were heading back to Belfast Lough. We were also heading for home but via Campbeltown where we had planned to put Tyl ashore.

The weather and wind direction still favoured us and we had a delightful sail to the sound of Islay leaving Colonsay and some rocky islets to starboard. As we approached Islay the wind fell light and speed dropped so that we thought if there were any mackeral about we might catch our supper.

We had hardly had the spinner in the water for fifteen minutes when Shane was hauling in something lively and then lifted a beautiful sea trout onto the stern deck which flapping furiously unhooked itself and if it had not been for Chris's quick reaction and sudden pounce would have been back in the sea! It made a beautiful meal for the four of us after we had moored up outside a timber jetty at Port Askaig, which, as we were to find out in the night, was a stupid place for me to choose. When we were all in our bunks asleep some large vessel passed us at considerable speed, in this narrow passage her wash picked up Brainstorm and seemed to hurl her at the jetty with two mighty crashes, the second occurring when we were already out of our bunks, from the glimpse I got of the vessel in the dark she looked like a naval vessel. (I could not find any damage at the time but I now believe it may have been the reason the rigging bracket which was glued to the hull failed in the later Irish Sea race which I have related earlier, the fact that the glued joint had been broken would not have been apparent). We just turned in again hopeing that no other large vessel would pass without seeing us and slowing down, but and as dawn was beginning to break it seemed unlikely.

In the morning we sailed down the east coast of Islay in bright sunshine and a light S.W. breeze heading for the Mull of Kintyre about 30 miles due south and hoping to reach the headland before the tide turned when I guessed the ebb would be hard to beat. The breeze slowly dropped and it was not until about 6pm that we arrived at the S.W corner of the headland with the Irish Antrim coast only eighteen miles away and with virtually no wind, and the ebb tide roaring up through the north Channel.

We started the little two stroke Vire petrol engine and headed into the now strong N.W going tide. Keeping right in to the rocks taking advantage of any eddys and with Tyl sitting on the bow most of the time guiding me and the engine going flat out we were only just able to make headway and at times were stationary. I don't remember how long it took us to cover the approximately eight miles along the south coast of the Mull, it must have been about four hours and for what seemed a noisy age of the engine, still with an open exhaust. At least it was perfectly calm except for the tide ripp. From time to time a light training aircraft from the airfield near Machrihanish flew low over us, the pilot giving an encouraging wave.

All things come to an end, and I thought it was going to be the petrol!

But miraculously it did not give out before a little breeze came in from the S.W. and we were able to get sailing slowly into slacker water and then turn up the east coast by which time the sun had set and it was beginning to get dark. By the time we were off Cambeltown it was quite dark, we had to round a high island to port and then try to locate the leading lights against all the lights of the town. Had it not been a clear night I would probably have anchored off and waited for light, because we only had a small scale chart of the port. Actually the harbour entry was fairly open and we soon found ourselves among small craft and using the echo sounder and the Aldis lamp as a spotlight picked a spot and let go the anchor. It had been a long day and we were glad to have a meal and turn in.

To wake up after a night entry in a strange place particularly on a brilliant morning is always exciting and so it was that morning as we ate our breakfasts in the cockpit. Cambeltown is a busy fishing port and we were lucky to have picked a place out of the route to the trawler section of the harbour or we would have had a disturbed night. After breakfast we all went ashore, did some shopping and exploring and saw Tyl off on the first available bus which would take him on the start of the complicated route by land and water to Glasgow.

I have no recollection of any headwinds, of strong winds or even rain of any significance on the whole of this, the only cruise Chris and I ever made together in our own yacht, weather conditions which must be quite unusual for that part of the world.

We decided to make Carlingford Lough our next port of call, a distance of about 120 sea miles, and to sail at night for the first and only time. So with just the three of us aboard we weighed anchor and were away before 9am. We had a fair wind again and a comfortable full sail strength, Shane and I did most of the steering, (unaware at the time that we were sailing over a vast ammunition dump which included chemical weapons), and by nightfall we were off or a bit south of Donaghadee. There we handed the helm over to Chris who always enjoyed being left alone on the helm at night, with instructions to leave South Rock light vessel to starboard and then to alter course slightly to the west. I came up after Chris had been nearly four hours on the helm and found her happy but tired and willing to go below. I made a hot drink for both of us and took over.

As the sun rose the Mountains of Mourne rolling down to the sea were wonderfully illuminated, it was another glorious day and I have photos to prove it! Somewhere about that time we noticed we were being shadowed by a Royal Navy patrol craft which eventually came up with us, had a good look from range of about 100yards and then without hailing us sheered off and soon disappeared in the distance, at that time I suppose they were concerned with gun running and the like.

As I turned westward I had to harden in the sails to make Carlingford entrance where fortunately the tide was still on the flood and a couple of tacks took us past the lighthouse and narrows. We turned north and anchored in what must be Whitewater Bay. We were all tired and made no attempt to land, just had a meal and were soon in our bunks.

Again and for our last day it was a lovely morning with a fresh west off shore wind which with the last of the fierce ebb tide ejected us from Carlingford. We had a glorious sail all the way down the Louth and North Dublin coasts on a close reach, cutter rigged with a staysail inside the genoa. We passed inside Rockabill, and outside Lambay's impressive cliffs. Then past Ireland's Eye and Howth Head and so to our mooring in DunLaoghaire Harbour. There to be ferried ashore by the senior boatman Sean, a man who had always been so helpful to me, a fairly obviously impecunious yachtsman.

And so home in our fairly well used Hunter Estate.

*

Chris, Shane and I did make one more voyage together.

It was never planned as a pleasure cruise, and it wasn't!

I had raced Brainstorm from Holyhead to Dunmore East where my crew had to leave me to get back to work. Chris had agreed to get there by public transport with Shane to help me sail home. (We had hoped weather might have permitted a landing on the Great Saltee Island off the Wexford coast, but that was not to be).

They duly arrived and, after a night aboard, we set off eastward about noon on a cold dull day, rounding Hook Head very close in, meeting a stiff north east wind coming out of Ballyteige Bay. Approaching Kilmore Quay it became pretty obvious that a landing on the Saltee was out, and that we were faced with crossing the long straight underwater ridge of I do not know what but which I believe is called St Patricks causeway.

I knew nothing about it or depths of water but the small scale chart showed what was apparently a deeper spot more or less about one third way out to the smaller Saltee, so with some trepidation we made for this as near as we could judge with a strong tide under us.

Brainstorm draws a good six feet of water and as we approached the quite definite long line of disturbance in the water it was a rather nail biting and not very seaman like thing to do, we passed over it without 'feeling' the bottom but shall never know what clearance we had. The recommended course is south of the Saltees, either right outside everything including the Saltees Light Vessel - now a large Buoy - or between the Great Saltee and the Brandies rocks. Because the wind was offshore and freshening we hugged the coast from Kilmore to Carnsore, anchoring on the way inside the Tersheen Rock and very close in to the steep shingle shore, in calm water except for the swell.

(A few years ago I tried to explore by car and alone this region of Carnsore westwards, with its tidal waters of Lady's and Tacumshin lakes, which seems to be all of sand or shingle. At one point rather late in the day and far from habitation I got stuck in shingle which was rather like driving over an endless bean bag! I only got out with the aid of the car mats).

We cooked up a good meal before facing what we knew was going to be a very hard windward passage, short handed up the Irish Sea. We took in a second reef and set No 1 jib, a very efficient sail with a reefed main, put on lots of warm clothes and oilskins, weighed anchor and headed for the Point where we could see conditions were going to be very unpleasant.

And they were!

The wind was about Force Six against the tide and the light was beginning to go. The only thing that was good was the visibility, everything else was really horrible! Perhaps we should have turned back to Kilmore, but we were both bad at giving up. I had complete faith in the boat and I thought we could cope. We made a leg out leaving The Tusker Rock about a mile to leeward and then back again to Greenore point making good progress with the help of the tide, but Chris was now below seasick and I was half drowned, totally unprotected in the cockpit.

The lights of Rosslare were so near and yet so far.

Never having entered the harbour and with the hard wind and sea driving straight into it I did not dare attempt it. The next leg was far out into the Irish sea where the seas were a little easier, Brainstorm somewhat overcanvassed and well over on her ear but going well. I managed to get her to steer herself by lashing the helm and got below for long enough to boil some water on the gimballed stove and, most difficult in the violent motion, make some strong Bovril for Chris and myself.

Boy was it good! The effect was marvellous. But I was definitely tiring and therefore very worried, feeling that we should not be here in a somewhat weak crew state and myself nearing seventy. However the Bovril had really put some beef into me and Chris had been able to keep it down which was a good sign. Although prone to sickness she was generally the first to recover and sometime in the small hours she came up and relieved me on the helm, the wind had eased a bit and backed into the

N.W. so we were making long and short tacks outside the east coast sandbanks, the graveyard of many ships in earlier days.

About an hour before light we found the Arklow harbour light bearing West and turned inshore but could not agree how far off we were, the shadow of the land deceiving us as to where it really was, so we hove too with the jib aback and the main hard in a moderating wind we sailed slowly landward until the light from the East gradually showed us our position. We were about a mile out and we were soon able to sail close hauled between the pierheads and to turn into the basin at Tyrells yard where we promptly ran aground in the middle in soft mud, let go the anchor, stowed sails and most thankfully went to our bunks. After a few good hours of sleep we had a hearty breakfast. We left the boat in charge of the Yard, Jack Tyrell being a good friend of mine, packed our bags and caught the train to DunLaoghaire and our car and drove home.

I sailed Brainstorm back to her mooring a few days later with the help of Andre Prieur of the Radio Eireann Symphony Orchestra, a lovely sail with an ideal off shore wind, and the lovely Wicklow hills as a backdrop.

IN '76 I GOT involved in a strange sea story. My friend Donal took on the job of finishing and fitting out a hull and partial kit of a "¾ ton" class "Shipman" of Swedish design, moulded by a firm in Limerick.

This was for a Dr Fred Sloane who planned to enter for that year's Trans Atlantic single handed race. He had not left himself much time and Donal had been more or less living on the job for a couple of months and as time was running out he thought I could help with the work of turning the finished hull into a seagoing yacht.

I moved in on the job on Fred's payroll and with very comfortable quarters in a local country hotel. Fred was in process of closing down a huge old linen mill near the town of Ballyclare in Ulster, a small section of which he had been using for weaving experimental mixes of linen and synthetics. His office was full of samples of made up clothing, of which he told me to take my pick!

Fred seemed to take little interest in the work Don and I were doing but provided anything and everything we required. Eventually the yacht now named Ballyclare was moved to the White Rock Yacht Club on Strangford Lough, rigged, and launched by his wife with little ceremony. The next day with Fred, Donal and myself and I think one other man, we hoisted all sail and although it was a horrible wet windy day set off down the lough into a considerable head sea which very soon had Donal laid out.

The surprising thing to me was that Fred insisted that I sail the boat and would not himself take over. Everything seemed to be in order, the boat was hauled back up the club slip and I departed for home.

One of the rules for the race was that contestants had to prove their seamanship and navigational skills by sailing I think was 500 sea miles in open water. This was not monitored and was apparently left to the individual's honesty. Don and I kept our ears open for any news of Fred having done his cruise, being very doubtful about his abilities as were some members of White Rock Y.C.

The first we heard was that he did set off and next we heard that he was in trouble off the North Welsh coast and had to seek the assistance of a lifeboat. Soon after that the yacht with Fred aboard was found by some men exercising horses!

It was stranded and somewhat damaged way out in the very shallow Morecombe Bay, from where it was lifted and carried by crane to Fleetwood for repairs. He apparently set off again to do his 500 but without insurance- Lloyds were not satisfied with the repairs!

He was next heard of on the Isle of Man!

He did eventually get to Plymouth and started the race arriving somewhere in America long after the race had been forgotten. Why he ever entered was the subject of much speculation!

*

Sometime in late 1976 I met up again with Patricia Dunkerley who had been with us on the disastrous first trip downriver in the St Brigid.

We struck up a friendship which just managed to be platonic. She was very much younger than I was, and had no intention of getting too involved with a married man! For my part I was determined to keep the faith with Chris.

Nevertheless I had no female friends and Chris had several male ones. John Weaving was a particular friend, and because he was working to some extent with us he was with her a great deal at times, to my anoyance. Patricia, or Tricia, had a very pleasant and spacious flat in Pembroke Road in Dublin which she shared with her twin sister Anita, they were both musicians in the Radio Eireann Symphony orchestra. Their parents, whom I got to know well, lived in Monkstown near DunLaoghaire. Mother was Irish and like her daughters full of fun, father was half French and the girls always seemed to have inherited Mediterranean genes!

Tricia took me to rehersals and introduced me to her fellow musicians both during rehersals and in the local pub afterwards. I have never really understood why we got on so well together because our lives were totally different but I did appreciate music more than she did boats! We had occasional evening meals out when I was in Dublin and because of her profession she was quite well known and being so outgoing we got V.I.P treatment in several restaurants and these occasions were always great fun.

I have always felt that it was natural for husbands and wives to have friends of the opposite sex simply to help develop their own personalities and those of other people but am old fashioned enough to believe in basic fidelity as an ideal.

Tricia married an Italian Count with a home in Venice - he was an oboeist and they played in several Italian orchestras and ensembles. They are now living in Bournemouth with two talented teenage musician children and I have twice been there when in England.

And she and I are still the best of friends.

*

My only source of income during the middle and late '70s was my work for Bord Failte. They gave me no retainer but paid me on a day to day basis, plus motoring and living expenses which were generous. I enjoyed the motoring and the opportunity of really getting to know Ireland's marvellous coast from Wexford south to north Donegal. The worst part was typing all the reports which no one seemed to really read or act upon!

Early in '77 Chris was badly injured by a kick from a young horse. She was with some horses in a field a long way from home but fortunately with Hazel Marsden, another horse enthusiast. The kick broke several ribs and badly damaged her spleen. The kick completely knocked her out, and Hazel had to get some local help and somehow got her to hospital in Longford. Next day she was transferred to The Mater Hospital in Dublin by ambulance which she said afterwards was torture every mile of the way. She was in hospital for three weeks but made a full recovery and was straight back with her horses.

My five years contract with the Dock Milling Co was up in mid '77 and as the company was really running at a loss it was decided to go into liquidation. My last and sad job was to clear up and clear out that almost ideal little plant for G.R.P. boatbuilding. It was particularly sad as I had planned it all and felt that as initial costs had been written off, and as we had some good work people, with accurate costing it could still have turned reasonably profitable.

Also that year I paid a visit to my now married daughter Tanya, living in Penrith in Cumbria with her husband Simon Moller. He was at that time a very skilled baker making a great variety of bread in a small bakery. After living together for several years, they were only recently married, in the village where she really grew up, Lower Heyford in north Oxford. It was a church wedding and I had given her away.

Unfortunately I got the impression on my visit that all was not well and not long afterwards they broke up and Tanya went to live with her mother Maud in Lewes, and is still there after Maud's death.

In late '77 I had a minor accident in my workshop which taught me a lesson. I was working on a big 14ft iron pipe for a staircase when it slipped from a vice and crushed the big finger of my left hand, breaking the joint and upper part. Simon who happened to be at home rushed me to the local doctor with it roughly wrapped up, he took one look at it and told Simon to take me to Roscommon hospital. There a pleasant young doctor did the painful necessary and then announced to my surprise that I was staying in the hospital. Simon was dismissed and I was put to bed - which was rather nice!

I was lying half awake in the small hours when I quite suddenly began to feel very queer and rang my bell, a nurse took my pulse and then there was an immediate emergency, things were stuck into me and I was on a drip! I had gone into delayed shock so I possibly owe my life to the wisdom of the young doctor.

Lesson; small very painful accidents should be taken seriously.

*

Once again in England I persuaded my son Finn to take me up in a glider. He had for several years had a half share in a high performance single seater in which he had done several notable cross country flights. Finn organised the use of the club's advanced trainer and one sunny morning I found myself shut in a rather cramped cockpit in front (I always wonder why tandem seated aircraft always put the passenger in front and have decided that it is to cushion the bump for the pilot in the event of a prang!) of Finn, with someone running alongside holding up a wing while a noisy little biplane pulled us on our single wheel on the end of a cable. We were off first, then our tug took off and we climbed quite steeply up to about 1000ft before Finn pulled the release and for a moment we seemed to stop and then we were freely and quietly gliding over rural Sussex. A glider is always flying down through the air but the air may be rising faster than you are gliding down.

This is where the real skill and knowledge of meterology and clouds come in. Finn told me to report from the rate of climb or fall instrument in front of me, it was not a good day for rising thermals, it was mostly down and after about ten minutes in the air Finn was turning into the light wind to land back on the flying field, a few gentle bumps and a wing drops onto the grass. We opened the hood climb out and trundled the thing to the hanger.

Since then Finn made a very heavy landing in a distant field while avoiding cattle, wrote off the plane and nearly himself, escaping with an injured back - which mended alright. Since then he has taken up paragliding with great enthusiasm and having watched him at it on the

Sussex South Downs I wish I was young enough to take it up. To be able to carry your 'plane' costing a few hundred pounds on your back, up any suitable hill with a moderate to light wind, spread it on the grass sorting out the strings, then inflating it above your head - it does inflate when headed into the wind- and then at the adjustment of certain strings lift off as gently as you like, take up your flying attitude and soar away on rising air to sail down or across the wind, and in the right conditions fly all day and far away!

*

Christine's first grandchild was born on the last day of '77, Simon's daughter was a bonny blonde baby and they called her Keelin.

Shortly afterwards in January of '78 I went to the London Boat Show, just to see the form, to get ideas and meet old friends in the boat business, a business which was really beginning to take off.

I have all my life been bad at timing!

Back home I now started working as marine consultant to the Northern Ireland Tourist Board, mostly in connection with Lough Erne developments. This made a useful connection between the two Irelands, boating tourism everywhere on the island was beginning to represent considerable national income.

And it also helped my income!

Later that year I was in England again, this time with a car, having crossed Larne-Stranraer and then through the beautiful country of Galloway on a lovely day. I drove through Durham to Richmond in North Yorkshire, home of my cousin Jack Plews and his wife Ruth. We had seen very little of each other since our late teen days and only met up on family social occasions. Now a retired Surgeon Colonel, Jack was at an advanced stage of spinal cancer and obviously living in pain. I was extremely fond of Jack and although he did not profess to be left wing like me he had seen enough of life to share most of my views. An extremely nice man, he must have been a very good doctor and surgeon.

I left them next day, very sad, knowing I would never see Jack again.

My next quest was to try to find another man of whom I was extremely fond, at yet another time of my life, Welfar of Westward days. All I knew was that, back in the '30s when I knew him, he had been a fruit farmer near Wisbich in Norfolk.

Rather vague information to go on! But I did track his two sons down via a phone directory, only to learn that my friend had died of cancer a few years previously. The sons were a couple of very tough young men,very different from their father, and they showed no interest in meeting me. They seemed to be running a rather run down business in hiring out boxes and crates for conveying fruit and vegetables, this being an intensive market garden area.

I finished that British trip as usual back in Lewes, before going home via Fishguard.

It was in this year that I stared the CND branch, mentioned earlier, in Carrick-on-Shannon. This grew rapidly, bringing in many young people with families. It is already hard to imagine the state of international affairs at that time. Germany was a NATO armed camp, with to the East an opposing camp, while England was a sort of American flying field with dumps of atomic weapons all over. Both America and the Soviet Union were pock marked with buried silos of nuclear weapons. Some day we may know the true facts of how near we were to universal destruction.

*

In '78 Simon had the idea of fitting out a suitable boat as a mobile base, with accommodation for a few divers, for scuba diving off our coasts. He was a qualified and quite experienced diver and Breda his wife was prepared to run the domestic side of the business. He located a big fishing boat named Virginia in the Dublin docks, which had already been used by the Garda as a diving boat. She was a beamy and rather shallow drafted 50footer with a Gardener Engine.

I inspected her and Simon bought her. With money I suppose, but I cannot now remember where it came from!

We decided to bring her by sea and river to Jamestown and there complete the partial conversion which had been carried out already. So with a crew of Simon, Breda, Shane, Shay Phelan and myself we made the trip to the Shannon estuary. We were lucky with the weather, calling in at Dunmore East and Youghal, thence the long haul to Crookhaven for a short rest. On that leg I remember being on a night watch with Breda when we decided to deliberately round the Fastnet Rock. This we did in a choppy sea under the great wheel spoke beams of the light. The next leg was all the way to Foynes, way up the estuary, passing round the wonderful scenery of the Kerry coast. After passing Brandon Head and as we had a good following wind we hoisted a spinnaker we had aboard to boost our speed. We spent a night at Foynes and then proceeded to Limerick, grounding at low water about three miles below the City, then waiting for the water to come back! Chris met us in Limerick and she and I changed over until I think Athlone which was one of the places where there was barely enough water for us, but we touched bottom at several other places.

LATER IN THAT summer of '78 I had an interesting cruise in a yacht called "Sybil of Kumai", some 60ft overall, rigged as a ketch - two masted - under the command of Ernest Nicolay. Commonly known as Nick, he was a retired civil engineer and wartime army Major Engineers.

Nick had been a friend of mine since student days at Southampton University, where he was a fulltime student and I was only a part timer (one day and three night classs).

Because we were both sailing enthusiasts we had struck up a friendship which has lasted a lifetime. Politically we were at opposite ends of the spectrum and agreed early on to amicably disagree on everything, including yacht design, he being for the classic, me for the most modern.

Of Nick professionally I have learned from his peers that he was a very clever engineer, responsible in the immediate post-War years for many important works, particularly in Africa, and also involved in the London Underground Extension.

The cruise started from Baltimore in West Cork. The crew besides Nick and myself were a teenage girl Sheila, and a long time sailing companion of Nick's, a Scottish friend Alan Willin. The weather was not good although it was June, not too much wind but lots of rain and Sybil had no shelter above deck whatsoever! She was also engineless - we had to do it all with wind and sail- which made the cruise all the more interesting and challenging. Below deck she was comfortable but not luxurious and for a yacht of her size rather cramped.

We started off in the early afternoon with a tricky passage through the islands to Schull and at one point when rather fortunately Nick was on the helm! - a long elegant tiller- and claiming to know the route he took us the wrong side of a rocky islet and we struck going quite fast but fortunately not much heeled.

Nick panicked slightly and wanted all sail off, but I suggested a trick we had learnt on the Shannon with no tides to help, so we hardened in the sails, heeled the boat over and reduced her draft and she came off and sailed clear. There was a risk of doing damage but the tide was on the ebb and worse damage might have been done if she had finished lying on her side on the rocks.

We spent the night anchored off Schull. The next morning was fine and we set off for Castletownbere sailing inside Long Island, green but almost treeless, and then in open water with the Fastnet Rock away to the south in the morning mist. (Bere island is on the north side of Bantry Bay and was one time an important harbour for the British Navy, the island itself being heavily fortified - forts and old guns are still there I believe).

Rounding Mizzen Head close in with its white lighthouse and dwellings and its bridge approach. I think it sad to think that all these lighthouses are now without human life (if you were in trouble within sight of them nobody would know), they are dehumanised by automatics and electronics. From Mizzen we eased sheets and bore away across Dunmanus and then Bantry Bay. To be afloat in fair weather in a large sailing yacht is joy almost unequalled. The blue-green sea deep and unpolluted, at this point quite near the continental shelf and benefiting from the warm water of the Gulf Stream the vegetation is almost tropical. To the east the Kerry mountains -the Reeks- balancing a few bunches of sunlit cotton wool on their summits. Travelling at seven to eight knots the only noise the bow wave peeling away and the burbling of the ship's wake trailing behind. By late afternoon Nick sailed us into the inner harbour at Castletown and head to wind we dropped anchor about fifty yards off the town quay and stowed sails. We launched the traditinal clench built "pram" dinghy which usually lives inverted on top of the coach roof, as did all dinghies in my younger days. Or, if the yacht was too small they were towed astern and in bad weather were always troublesome, either getting swamped or trying to climb aboard. But in use they were better than the inflatables.

I think Nick stood us a meal!

We cetainly had a drink or two before returning aboard without Sheila who had to go back to Cork to take some exam. We had some fun the next morning when it came to getting under way. Mainsail hoisted and jib ready, Nick orders the anchor weighed, quite a big one and no such luxury as a winch so Alan and I heave away manfully and take up the slack chain. Then it's up jib and breakout the anchor but it won't budge. 'Go on pull harder' from the other end of the boat, we go through the motions heaving, but quietly agreed that it is foul of something we have no intention of lifting.

Nick comes forward to show us how!

But he has to agree with our analysis so we hitch a stout rope to the chain and take it to one of the big sheet winches aft and start grinding it up. Just then a couple of local fishermen arrive alongside in a boat with offers of help, and looking down in the clear water we see we are lifting a huge chain cable from some ancient time, they get another rope under it to hold it off the bottom, we clear and hoist the anchor aboard, the fishermen are duly awarded, quietly blessing the cable no doubt for the umpteenth time as they depart!

There is great satisfaction in manouvering a sailing yacht especially a big one out of a tight corner under sail and it came off well this time, but can go horribly wrong, especially in fluky wind conditions which may catch you unawares and put you on the wrong tack and you may end up tangled with other yachts and their moorings or run ashore or into something solid.

After rather an awkward beat through the narrows to the north of Bere Island we were able to sail close hauled past the ruins of the first Transatlantic radio station on Black Ball Head. Going north it is usual to go through the Dursey Sound if the tide is right but there is a cable across the sound which I think carries a cable car and we did not know if Sybil's 60-70 ft mast would clear so we sailed round Dursey Island and headed up the Kenmare estuary. This is really a very long bay on the northside of which is Parknasilla and its famous hotel. We had a light following wind, it was a pleasant warm but dull evening, I was on the helm and suddenly became aware that we were not moving and a glance over the side told me we, we were caught in a drift net. These are filament nets of green nylon and almost invisible under weter 8 to 10ft deep supported by many small floats. They may be half a mile or more in length and are set across the tide and allowed to drift with it. Set for salmon they also catch other fish and also unfortunately diving seabirds and occasionally young seals and porpoises which fishermen don't like drowning in this way.

We got the sails down and set about trying to clear ourselves but it was soon evident that the net had tangled with something, probably the useless propeller and I was just contemplating going overbard when the net owners arrived in a half decked fishing boat and first demanded booze, they had taken us for a Frenchman. The south and west coasts of Ireland are very popular with French yachtsmen. We told them that we were Irish and had no booze to give away and rather surly they came alongside and soon had us free to up sails and claw out and sail round the end of the net and continue up the bay. When nearly up to Parknasilla, we jibed onto starboard tack and sailed into the delightful bay of Kilmacilloge and in the twilight dropped anchor off the semi ruined coastguard station. It was a lonely anchorage in beautiful surroundings (I made up my mind I would someday visit the place by road, but have yet to do so).

After breakfast we upped anchor and beat slowly out of the bay, avoiding drift nets and heading for Derrynane, again an anchorage well known to Nick so that the entrance through the offlying islands and rocks was easy. Once inside one is beautifully sheltered from the sea but not from all winds.

To the North the land rises to the mountains in a steep slope up, down which most violent williways sweep in stormy conditions not experienced by us, because although we were held up by strong winds they were from the south and west. The weather was sunny and conditions allowed me to make a lovely photographic record of the place. The south of Derrynane Bay is a beautiful silver strand with a pier of sorts running down to about the half tide mark. Just inland is Derrynane Abbey and the house where Daniel O'Connell grew up, now a sort of museum. There is a story I can believe to be true of the times, just after the first world war a certain titled gentleman in command of one of HM destroyers took his ship into Derrynane for a bet.

During the evenings and while sharing the domestic work we had long political-economic discussions, conclusions were never reached but although we had very divergent views on nearly everything we always amicably agreed to differ!

On the third day Sheila rejoined us at the top of the hairpinned road climbing from the bay to the main 'Ring of Kerry' road above.

The next move was a fairly long one to Smerwick harbour, just a big bay open to the north, but as the winds seemed to be set in the south and west we reckoned it would be safe and comfortable for a night. It was a spectacular trip, past the Skelligs and paricularly the Blaskets, accompanied by thousands of seabirds, gannets, fulmar, terns and puffins mostly. And then bearing away round Sybil Head after which our ship was supposedly named, but why was not known. Then jibing round and going south into Smerwick where we anchored well off shore in this somewhat uninteresting place. We did not go ashore but did not up anchor until quite late in the afternoon of the next day for the Aran Islands.

Nick was feeling off colour and asked me to take charge and stayed below himself. The conditions were decidedly unpleasant, rain and heavy sea mist, but a fair and pretty fresh wind promised a fast trip through the late evening and short night. I set a compass course and Alan steered until dark and I for the rest of the night alone on deck, a bit cold but happy and wide awake because no land was in sight and the poor visibility meant watching for trawlers and keeping an eye on the compass. It was a straight line course with no tacking to complicate the navigation and nothing but my own thoughts for company. The visibility was not a worry and I was well offshore in the open Atlantic but I could not help thinking of the position of ships captains of the past approaching land in really thick weather with only a somewhat vague idea of position and a lee shore somewhere ahead. Far more ships have been wrecked than ever were lost at sea. There is a true saying that while the landsman fears the sea, the seaman fears the land.

Soon after first light the Aran Islands showed up about a mile and a half off with the Gregory's sound dead ahead, and as we sailed through this I called Nick up to take us into Kilronan. As soon as we were safely anchored and sails stowed we had breakfast, then I turned in and the others launched the the little dinghy and went ashore. I went ashore later and we hired an 'outside car' to take us to the remarkable cliff fort of Dun Aengus. We walked back to Kilronan and spent the rest of the day between the village and the ship and had a pleasant evening in one of the smoke filled pubs.

The next day Roundstone was our objective and it was perhaps the most pleasant day of all. Nick took us across to the mainland at Golan Head and then through what is known as the inner passage, inside many islands and rocks, favoured by the fair wind we had through most of the cruise. Past Saint McDaragh's island with its tiny all stone church and so to anchor off Roundstone where I was to say goodbye. They returned to Baltimore while I made my way home.

That cruise a pleasant memory.

THAT VISIT TO the Arans was only my second, a previous visit had been by air, a 'spur of the moment' decision. In Galway city alone and with nothing urgent to do, I bought a return ticket and motored out to the small airport which was then a few miles east of the city. There I waited for the return of the little 'Islander' aircraft, a 10-12 seater built on the Isle of Wight by a man I had met in India when he was engaged in crop spraying.

The plane came in and after the few passengers had disembarked the single pilot climbed down onto the tarmac and I got into conversation with him. He was an elderly man for a pilot - Wallace by name - and we found we had several past friends in common and so, when we took off again I was in the co-pilots seat, continuing on the conversation. Wallace had been a commercial pilot since the war and now lived alone in a caravan on the airport, a lonely man with a past of some note I would judge.

There were only three other passengers and quite a lot of goods on that flight. We landed first on Inishmaan on an upsloping grass-on-sand runway pockmarked with rabbit burrows, these marked by little red flags!

One person got off there and we taxied back to the edge of the 'field', actually the edge of a low cliff, and took off up a considerable slope, a low stone wall at the top. It all looked a bit hairy to me but the Islander had no problem and flew low over the half mile of the Gregory Sound, to land on another grass-sand-burrows field.

We quickly turned round and with only two other passengers aboard, Capt Wallace flew south east over the Burren, circling a few times, pointing out features of interest which one could only see from the air, mostly ring forts and collapsed natural caves in the limestone of the area. An extremely nice man, Captain Wallace, and I was very sorry to hear sometime later that he had been badly knocked about in a crash somewhere else and when not in command.

*

It was at the end of '78 that Chris lost her horse Jo, a sometimes brood mare, at other times a nice riding mare. She was in a field with someone else's mare and apparently they had a kicking fight and Jo broke a foreleg. John Mack - owner of the other- came to the door and in considerable distress told me the news.

Chris came in shortly afterwards and we went to the field which was along the canal bank near here. We found Jo standing in pain and misery on three legs. The local vet had been called and we waited with the horse until he arrived. There was nothing to be done but put her down, we couldn't move her and although she was rather close to the bank he gave her the lethal injection. Christine and myself were in tears. Almost immediaely the horse collapsed, rolled over and fell into the canal and sank!

Shortly afterwards some busybody reported to the Gardai that we had thrown a dead horse into the canal! A young Guard came to the house and accused us! I was furious and said of course we would never do such a thing. But there was nothing to be done until she floated, when we got her out with the help of a tractor.

*

Early in 1979 I had a call from a Father Murphy, Parish Priest at Prosperous in County Kildare. He wanted me to design a river cruiser of about 34ft for construction in steel. This was for some Australian people who were proposing to start a hire company on the Shannon. The boat or boats were to be built by a family of steel workers, ex Harland and Wolfe, now living at Robertstown on the Grand Canal and this family Fr Murphy had 'taken under his wing'.

I went ahead and designed a cruiser 34ft by 12ft. Then Fr Murphy informed me that the clients had cried off, and could I change the design into that of a fishing boat!

I said yes, I could, although it would be a bit narrow. Nonetheless with his finance the job went ahead and I spent some time with Murphy and the builders Downeys, father and two working sons who were very skilled. At this same time I had Brainstorm at DunLaoghaire and was racing her twice a week, and also doing a lot of inspection work for Bord Fáilte.

I was 67 or 68 years old, and it caught up!

I had a heart attack in '79, later followed by another in 1984.

*

One Thursday morning I set off fairly early with Simon, heading for Tullamore. But, having gone a few miles, I was bothered with rather severe 'indigestion', so I changed my mind, returned home. There I took a Rennies and, feeling better, decided to carry on and set off again. I drove to a hire base near Tullamore and inspected two recently imported cruising barges, and then headed for DunLaoghaire, letting Simon drive as I was not feeling very well again. We had a meal on the the way and although we had plenty of time before the 6 o'clock start we went aboard Brainstorm and did a lot of the little jobs that are always waiting to be done on a sailing yacht.

Daphne and Stephen Wynne who had crewed on Brainstorm before came aboard to complete the crew and we duly started in the race, myself on the helm. We had been sailing in light conditions for about half an hour when my discomfort really became a pain in the chest which I just could not ignore.

I said 'sorry chaps but I'm afraid you will have to take me in', and I went to the cabin and lay down!

The others took over and as soon as they reached the harbour entrance they fired an emergency flare which the club boatmen saw immediately. A launch was alongside before we reached our mooring and Simon and I clambered aboard. I was almost immediately violently sick, over the side! Once ashore, somehow I got up to the club bar and there asked the very pleasant barman Christy to try to find a doctor if there was one in the club. I went and sat in the library, while Simon went to bring the car to the door. By good fortune there was a doctor in the club. He took one look at me and said 'you know what is the matter with you' and I said 'I think so'. He said 'never mind, we'll have you in intensive care in ten minutes' and went to the phone.

Simon took me immediately to St Michaels in the town and almost within ten minutes I was doped and in bed, hitched onto cathode indicators and, not knowing the real situation, comfortable and half asleep. Chris drove up in the evening and I was very glad to see her.

Next day when I really did not know my condition I was thinking of the situation. If I did not recover, I calculated, I would be leaving Chris on an old barge with extremely little money to her name. There and then I made a resolution that the first thing I was going to do when I recovered was to design and build a house in our field so that we had some security and, so to speak, some real real estate!

I was about a week in the intensive care ward and very well looked after, and then moved down to a ward with about eight beds where I found myself next to a very pleasant elderly priest with whom I almost immediately struck up a friendship, centering on the sea and ships and boats in which he was very interested, but of which he admitted total ignorance.

In this ward I had quite a number of visitors. Chris brought me up a portable radio which I used with a headphone and the book 'Sailing Alone Around The World' the famous piece of marine literature by Joshua Slocombe. This I lent to my priest friend who was facinated with it. I seem to remember that the weather and the ward were extremely hot and I was delighted with a huge bottle of fresh lemon juice brought me by my crew Daphne.

It happened that in the second week (I was there over four), the disastrous Fastnet yacht race took place, in which everyone was interested and I with my radio was able to give an hour to hour commentry. Some friends of mine and ex-crew were sailing one of the Shamrock class boats-same size as Brainstorm and smallest size in the race - they missed the worst area of the storm but retired to the Irish coast.

As soon as I was allowed out of the ward I was trying to climb stairs but was amazed how weak I was. After the fourth week Chris came and drove me home and I annoyed her by asking her to drive more slowly, I found that for some reason, probably weakness, that I was extremely nervous! When we got back to the barge I was very pleased and happy at how much trouble she had taken to welcome me back with small domestic improvements.

*

I was apparently given a pretty stout heart with a very slow beat, sometimes known as an athlete's heart, maybe good when you are young and athletic but not so good when you are old. This has rather let me down twice in embarassing circumstances. The first when I was in court in Clifden in Galway as a technical witness in a court case between a Dutch fisherman and a local boatbuilder. I was on the boatbuilders - the defendant's - side.

The case was before the Circuit Court Judge. I had gone to quite a lot of trouble preparing notes and sketches for our counsel and solicitor and for the Judge to help them understand the problem. When I was called I had to sit in a big chair on a raised platform facing the judge and with the opposing counsels sitting on either side of me and the gallery behind I found it a bit daunting! I answered questions from both sides and handed the Judge my notes and sketches. When I'd said my piece I returned to the seat beside my client.

Somewhat deaf even then I could not hear the Judge's summing up and verdict and leaned over to my client and whispered 'what did he say'?'

'We won with costs'.

The next thing I knew I was lying on my back on a floor somewhere looking up at a very high ceiling surrounded by very concerned people, including a Garda officer, most of the court and the Judge without his wig. (I hoped this uncovered head was to be informal rather than because he thought me to be a corpse!) Actually he was very pleasant and took charge of the situation, expressing surprise at my apparent stress and reaction. I was helped from the court and carted to the small local hospital. When the doctor turned up and checked me he insisted Simon who was now with me should take me to hospital in Galway City where I spent three days feeling perfectly well, though technically apparently not so!

The second time my heart let me down was in the Sligo Courthouse in a somewhat similar case, when on hearing of my client's success I began to feel I was going to pass out...so I got up and headed for a door at the back of the court. There I spread myself on a table I found in a quiet passage. I was not allowed to make a quiet recovery, however, a lady doctor who happened to be in the court had noticed my escape and my appearance and had followed me out. She very kindly took charge of me, checked my pulse, and an ambulance was called and again I was carted off to hoapital for a few days.

I think I reported that away back in India days I was struck by Menieres Syndrone, a condition which left me with depleted hearing and a balance problem, particularily in the dark. The only time this complaint had caught me out up to the time of which I'm writing- late summer of 79- was when I was returning from Belmullet in west Mayo.

The night closed in after a hard day's work. I had just left Tobercurry with about two thirds of the journey behind me when I began to feel seriously giddy, and for a moment was in a bit of a panic, I pulled up in open country wondering what to do. Finding that I could still drive with concentration, I drove back to Tobercurry and, picking a reasonable looking pub on the outskirts, I got out locked the car.

Balancing with a hand on the wall I entered the bar. There were two men at the bar and a young woman behind it.

I announced that I was not drunk!

But I was rather ill and asked the young woman if she could possibly give me a bed for the night and call a doctor. She gave me a bed and about an hour later a doctor came, heard my story and gave me an injection which put me to sleep. The next morning still feeling groggy I was able to drive myself home.

*

While I was in hospital boatbuilding was going on at Robertstown, and the fishing boat was nearly finished. Father Murphy came to visit me and asked me if I thought Simon would deliver the boat to a fisherman he knew living at a place called Doohoma in west Mayo, a very out of the way place on the coast facing the southern end of the Mullet Peninsula. He also asked particularly if I thought Simon would take him as crew, although he admitted he had never before been to sea in a small boat!

I said 'you had better ask him yourself' and gave him his phone number.

They came to an arrangement that the builders the Downeys would take the boat to Limerick by water, and that Simon and Murphy would do the sea passage. I was disappointed not to see the boat completed and launched, but news filtered through to the hospital that they had left Limerick and about a week later Fr Murphy came to see me again, very full of himself. He told me about the voyage and its sequel. They had had a very rough trip from the Shannon Estuary to Inis Boffin- about 100 miles- it was actually at the time of the Fastnet race and in part of the same weather. Simon told me afterwards that Murphy was obviously very scared and he did not blame him, it was very rough for so small a boat. But, scared or not, he did relieve him at the helm several times. From Boffin to Doohoma the weather had been much kinder.

The outcome was that Murphy was so impressed with Simon that he offered him the boat if he would share it with his friend. The latter anyhow was not really interested in having the boat, so it became Simon's with some vague and never enforced repayment scheme. Doohoma, where the boat was, was quite a good area for potting for lobster, cray and crab. And so Simon and Breda and baby Keelin -augmented while there by the arrival of baby Lorna- moved into a rather miserable damp little cottage there. I think they were there for about a year before moving boat and home to Letterfrack in Connemara, to a much more modern cottage which Simon and the girls still occupy.

AT THE END OF the 1983 sailing season in DunLaoghaire I decided it was time to give up racing as being rather beyond my means and physical strength and that we could have more pleasure from the boat if she were near Simon at Ballanakill in Connemara. There he could keep an eye on her on a mooring, and it was a lovely day cruising area.

I would sail Brainstorm around to the West.

Planning to go Northabout and to leave DunLaoghaire early on a Saturday, the 28th August, I spent all day Friday readying my little ship and stocking up with food. My crew on the trip as far as Lame were to be James and Luke and Brendan, all of whom had been with me before. After Larne there was a bit of a query about crew, but I hoped to pick up someone prepared to do at least part of the other two thirds of the passage.

We got away by 0900 as planned, picked up Brendan as planned, and headed for Kilkeel, our first stop. There was a good offshore breeze and rain which had become a deluge, and the early night was very dark until we were under the sodium lights of the port. We attempted to enter at dead low water only to run aground just short of the outer pier steps, the pier itself towering above us.

Fortunately the tide was on the turn and the engine was soon able to push us through the mud to let James jump ashore. His role was to locate a Mr Collins, a solicitor, owner of one of my Kerries in which he had recently completed a cruise to Spain with his son Kevin.

I had asked him to expect us and to advise us of the best berth in this crowded port, very much a fishing port. James was soon back with Mr Collins who helped us berth alongside a big trawler which was aground in the inner harbour. He then invited us all up to his house where his wife most kindly gave us a splendid meal.

We had a quiet night aboard as being a saturday night none of the trawlers were moving but it wasn't until about 10.30 that we floated again after nearly falling half under the very big boat we were alongside. We motored out of the harbour which must have one of the biggest tidal range of any Irish port, it happens to be at about the area where the flood and ebb coming round Ireland meet and seperate.

We had a moderate offshore breeze up to St John's point, the Mourne Mountains partly covered in cloud sending us rain all the way to Portavogie. We had planned to go ashore there for an evening meal. Portavogie is another busy fishing port but, unknown to us did not have any town associated with it. We moored up in a vacant berth and all went ashore in search of food, reckoning that we would have time to have a meal before Brainstorm went aground and trapped us for the night. We found no sign of an eating place and when we enquired at a small shop we were told in a strong Northern accent that there were none.

And there were certainly no pubs!

We were to learn later that this place was known as being very strongly Presbyterian. There was not a pub within three miles of the port, an extraordinary situation in Ireland or anywhere else! We went back aboard and in our rather cramped quarters cooked up a giant fry, while I kept an eye on the echo sounder. We got away with very little time to spare for a night sail to Larne. For a time we used the little B.M.W. diesel as there was little or no wind but soon shut it down as sleep was hardly possible with it running. It was a most beautiful star filled night which I sat right through, as a pleasant light northerly breeze set in...I really enjoyed night sailing under those conditions.

During the night we tacked west round Mew Island after passing inside Copland and stood on into Belfast Lough until we could make Black Head on the port tack. We were tacking slowly up Island Magee shore as dawn began to break. It came up in a wonderful band of colour like a horizontal rainbow in the mist over Scotland, the sun just peeping over it as we turned into Larne.

We berthed alongside a big yacht-converted-trawler in deep water and after breakfast my three crewmen departed with regret to seek public transport back to Dublin and their work, leaving me somewhat disconsolate without a crew. I went ashore to ring Mr Collins to ask him if his son Kevin, a pleasant young man still at college, would be interested. Luckily he was, and he turned up the next afternoon. While sitting in the cockpit the first afternoon I noticed among other moored yachts one with a profile which seemed very familiar, and getting my glasses on her confirmed that she was one of my eighteen Slipway Five Tonners (already about 40 years old).

I did a bit of shopping and exploring that evening and the following morning. Then, while waiting for Kevin, sitting in the sun I noticed a man rowing a dinghy out towards the 'Slipway'. Sure enough he went alongside, climbed aboard and went below, and then I heard the engine start. When he came on deck I started shouting and trying to attract his intention. He was obviously dropping his moorings, so I started Brainstorm's engine and frantically cast of and started in pursuit, trying to attract his attention without success. He had more power than I had and was leaving me behind! Diasppointed I returned to my berth and soon afterwards Kevin arrived. We went ashore for an evening meal and after a good night made a fairly leisurely start on a beautiful morning, a light southerly wind.

As soon as we were clear of the harbour, with Kevin steering, I set our big masthead spinnaker and this hauled us up this very beautiful coast, headland after headland, past the vales of Antrim at a steady 5 knots all the way to Torr Head with the Mull of Kintyre clearly visible to the north east. At Torr we changed the spinnaker for the genoa, and then hardened into make Rue point on Rathlin Island, a crossing with only a suspicion of what it could be like in stormy weather. We shortened sail to mainsail and rounded up head to wind alongside the short stone pier within Church Bay behind a fishing boat. Before nightfall the weather had deteriorated, the wind going round to the S. W., freshening and bringing rain.

We went ashore and walked up to the pub on this rather bleak island with not much evidence of population. Although it was after 1800 the pub was closed, but we had been seen and after a few minutes the door opened we were welcomed by the publican and after a short time were joined by two islanders.

I believe quite a lot has since been done to improve the lot of the inhabitants, but then the talk in the pub was mostly about hardships and lack of facilities. What interested us most was the story of the British battleship HMS Drake, the remains of which lay in the middle of the bay, now reduced by wind and weather so that she was no longer a hazard to small craft. As I remember it the story was that she was torpedoed north of the island soon after taking on a full load of ammunition, and her captain brought her into the bay and scuttled her. Everything worth salvaging had been taken but the explosives had been left to be taken later (so the story goes) for doubtful purposes!

It blew a gale from the SW in the night, and we on the lee of the low pier were douched with spray all night, the boat fidgeting against her fenders, so we did not have a very good sleep. By morning the wind had moderated somewhat, and as it was offshore the seas were not bad. We were away well reefed down by 0700 and closed the land and stayed with it to Benbane Head and the Giants Causeway. With the sheets eased a bit we made a fast very wet passage across to the Donegal coast, and then with the echo sounder going worked into Culduff Bay and dropped the anchor off a slipway. Here we were in the stream of quite a sizeable river of brown bog water flowing over really golden sand on a beautiful strand. This stream held us nice and steady into the wind, now moderated somewhat although still squally off the land.

We inflated our rather miserable little dinghy, (My good Avon had been stolen from my locker in the gents at the R St GYC) and I rowed ashore to put out a call to Chris. I was met on the slipway by a young woman who turned out to be a Miss O'Rahilly, sister of Michael, The O'Rahilly, who happened to be also the Dentist we used! We had known the whole family when we were much younger and they had the Barge Gilaroo at Jamestown Quay. In charge of a party of geological students here, she kindly helped me carry the dinghy up the slip and then drove me in the rain to Culduff to the phone, and back again.

Culduff Bay was a lovely anchorage with an offshore wind but anchoring there one had to consider what if the wind should shift to the North in the night? Being an open bay with no offshore obstructions I decided that Brainstorm could easily beat out of it going either North or South so we stayed put and had a very good night. The only mishap was that Kevin, going ashore after me in the hope of finding some life in the village to make up for the generation gap between us, dragged the dinghy up the slip and wrecked the "deck". The water level inside it was the same as outside and it was shoes and socks off from then on!

The wind remained off shore and we sailed away in the morning to make for Portsalon, someway into Lough Swilly on the west side.

It was quite an exciting sail through Inishtrahull Sound and round Malin Head, the most northerly point of Ireland. (On a magnificent day recently I stood atop this high headland with its views in every direction. And I imagined Brainstorm rounding it about 15 years before when I was still fit and strong.) As we came round the head we found ourselves in the very close company of one of the big clench built fishing boats so typical of the North Donegal coast. Because we now had got no shelter from the land it was extremely rough and both boats were rearing and plowing dramatically side by side and almost at the same speed, both crews enjoying the view of the other. We soon drifted apart, the fisherman with a big diesel slowly drawing ahead and sailing a course up the Lough while we were crossing it.

We noted several big dorsal fins some quarter mile away, these we decided were almost certainly Killer Whales, an indication of mackeral. It was some time in the early afternoon that we moored up at the outer end of the pier at Portsalon. Checking depth of water and tides I reckoned we would ground at low water but as we had some time in hand we walked up to the big hotel with food on mind.

The hotel was closed for the winter!

Instead we found a small cafe in the village which was able to satisfy our needs. We went for a walk which kindled a wish in me to return some day by land to explore the peninsula. The wind had fallen light and Brainstorm's keel was getting near the bottom...and as I knew what an awkward boat she was to ground alongside a pier (due to her aft keel position) we cast off and sailed quietly up the lough trailing a spinner, conveniently soon landing two fish.

Noting a small creek, under a Martello tower which had been converted to a dwelling, we decided to spend the night there and dropped anchor. We managed to get ashore in our floating bathtub for another lookaround before cooking the fish and turning in. The idea was to make an early start on the morrow and a sail round to Sheephaven and Downings where Kevin might find company more to his liking -not that we didn't get on quite well together, and from my point of view he certainly was very competent.

This trip was the shortest of the voyage, sailed close hauled in a full sail breeze past a number of fishermen and then tacking in to the landward side of the south facing pier at Downings. I again checked depths for our 6ft keel and decided we had to lie at the outermost end of the pier. There we were befriended by a fisherman and his wife who invited us into their house and later presented us with half a bucket of cooked crab claws, most welcome. We also got a weather forecast while at the house which warned of a severe gale from the west backing SW and imminent. This brought three fair sized trawlers in to the pier and we had to moor on the outside of the last one, putting us more or less outside the protection of the pier.

Later I left Kevin in one of the pubs, where there was music and company, and I went back to Brainstorm, anticipating a rough night, and did the best I could with fenders and 'springs'. It was indeed a very rough night, I do not know how Kevin slept through it but he did. I was up almost all night trying to cope with the heavy surge coming in from the Atlantic, the wind and the rain and the movement of my neighbouring trawler, chafing through some of my best warps the while.

The wind eased a bit and went more southerly in the morning which reduced the surge but as the forecast was still bad we decided to stay put. I rang Chris to ask her to see if she could borrow a better inflateable. She got a friend in Westport Mike Roberts to drive up with one which turned out to be too big to stow or even inflate on Brainstorm's deck. He stayed the night with us before driving home with his dinghy and my thanks.

The next day was a Sunday and our neighbouring trawler went out to catch some bait, and we decided to go out to Horn Head and assess conditions for going on, with the idea of making for the lifeboat station on the inside of Aran Island.

There was still a lot of wind, I reckoned it to be nearer force 7 than 5. We put two reefs in the mainsail and set no 2 jib and set off passing our trawler fishing in the lee of the headland. I think they were surprised to see us heading out. We did not meet or even see another vessel all the way to Aran. As soon as we cleared the Horn (on the top of which Chris, I and the boys had camped some years previously) we met the full force of the wind and a rough sea on top of a really big Atlantic swell with moderate breakers atop.

We hardened in both sails and pointed Brainstorm into it on a WEW direction to take us between Tory Island and Inis Beg and without saying anything just kept going. With her long fine entry the boat seemed to love it and it was thrilling sailing, although extremely wet. We went down the valleys and then up the blue green hills, crashing through the breaker on top, sluishing down the deck and dousing us with heavy spray.

It was so exciting that we were both shouting encouragement as we soared up each wave and Kevin was humming to himself. The boat was logging nearly five knots. We never thought of turning back although the weather was not improving and it was beginning to rain heavily, reducing visibility from time to time. Passing south of Tory we stood on out into the open Atlantic, leaving the Bloody Foreland far to the south east until we thought we could weather the small island of Owey on the starboard tack.

The next hour was the toughest I remember on Brainstorm or on any other boat. The wind was increasing and the rain becoming a horizontal deluge, landmarks being blotted out in the squalls which rattled on our oilskins like buckshot. We huddled high on weather deck with the boat over on her ear and as we neared the land, islands and danger again, with huge breakers to leeward, I admit fear was not absent from my thoughts.

I knew the entrance to Bunbeg was somewhere to leeward but didn't know the passage and to consult the chart would have been impossible. I could see that we were not going to weather Owey and would have to put in two more tacks before we could hope for some shelter from Aran. My two fears were gear failure and that Brainstorm would not come about in the very severe conditions of wind and sea. (Gear failure, mainsail splitting and so forth in these conditions are a sort of nightmare.) There came a time when I had to find out if she would go about, or we would sail into unknown waters and probable disaster. She did go about first time I put the helm down, to my relief and gratification.

(Previous page) Brainstorm racing, Dun Laoghaire 1981
(inset) Brainstorm in final trim

(This page) (above) Kerry at Earlscourt. (below) Kerry 'Margaret', Brien and Christine Kennedy with Matt Kennedy

(Facing page) Junior Shannon design

JS

(Top) Christine Kennedy
(Left) Grandchildren, Keelin & Lorna Kennedy
(Below) 'Serena' 1991

We sailed clear of danger and tacked south again. I remember that it seemed to take a painful long time to get any benefit from the island, not until we were nearly into the mooring where the lifeboat lay. It was good to go below where it was surprisingly dry and warm, to get out of our wet gear and clothes, light a cooker burner or two for heat and then make some Bovril as a starter and cook up a good fry.

After that I just wanted to relax but Kevin wanted to go ashore, the rubber dinghy being almost useless he was lucky enough to get a lift from a fisherman. (We did carry an inflateable life raft in a valise but this was strictly for dire emergency only). It was an hour or two later and after dark when I heard him calling from the small pier to come and pick him up. I'm afraid I had no intention of doing this alone, not knowing the depth of water, and shouted the suggestion that if he could not get a boat or a lift that he found a bed ashore. He did manage to borrow a dinghy for the night but by the time he returned he found me asleep in my bunk. In the morning Kevin told me that some of the locals had been watching us coming across, were impressed and said we "came in like a bullet". I was certainly well pleased with the boat's performance and that all her gear stood up to a test which I was never likely to repeat.

By morning the weather was much improved as had the forecast so we decided to press on to Killybegs where Kevin was to leave me and make for home. The wind was WEW about force five when we weighed anchor, and under full plain sail we set off south inside Aran, passing the entrance to Burtonport, another very active fishing port. We made good speed helped by the ebb tide. (Some years earlier we had brought a good dinghy on a trailer to this area and explored the tricky waters between the port and Island). Leaving Inishfree Island to starboard and Roanish to port, we went on down the exceedingly rugged and mountainous coast to Mainmore Head. Then close hauled in very pleasant weather we passed inside Rathlin O'Byrne Isle. Here, due to some wind-tide conditions a very big steep swell was running and we met a big trawler north bound, lifting nearly half her length out on the crests, we just went up and down as in a lift.

From there to Killybegs was just a very comfortable broad reach passing close under the very impressive and remarkably coloured Slieve League cliffs. We were in sunshine, of which we had seen very little since our sail to Rathlin. The natural harbour of Killybegs, where the inner end is competely sheltered, is probably the most important fishing port in Ireland and certainly harbours the biggest vessels.

We moored up to a trawler which seemed to be out of service on a west side pier. I phoned Chris as arranged and asked her to motor over the next day to collect Kevin. The weather forecast that night was pretty grim so I decided I would go home for a few days rest and try to find another crew to finish the trip with me and to wait for better weather.

Chris duly arrived the next afternoon and we all went home, Kevin spending the night on our barge. We sent him on his way the next morning with my thank for his help and company. By phone I got onto Stephen, a friend of my friend James Cahill, solicitor, seaman, amateur boatbuilder with a double Atlantic crossing under his belt. Stephen was a ship's radio operator on a tanker and owned a Dragon class yacht converted for limited cruising, he lived at Rosmoney near Westport and being on leave agreed to join me if he could bring his girlfriend Kaya and another young man. It was agreed that I would contact them when weather outlook was better. My old friend Donal Conlon drove me back to Killybegs, helped me with a few minor jobs and went home. Brainstorm was now very foul with weed and I wanted to scrub her but there was nowhere suitable for drying out a small boat in the port. I thought I would sail her single handed to the tidal yacht harbour of Mullaghmore north of Sligo. This would also much reduce the distance the others would have to drive. There was still a lot of wind the next morning, but I sailed out to see what conditions were like outside and the true direction of the wind relative to entering Mullaghmore. As I cleared the entrance I met the full force of a west wind, and in rough sea I found myself in amongst a great quantity of wreckage and fish boxes. I learned later that a trawler had somhow missed the entrance in the night and was totally wrecked, no loss of life. It was pretty evident that I would have a very tough crossing and that Mullaghmore would be a very uncomfortable if not a dangerous place - later confirmed by friends Lomax living there- so I went back to my berth. Towards evening the weather improved and the forecast for the morrow was light to moderate easterly which would be ideal so I rang Stephen and they came tumbling aboard about one am, complete with a good inflateable dinghy, sleeping bags and sailing gear.

I gave them something to eat after their long night drive and we all bunked down until about 0800. Then we quickly got underway, cooking a breakfast as we went, sailing on a broad reach with the big spinnaker set (we carried it for the whole day) for the North Mayo coast on a glorious morning. Keeping up an average speed of about six knots we were close to the coast west of Downpatrick Head by about 1500, and then sailing on a run about a mile off the rugged coast inside the spectacular Stags of Broadhaven. Nearby the small fishing ports of Belderg and Portacloy, at both of which Chris and I and the boys plus dogs and canoes had camped in the past, a wonderful coast for cliff walking. Then it was down spinnaker to round Benwee Head and Kid Island at dusk to anchor off a small concrete pier, a little too exposed to the Easterly wind to offer a safe and comfortable berth. We were below a tiny village marked Stone Field on the road map and after a good meal the three young people went ashore in the dinghy and walked up to this place in the dark looking for the pub. But there was none so they returned and we drank what we had aboard and turned in for a quiet night.

We were now nearly into October but it dawned another brilliant morning, still with the light easterly. I was keen to explore the unmarked entrance to what was called Ross port, with a very long shallow inlet beyond it, hoping to add a small item to the Irish Cruising Club's journal (Pilot). After a leisurely breakfast we started the engine and weighed anchor, Stephen went aloft and sat on the crosstrees to act as pilot as we headed for the bar, it being nearly low water but conveniently rising. A low surf was breaking on it, indicating where the channel might be and as the water was beautifully clear Stephen had no difficulty in guiding us through into the deeper water beyond. I made some notes and took some bearings to forward to the ICC. The tide was too low to allow us to go any further so we turned about, set full mainsail and the big spinnaker and sped away in the sunshine for Erris Head the 'topknot' of Belmullet Island.

Then it was down spinnaker and a close reach under genoa through Eagle Island sound with its famous lighthouse and whitewashed buildings bright in the sunlight - all uninhabited now I suppose - on past Annagh Point and inside Inis Glora rocks where we only avoided running on its Eastern inshore tail by making a violent tack to port when I spotted a swirl in the water just ahead of us. In rougher conditions we would all have seen it sooner. I had set my heart on landing on the Iniskeas if weather permitted and it was ideal so we sailed into the crescent bay of lovely silver sand. We dropped anchor about 30 yards off, inflated the little 2-3 man dinghy and all four piled in leaving a few inches of freeboard!

We explored the island and its ruined village, walking up the gently sloping grassy field behind it, which had a spring at the top and a little trickle down a ditch where grew the highest vegetation, some reeds which would have produced the yellow flags (Irisis in the summer). This was as far as we could see the only source of fresh water. There was a windbreaker wall of loose stones at the top of the field and beyond that a wilderness of stones and boulders thrown up by thousands of years of winter storms.

Iniskea must have been one of the most storm exposed habitats in the world, being very low and really without any natural shelter, yet at one time in the beginning of this century when it was a whaling station around

50 to 70 people lived there, though probably for only part of the year. (This whaling was essentially run from Norway, a country which still cannot stop killing these wonderful beasts of the sea.)

The whaling station itself, I read, was entirely timber built. There was a pier for the small steam whalers to berth alongside the slipway and a large timber building for melting down and storing the oil and baleen, other bones and so forth. We could find nothing of all this except rusty remains of boilers and steam engines, winches half sunk in the rough grass.

On this beautiful late summer's day we all felt there was something of magic about the island. A well known breeding ground for seals and stopover for migrating geese, whooper swans and other birds, it has quite a good little harbour on its SE side and a sort of tidal marine bench which must have been where the islanders kept their Currachs. These would have been the fishing boats and ferries to the mainland. I have visited the island since this time and learned that it is owned by a consortium of people including a young friend of my sons who has assured me that it will never be 'developed'.

I hope that remains true.

We spent too long on this little summer paradise and the evening was beginning to draw in when we re-embarked to set sail to round Achill Head. I watched the island growing higher and higher as we approached, it rises up to two thousand feet straight out of the sea, and I remembered how a year or two earlier Chris I and the boys had stood atop this mighty cliff and watched the seabirds sailing about far below.

I had only a fairly small scale chart of this area on board and as it seemed clear, and as we wanted to try to make Clare Island before full night, I sailed through the sound between Carrickalin Island and The Head. The chart indicated with a cross something called Priest Rock to the west side of the channel, so we kept east and were swept through by a fierce south going tide, passing rather too close to an eddy which must have indicated the rock. We now had a headwind and as night slowly fell we beat eastward passing north of Clare Island, then sailing west again to anchor off under Grania's Castle in almost total darkness. (The story of Grania herself is one of a very tough queen and pirate in her day.)

Although it was almost midnight by the time we had had something to eat my young friends decided to go ashore and find their way to the pub which, well known to all of them, was not too worried about closing times!

I wriggled into my sleeping bag and cave bunk- guaranteed to contain me in the roughest conditions. Then, after a good night I went ashore early in the morning for a breezy and somewhat wet walk on this interesting Island. Back aboard for breakfast and then an exhilarating wet sail hard on the wind to Rossmoney. We went to Stephen's home for a dryout after a trip enjoyed by all. Then it was a drive to Westport and the train to Claremorris where Chris met me.

And so to home.

*

After bringing Brainstorm round from DunLaoghaire to Westport-Rosmoney, I left her for a week or two on her anchor off the yacht club. Not a good idea, she dragged it and did a little damage to herself and another yacht.

Nancy and her husband Reggie Cooke visited us and we drove them down first to Rosmoney and went on board Brainstorm and then on down to Letterfrack, when the clouds simply burst in torrential rain. This turned the mountain streams we passed to foaming rivers in places depositing rocks on the road and in one place it was so flooded that it stopped the car and we had to roll up our trousers and, shoeless, push the car out.

After the Cookes had gone home I sailed single handed from Clew Bay to Ballinakill in moderate weather with quite a lot of sea mist. This closed me in from time to time, putting me on compass to avoid the several islands on the passage. Arriving off Ballinakill, which I did not know at that time and so nearly turned into a no go area before getting the correct bearing and sailing up the bay for Derryinver, I ran on a sandbank but as the tide was fortunately rising I was soon off.

Simon saw me coming and had the mooring ready for me and ferried me ashore. I managed to scrub the boat there against a quay, and shortly after that Simon and I sailed her to Roundstone with a good favourable wind, round the rather awe inspiring Slyne Head with its great offlying reefs, a heavy swell breaking on them and later on the many rocks on this particular passage well indicated by the white surf of breaking seas.

We left Brainstorm well moored and Breda came for us with the car. A few days later Mike Roberts an old friend living near Westport joined me at Roundstone and in two hops in beautiful weather- although almost windless on the second day - we sailed to Galway docks, where I had left her road trailer, and had her lifted out.

The following summer she was back in Connemara and Chris and I alone and with other people had some lovely day and overnight sailing off this beautiful coast for two or three summers, wintering her afloat and also hauled out at O'Connells Boatyard and delightful tidal lagoon.

We also had a few races locally and inside Boffin. One of these was nearly her last! By this time she was no longer mine but belonged to a partnership of two women, neither very experienced with this type of yacht. So when it came to racing her back from Boffin to Clifden they asked me to sail her. I agreed, provided I could have Simon in the crew. The crew thus was the two owners plus another fairly elderly lady, and Simon and me.

We led away from the start in good clear weather and I sailed a course which turned out to have been a mistake sailing - it was a beat all the way-up the open water in the middle of the outer Clifden bay. The other four or five boats followed the local man O'Connor who sailed close to the islands on the north side of the bay. Quite suddenly the wind started to harden, it began to rain a heavy misty rain which closed in until visibility was down to fifteen yards. As we were tacking and approaching the middle ground and planning to pass it to port, I put Simon up in the bow to watch out for danger, and he hadn't been there for more than fifteen minutes when on the Starboard tack he suddenly shouted 'go about' which we promptly did. I had seen nothing but Simon came aft and told me I had almost sailed onto the rocks.

Now not being sure where we were in relation to the middle ground we sailed clear and short tacked until in improving visibility we picked up one of the islands familiar to the women and were soon off the yacht club but last boat in and causing some concern.

Brainstorm remained in that area, either off Derryinver pier or in Clifden Bay off O'Connor's yard, or wintering in his little tidal cove until I sold her to help finance my house building. In the meantime we had a lot of pleasure with her, cruising the Clifden, Boffin, Turk area with occasional not very serious racing.

I also spent many nights aboard, always with the pleasure of waking afloat in my own little ship. Selling her was a hell of a wrench, especially when I saw her being altered in a most ignorant way!

But then a following owner walked into the house in October of 1996 and told me he now had her in Wicklow and was partly rebuilding her.

I had thought of her as being a sad wreck in some boat graveyard, after all she is 25 years old and was cheaply built - as she had to be.

I was delighted.

*

In the winter of 80-81 we had to put down a dog we will always remember, 'Bungi', a brindled Stafford bull terrier bitch. There was never a more intelligent or sweet natured dog of the many we had. She was quite an old dog when she had some sort of heart attack and for two days we suffered for her, she was obviously in great pain, would not eat but never made a sound. So Chris, who could well have been a vet, went to our doctor who was also a personal friend and got a syringe and a lethal dose from him, and with Bunji on my lap she administered the merciful dose.

I sat quietly in the arm chair. She died peacefully, after about twenty minutes the little movements of her nostrils indicating breathing slowly stopped and I said to Chris she is off to meet St Francis, we were both crying, and I have to hold back my tears now!

She was the dog of our prime and a constant companion.

I had one of these dogs I called Sammy when I was still a teenager, we were the greatest pals, he was killed on the road when I was in England 'serving my time'. I did not have another dog of my own until after the war. I was living on a boat at Lymington and bought a Stafford puppy. She became Sally, another well-loved dog.

*

DESIGNING THE house, after so many boats! I had intended to build something 'different' and 'original'. I am sure now that this would have been awful and luckily, through Christine's intervention, I came up with a simple cottage-style house. Getting planning permission was another question entirely, my land being between a river and a road and strictly speaking in planning terms, an unacceptable site for a house, although, in fact, the boundary was well back from the river.

I turned up at the planning office in Roscommon with basic outline drawings which I had prepared for my own guidance in estimating quantities and so forth. The planning officer I saw was an elderly man like myself and we started off chatting about things in general.

I mentioned my son in Letterfrack and then showed him a photo I had taken of my little fairhaired granddaughter Keelin. This showed her sitting in the heather with Simon's little home in the background and the mountain called the Diamond in the distance. That really set us off and in no time we were walking, climbing and fly fishing in the west. For a time we quite forgot who and where we were!

After about half an hour he picked up my drawing, looked at it's obviously amateur nature and said "I think it will be all right Mr Kennedy, but keep it well back towards the road. And make the roof tiles and the wall colour blend with the surroundings".

I said I certainly would, and so it is, well back towards the road, with colours blending!

We shook hands and I brought the good news home to Christine on St Brigid.

Planning was one thing, but finance was quite another!

The local priest had himself built two houses near me on spec and his advice was 'start it and you'll find the money'. Whether this was the promise of divine intervention I've no idea, but I did start, and I did find the money.

Workwise I was actually frantically busy in 1982. I was working as a surveyor for Bórd Fáilte both on the Shannon and on the coast, also for the Northern Ireland Tourist Board on Lough Erne, and for independent sea fishermen when they were having new boats built, particularly at Hickeys of Galway. On top of all this I was also that year much involved with C.N.D.

The work brought in quite a lot of money which, apart from living expenses, went straight into the house. My sons Finn and Tyl gave me £5000 -£6000 between them and this allowed me to purchase just about all the structural timber I required, plus pay for the foundations and really get started. The middle bit of construction financed by my work and to finish the house I had to sell my boat!

The total cost in 1984 was approximately £17000 at move in time. In building the house I had the manual help of Mick. As well as helping me he helped Chris a great deal making and mending fences, building a little shed as a loose box for the horses and a store for hay. Chris and my four sons helped at different times when they could. I was lucky in that I had my big boat shed which I was able to clear out enough to allow me to prefabricate all the inner and outer plywood wall structures, Tyl was with me when we started the roof which was a crazy and dangerous operation trying to assemble the loose rafters and hold the ridge piece up at the same time. Chris and Shane helped me with the battening and felting and I got two professionals to do the tiling and we had a roof! Our methods and equipment would have made a proper builder laugh his head off ...or cry!

*

Life went on.

That year I visited the UK several times to see my families at Glynde and Lewes in Sussex. My son Finn and his wife Anne were building up their most successful Clothkits business which at its peak was employing nearly 250 people. My other son Tyl's own business was also doing well, exporting spiral staircases worldwide.

I did some commercial fishing with Simon in Julia, the boat he got from Fr Murphy.

And I visited Clare Island off Clew Bay in County Mayo to inspect a diving or sea angling boat there. It was high season and there were a lot of people coming off the Island on the return journey, far more than the twelve the boat was supposed to carry. In addition there were empty gas bottles and beer crates. The helmsman knew his job, just as well, it being pretty rough in the channel. He was luffing up to all the bigger waves but nonetheless we were all getting doused with heavy spray and while the passengers thought it was great fun I felt the situation was dangerous. Although a good boat, it was overloaded. I had seen this sort of thing and worse previously on ferries and I took up the matter with the board. The situation on these tourist ferries is different now... but probably not so profitable!

*

My overdraft in 1982 was £2700!

I wonder how I was allowed even that, I didn't play golf with my manager or anything! But still I managed to buy a little DAF car for £100! This had been lying in the village, in a side damaged condition but otherwise good and with a low mileage. I had it straightened up and resprayed and for several years drove it with pleasure, except when overtaking a long vehicle with a blind bend to the left coming up, then its two little lungs seem a little inadequate!

When finally something big went in the engine I bought two more DAF's cheap and cannibalised them. The parts kept me going for another while. Chris favoured her own brands of jaloppies, Hillmans and Vauxhalls which I was forever patching with fibreglass. No wonder the Japanese took over!

*

On April the 6th my very dear sister Nancy died of cancer in Wallingford hospital in Oxfordshire. Her death followed a long painful illness at her home, during which my daughter Tanya lived with her and her husband Reggie. Then death came so suddenly that I failed to be with her at the end.

*

At the end of the year I heard of a cheap two week tour in the then USSR. Organised by the Huddersfield Trades Council and run by an elderly couple of communists it cost £250 all in. I made a booking for two!

Chris was not very enthusiastic, and not very fit at the time, and she said if I could get someone else in the area to go she would drop out. Brought up a Socialist by her accountant father, she was somewhat anti my communist leanings principally because she did not agree with my then belief that human nature can be changed by environment.

Current evidence suggests she may have been right!

I do however feel as an idealist that some day if the world can solve its population problem and distribution of wealth satisfactorily it will change for the better.

So, for the USSR trip it was agreed that Joan Maidment, a friend and fellow CND member, and I should travel together. We would share bedrooms but not beds!

*

The journey to and from Russia was to be partly by coach and partly by train.

The first part of the journey was by coach and we were to join it at Euston in London. The prelude to this was a drive from Ireland in the little DAF I had at the time, crossing to Holyhead, followed by the long drive to London via Snowdonia, snowy at the time and very beautiful.

We had a night and a day with one of Joan's married daughters at Greenwich. (While there I took the opportunity of visiting Greenwich Museum and Observatory.)

We duly climbed aboard the coach at Euston and took our seats, the co-travellers being a very mixed 35 of all ages, which included a very nice Burmese couple and their two most well behaved and attractive kids. We were greeted by the very pleasant elderly couple acting as tour guides. We also had two drivers aboard as it was virtually to be a non stop- except for snacks at some border posts- to Budapest once we had crossed the channel. We were timed to drive almost straight onto the ship, there being little or no coach traffic in late December.

The coach was a big Volvo with fixed seats which were not particularly comfortable, and the heating was not good, being either too hot or not hot enough. We off loaded at Calais and then set off on the thirty hour drive accross Europe.

The route took us right through the battlefields of the First World War, towns with very familiar names in France and south Belgium, familiar to me as a schoolboy in England in 1922. (The school library had all the bound copies of the London Illustrated News of the war period, all war propaganda and totally biased!)

Then we had a long run into night across Germany and Austria. My memory of that night is pretty grim. The country was snow covered and much forested, and no doubt teeming with wolves but our gallant drivers kept up what seemed a very high speed in the conditions.

I was still a little under par with my heart and I passed out briefly twice that night, I think because the coach was too hot and badly ventilated.

We passed right through Vienna that morning without stopping, only getting a glimpse of the not so blue Danube, and then through the Austro-

Czech border where there was a nice cafe. We has a good breakfast and were impressed by the very smart and efficient Czech border guards. A short run through Czechoslovakia and across another border into Hungary, and by later afternoon we crossed the Danube again in Budapest. Here we said good bye to our drivers and coach for two weeks.

Having a couple of hours to wait for the Moscow train the party broke up to do some sightseeing. Joan and I decided to try the local food and went into some sort of restaurant which turned out to be very much a proletarian eating place. The food was disappointing but cheap, it obviously did not normally cater for tourists, in fact it was rather typical of conditions in the country at that time, poor.

We were then rounded up by our guides and walked up to the big central station, collected our luggage from where our drivers had left it and proceeded to board - climb up into this by Irish standards huge broad gauge train which seemed endless. We were allocated compartments, four persons to each very roomy one. Joan and I were together and there were two other young women with us - there were more women than men in the party. There was no food to be had on the train at that point but when it eventully got started - on time - we found that there was a samovar at the end of every corridor for tea making and also the equivalent of tea ladies who I seem to remember also acted as sort of hostesses doling out bedding, all very clean and showing us how to make the upper berths.

This was our first real opportunity for meeting the other members of the party, which occupied nearly the whole of our carriage and so we socialised in the corridor, and began to enjoy ourselves on this long journey through part of Hungary and then right across the Ukraine through Kiev and southern Russia, cutting through the Carpathian mountains, which we must have done both ways at night because I can only remember the Steppes and pretty flat country. The journey involved two nights and a whole and a half day. All meals were taken in the restaurant with the Soviet Citizens, and with the help of our guide in selecting food, (they were both pretty good Russian speakers). And although the food was somewhat strange it seemed to nourish us alright!

Perhaps the most interesting part of the journey was crossing the Hungary Ukraine border in the small hours of the morning. The train pulled up and lightly armed Russian customs and security men boarded the train. They politely but firmly turned us out of our berths, compartment by compartment, examined our documents and went through our luggage, while we stood around in our night clothes finding it all very funny! I with my three women seemed to amuse the men, but our passports did show they were not my wives!

While this was going on and without us being physically aware of it, the whole train, which has been running on what was called narrow guage track, was lifted off its bogies bodily moved sideways over its whole length, and placed on a set of broad guage wheels. The whole business seemed to take well under an hour, and we were again rumbling through the night over a dark landscape with only the very odd feeble light to be seen from the window of my upper berth.

I got up early to get in first with the toilet and out of the way while the women dressed, standing in the corridor watching the flatlands go by, gradually becoming more snow covered and thinking that I was again looking upon part of another and even vaster battlefield, the one of which the Russians refer to as "The Great Patriotic War".

We pulled up for a short stop at Kiev but saw little from the train, a huge city, it was the third city of the USSR at that time and now the capital of the independent Ukraine. The second night was undisturbed. The track as far as I can remember was electrified overhead the whole way and we were being hauled by two huge electric locomotives which I think had crew accommodation.

Arrivals are always exciting, and coming into Moscow it was a very prolonged arrival. First we passed through a snow covered land of dachas in silver spruce woods, then suburbs gradually becoming denser and denser, those well recorded ugly concrete multi-storey blocks of flats (a lot of them built by German prisoners of war), and finally then the city proper and the huge covered stations swarming with warmly clad humanity.

The train had been well heated and we were surprised to find as we clambered onto the platform that the weather was not as cold as we had expected, in fact what little snow there was was melting. A coach took us a few miles to a big multi-storey hotel in plan built in a crescent. We were travelling and touring quite independent of the "In Tourist" organisation and this hotel was one used by the ordinary travelling public, I think in co-operation with trade unions. At that time trade unions seemed to have a hand in most things, particularly in the matter of the allocation of tickets for all such entertainment as Ballet, Opera, Theatres and the Circus. As far as I can recall we had two days to do as we pleased. Joan and I used the truly beautiful and famous Moscow Metro, which was immaculately clean and the trains ran like clockwork on timed schedule, five kopeks to anywhere.

I had the misfortune to have my little Rolli camera jam up when attempting photography from the train, and failed to find any place where it could be put right, so I bought a Russian-made camera in one of the shops that took foreign money. Much to my surprise they were perfectly prepared to take my bank card without any delay after a brief phone call. Unfortunately the instructions with the camera were only in Russian and I missed a vital piece of information which meant that the lens was normally wide open! The result being that on the four rolls that I took on the trip all were totally over exposed except those taken indoors, principally at the circus to which we went on the second night.

I went alone for several runs on the Metro exploring the fantastically decorated marble halls called stations. I was very pleasantly surprised at the behaviour of the passengers, there was little pushing and shoving, they were all well and sensibly dressed. I was getting a bit lost by the odd way stations names were indicated, and if the person I asked could not understand English he or she called for some in the carriage who could! (That made me feel my age). I also found the impressively dressed police, in their long grey coats and furry hats in blue grey, as helpful as limited conversation would allow.

I was still under doctors orders to the extent that I was to take a walk before retiring every night. This I did sometimes close to midnight in Moscow, Tashkent, and Samarkand - near the Afghan border. And although I do not recall seeing any police on the streets at that hour I felt perfectly safe, was never molested or approached by anyone and the only beggar we saw on the whole of the trip was a somewhat demented poor fellow outside one of the big churches turned museum.

Full employment which existed at that time was no doubt thoroughly inefficient by Western standards where profit is the criterion for all activities - even sport to-day. Nonetheless there was a certain stability and security and it is therefore not surprising that the oldies at least are still voting Communist to this day.

So far as Market economy went at that time it existed only in the matter of garden products, there were huge market places in both Tashkent and Samarkand, selling every conceivable kind of vegetable, fruit, breads of all sorts and cooked food. I took many shots there of beautiful old and young people and their produce.

And they were all hopelessly over exposed!

Getting back to the hotel, our party was sorting itself out and I personally became very friendly with a London practising or semi retired architect and his wife. He was about my age and of course in the same sort of trade and we shared the same silly sense of humour and had some hilarious meal time laughing sessions in the huge dining room, I am sure some of the Russians, and the (buxom) waitresses must have thought us slightly mad!

We would have liked to have seen something of the Bolshoi Ballet but, no tickets being available, we went to the famous circus, in a permanent building built to look like a big Big Top. The performers were very good but for my liking there were too many performing animals which I hate. Our itinerary included a train journey down to Tashkent which is one of the most southern major cities of the then Soviet Union, a day or two there and then by coach to the romantic sounding city of Samarkand which was on the ancient silk route from China to Europe and also the invasion route of Genghis Khan and his mongol hordes.

We were due to leave on the third morning, but got a message on the night before that due to some trouble on the track we had been booked to fly down at no extra expense. It is my belief now, that trains were being used as troopers or were carrying military supplies for the war that Russia was involved in Afghanistan.

So in the late morning we were coached to one of the non international airports on the south side of Moscow and with the minimum of formality were airborne. It was a big quite comfortable fully loaded plane with propellers. I don't know how long we were in the air, but looking at the map I have before me as I write, it must be more than twice as far as Budapest-Moscow, so if we had gone both ways by train most of our holiday would have been spent on trains. We flew at no great height over terrain which became more and more just a desert, with no apparent habitation or roads, arriving at Tashkent after dark, where some military activity was apparent. We were then driven to our hotel, in several cars. (As it happened I had been at Tashkent airport about eighteen years previously when returning with my family to England from Delhi via Tashkent, Baku, Moscow and Paris).

The hotel was of a similar standard to that in Moscow, externally very impressive, but I could not help noticing the poor quality of some of the workmanship, particularly the tiling in the bathroom of our room and the plumbing .

But it did work!

In Tashkent we were very definitely no longer in Europe.

The national dress worn by many men and women was middle eastern in appearance, the city being on the borders of Uzbekistan, Kazakistan and Kirgistan. Not all the people wore national dress, women who did wore headscarfs but under Soviet rule they no longer covered their faces. Men and women alike tended to wear embroidered pillbox hats - one of which I brought home. The women wore long loose dresses, sometimes of silk and of many colours, the men loose baggy trousers and embroidered waistcoats. This form of dress was universal in the markets I have mentioned. In the city itself dress was more generally western and many of the people were obviously Russian. The city was very modern and possessed many really beautiful buildings, and also an underground rail system which gave little or nothing to Moscow. But then it was a new city, new even since I was last there because of the calamitous earthquake which had occurred in the meantime. There was still evidence in a preserved section of the old city where the dwellings were mostly mud huts that casualties were not so heavy. From an architect's point of view the bigger buildings - there were no skyscrapers - were designed, hopefully to withstand earthquakes, some of the buildings we noted had external steel structure. We were told that a lot of research was being done to minimise earthquake damage but as we know now most of the older towns with old buildings are very vulnerable. We toured the City for a day visiting places of interest, particularly I remember the beautiful new library and the spaciousness with which the city was laid out.

Tashkent is also a city of industry, engineering of every sort, notably that of aircraft, no doubt for strategic reasons. The Tupolov factory is there and it must be a huge establishment as there seem to be Tupolov civilian and military aircraft everywhere. Tupolov was of interest to me because I was at one time involved in the aircraft industry and also because it was a TU 104 that flew us most of the way home from India 18 years previously. These planes which were jet propelled were coming into production very soon after the British Comets started to literally fall out of the sky in bits! The TU 104 on the other hand was a highly successful plane and hundreds were built. Although it is fair to say that at that time things like aircraft were made to do a job and not basically to make a profit for some company shareholders, so I do not know how cost effective they were.

The next day we set off early by coach for Samarkand, a town about 150 miles south and west. It was an interesting run through semi-desert, mountainous country, at first through apparently endless fields growing cotton and then miles and miles of mulberry bushes. Mulberries being the food of the silkworms, silk next to cotton being the most important product of this area. There was evidence of considerable long distance irrigation in the form of concrete flues carried above ground for miles parallel with our road, but these appeared to be going derelict, sections being broken. We had one quite long stop near a lake and in a not very impressive pass, which was on Genghis Khan's route to the west where he met some opposition and (I think!) won a battle. There was a sort of rest house at this place where we were able to get some refreshment but not much solid food. The very large disc of unleavened bread which I had bought just before we started, almost fed the multitude - every one on the coach had a bite!

As we approached Samarkand we began to see the minarets and cupolas shining in the sun. Although it was mid-winter down in the south the sun shone all the time but it was not too hot, in fact the weather was really beautiful, as indeed were these amazing mozaic and gold covered buildings, some of which were being restored. We were also shown what remains of what must have been a huge astral telescope in very early times.

I do not know who was responsible for all the restoration of beautiful buildings throughout the Soviet Union but the Russians seem to have a fine 'Office Of Public Works', or did so at that time.

The town had its modern side and our hotel was pretty new but again the standard of detail workmanship was poor, surprising when seen against the restoration craft work being carried out everywhere. People in this part of the world are all of course Moslem, I am not sure to what extent this was restricted at the time we were there but I cannot recall any outward evidence of its being practised. In Samarkand as in Tashkent we were on several occasions taken to schools and academies of dancing and entertained with national dancing by lovely children and beautiful and beautifully dressed young women.

Somewhere in Tashkent I must have left my name and address because right up to the time of the break up of the Soviet Union I regularly received an illustrated periodical in English with local news of all sorts, I am very sorry now that I did not communicate with the editors.

Samarkand was the end of the trail for us, and since I am trying to write my life story and not a travalogue I had best cut this expedition short by saying that we retraced our steps all the way back to England without a hitch. All in all it was a thoroughly enjoyable and instructive holiday which genuinely left me feeling that all was far from wrong with the Soviet system. As mentioned, we were not with Intourist and were not restricted in any way as to where and what questions we asked. We lived in hotels with ordinary citizens, and while language was of course a problem we had very good interpreters in our two English guides.

I have in fact very little recollection of the return journey. For Joan and I and the architect and his wife it ended when we were dropped off near Gatwick and took a taxi to Joan's daughter's house. I was going south to East Sussex and these other people lived on my route near East Grinstead. We said goodbye to Joan and I drove the others home in the Daf and had a very pleasant lunch with them, most congenial and intelligent friends.

THE RETURN from the Soviet Union took me into 1983. It turned out to be a year of little consequence. I was involved with much CND activity that year. I don't know that the movement had much influence anywhere but it certainly had nuisance value and, I suppose, helped keep democracy alive through very critical times.

My 'Irish' sons carried on developing their own lives. At the end of January Shane was sent by his firm to do a stint at their Seattle plant. He had his Garda girlfriend Frances over to stay with him and with a motorcycle they got around, even down the west coast of the US to California. While in the meantime on the west coast of Ireland Simon tried his hand at mussel farming . I don't think this was ever in his line and I think he lost more money than he ever made. Some coastal people have done well from this but it does not suit the genuine fisherman's temperment. One fisherman I asked about taking up the trade said "what, sit and watch the -%$£^% things growing? No %^&$* fear!" (In actual fact there is not much sitting about but a lot of real hard physical work which I suppose some people don't like either!)

(Shane and Garda Frances were quietly married the following year by the PP of Wicklow Town, a friend of ours, only one of her sisters and Simon were present.)

The house building was going ahead in every spare minute. I was still earning quite good money, if at considerable expenditure of energy, shuttling about Ireland's coastal and inland waters. The work involved the surveying of boats, though I had one job out of the ordinary from Bord Failte. They asked me on behalf of the Howth Yacht Club to meet the club boatman whom I knew quite well and between us make a chart of our suggestion for the positioning of the Marina approach channel markers. I had a very nice letter from the club's Commodore of the day thanking me for my work, though I never heard if my suggestions were implemented.

I never heard any more from the Bord itself, not unusual. I never did get any reply to any of my suggestions!

*

Brainstorm was at Derryinver and we had some day sailing. I particularly remember a pleasant and happy little cruise Chris and I had in good weather to Inis Boffin for one night. And then round Inis Turk and back to Little Killary for the second. We cruised back through the island rocks off the Renvyle Hotel in misty conditions. But I guided the boat and a worried Christine safely back to our mooring off Derryinver pier. On September 30 of that year, with a crew of John Pearson and Olaf we sailed Brainstorm round from Derryinver in a very strong headwind and rough sea (but fortunately in fairly good visibility) to O'Connors yard near Clifden, for winter storage. Olaf was Olaf Tyarensen who visited us in Drumsna from time to time. He and I and sometimes Chris had great discussions solving all the world's problems and affairs from our different and divergent points of view. When things got hotted up (as they occasionally did) Chris usually retired and left us two to hammer it out, but the spirit always remained friendly.

*

On the seventh of July (some dates are well remembered!) I had my second heart attack. The timing/location was rather better arranged than the first, which it followed by nearly exactly five years.

I had spent the night with my cousin Joan Plews and had got her to drive me to Blackrock station on the Dart with the intention of catching the main line train to Dundalk for a CND meeting. It was about 10.30am and by a streak of good fortune I found there were no trains, for whatever reason. I left the station to see that Joan was only just leaving. I was delighted because just at that moment I began to feel that familiar pain in the chest. Had I caught a train, goodness knows where I would have finished up!

By the time I was in her car the pain had become really severe and I said to Joan ' I'm in trouble, please take me to St Michaels'.

I stayed there again in intensive care for about a week. There was a break in the middle when they decided it was not an attack and sent me down to an ordinary ward! I was extracted from this again in the middle of the night when the lab found evidence to the contrary!

I stayed in overall for two weeks and I made a quicker recovery than the previous time. I convalesed partly on Brainstorm, not sailing, just happily living aboard.

On the 22nd of December (another date to be remembered) we moved into the house. My daughter Tanya was with us and helped us with the move. A protracted affair, if only over a distance of about 100 yards!

After three and a half years building (and at time of move in an expenditure of £17,500) the house was not quite finished, of course, and thirteen years on it is not really finished yet! But a good house is never 'finished'.

*

The fifth of April, 1985, a sad day!

Brainstorm, sold for £7500, was trailed away from her shed here, never to return. The only seagoing yacht I had ever owned, she had given me enormous pleasure in the designing, building, modifying and sailing, but the money was badly needed for the house and I was getting too old for racing or serious cruising.

But not too old to be still dashing about in my little DAF cars. Surveying work took me throughout the Shannon basin, to the Erne, and to coasts, north, west and south. The DAFs were great money earners because I was paid the same - quite good mileage rate as all other civil servants, and this worked out very well for the little DAFs. I reckon that up to about the middle of this year I had inspected and reported on well over 600 boats, though admittedly the 420 or so hire craft were reported in pre printed duplicate books, me ticking boxes which covered every particular.

Around this time another unusual and interesting task came my way.

The ESB (Electricity Supply Board) had recently started up their new coal burning generating station at Moneypoint, on the north side of the Shannon Estuary, a few miles east of Kilrush.

There had been complaints about the effect on the area and the ESB had offered a considerable sum of money to the Clare County Council for any project it thought fit as compensation. The Council had come up with the idea of a yacht marina at Cappa, just to seaward of Kilrush.

ESB engineers were preparing a plan and specification and I was appointed by Bord Failte to investigate the matter on their behalf.

I was given carte blanche on expenses, always an incentive.

On my first visit the weather was wet and windy from the SW and this gave me a bad first impression of the proposed site. This was on the east side of Cappa pier and inside Hog island. It was a bleak, very exposed, stony shingle beach. As far as I could see there were no redeeming feaures.

I took a number of photos in the dull conditions and noted the tide at the top and the bottom, about 17ft difference. Conversations with several locals confirmed my impression that a marina in that situation would take a severe if not catasthropic beating in a South Westerly storm, and this if nothing else would rule it out.

I then had a good look at Kilrush creek and came to think that the place for the marina was in the creek but above a dam with lock gates. This idea was reinforced when I had lunch in an hotel at the bottom of the town where I saw a number of old photos showing sailing vessels moored to the old quay at the top of the creek both afloat at high water and aground. At low water the creek was just a huge muddy ditch with a small river running through it but at high water it was and could be a very pleasant feature of the town.

I drove home and in spare time set about preparing a reply to the ESB and also acquiring a large scale map of the creek and planning my own suggestion. Later in the month I met about six members of the Clare County Council, these included the County Engineer and the District engineer and one member who happened to be a yachtsman Hugh Mc Kirnan. He was delegated to meet me at Cappa in the evening. I said that I had made a preliminary visit about two weeks previously and that I was not at all impressed with the site which was unattractive and far too exposed in my opinion and we left it at that. I duly met Hugh, walked the beach at the proposed site and I think convinced him that it was not a good idea.

He arranged for an overnight stop at the Gallion pub just off Cappa pier and spent the evening there with me talking sailing. I don't think I mentioned my alternative ideas because the very friendly publican was most interested in having the marina at Cappa! The next morning I spent having a much more detailed look at the creek, its surroundings and the approach from seaward. I also met the Chairman and other members of the Kilrush town council who all liked my ideas.

After that I drove home and got down to writing off the ESB scheme and preparing my own with a good map and a detailed written description, which I forwarded to Donal Guilfoyle of Bord Failte.

I heard nothing more for several months when I had a phone call from the Shannon Development Company in Limerick, requesting a copy of my plans and description. The Board having apparently lost what I sent!

I did this and it was the last thing I heard until it was announced that a Marina was to be built exactly on my lines in Kilrush creek. When eventually built the only difference was that the dam was further down the creek (where I should think the entrance to the lock would be more exposed in rough conditions). Neither my name or that of The Bord have ever been mentioned in connection with the project, the credit being taken by the Development company.

*

In late April I had a message from the Bord to the effect that Ronnie Kearsley was going to try his hand again at operating a Floatel on the Shannon. He had bought a very big Dutch commercial cargo barge, got it up to Killaloe on the lower Shannon, and was about to commence converting it into a 12 passenger boat.

Aimed principally at America and the elderly people who could afford a high rate, the conversion was to be of a very high standard. Cabins en suite, Cordon Bleu cooking and so forth.

My role was to vet the layout and details, largely from a safety point of view. The plans were largely drawn up by Ronnie's recently acquired Filopino wife, a very smart young woman. The actual work was carried out professionally by a good firm of builders and when completed presented a very luxurious appearance. With a fine main engine and a fully silenced highpowered 220 volt A/C generator installed, the vessel had all the facilities which might be expected in a small high class hotel. Ronnie's timing was unfortunate in this project. He ran into a period of aircraft bombings and the type of people he was targetting just did not want to fly. I don't think the project ever got going on a scale to be profitable.

*

This was the summer when I met up again with that great character, Michael Jones of Kerry. He had a few years previously built one of my Kerry yachts from a kit and was a very enthusiastic owner of this little boat which he kept on a mooring at Fenit. Reputed to own a lot of property in Tralee, he spent all his time in a little cramped old shop on the old market square, selling outdoor, heavy weather and service disposal gear. And although he had a very nice house out of town he seemed to prefer to live in his minute back premises. There he held court with his friends. Whom I'm glad to say, and glad to remember, included me!

Regrettably I have not managed to keep in touch with many of the Kerry owners, so far as I know all except Margaret are still afloat, and I hardly ever see one on the market, any owners I have met were very happy with the little boat and she certainly has a good reputation as a seaboat, I know several had made extended cruises.

Some twenty-three 'Kerrys' were sold, either as kits or as finished boats.

As well as the London show we exhibited three times at the Dublin Boat Show, the first time with Kerry as a finished composite boat, plus the first

GRP moulded bare hull beside it. Looking rather nice, I thought, with the extra beam but it did not attract much attention, a disappointment.

At the second show we won the prize for the best Irish built boat and at the third the prize for the best boat in the show, to my satisfaction beating the Swedish designed 'Shipman 28', which were in series production in a Limerick factory and absorbing part of the market which might have been ours.

They went out of business at about the same time we did!

*

Chris and I both crossed the Atlantic in '86, but to different places and at different times. I to Toronto in Canada in June, and she to Seattle in the USA in October.

Although it was interesting , my trip was not one for pleasure, but to see my very dear sister Doreen who was dying of cancer of the spine, just at a time when she and her husband had planned to come the other way and stay with us.

The matter was urgent and the best and cheapest way was by Air Canada on a flight from Amsterdam. As the connections were not very good I had time to see a little of this city and its waterways which are of course very dramatic. I also took the standard waterbus sightseeing tour through the canals of the city.

The flight out was as uneventful as one always hopes flights will be! Even though it was mid summer we passed far enough north to fly over broken sea ice and snow. I was met at the airport by my niece, Doreen's daughter Denise. She took me by bus to the home she shared with her Chinese husband and four children. (The next day I had a real Chinese dinner with Denise and her family.) Brian her brother came and collected me later and took me to the house he shares with a girl he had been living with for years, he works in Toronto for the famous German camera company of Leica.

Brian drove me in his precious open MG to London, a large town about 100 miles sw of Toronto where Doreen lived in the outer suburbs, in fact right beside some hills, each with its own ski lift. I found Doreen more or less invalid and obviously in pain but sedated. She was delighted to see me as I was to see her, although it was distressing.

A friend of hers Pam took us all for a long drive and picnic on the shore of Lake Superior on a beautiful day. There were lots of yachts in Marinas but none sailing, the bigger fishing boats I saw were all to my eye very crude looking craft but apparently they can catch fish from them!

At the week end Brian drove out from Toronto and took me to a pretty spectacular air show quite near the Canada US border, the show completely dominated by the US Airforce. A few days after my arrival Doreen was carted off to hospital in the town and as her husband Freddie did not drive due to a severe shoulder war wound, I was dependant on busses or on Pam to get me to the hospial which I think I visited every day.

I became very friendly with Pam, German and a widow, and had several pleasant walks in the area of the Ski slopes with her. There were lots of chipmunks and birds with which I was not familiar to be seen.

I had my return flight booked and too soon the day arrived when I had to say a final good bye to Doreen, which was cruel for both of us.

She died 15 days later.

THIS AMSTRAD came in 1987. I got it with the help of my son Tyl, although he did say 'you're mad...it'll drive you crazy... and you'll throw it in the river!

Ten years later I still have it. And though many times I felt that the river was the best place for the computer, it did give me a new lease of life.

Instead of Chris doing my reports from handwritten drafts, I started writing them myself. I founded a new company. And I started writing this, my life story. And, if truth be known, I started wondering at the same time just who would read it!

But not to worry, writing in itself is half the experience, and a great aid to memory. Though, of 1987, there appears to be little to remember. Though I do recall a cruise off the west coast.

Sheila and Mike Roberts had a comfortable auxilliary yacht 'Blue Mack'. In July I was invited to go cruising with them. The yacht was kept in a snug berth in Clew Bay, about a mile's crow fly from their delightful chalet home. This was high on the hills leading to Croagh Patrick with the most magnificent view across the bay.

The island of Inis Skea had won my heart on a beautiful afternoon a few years previously and I persuaded the Roberts to head in that direction.

Lucky with the weather, we spent the first night in Achill Sound, lying to our own anchor in a fierce tide. This kept me kept me peeking out all night to see if a nearby tower was staying in the same place!

'Blue Mac' could just as easily have been called Cordon Bleu. Spoilt with Sheila's good cooking, we got to Inis Skea on a beautiful afternoon.

Ashore we thoroughly explored the island and I took a lot of lovely pictures. After a night in the sandy crescent of a bay on its east side, we sailed home in one hop the next day.

Apart from that cruise, another year, and the next very similar. Though in 1988 there was a high point, my second visit to the USSR. This came about through my membership of the Communist Party of Ireland. Although a very inactive member for some years I still held a card and when a group of about twelve Irish members from north and south were offered a free holiday in the USSR with free transport to and from, and the wife of a friend did not want to go, someone suggested me and I was happy to take her place.

The flight was to be a direct one, Shannon to Moscow on a big Russian Jet. Packy and I drove down to Shannon spending a night there to catch the plane in the morning, where we met up with the rest of the party and got our tickets. The plane was already pretty full of Cubans, men, women and children all in holiday mood, though already tired by the long Transatlantic flight.

The sky was clear and we could see the ground practically the whole way. We flew over central England the North Sea, over part of Denmark and the Baltic states and a part of north Russia which from a height looked little cultivated but considerably afforested.

Landing at Moscow's western airport, we were given total VIP treatment being met by an envoy who took our passports and brought us straight through immigration as a party. A mini bus was waiting for us, our luggage came through with the minimum of delay, and we were whisked into the city to the most magnificent hotel any of us had ever been in. Our spacious suite twin bed rooms were equipped with T.V. and phone, a big refrigerator already loaded with soft drinks and milk, an electric samovar, tea and sugar and coffee, and fresh fruit and fresh flowers on the table!

The evening meal was in a very large dining room, our party and the men and women who were our hosts together at one table, while other tables were occupied by other groups from different countries. Afterwards we socialised in the comfortable lounge but no alcoholic drink was offered -in fact during the whole time I was in Russia I never even smelt any! No doubt if I had been interested I'm sure it could have been got at a price; actually on top of free travel and everything else we were given a present of a useful sum of roubles to spend.

After a comfortable night and a good breakfast we were driven a short distance to a clinic which inside seemed like some huge ministry building, although the waiting room was extremely comfortable and beautifully decorated. We were all given a most thorough medical check, including blood tests (we wondered if they were on the lookout for AIDS). They spotted that I had some heart trouble, as did one of the women in our group, so they told us they would not recommend us to go to Sochi on the Black Sea, as had been arranged, as it would be very hot there. So I and the woman and her husband were offered an hotel on the Gulf of Finland- part of the Baltic - as an alternative.

This of course we accepted, although it meant an overnight train journey to Leningrad (as was!) the next afternoon. I was disappointed as I would have liked to have seen the Black Sea coast which I believe is very beautiful, and also I had not taken to the couple who would accompany me, middle aged and to my mind as they proved to be, extremely dull. They would have enjoyed Blackpool very much more than the Baltic Coast!

We were installed on the train, alone in one of the spacious four person compartments which make first class travel in Russia so comfortable.The berths were arranged for us and we slept or read as we wished most of the way to Leningrad. Actually I stayed awake most of the night- which wasn't- looking out of the window of my upper berth at the passing scene which on the whole was flat land and pretty drab, but one forgets that it is under snow for much of the year. However I did feel that that was no reason why the people had not shown more initiative. There was plenty of standing timber and plenty that could be done with it, but no signs in the villages through which we passed of any sawmills. The roads were in a poor state and there was little sign of any attempt at flower gardens, only of vegetable growing in a small and rather untidy way, in other words the picture was not of a bright and intelligent peasantry.

Also in the broad summer sunlight the houses all seemed shut in by trees, dark and with lights on, no doubt as a protection from winter blizzards. However I could not help remembering London Ontario where the winters must be nearly as severe at times, and there the attractive bungalow-style houses, many all timber too, all have grass surrounds and a basement living room.

Different peoples!

We were roused for breakfast in the dining car before we got in, and were met on arrival by a very pleasant young woman, Tamara by name who was with us off and on throughout our stay, particularly at meal times to help out with ordering food which had to be done the previous day!

There was a mini bus waiting for us and at our service during our stay on request. Tamara spoke good English and was very keen to improve it, with which I went out of my way to help her. (The others seemed pretty indifferent to their surroundings the whole time!) Tamara lived with her family in a block of flats between the hotel and the city. On the way out we saw a little of this beautiful water surrounded city which had largely been re built since the War, and its pleasant treelined suburban streets.

We stayed at a beautiful brand new Finnish built hotel called White

Nights (because in mid summer the nights are light). Situated on sand with imported earth flower beds in a forest of smallish conifers, where I spotted red squirrels. Again we were installed in very luxuriously furnished en suite rooms with a balcony, mine on the second of five or six floors.

As usual my first reaction was to explore my surroundings. Paths radiated every which way, and it took me quite a time to find the sea! By which time it was midday meal time. We four had a table to ourselves, and were quite obviously the only non Russians in the big pleasantly open room. I should say at this stage that all the people, men, women and teenagers - no children - were all well dressed and of what one would call middle and upper middle class at home, and very friendly to me in lifts etc. In spite of my age, or maybe in spite of it, I could not help being attracted to a very beautiful youngish woman sitting in profile to me at an adjoining table, she was obviously with her husband, teen aged daughter and an elderly woman.

Naturally I did not like the look of the husband and thought she looked unhappy!

After the meal, wearing shorts and a shirt - it was very hot - I took a bicycle from a rack of ready to use bikes and rode down to the bathing pavilion, an extensive permanent structure, there I kicked off my shoes and waded into the tepid and none too clean-looking sea. Further out people were bathing in what was still very shallow water, it did not tempt me.

I was standing thinking that in winter this sea is frozen right over, when a young woman in a bikini walked past me and a bit further out and then turned and walked up to me and introduced herself as Elena in very good english. And, from my point of view anyhow, so began a sort of dry land shipboard romance!

Elena was with her husband who was Pravda's correspondent in New York and they were home on leave, and they had fairly recently been posted in Belfast.

We stood talking about ourselves, an old man and a very beautiful slim athletic young woman in a bikini until suddenly her daughter came running out through the shallow water and joined in the conversation. She spoke English with a very strange accent and was altogether a very effervescent girl.

The next time I met Elena was on the sandy beach, I was looking for a spare board to sit on when her daughter ran up to me saying her mother wanted to speak to me so I followed her and we sat together, the girl obviously wanting to exercise her English, until she quite suddenly decided a friend was leaving and rushed off leaving us together again.

I don't know what we talked about.

We met again several times during my stay.

But I had a feeling that Elena's husband was mocking her over her friendship with me. She did publicly introduce me to him in the dining room and when I was leaving they all three came out to bid me good bye: no I did not get her phone number or address!

Apart from that little episode, and friendship with a man who was a Siberian son of a forester and in one of the ministries in Moscow, very interesting to talk to, I found the two and a half weeks in the sun rather boring. I used to get up very early and go for long walks in the cool along the almost endless strand. There was such a small tidal range that the rather dirty highwater mark never got flushed and it had to be manually cleaned from time to time.

On the South Western horizon I could just see the outline of the island of Kronstadt which was never captured by Hitler although Leningrad some miles inshore was totally besieged. In winter during the siege a trickle of supplies did get into the City across the frozen Lake Ladoga. This siege lasted nearly two years and thousands died of starvation and enemy action.

The location of the hotel was significant, as it was virtually on the old pre war border between Finland and Russia. The dispute which was the cause of the Finno-Russian war of 1939-40 was when Stalin, justifiably as things stood, with the Finnish fascist Mannerheim closely linked with Hitler, and in possession of this otherwise useless territory which was within easy artillery range of Leningrad, offered a much larger area of territory in exchange for a new boundary.

Within the grounds of the hotel there were still the remains of half buried pill boxes. At that time England heavily supported the Finns even to the extent of giving them a squadron of Hurricane fighters, which were already needed in England. Of course when the war really got going the Finns were against the British, Sweden was neutral, Denmark was occupied and only little Norway really put up a fight before occupation.

The hotel had a splendid heated indoor smimming pool which we and Tamara made use of several times. Tamara did not approve of me diving into this because of my heart condition so not to offend her I climbed sedately down the ladder. There was also a very nice little theatre and we had frequent performances by visiting musicians and dancers from distant parts of the Union. There was also a big library but few of the books or periodicals were in English. The Russians seemed to make extensive use of it. I also noticed that they are great drinkers of what we would call buttermilk and last thing at night before everyone retired to their rooms they all assembled informally in the dining room and from wheeled trolleys drank glasses of it, as I did myself! They are also very keen on physical fitness, jogging on the sands in the early morning and doing what we call P.T. (The last time I saw Elena she was at one of these classes doing all the exercises with ease and grace, I remember thinking she would be good on skis.)

While at White Nights I had a dose of quite severe earache, something quite unusual for me. I reported this to Tamara and that evening I was attended on by a very attractive and immaculately dressed nurse-docter who administered drops and an ear pad and wrapped me in bandages for the night. She did not seem able or willing to speak English so I thanked her with a little Irish brooch I happened to have.

Right from the start in Moscow it was obvious to me that the members of the Communist Party were an elite, probably numbering 25% of the population, an upper class rather like the Conservative party in England, it was a matter of the CP and the rest!

I discussed this with my Siberian friend and he pointed out that it was by no means a closed party but was open to all with the education and ability to be leaders in their sphere, however it was clearly not the classless society of the Communist ideal. Perhaps this goes to show that this is rather an impossible ideal, human nature being what it is.

We had excursions in our mini bus, the first to Leningrad to visit museums, including the must, the Hermitage, very well reported on elsewhere but the contents are really quite fabulous. We also visited the Cathedral of the Russian Orthodox Church. (It was outside this building that I saw the only beggar in the whole trip.)

Another day we visited the house which had been the home of the famous Russian painter Rabi, known worldwide, a unique house maintained as a museum to him. The third excursion involved quite a long drive right through Leningrad, including the rather dilapidated western end and then some 15 miles out along the coast to the west to Petrodvorets which I think is also called the Summer Palace of the Tzars. Another fabulous place, although it was a dwelling and is kept as such, it is really a museum of beautiful things. There were splendid gardens too, with artificial waterfalls and fountains of great beauty everywhere, all created by Italian sculptors and gold plated. Incidentally this palace was utterly destroyed by the Nazis, when they discovered that the whole building and gardens had been completely cleared of everything. However the plans had been kept, and the location of everything meticuously photographed, and it has been rebuilt and restored in every detail, some of the work was being completed when we were there.

Just as I was getting very much used to the leisurly if boring life of the seaside visitor it was time to retrace our steps to Moscow. We said a fond farewell to Tamara at the station and, after another night trip, we were met in Moscow and taxied to the other hotel. There we met up with the other party who had just flown in from Baku, all looking very sunburnt. We visited a Palace of Achievement which had an interest for nearly everyone in the party including my friend Packy who was a farmer, there being an area of farmyards and cattle breeding estabishments.

In the evening it was the inevitable circus (no ballet tickets we available!)

In the morning it was off to the airport, again a fond farewell to the really very nice elderly lady who had been our principal hostess and ran the whole visit without a hitch.

And in five or six hours we were back at Shannon and motoring home.

IN THE WINTER of 1988 I bought for a song a stand of fifteen or so small ash trees. We cut these three to four feet off the ground so that the butts could be cut into hurley sticks. Much fun was had in felling these among the other trees, cutting them up with a chain saw - brutal instrument - and getting the logs out of the wood... great work for winter days.

Kennedy International Boats was re-registered as a company in 1989. The idea was to start off by building essentially steel cruisers. I had been sounding out the reaction to the idea of these as an alternative to the imported GRP boats. My feeling was that in the hire boat business they would stand up to the rough treatment and frequent grounding better. Furthermore, their construction in Ireland would keep the money in the country and give employment locally.

The only hurdle in the way of getting started was my usual one, a lack of capital with which to prove my faith in the idea and to have some control of the way the company developed.

It was suggested that I engage a Dublin accountant who was young and up and coming! He would be in a better position in Dublin to find shareholders...people who could put up money! Or so the notion went! I took him on on the basis that he would be paid according to results.

From the start I had been in touch with the Industrial Development Authority (IDA) and the County Leitrim development team. I had spent a lot of time trying to find a suitable premises in which to build boats of about 40 ft length. Also in the meantime I had designed in outline a craft which I believed would fit the bill. And I actually got a note of intent to purchase five of these craft from a hire boat operator whom I had known for some time.

This last thing tipped the balance in favour of the scheme and we were promised some help from local development funds and also an investment by the Electricy Supply Board (ESB). Then, with a lease of a small IDA factory unit outside Carrick we got started.

I designed a jig for building a standard 38ft steel hull inverted and we got underway. This type of work was completely new to all but one of the construction team. First the bare shed was turned into a proper workshop with office and drawing office, storerooms and work benches. What with this and then buying ply for templates, steel for the jig and the frames and steel plate for the shell, we really only got started on the boat proper in May. Even then I was still completing the drawings at home in the evenings while supervising the work in the workshop all day.

We had secured two first class welders and had bought good welding and cutting equipment People soon adapted to the new work when they realised a hull was not much different from a tank.

The building went ahead, and we were soon able to turn the hull over having just enough room to rotate its 14 ft beam - breaking a few overhead lights in the process! - and work of fitting out and decking commenced.

As did my (short-lived) television career!

Earlier in '89 we had had a visit from a young woman from RTE Clare O'Loughlan was proposing to make a feature film in the series 'I Live Here'. She thought we might be the right people to feature. We agreed but heard nothing more for several months... and then had a phone call announced that the film team would be coming to start things in a few days.

This was the beginning of a very happy series of filming sessions around Drumsna and elsewhere on the river. Godfrey Graham the cameraman had been in ballet at one time and he struck up quite a close friendship with Christine. The RTE people generally were all most pleasant and easy to work with.

The film when it came out ran for nearly an hour and was generally voted one of the best of the series with Christine the Star. Everyone in the district has called me by my first name ever since!

However, in the meantime, the business and management side of the boat building business were not so happy.

This was essentially due to my lack of experience, not helped by our accountant's growing interference with the running of the plant. From the first I was chairman and managing director and Christine was (reluctantly) company secretary. She did have the experience of running the business side of our previous boat hire enterprise and was efficient. (And her father had been an accountant!)

I found that I was sometimes at loggerheads with some of the other directors. They even interfered on technical matters of which they had little undertanding. Then we reached a crisis over cash to carry on, that letter of intent never having came to anything.

Just at this time Tyl happened to be visiting from England and I arranged for him to sit in at a board meeting at which the question of money to finish the boat came up and to my amazement Tyl said 'I will buy it'.

There and then an extremely low figure of £55000 was agreed and we built the boat for him on condition that the Company could have it to exhibit at the forthcoming Dublin Boat Show. It was duly launched and it floated as per design... always a dicy moment! We ran trials and photographic sessions, and then she was towed to Dublin and exhibited afloat on the Liffey with Gay Byrne on the helm wearing my nautical hat!

After the Boat Show the cruiser was operated on Lough Erne as part of a hire fleet run by ex RN Captain Trevor Clayton. She remained there for nearly three seasons as Tyl did not really want to have a big cruiser on the Shannon while he was living in East Sussex! He in fact only used her once before we brought her back to the Shannon in 1994 via the new Shannon Erne Link.

In the meantime Chris and I had resigned our positions in the boat building company, being thoroughly fed up with the way things were going. However the company managed to secure a contract with a new cruiser company and eventually built some 22 boats. Based on my original design with certain superstructure and interior changes, these became the TARA Cruisers and have proved very popular with German hirers.

Another disappointment of this period was my work on the design of a high speed passenger and rescue craft for Tory Island. This was to have been in conjunction with a proposed big holiday development scheme for the Gortahork area of North Donegal. As far as I know nothing came of it but nobody ever told me I was wasting my time!

A pity because it was an interesting scheme and an interesting boat of the sea sled type and I spent a lot of time on it, and got no cash nor credit from anyone!

Story of my life?

*

While Tyl's cruiser 'Serena' was still operating from Kesh in Fermanagh I arranged to have her (at a much reduced rate!) for two weeks. The crews consisted principally of the older generation of Royal St George YC members and of older Shannon enthusiasts. Our good friends the Denhams, particularly Dr Peter, - then a sick man - were very keen to navigate Lough Erne and the recently reopened canal now known as the Erne - Shannon Link. Their family like mine had in the '70's explored the line, closed since 1880.

We had explored the area of interconnected lakes and then, with canoes and a Landrover, the Ballinamore - Ballyconnell section of the canal which had been closed since the 1880's .

Those were very happy weekend exercises, with the aid of an old map which indicated the line of the canal. We could always find traces of it, maybe just a trickle of water in a shallow overgrown ditch and sometimes the fairly intact remains of a lock with inevitably the river weir beside it all overgrown with reeds and moss, even big trees.

I remember finding the lock and weir at Ballyduff which was also Ballyduff Railway Station. It was evening time and very quiet, we were standing on the old track by the remains of the platform, the boys were young. I suddenly said I think I hear a train we'd better get off the track. Of course it was only a ghost train but I think we all had a shiver! The lock and weir there were beautifully overgrown with a little waterfall over the cill running away through the moss covered masonry.

A moment to be captured!

Long years later we cruised the reopened waterway in Serena. Peter Denham organised the crewing (some 14 people at various times) and Maureen his wife the catering. Different people including myself and Christine joined at various stages. The cruise was from Kesh to Keshkerrigan. This is not far from Leitrim village at the top of the multilock drop down to the Shannon. From here we returned to Kesh.

At one stage I and Chris rejoined the party at Ballinamore. Taking over the controls in the upper steering position I asked someone in the cabin to do the simple indicated switch over and was castoff before I had checked everything. The boat went ahead and I did not try the reverse. The first 'up lock' is very close to the town and was open so I drove slowly into it but there was a strong breeze behind me. I put the lever into neutral and then reverse, nothing happened except panic!

It was a situation where nothing could instantly be done to take way off the boat and there was nothing to grab hold of. I thought that it wouldn't be too bad as we would hit the upper timber gate which would yield a little! But instead we hit the corner of the new concrete cill which was standing about 7" above water. There was a horrible crunch as the eleven tons of boat met an immoveable concrete mass.

One could only be philosophical about it.

Chris scrambled up onto the lock and reported that I would be very sad, the damage was extensive. The lower stem was crumpled and the whole of it somewhat distorted. However it was above water and was not open and it didn't spoil the cruise. We decided to ignore and say no more about it. (It was not until nearly a year later that that my friend Donal Conlon built in a new stem.)That cruise itself was thoroughly enjoyable and the mixed company very congenial.

In early September of 1994 Tyl and Janet plus another couple and their little girl brought Serena all the way to the Shannon and finally to Jamestown in beautiful weather. There she lay alongside our old home, the barge St Brigid, going into decay under new ownership.

*

Earlier than this I did have a brief holiday on the Lower Erne with Tyl and Janet in Serena. It was rather mixed weather and the main part of the lake is big and open. When the wind blows (which it did!) it kicks up a sea which taken on the beam has the boat rolling violently...and when taken head on means clouds of spray! But it is usually possible to make a way through the islands in calm water. Virtually all these islands have landing stages and some are well worth exploring for their archaeological remains, others just for the peace and the bird life.

Lough Erne is a lake with a wartime history of Atlantic patrols by flying boats based here. At Killadeas the RAF had a base, the Americans were at Castle Archdale, and they flew Sunderlands and Catalinas respectively. The remains of the bases are still to be seen and have found peacetime use.

Between the upper and lower lakes the river winds its way through Enniskillen. This is the main and really the only accessible shopping centre on the whole Erne waterway, except for Belturbet at the southern end. There is nothing on the upper lake except a house on one of the small islands where given plenty of notice an evening meal may be had. But this lake itself on a peaceful sunny summer afternoon is delightful with its mirror lakes, its islands and bird life... and the ship's wake astern.

The new canal as a navigation is no chore. (In fact as an old canal hand myself I rather missed leaning on the gate beams and winding up the sluices.) The country in the river section is low lying callow grazing land, very pleasant. South of the market town of Ballinamore the navigation becomes mostly a series of shallow lakes connected by canal cuts, the levels between being controlled by locks. The country here is hilly, heavily wooded. On the trip we sought out the terminal of the still totally derelict Ulster Canal. There appears to be definite moves to have it too restored.

But that is something I shall not live to see!

I SUPPOSE THERE are many things going on around which one will not live to see completed. In late '92 one such project got underway to bypass our two local villages, Drumsna and Jamestown. Both of these have bridges over the big loop in the river here and Jamesown Bridge forms our northern boundary. Christine and I were longing for this work to be finished as it would mean our beautiful bridge would be just a quiet country road instead of a main arterial one. The bypass is now complete but Christine didn't live to see it finished.

She hadn't been well for quite some years.

In 1991 she had spent three weeks in Spain. I was touring in England where I visited the Southampton Boat Show, doing a stint on the stand of an old friend, Conrad Natzio.

Christine stayed with another old friend of ours, Hazel Marsden. She lived with her ex-naval husband in a country area and we had a faint hope that the dry climate there might help Christine's lung trouble.

Her hosts kept horses and she enjoyed the visit but it did not seem to help her condition. When she returned she got right back to doing the work with vinyl material, this in hindsight may have been a major cause of her trouble. I also have on my conscience another incident from an earlier time when I quite innocently asked her to apply the Cuprinol to the inside of Brainstorm's hull. This meant working in confined spaces with the fumes from this copper based wood preservative which are now known to be dangerous. She was quite a heavy smoker and was also handling hay for her horses which when somewhat musty can be a cause of 'farmers lung'. All in all she did not give herself much of a chance, but she never complained. Over her last years she was gradually running out of natural oxygen supply and depending more and more on oxygen bottles, then finally upon a machine to keep herself alive.

*

Christine's illness was echoed by the passing of my first wife, who died a few years before her in 1991. I attended Maud Cooke's funeral with very mixed feelings. But she was the mother of three very dear children who have always been close to me. Shortly afterwards I also 'lost' my cousin Joan Plews. She didn't die then, but moved into a nursing home, a sort of living death in my view. She was persuaded by her solicitors to sell her house Bellevue in Leopardstown and move into a nursing home on Killiney Hill. It was largely my job as the nearest interested relative to clear out the house of the residue of the auction and I benefitted to the extent of useful things like ladders and a mowing machine!

During her few remaining years I managed to pay her fairly frequent visits although it was very depressing to see her go downhill so quickly in the environment of the home and her treatment there.

She died early in 1996.

Aisling Kennedy was born in 1993, child of my son Shane and his wife Frances, another grandchild for me. This was my 80th year and a time to start running down my story.

A man of eighty is not going to lead a very interesting or exciting life. In fact I had always said I did not want my life to continue beyond a point where I had done everything I wanted to do that I was capable of doing.

I was working on these memoirs and doing some boat designs during the year. And I took it into my head to finally try to find out something of the life of my first love, Peggy. I didn't intend to meet her again or even communicate directly with her but, through an intermediary, to learn a little of a life which had run parallel with my own. I told Chris of my intentions. Whilst not encouraging me, I think she accepted that I had a right to do this.

I had last met Peggy in 1938 and had had no contact with her whatsoever since then. I had no idea what Peggy's married name would be, assuming even that she was married. I didn't know where she lived, whether Ireland or perhaps more likely England... but possibly anywhere else in the world.

The only practical starting point from which to track her down was with the present occupants of Knockmore. This was the house which had belonged to her aunts the Miss Mays. I visited there and met a Mrs Ross who was extremely kind. She knew something of the Mays and the Actons, Peggy's family name. But she knew nothing of their whereabouts. She did however remember a visit of some fifteen or twenty years previous. A lady who seemed to meet the description of Peggy herself had visited, telling her of holidays spent there and how she had loved the place.

She thought her name was Nicholson and that she said she lived in Co

Louth. I scoured County Louth by car and by post. I inquired of the Protestant clergy, the Garda, even The Country Women's Association! But I drew a total blank! I wrote Mrs Ross accordingly and let the matter rest for a time. I seemed to be at the end of a trail which had no real beginning.

Then one day I had a letter from Mrs Ross who had not let the matter rest. She sent me the addresses of two ladies of the May family. I wrote to one and had an almost immediate reply giving me the address of a man living in London. Strangely enough I had known this man slightly in Bombay.

He had never met Peggy but knew of her as a Mrs Hacker. And she had died in 1980. He gave me the address of her sister Jill whom I have now met several times times and thus know something of Peggy's life in India, in war and in peace.

In India as the eldest daughter of the police superintendent of Dehra Dun she had a good life but a useful one, helping her father. I have a self typed note in which she describes herself (with a high powered Magnum rifle, a heavy weapon for a woman) dealing with a tigress which was marauding in a neighbouring village. During the war she was for a time working from Blenheim Palace, the headquarters of the Free French with the rank of ATS Lieutenant. Even her husband whom she married at the end of the war- aged about 32- never found out what she had been up to!

*

1993 was a very uninteresting year.

I was kept busy inspecting boats up and down the river, it being a requirement of marine insurance that the boats should be professionally inspected with safety in mind and a certificate produced before cover could be granted. This was a good source of supplement to my meagre combinations of British and Irish state pensions. Uninteresting workwise for me, 1993 was also the first really bad year for Christine. At least four times I took her to Sligo General Hospital on doctors' orders. But she always insisted in discharging herself as soon as she thought she was better ...and it was always too soon! When at home she still insisted in doing some of her work and cooking our main meal. I did breakfast for her in bed and handled the evening meal.

The year merged with 1994.

I designed some steel barges. And some cruisers. And two yachts. One of these was a multi chine steel 40 footer, built in Dublin. The other was for a design competition, a new class of 30ft small offshore racing machine to the same class of rules as the 60ft Whitbread Class. This was quite a challenge and I think I designed a very sweet little boat with lots of new ideas.

There were 34 entries from all over the world. Four designs were judged the best and then mine with four others were judged equally next, so I claim only four were judged better...but only on paper! I would love to have seen it built, or better still to have built it myself.

But...my boat building days were over.

*

Christine made one last trip to Connemara to see her grandchildren and the two ponies she had given them. Of course she knew she was not fit to drive but nothing would stop her and in fact she did have a minor accident on the way back. Emergency breaking on a gravelly road she slid into the back of another, disimproving her own car but making no impression on the other. She told me the driver of the other vehicle was very concerned, but not about any damage, rather about her own really wretched appearance.

In September 1994 we went to watch the gathering of hot air balloons at the Forest Park near Boyle, the old Rockingham Estate. This gathering has become an annual event and generally seems to be blessed with ideal weather.

Twenty or so balloons of all shapes and sizes were spread out on the grass and being inflated. Christine and I picked upon one to follow. Then we took off after it by car through the highways and byways of County Roscommon. It travelled at perhaps about ten miles per hour, twelve hundred feet high in a south easterly direction. And we followed excitedly, trying to decide which roads and lanes would keep us most nearly beneath. And wishing we were up there too.

For a little while we forgot our troubles and our age, and we were happy together. But of course in the end the balloon like a dream got away from us. It drifted across the Shannon at Lough Bofin.

Christine died on the 14th of October. Having just refused to go to the hospital again, she died alone with me in the afternoon, ever so quietly in her own bed at home as she had wished. She just went to sleep and I knew it was right for her. And I did not pine but something precious drifted away for ever.

Now I live alone and what happens now is not worth writing about. So I will leave it at that.

My two little acres on the riverbank are quiet. It is all a happy dream.

And life closes in.

APPENDIX

postscript

For some year before her death my sister Nancy had been compiling our family tree. This resulted in her contacting Elizabeth Caldicott who was a Kennedy. At the time of my early childhood the branch she descended from had seemed to take a separate course to ours and in our teens and adult times we did not seem to have much if any contact, although we were all cousins with a common great grandfather, Frederick Kennedy of Dublin. (I was to learn later that this great-grandfather Frederick was one of the Kennedys of Cultra, at Holywood in County Down).

Through Elizabeth I met her father Gerald, who was of the same generation though much younger than my father. A family gathering of these Kennedys was held at which myself, Joan Plews and Henry Kennedy were the sole living representatives of our generation of our side of the family. There I met Elizabeth's brother Gerry, aka the writer Conan Kennedy. He has edited and unscrambled these writings as best he could.

I am presently working on drawings (below)for the rebuilding of a Droleen, the historic (1895) dinghy associated with Bray Sailing Club.

Jamestown Bridge, October 1997.

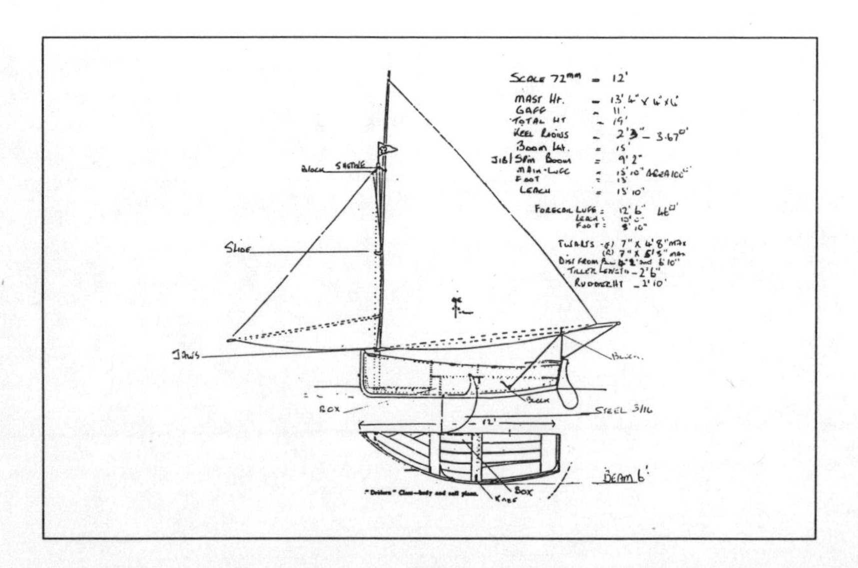

Boats Designed and Built by George O'Brien Kennedy:

{(b) after an entry signifies boats built personally by G O'BK}

Pre-War and during 2nd WW:

Rusheen	10ft Sailing sharpie.	1(b)
Evolution	14ft International	1(b)
Dawn	14ft International	1(b)
Hiltrau	14ft International	1(b)
National 12		3(b)
Camping Cruiser		9(b)
Dragon Class (not designed)		1(b)
Naval Dinghies (wartime)		24

Post-War, Lymington:

Slipway 5-Ton, 26 footer.	18
REB 14 Footer	6(b)
Frostbite Dinghies	2(b)
Swallows (joint design)	6(b)
Merlins 14 Footer	2(b)
Binker 32,	1(b)
IDRA 14's	c80
Yachting World Day Boat	c700

India (Varuma):

Car Passenger Ferry	2
Police Launch, Fast 26	1
Launches	6
Merlin Rockets	2(b)

India (Alcock Ashdown):

Fire Float & Salvage Vessel	1
Yacht 'Tir', 42'	1
Seagoing Tugs	4
Small Tug	1
CBK's, Indian National OD.	c50

Ireland (post war)

Otters 10ft	20 approx
Inis Cealtra 30'	1
Inismore 32'	1
Inis Bofin 32'	1
Mallard 25'	1
Curlew 25'	1
Catavan (for JKR) 40'	1
Flagline Cruisers 26'	4
Flagline Cruisers 32'	2
Kerrys 27'	26
Brainstorm 30'	1
Serena Class 38'	3
Tara Class 38'	20
Steel Cruisers 36'-38'	6
Lobster Boats 32'	2

The Slipway 5-Tonners:

18 of these boats were built by the Lymington Slipway & Engineering Co.Ltd, in Lymington, Hampshire. (Illustrated below is the first built, off Lymington in 1948, Brien Kennedy at the helm).

The following is reproduced from a brochure of the period:

This little cruiser has been designed to be faster, have better windward ability, and balance on the helm than is usually found in boats of this size, without sacrificing handiness or interior accommodation.

Most small cruisers carry about a lot of useless timber which has, generally, an adverse effect on speed and comfort in a seaway whilst adding nothing to the strength.

Therefore in the Slipway 5-tonner this has been cut out and with adequate scantlings she has a ballast ratio of nearly 50 per cent on a comparatively light displacement.

To give good accommodation and reasonable headroom without too much freeboard, the hull is wide in the garboards and the bilges rather easy, which makes for smaller wetted surface and a hull easily driven with quite a small sail area and engine. For windward ability and handiness, the fin is fairly short and of a carefully considered section.

The raised topsides are much better than a coach roof from the strength point of view and give extra roominess below. There are three full length berths, one of which is a quarter berth opposite the galley. The headioom in the cabin is 5ft. and under the doghouse at the galley 5ft. lOin

The cabin table fits on to the mast and when not in use stows neatly out of the way. a Baby Blake WC is fitted forward of the saloon, and double doors ensure privacy. Forward of the WC there is ample stowage space for sails and gear, with access through a hatch in the foredeck.

The 6 h.p. Watermota auxiliary engine gives her a good 51/2 knots under power.

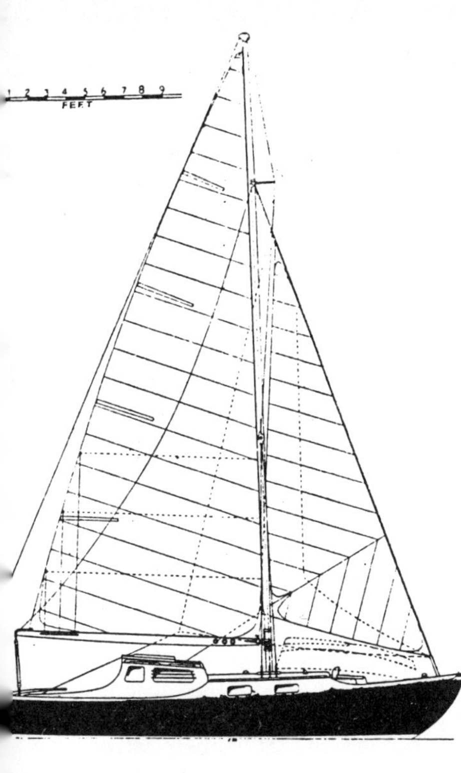

Specification & Inventory

Length O.A	26ft
L.W.L.	2Oft. 3in
Beam	7ft. 3in
Draft	4ft. 6in
Displacement	3.48 tons
Working Sail Area.	280 sq. ft

Key

1. Laminated stem.
2. Fairlead and backstay fittings.
d. Feathering reversing propeller.
4. Compass.
5. Laminated stern member.
6. Cockpit.
7. 6 hp Watermota Auxiliary.
8. Propeller pitch control lever
9. Petrol tank, 3 gallons, under seat.
10. Fresh Water Tank, 12 gls. under seat.
11. Bilge Pump.
12. Mainsbeet block eye bolts.
13. Quarter berth.
14. Sliding hatch.
15. Cooker, with cupboard under.
16. Doghouse extending over cockpit.
17. Stowage for crockery.
18. Fresh water tap.
19. Saruson posts fore and aft.
20. Windows.
21. Berth settees extending under cup boards
22. Double doors
23. Portable table attached to mast
25. Chain locker
26. Cupboards
27. W.C. Baby Blake
28. Fore hatch
29. Handgrips
30. 'Dorade' type cowls & vents. P. & S
31. Sail stowage.
32. Iron keel.

Note. The mast can be alternativly stepped on deck. On later models this will be standard

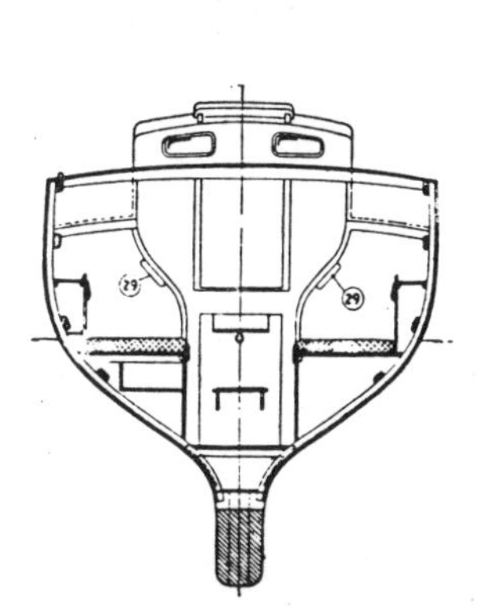

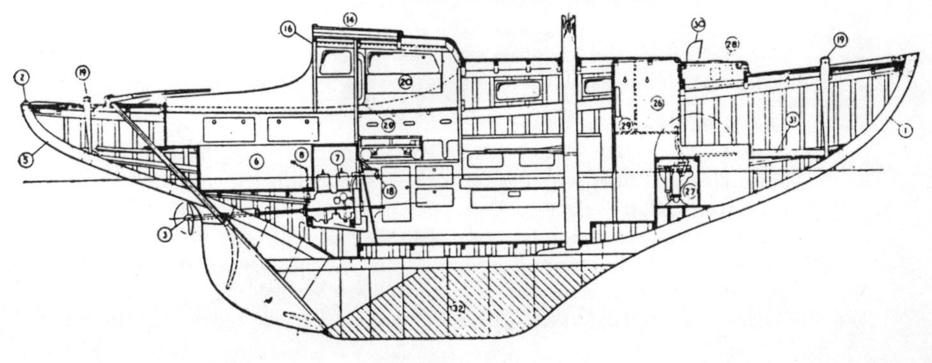

IDRA 14

Some 80 of these boats have been built. Drawings on facing page are

The following (by the late G.H.Gray) is reproduced from The Irish Field of 2/2/1946.

NEW DINGHY CLASS FOR IRELAND

Writing about the new 'Yachting World' 14-foot restricted dinghies a few weeks ago, I commented on the fact that for the past couple of years Irish dinghy men have been looking for a suitable prototype for an Irish one-design dinghy class, and I suggested that this 'Yachting World' 14-footer might prove the answer to the problem. A few days after the article appeared I got a note from Mr. W.J. McClelland, of the Sutton Dinghy Club, to say that a suitable design for a new Irish dinghy class had at last been found, a new association - the Irish Dinghy Racing Association - had been formed, and some sixteen of the boats were already being built, and were due for delivery in May.

The design would not be confined to any one club, but would be adopted by various clubs around the coast, making inter-club matches possible. About twelve of the dinghies would be racing in Dublin Bay this summer, it was expected.

The design which has been approved by representatives of all sailing centres immediately interested is by Mr. O'Brien Kennedy, of Poole the son of Mr. F.A.Kennedy, captain of the Water Wags. The first of these boats was designed as a one-design racing class for Poole Harbour, in 1939, but the war intervened. One boat was built and was thoroughly tested during the 1939 season, and raced with great success in regatta and handicap events. The dinghy, called Fuss, was not built with speed as a primary consideration, but rather with the idea that she should be a practical day boat which would be suitable even for comparative beginners, and yet would provide good-class racing.

ITS BIRTH

Mr. McClelland writes: 'The new Irish Dinghy Racing Association's 14-foot dinghy was thought of over two years ago, when a group of small boat-owners from various clubs met to consider post-war developments in small-boat sailing. At that time it was obvious that, because of the lack of materials, a large demand was banking up for small boats, particularly class boats, and that as soon as supplies permitted, there would be a rush to build. There was, therefore, a unique opportunity to agree on a design to which a new and large class could be built in the post-war period. A suitable boat to meet this popular demand would be dual purpose, rathern than an out-and-out racing design. It would be a good sea-boat, weatherly, reasonably fast and, above all, moderate in cost, while attractive in appearance and modern in design. Furthermore, it would be sturdy and capable of taking the ground in exposed achorages.'

Mr. McClelland and the other small boat-owners interested in the project are satisfied that Mr. Kennedy's design meets their requirements.

SOME NOTES

Here are some notes which Mr. McClelland has given me on the new dinghy.

Several sets of lines were drawn, each with a slightly stiffer section than the previous one, before the designer was satisfied that the dinghy would make a really safe and serivceable boat. The hull is half-decked, with a small side-deck, and leaves ample room for four or five adults; for racing, the crew is two. The beam is 5 foot and the hull is strengthened with grown floors, to enable it to take the ground in tidal moorings without strain and for road towing. The rudder is pivoted and ballasted, to avoid damage in shallow waters.

The rig is Bermudian, with a hollow mast 21 feet above deck level. The boom is also hollow and both mast and boom have internal tracks.

The centre-board is of the wooden ballasted type, with 25 lb. of lead set into the lower third, and it will work on rollers instead of a pin. The wooden centre-board avoids the necessity of ballast tanks, as the hull itself will have adequate positive buoyancy to support its crew.

The batten side seats are fitted with hinges, so that they fold out of the way when racing.

PRICE CONSIDERATION

Price has been made a prime consideration and all unnecessary expense in fittings has been cut down. For example, a spinnaker will not be included in the one-design specification, although individual clubs may, if they choose, decide to use spinnakers in club races. The sail area without the spinnaker is 120 square feet - 84 square feet in the mainsail and 36 square feet in the foresail. The price of a suit of sails from a first-class sail-maker will, it is expected, be in the region of £10.

The specification will permit boats to be built of any wood, provided that the hull, stripped, is not below a certain weight. The boat, complete with hollow mast, hollow boom, and all gear, including designerís royalties, but excluding sails, will not exceed a maximum of £65, delivered in Dublin, and there is every hope that it may be kept as low as £55.

It is expected that the first boat will be delivered early in March, and will be available for inspection. It is certain that at least two classes of these dinghies will be sailing in Dublin Bay during the coming season - in Dun Laoghaire and at Clontarf.

Plans and specifications of the dinghy will shortly be available through the newly formed Irish Dinghy Racing Association, at the cost of reproduction, plus a a royalty to the designer of one guinea per boat.

Since this will be a one-design class sailing not only in Dublin Bay, but also in Cobh, Cork and other centres, including the North, where at least three clubs are interested in the design, the possibilities for inter-club competitions are enormous.

For example, Mr. McClelland suggests that an annual championship should be promoted, to be held at a different centre each year. Furthermore, the design offers great possibilities for team racing, not popular in this country up to the present, probably because the 12-foot international dinghies are the only one-design class sailed by different clubs.

At any rate, team racing between the Cork Harbour and the Sutton Dinghy Clubs, has been very successful, and there is every possibility that this sport, which combines team work with the individualism of straight yacht racing, will increase in popularity with the introduction of the new class.

THE OFFICIALS

The president of the new Irish-Dinghy Racing Association is Mr. R.D. Heard, a member of the Dinghy Council of the Y.R.A., and a well-known helmsman in both 12-foot and 14-foot dinghies. The Committee is widely representative, and includes members from Dun Laoghaire, Clontarf, Sutton, Cobh, Cork Harbour, Belfast Lough and Strangford Lough. Further information about the dinghies can be obtained from the hon.secretary of the association, Mr. A.J.Mooney, of 26 Upper Fitzwilliam Street, Dublin.

The IDRA 14

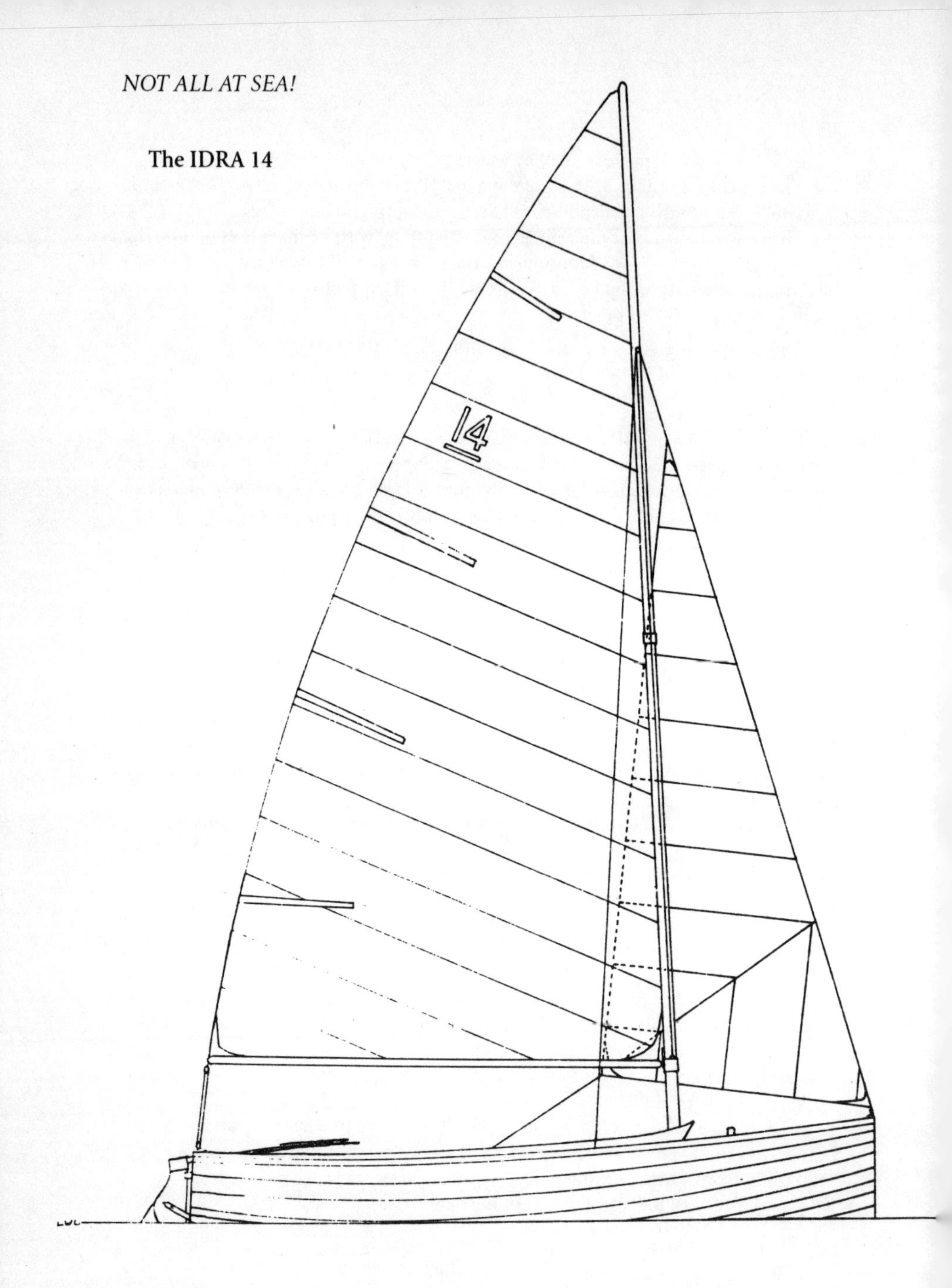

The IDRA 14

Length overall - 14 ft.

Beam - 5 ft.

Minimum weight - 325 lbs.

Total sail area - 120 sq. ft.

Designer - Mr. George O'Brien Kennedy - 1938

I.D.R.A. formed - 1945

Scale

feet

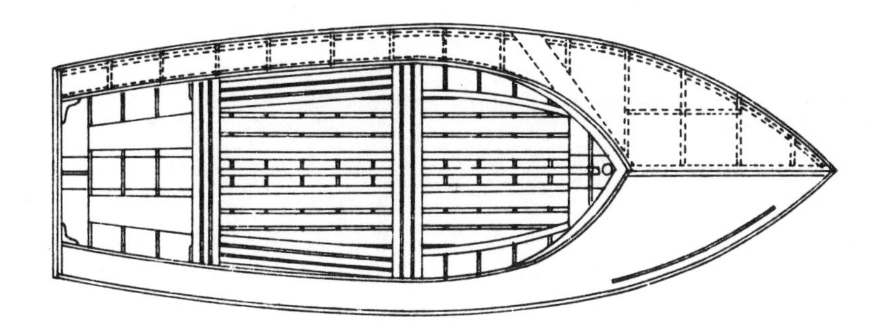

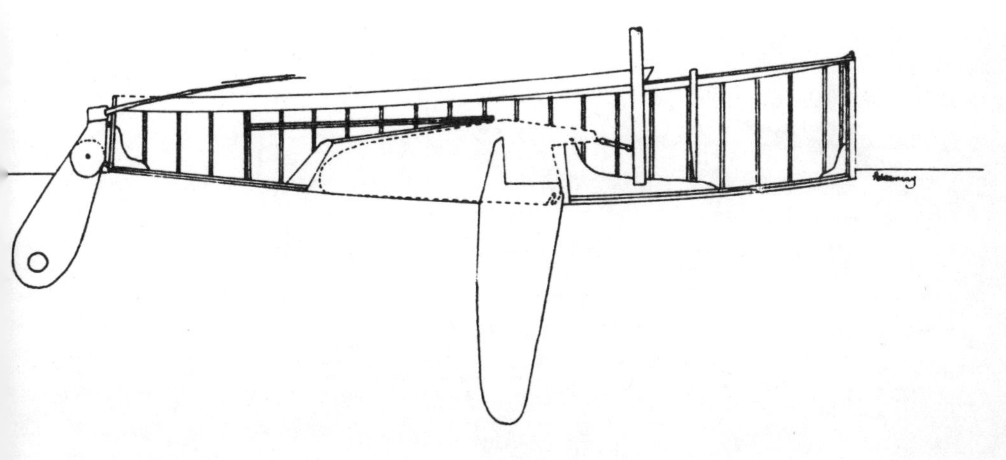

Kerry 27' Sailing Cruisers:

These boats, 26 built to date, resulted from a design competition in **Irish Yachting and Motorboating.**

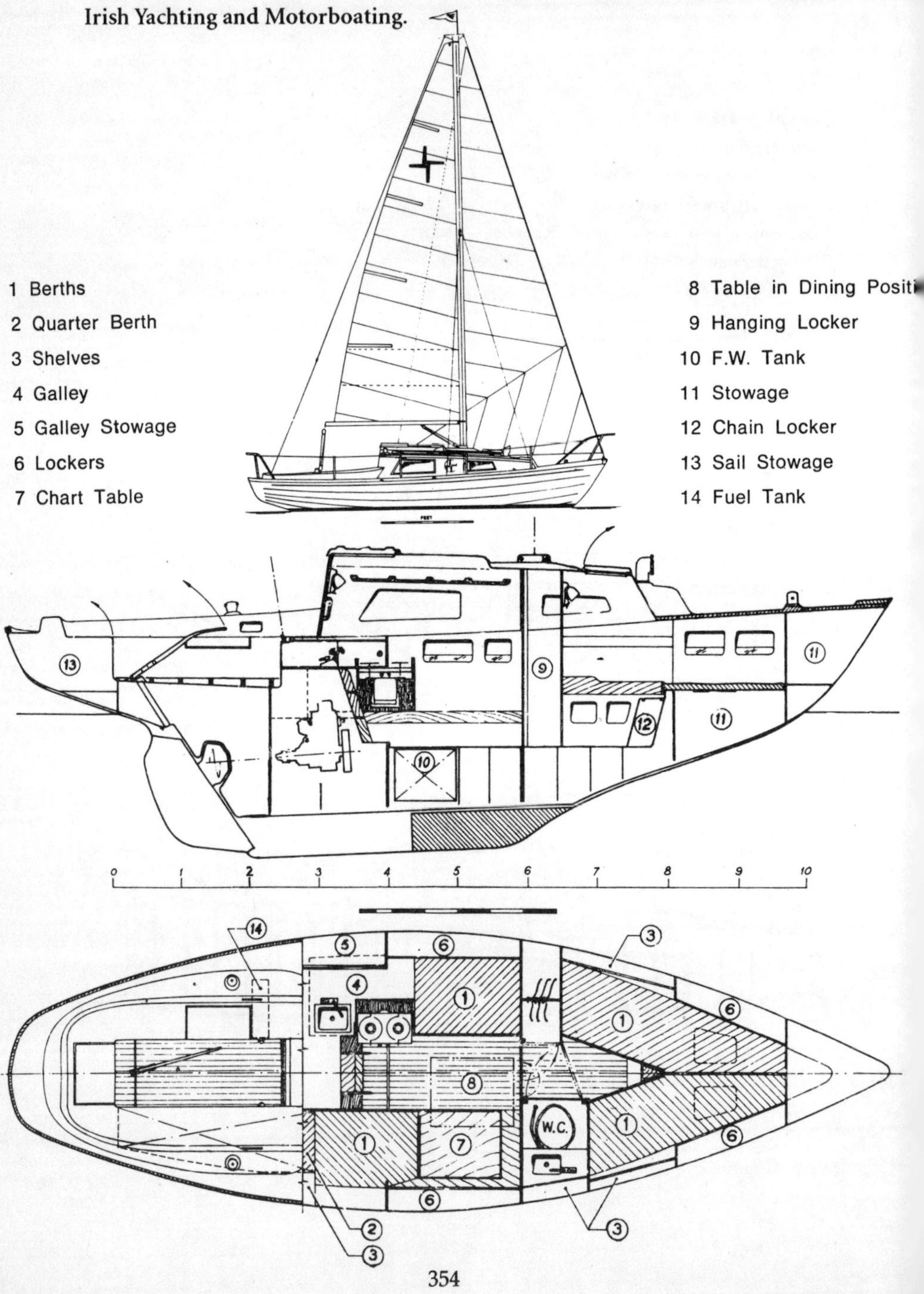

Kerry *(from the original brochure)*

Probably the most rugged and seaworthy production yacht of her size and time anywhere, proved in the tough 1970 Round Britain Race. The yacht for the man or family who cruises in exposed waters and who likes to know that they can take anything that comes.

Two seasons of cruising and racing the first G.R.P. and Timber Kerry, and two of the Mark II, have gone into the design, construction and interior layout of Kerry, which is based on actual experiences at sea. we are convinced that no better value for money is available today in this class of yacht.

When caught out, Kerry wil really take care of you, and be manageable at all times. With her most practical interior layout you will be really able to live comfortably at sea, cook a meal under bad conditions, navigate efficiently at all times, and sleep secure. Particular attentin has been paid to ventilation and storage of all gear, wet or dry.

Should you wish to race, you will find Kerry a remarkably fast close-winded boat under all conditions; add a spinnaker and genoa, with her low rating yu have a winner in class IV and JOG racing.

Price £4,400 including all electrics and navigational lights, with Couach 6 h.p. Petrol Engine.

Standard Kerry Specification

Unique simulated clinker-stringer construction ensuring an immensely strong hull which is remarkably dry in a head sca, serves as a most effective damper to pitching, and produces an attractive workman-like appearance.

Hull and superstructure moulded in glassfibre reinforced ploysters rein to Lloyds approved plans and specifications, under controlled conditions and under expert supervisions and inspection.

Boats can be supplied, built under Lloyd's survey if required at appropriate extra charge. Ballast Lead 22 cwt.approx., main bulkhead B.S.S. 1088 Mahogany doubled and reinforced to take all sailing strains. Interior partly glassfibre sub-mouldings, trimmed with Mahogany and lined throughout for warmth and elimination of condensation, 12 gallon F.W. tank in keel. All deck and sheer trim of Honduras Mahogany. Deck fittings including life line stanchions, pushpit and pulpit stinless steel or chrome bronze. spars anodised light alloy, mast sound deadened, sail terylene. Main sail and numbner 1 and 2 jibs. Running rigging stainless wire with terrylene tails, sheets, etc., 25 Ib. Sanforth or C.Q.R. anchor, 3 fathoms of chain and 20 fathoms of nylon anchor rope.

Interior equipment includes: fitted gallery with sink and water pump, Gimballed gs cooker, stowages etc., sepatate toilet with yacht-type w.c. and wahbasin. All five bunks have 4" foam mattresses with attractive and practical covering. Chart work and navigation can be comfortably carried out sitting or standing at special chart table.

DIMENSIONS

Length	27.0	8.23
LWL	21.0	6.40
Beam	8.3	2.5
Draft	4.3	1.32
Disp	5,400 Ibs	2,475 kgs

Ballast ratio 45%
Sail area 320 sq. ft. 29.76 sq.m.
(Main and Fore Triangle)
I.O.R. rating without engine
20.60 ft. 6.25m

BRAINSTORM

Loa 29.25ft Lwl 22.5ft
Beam 9.5ft
Draught 5.4ft
Diaplacement 2.6 tons
Sail area 382 sq ft

(Details of this boat are given on page xxx)

The following article is reproduced froom **Yachts and Yachting** *of June 1973.*

BRAINSTORM, a highly unconventional half tonner.

It is probably fair to say that most modern offshore racing boats are designed in the shadow of evolution as opposed to innovation. They are usually gradual developments along known parameters, increasing this and decreasing that as rule and performance incentives dictate. One notable exception is 'Brainstorm', a Half Tonner designed by G.O'Brien Kennedy MRINA, an Irish naval architect of repute who has to his credit a number of successful dinghy designs as well as the comfortable production cruiser 'Kerry'.

Brainstorm is an exercise in what you might call letting one's hair down. It is quite evident from the boat that the designer has thought very deeply and inquisitively into the most basic principles of performance and handling under sail, largely without influence from the traditional run of offshore racing boats. 'Brainstorm's' configuration is consequently very unconventional, a new concept in a somewhat stereotyped world.

The most characteristic deviation from convention is the forward rudder which the designer has adopted in an attempt to improve downwind directional stability to the banishment of broaching tendencies, with a possible bonus of increased windward performance. Having committed himself to this bold step, Kennedy has had to design the boat around this appendage that has its own demands which a conventional hull cannot fulfil. To be efficient the rudder must always stay immersed.

Therefore sailing to windward in a chop dictates that it should be well aft on the forebody. At the same time to enable it to exert sufficient turning moment it must be as far away from the centre of lateral resistance as practicable; this decrees that the lateral resistance provided by the keel must be located further aft than usual. With all good design everything must be considered as a whole and all factors are interrelating. Consequently with the centre of lateral resistance placed aft the centre of effort of the sail plan also has to be well aft in order to retain the right balance for the boat to sail well

However, it doesn't necessarily follow that the centre of gravity should be

Continued on page 358

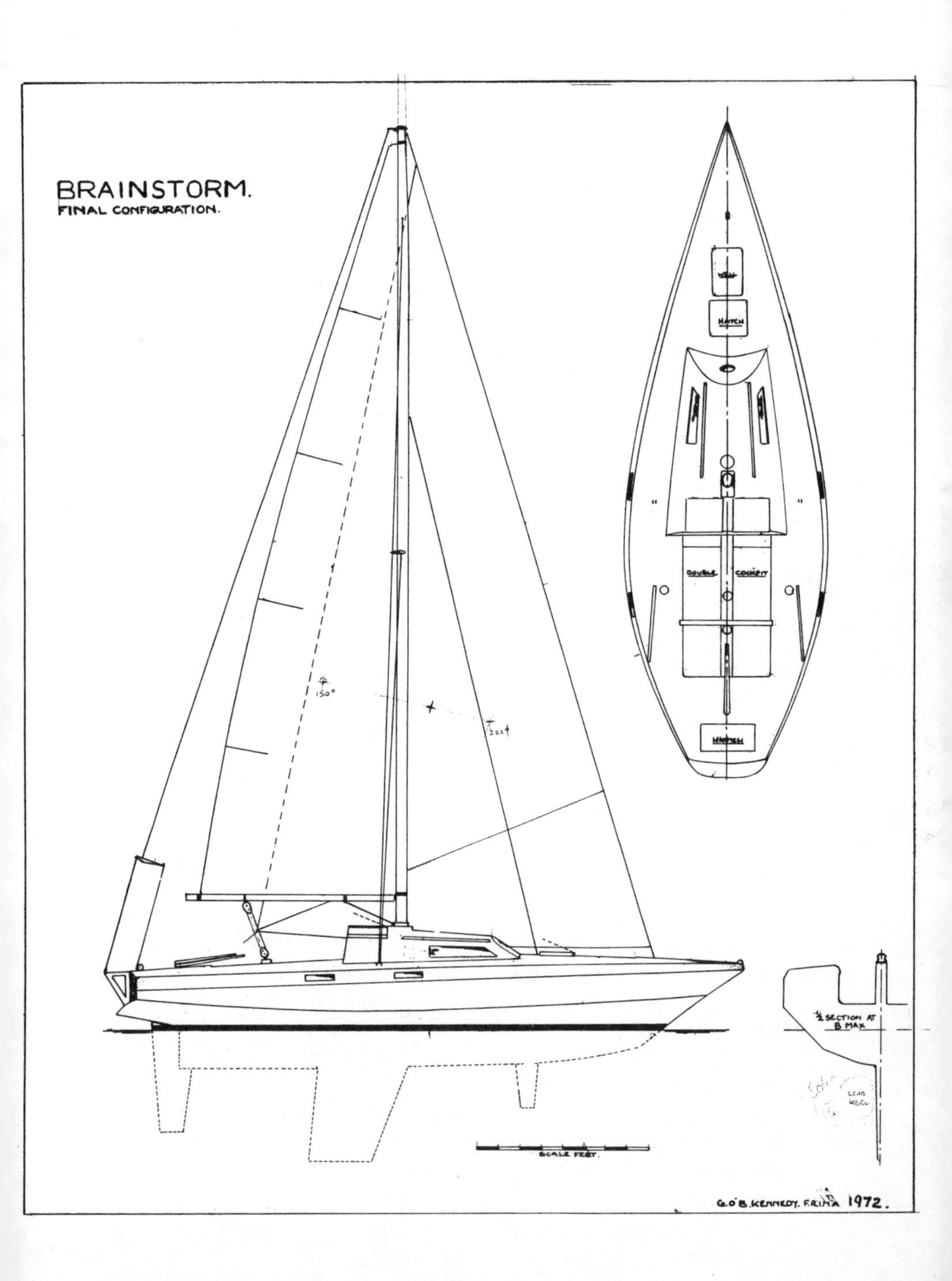
BRAINSTORM.
FINAL CONFIGURATION.
150°
HATCH
DOUBLE COCKPIT
½ SECTION AT B MAX
SCALE FEET.
G.O'B. KENNEDY. F.R.I.N.A 1972.

further aft than in any other boat. The rather peculiar keel profile is therefore the result of an unusual balance struck between the centre of lateral resistance of the fin and the centre of gravity of the ballast bulb. O'Brien Kennedy adds: 'The position of the centre of gravity of the whole boat, of the ballast and of the mast are all more or less in the same vertical plane, as is the point of maximum beam which seems to me to reduce couples between dynamic forces to a minimum. It is also possible thereby to give the boat a very long, fine entry which is considered desirable in a relatively light boat which is expected to go well to windward in rough conditions.'

'Brainstorm' does have a rudder aft but though this has more area than the forward rudder it is intended primarily as a balancing rudder, a trim tab of sorts. Most of the time the forward rudder will be used for steering, with its own tiller and helmsman's well on the foredeck, giving him the advantage of an unobstructed view of the luff of the genoa and of the seas the boat is going through. The boat also has a double tiller system aft so that both rudders can be worked in unison or independently as required.

'Brainstorm' is noteworthy in other aspects. Her hull for instance is very refined in terms of the IOR with a flat bottom out to the centre mid depth position and then a straight flare to the chine at the point where the rated beam is taken. In this she is somewhat similar to the Scampi, though 'Brainstorm's' sections are more extreme.

Wide waterline beam is advantageous under the IOR so 'Brainstorm' with her slim immersed body tends to suffer in this respect, having to accept less sail than most recent Half Tonners. However, with a displacement of only 2.6 tons and a low wetted area she is a very easily driven shape. Her sail plan uses a large foretriangle and relatively small mainsail, with an option for cutter rig. Total area of main and genoa is 382 sq.ft.

Construction is entirely of plywood, the compound bottom shape being of double skin ply planked, and the flat surfaces single ply. Her freeboard is low by modern standards and tumble-home in the narrow panel between the sheer and the topside panel reduces windage when the boat is heeled.

'Brainstorm' was launched towards the end of last season, too late for her to be raced and with a dismasting to hinder trials. However, the designer is satisfied with her performance, proving to be very stiff in a blow and well-mannered downwind. A few modifications have been carried out over the winter, including reducing the ballast weight, installing a lighter engine and fairing the fin

She will be campaigned hard in the Irish Sea this season and may go down to the South Coast around Cowes Week/Fastnet time. We hope that if she proves to be a flier the designer might contemplate taking her to Denmark for the Half Ton Cup to contest against the best the world has to offer. Certainly in terms of inventiveness she stands head and shoulders above the Opposition.

K line Cruises On The Shannon

Weekly Hire Rates Per Boat For 1971

Weeks commencing	Inis More Inis Bofin	Inis Cealtra Curlew	Mallard	Grebe	Plover
May 8,15, 22 29 Sept 4, 11	44	35	42	19	17
June 5, 12, 19	55	45	54	27	24
June 26 July 3 August 28	75	55	60	29	25
July 10, 17, 24, 31					
August 7, 14, 21	78	62	66	31	27
Special rates for periods outside the above	33	25	30	15	13

5% reduction for two or more weeks booking Rates include dinghy with all boats. The only extra charges are for diesel oil or petrol and a refundable insurance depost of £10.

Ireland - Places mentioned in text

MULL OF KINTYRE
MALIN HD
RATHLYN I
TORY I
L. SWILLY
CULD. F.
BLOODY FORELND
DOWNINGS
L. FOYLE
DERRY.
ARAN I
LARNE
BLACK HD.
BELFAST
KILLYBEGS.
BELFAST
DONEGALL BAY
BALLY SHANNON
L. ERNE LR
STAGS.
L. MELVIN
BELMULLET
ENNISKILLEN
SLIGO.
L ERNE UPPER.
KILLALA
INSHSKEA
BALLINA
BELTURBET
NEW CANAL
NEWRY
ST JOHNS PT
ACHILL
LEITRIM V
KILKEEL
DUNDALK
CARLINGFORD L
CARRICK ON SHANNON
JAMESTOWN
CLEW BAY
WESTPORT
DROGHEDA
KILLARY HARBOUR.
SKERRIES
LEANANE
BALLANAKILL B.
LETTERFRACK
L. REE
ROYAL CANAL
UNDER RESTORATION
O LAMBAY I
CLIFDEN.
SLYNE HD
HOWTH
GRAND CANAL
DUBLIN
DUNLAOGHAIRE
TULLAMORE
GALWAY CTY.
SHANNON HARBOUR
BRAY
GALWAY BAY.
BANAGHER
ARAN ISLES.
BARROW CANAL
ATHY
L. DERG.
WICKLOW
DROMINEER.
BARROW RIVER & NAVIGATION
ARKLOW
KILROSH
LIMERICK
KILKENNY
LOOP HD
CARNSORE PT
SHANNON ESTUARY
BANKS
WEXFORD
ROSSLARE.
WATERFORD
DINGLE
DUNMORE EAST
CARNSORE POINT
SALTEE ISLES.
HOOK HD
DINGLE BAY
KILARNEY
VAUGHL
CORK HARBOUR
KENMARE
CASTLE TOWN BERE
KINSALE
DURSEY I
BANTRY BAY
OLD HEAD.
MILES.
0
10
20
30
40
50
60
70
MIZEN HD
FASTNET RK

Merlin Dinghy, designed by G. O'B. K. in 1947

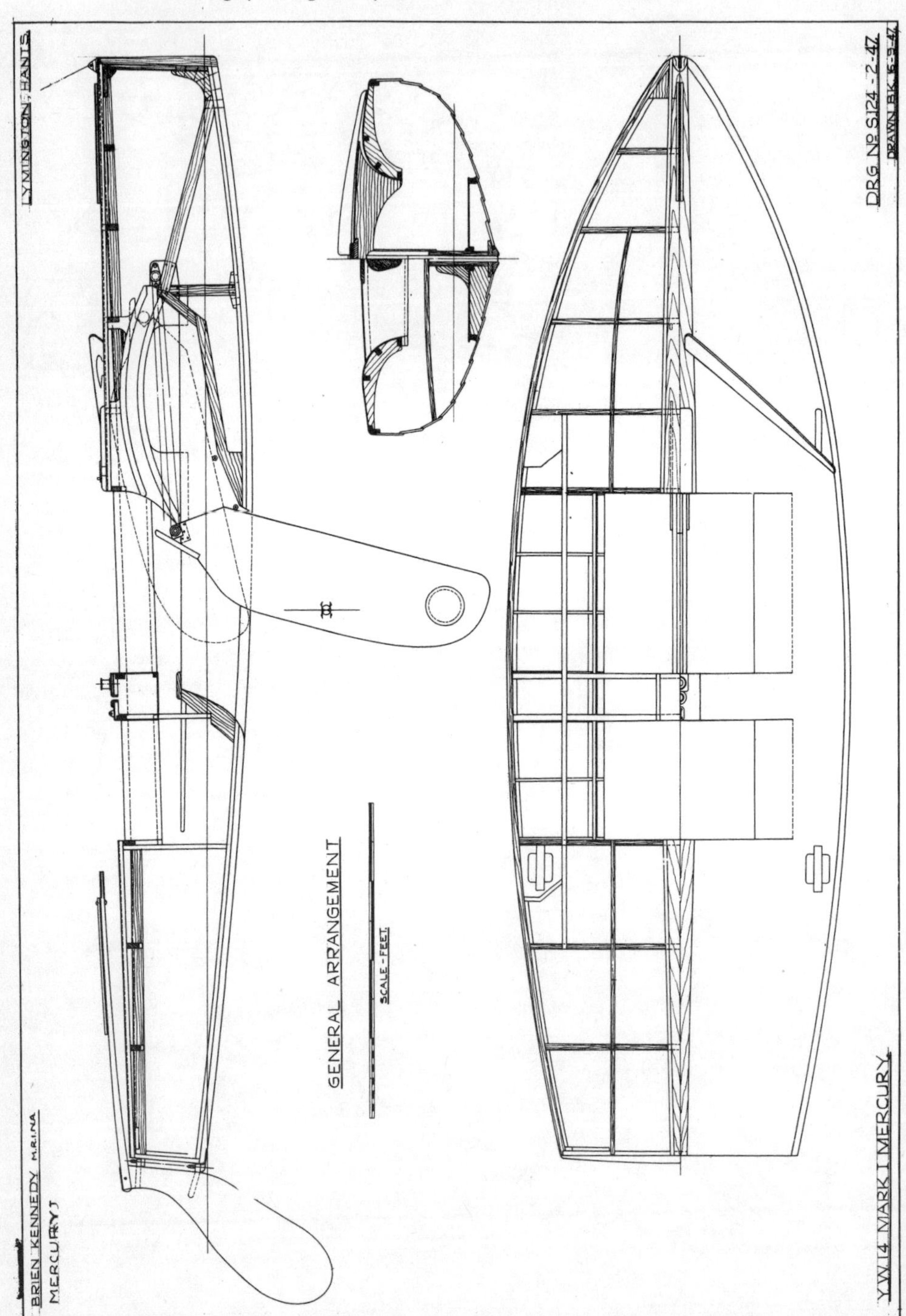

Merlin Dinghy, designed by G. O'B. K. in 1947

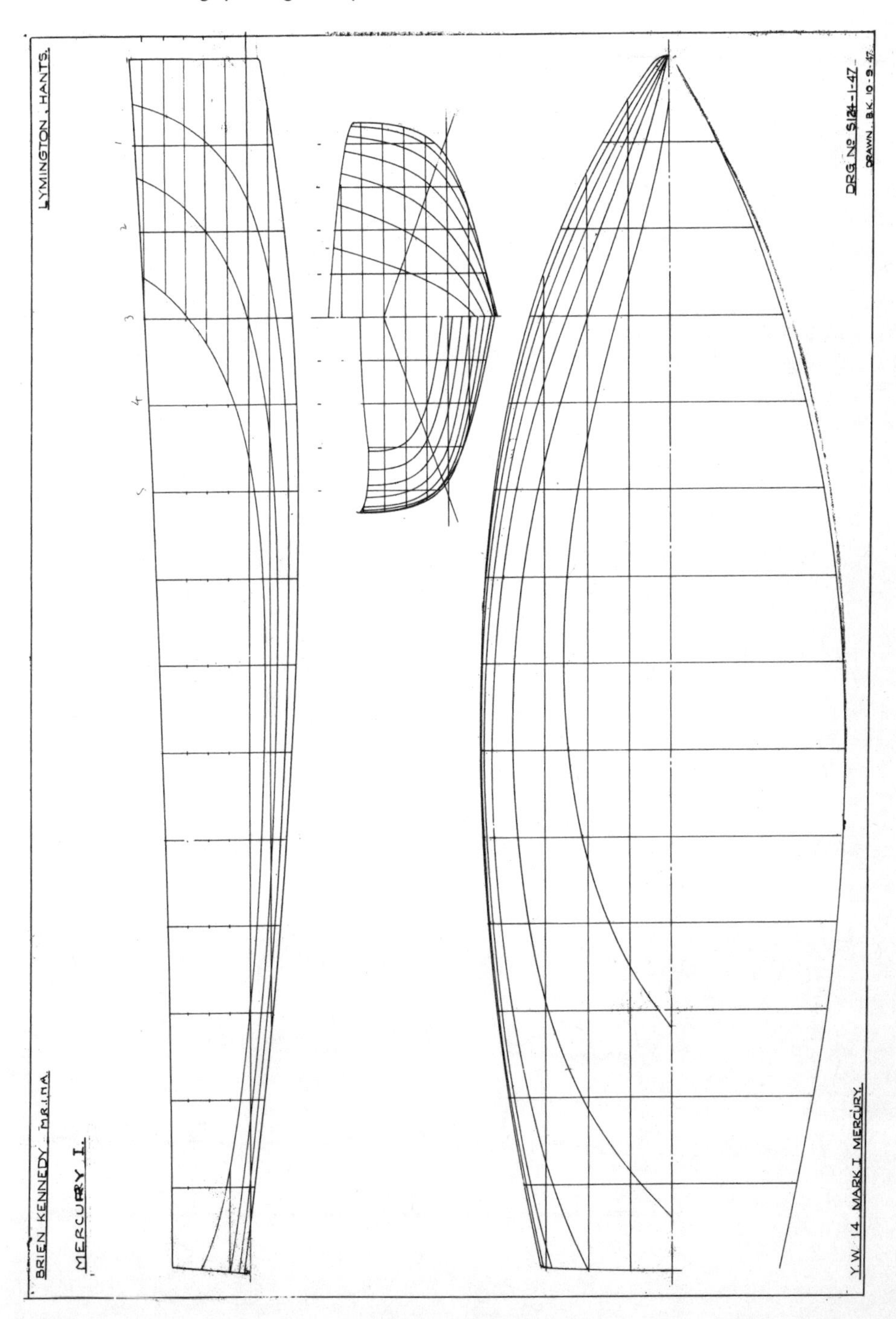

'Binker' 1948, winner of RORC Channel Race

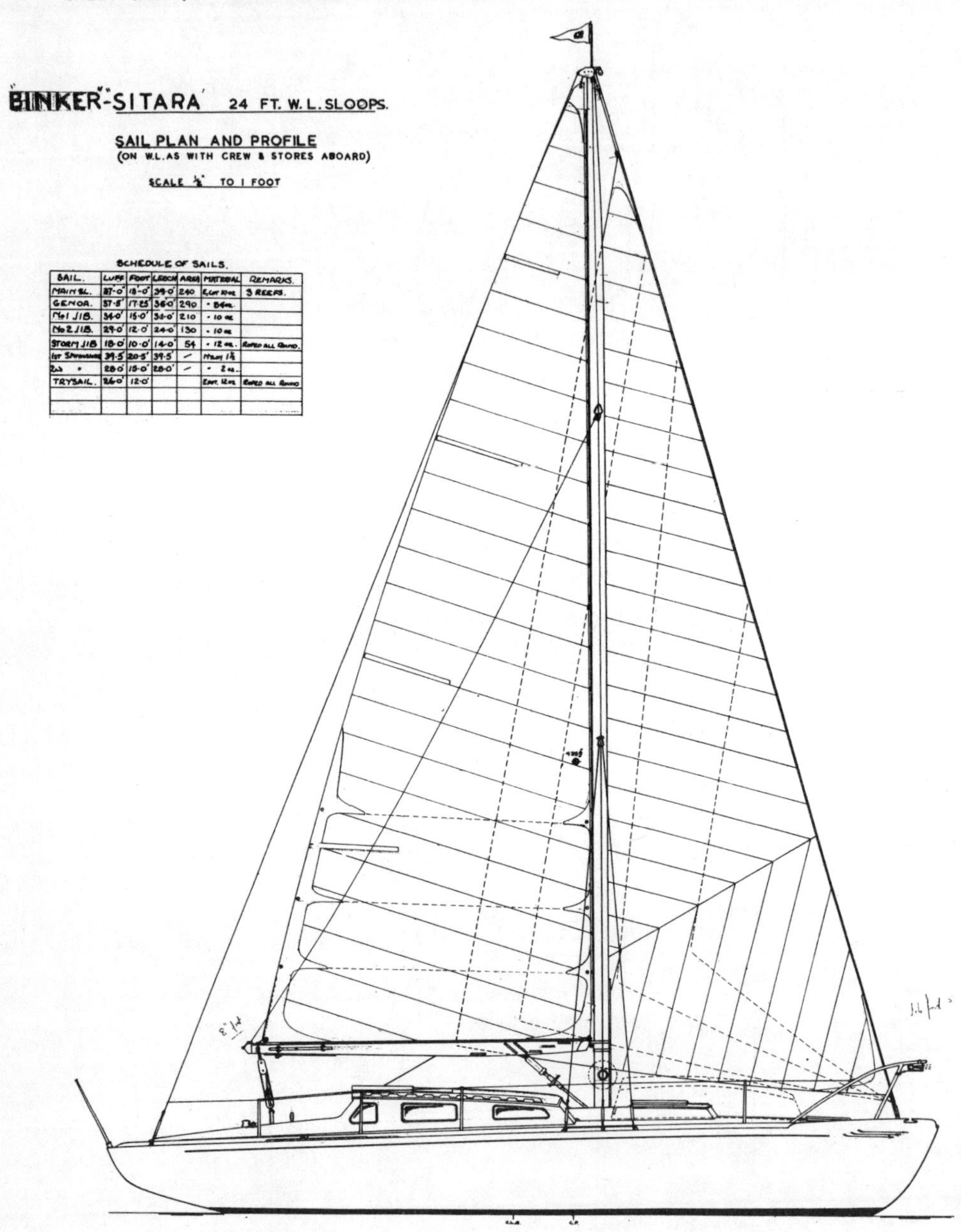

SAIL.	LUFF	FOOT	LEECH	AREA	MATERIAL	REMARKS.
MAIN SL.	37'-0"	18'-0"	39-0'	240	E.cot 10oz	3 REEFS.
GENOA.	37·5'	17·25'	36·0'	290	" 8 oz.	
No1 JIB.	34·0'	15·0'	34·0'	210	" 10 oz	
No2 JIB.	29·0'	12·0'	24·0'	130	" 10 oz	
STORM JIB	18·0'	10·0'	14·0'	54	" 12 oz.	ROPED ALL ROUND.
1st SPINNAKER	39·5'	20·5'	39·5'	–	Nylon 1½	
2nd "	28·0'	15·0'	28·0'	–	" 2 oz.	
TRYSAIL.	26·0'	12·0'			Egypt. 12oz	ROPED ALL ROUND

Shannon Cruiser Inis Cealtra, 1960

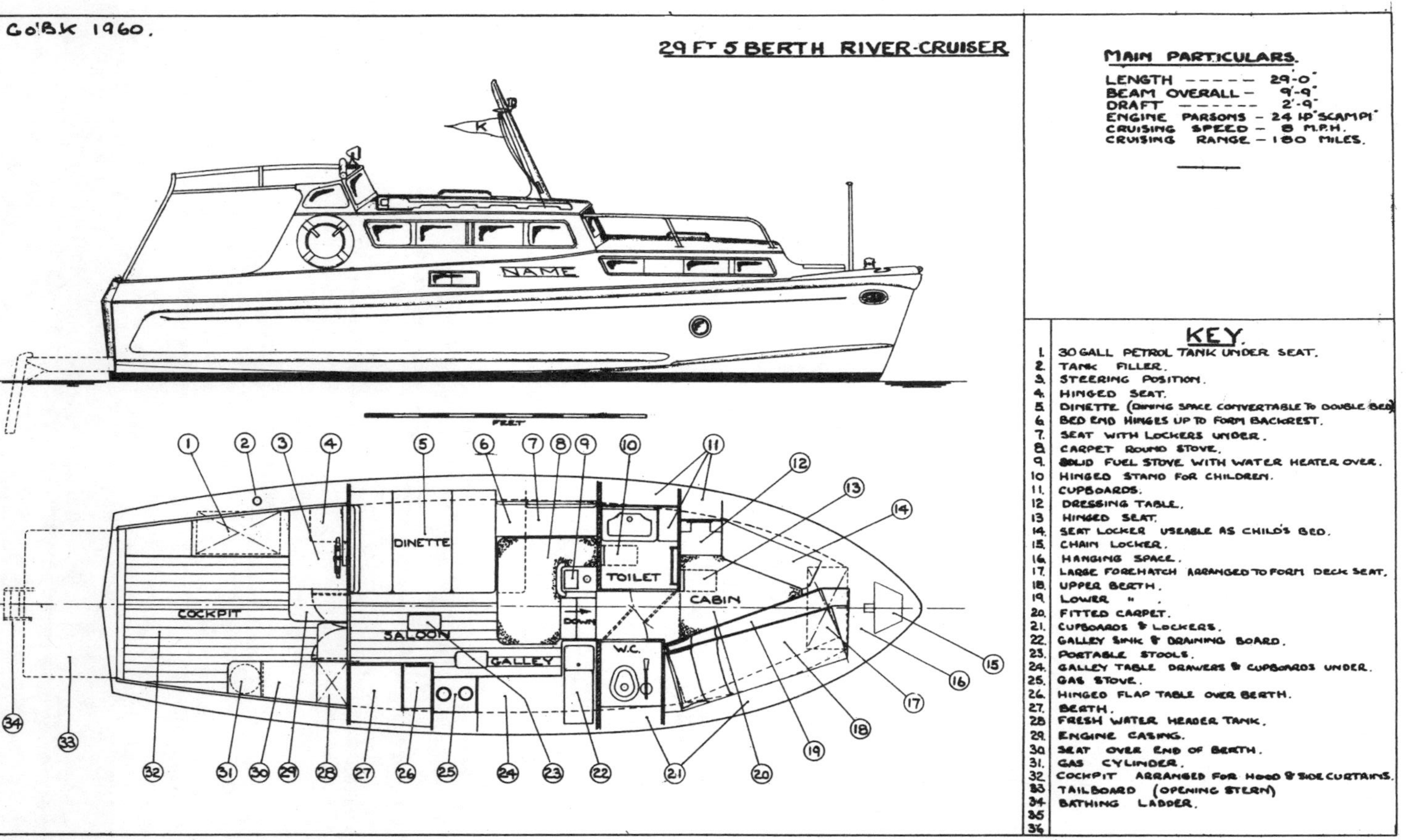

Go'B.K 1960.
29 FT 5 BERTH RIVER-CRUISER
NAME
K
FEET
MAIN PARTICULARS.
LENGTH ----- 29'-0"
BEAM OVERALL - 9'-9"
DRAFT ------ 2'-9"
ENGINE PARSONS - 24 HP 'SCAMPI'
CRUISING SPEED - 8 M.P.H.
CRUISING RANGE - 180 MILES.
KEY.
1. 30 GALL PETROL TANK UNDER SEAT.
2. TANK FILLER.
3. STEERING POSITION.
4. HINGED SEAT.
5. DINETTE (DINING SPACE CONVERTABLE TO DOUBLE BED)
6. BED END HINGES UP TO FORM BACKREST.
7. SEAT WITH LOCKERS UNDER.
8. CARPET ROUND STOVE.
9. SOLID FUEL STOVE WITH WATER HEATER OVER.
10 HINGED STAND FOR CHILDREN.
11. CUPBOARDS.
12 DRESSING TABLE.
13 HINGED SEAT.
14. SEAT LOCKER USEABLE AS CHILD'S BED.
15. CHAIN LOCKER.
16. HANGING SPACE.
17. LARGE FOREHATCH ARRANGED TO FORM DECK SEAT.
18. UPPER BERTH.
19. LOWER "
20. FITTED CARPET.
21. CUPBOARDS & LOCKERS.
22. GALLEY SINK & DRAINING BOARD.
23. PORTABLE STOOLS.
24. GALLEY TABLE DRAWERS & CUPBOARDS UNDER.
25. GAS STOVE.
26. HINGED FLAP TABLE OVER BERTH.
27. BERTH.
28 FRESH WATER HEADER TANK.
29. ENGINE CASING.
30. SEAT OVER END OF BERTH.
31. GAS CYLINDER.
32 COCKPIT ARRANGED FOR HOOD & SIDE CURTAINS.
33 TAILBOARD (OPENING STERN)
34. BATHING LADDER.
35
36
COCKPIT
DINETTE
SALOON
GALLEY
TOILET
W.C.
CABIN
DOWN

Whitbread 30, designed by G. O'B. K. in 1993

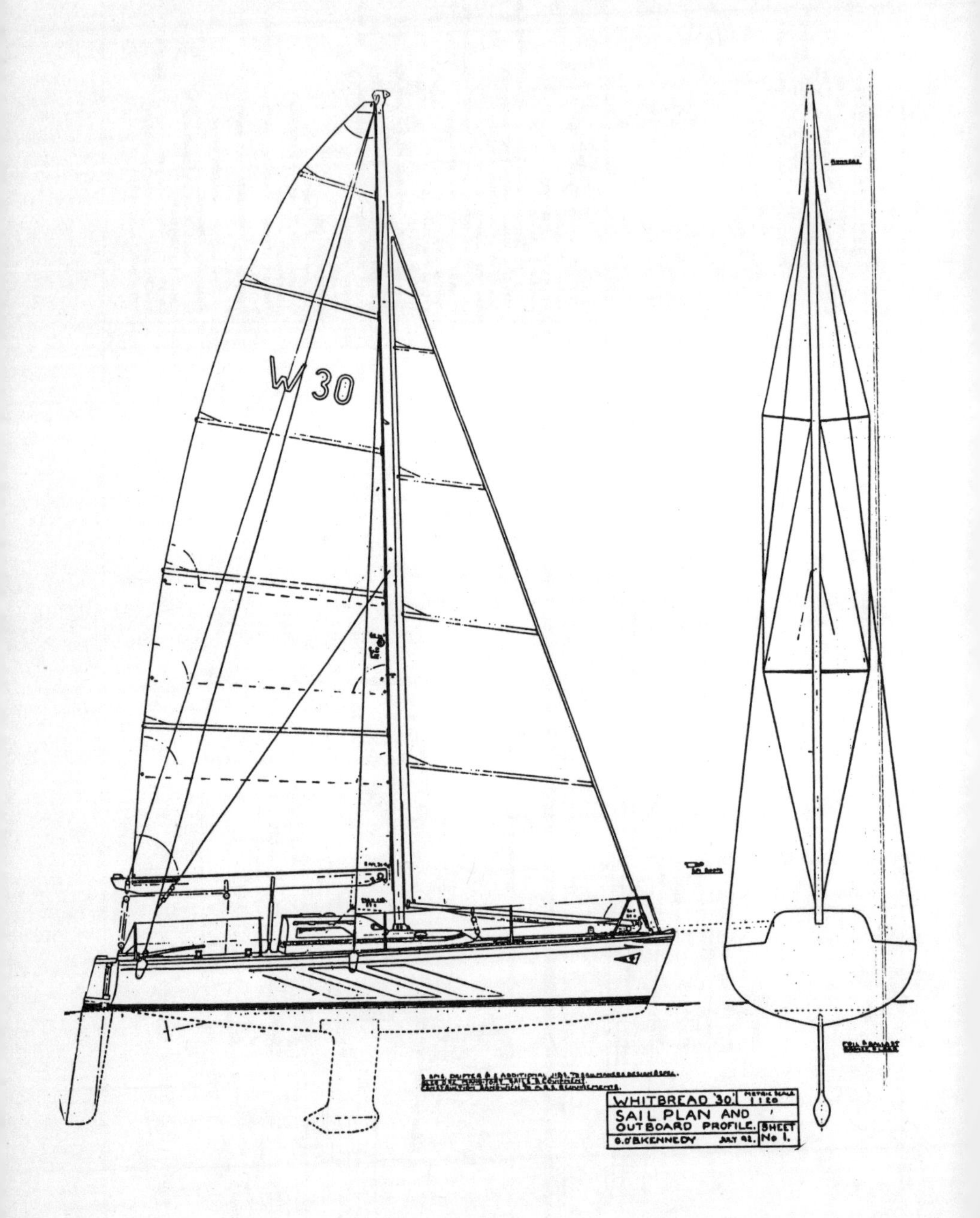

Whitbread 30, designed by G. O'B. K. in 1993

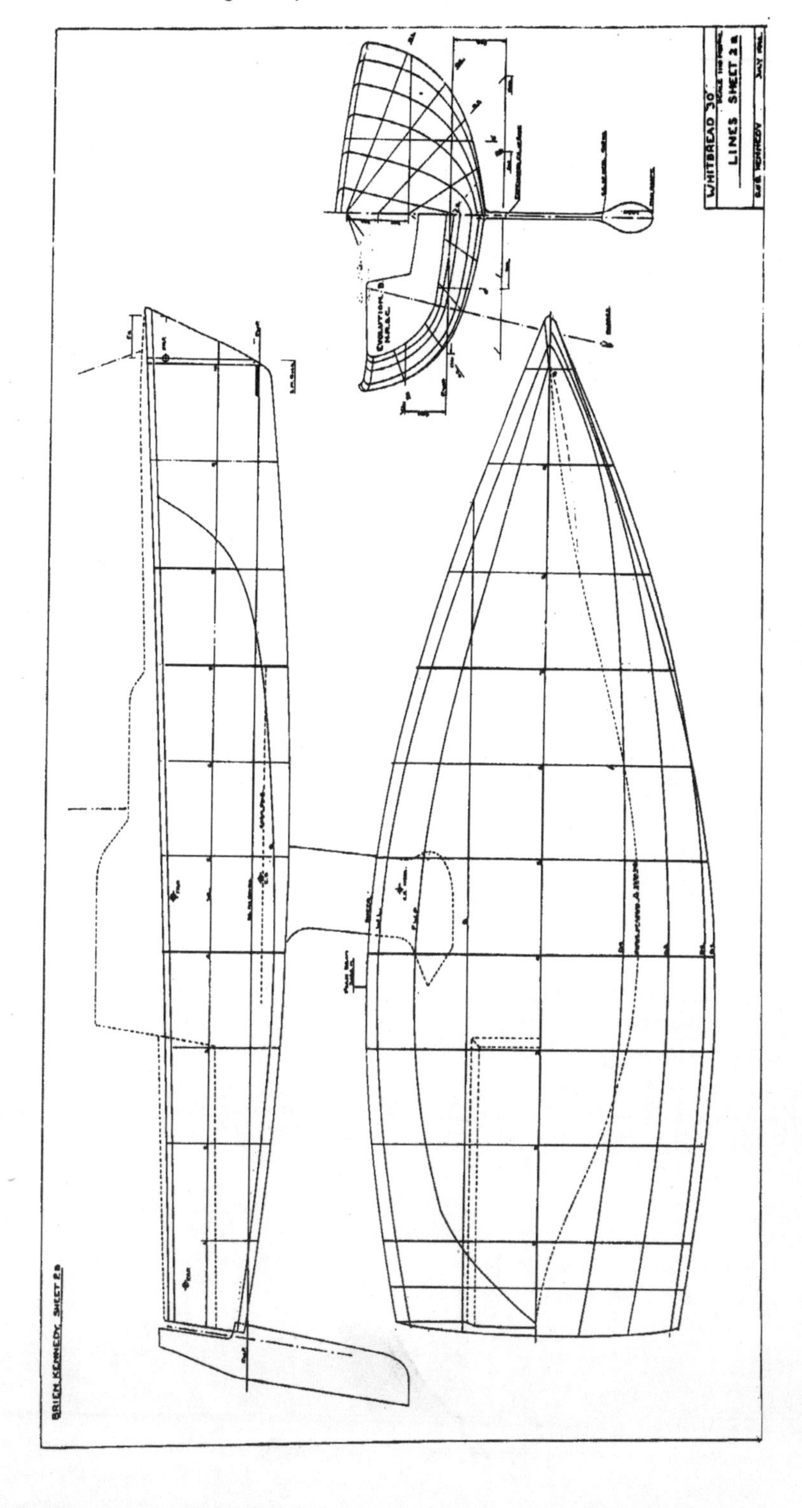

Steel Cutter, building in Dublin, 1997

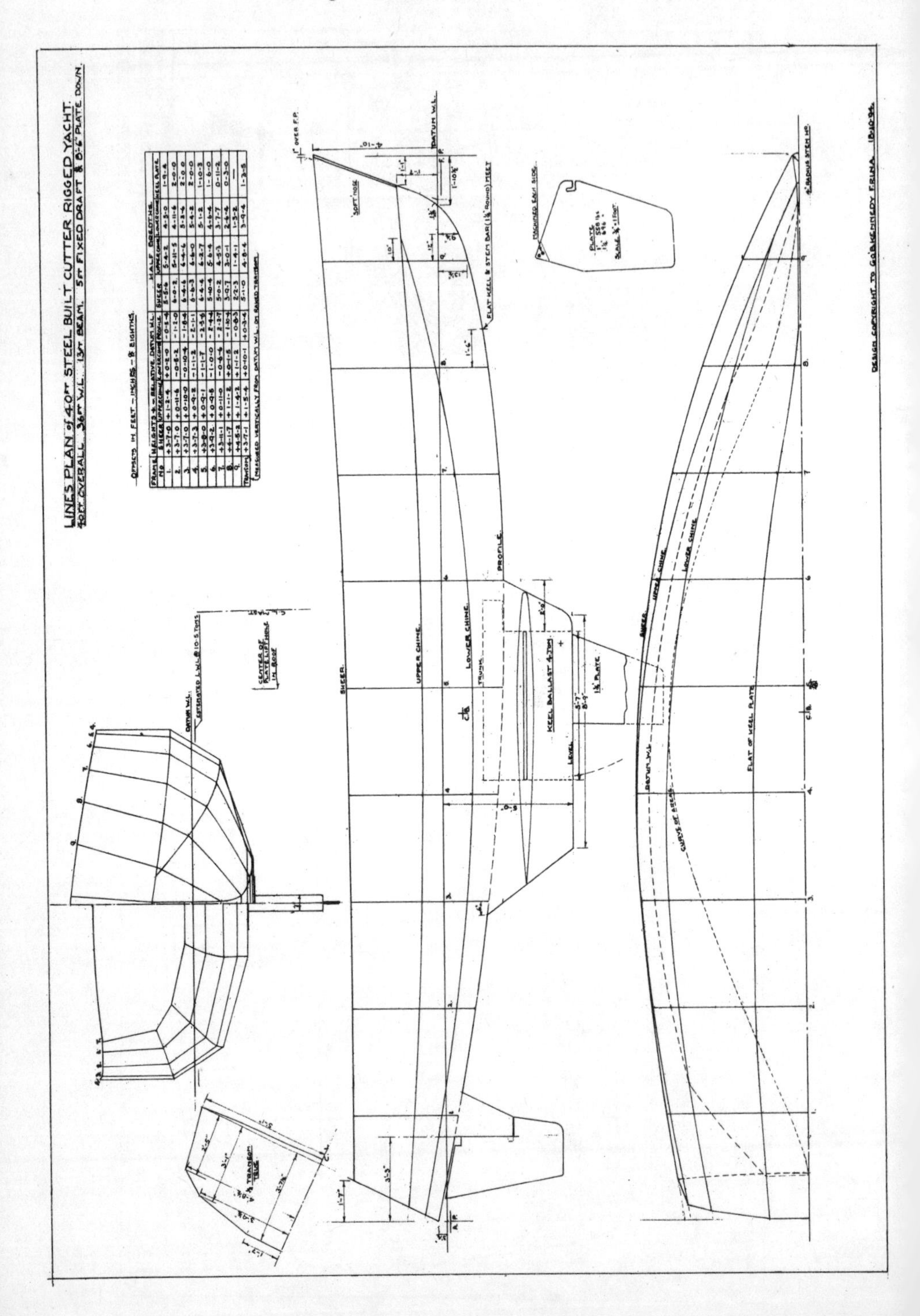